INVENTING A SOVIET COUNTRYSIDE

**Pitt Series in Russian
and East European Studies**

JONATHAN HARRIS, *Editor*

INVENTING A

SOVIET COUNTRYSIDE

State Power and the Transformation of Rural Russia, 1917–1929

James W. Heinzen

UNIVERSITY OF PITTSBURGH PRESS

Published by the University of Pittsburgh Press,
Pittsburgh, Pa., 15260

Copyright © 2004, University of Pittsburgh Press
All rights reserved
Manufactured in the United States of America
Printed on acid-free paper

10 9 8 7 6 5 4 3 2 1

Heinzen, James W.
  Inventing a Soviet countryside : State power and the
transformation of rural Russia, 1917-1929 / James W. Heinzen.
    p. cm. – (Pitt series in Russian and East European studies)
Includes bibliographical references and index.
  ISBN 0-8229-4215-1 (cloth : alk. paper)
  1. Agriculture and state–Soviet Union–History. 2.
Agriculture–Economic aspects–Soviet Union–History. 3. Russian
S.F.S.R. Narodnyæi komissariat zemledeliëïa. 4. Rural
development–Soviet Union. 5. Peasantry–Soviet Union–History. 6.
Soviet Union–Economic policy–1917-1928. I. Title. II. Series.
HD1992 .H45 2004
338.1'0947'09042–dc22

2003015074

For Becky

Contents

	Acknowledgments	ix
	Introduction	1
1.	A False Start: The Birth and Early Activities of the People's Commissariat of Agriculture, 1917–1920	11
2.	A Struggle for Identity: The Uncertain Transition to the New Economic Policy, 1921–1923	47
3.	"Too Many Comrades Misunderstand the Countryside": A Commissariat Comes of Age, 1923–1926	91
4.	Socialism in One Countryside: Architects of a New Rural Russia, 1923–1926	136
5.	Professional Identity and the Vision of the Modern Soviet Countryside: Local Agricultural Specialists, 1927–1929	171
6.	Better Red than Bread? Purge, Collectivization, and the Defeat of the People's Commissariat of Agriculture, 1927–1929	185
	Conclusion	220
	Glossary and Abbreviations	229
	Notes	231
	Bibliography	280
	Index	291

Acknowledgments

I owe a debt of gratitude to many individuals and organizations for their support. Moshe Lewin and Alfred Rieber set high standards and provided intellectual inspiration during my time at the University of Pennsylvania. Thomas Childers, Lynn Lees, and the late Jack Reese offered useful comments and invaluable moral support. Conversations with a remarkable cohort of scholars during a research year abroad (and since) were invaluable. Among those who spent that year in Moscow were Daniel Peris, Marshall Poe, and Peter Holquist. Each of them also offered comments on parts of this book.

I would also like to thank my colleagues in the history department at Rowan University, whose friendliness and enthusiasm for teaching and learning history are infectious. I am also fortunate to have worked for a time in history departments at several universities. During my years as a lecturer at Princeton I was incredibly lucky to work with and alongside Stephen Kotkin and Laura Engelstein, whose generosity will never be forgotten. Stephen Kotkin also read a draft of this book and offered invaluable suggestions. At Princeton, Phil Nord, Bob Tignor, Bill Jordan, Dan Rodgers, Harold James, Michael Mahoney, Peter Lake, Molly Greene, and others offered friendly advice and provided a genial atmosphere for a young scholar who felt far out of his element. At Yale University, another remarkable group of historians helped me feel welcome, including Ivo Banac, Paul Bushkovitch, Katerina Clark, John Merriman, and Lee Blackwood.

I am grateful to the participants in the Delaware Valley Historians of Russia seminar for their careful readings of drafts of many of these chapters. Bob Weinberg, Laurie Bernstein, Adele Lindenmyer, Michael Hickey, Lisa Kirschenbaum, and Barbara Norton are thanked for their creation of a smart, supportive group of Philadelphia area scholars. A number of people have offered valuable comments on the manuscript over the years, including Daniel Orlovsky, Don Rowney, Jonathan Harris, Ron Suny, David Kerans, Lars Lih, Andrea Graziosi, Alessandro Stanziani, and Bill Heinzen. In Russia, conversations with V. P. Danilov, V. V. Kabanov, and Viktor V. Kondrashin were of great benefit. Special thanks must go to David Shearer, who has been an unofficial mentor and a good friend since my years at Penn.

Several institutions offered substantial financial support in the course of writing and researching this book. A grant from the International Research and

Exchanges Board (IREX) made my research in Moscow and Penza possible. The Kennan Institute for Advanced Russian Studies, Princeton University, the Yale University Center for International and Area Studies, and Rowan University supported parts of the research. I am grateful to these institutions.

My parents and my brother, Robert K. Heinzen, shared my love of history, and helped to instill in me at a very young age a fascination for the events and personalities of the past.

The greatest share of my appreciation goes to Becky Griffin-Heinzen, Conor Heinzen, and Julia Heinzen, who have had to endure my absences and who have been unfailingly supportive. Through some challenging times Becky helped me much more than she knows, never wavering in her strength, sense of humor, and love. This book is dedicated to her.

INVENTING A SOVIET COUNTRYSIDE

Introduction

Inventing a Soviet Countryside examines the urban-based Bolshevik regime as it confronted what its leaders viewed as two critical problems in the first dozen years after it seized power—a countryside that seemed to them to be profoundly underdeveloped and decades away from reaching socialism; and the personnel of the state administration they inherited across the revolutionary divide, which they regarded as untrustworthy, alien, and often thoroughly bourgeois. Between 1917 and 1929, in the aftermath of the largest peasant revolution in history, the Bolsheviks undertook the mammoth task of peacefully recasting the economy and political loyalties of the Russian peasantry. This period included both the great famine of 1921–23 and the prelude to collectivization of agriculture launched at the end of 1929, a cataclysm that contributed to a second famine in 1932–33. During this time, the revolutionary regime mobilized state power and institutions in an attempt to "modernize" and ultimately "socialize" the Russian village.[1] A principal question is why the state agency in charge of modernizing the countryside was vanquished and rendered impotent in 1929. This is a critical issue since the state's failure to come to terms with the peasantry helped to cause the collectivization catastrophe with its countless victims and the ruin of Soviet agriculture for decades. Indeed, the post-Soviet countryside has not yet recovered from the legacy of those years.[2]

Reshaping the modes of production and the mentalities of the peasantry, who still comprised the great majority of the population, was central to the Soviet socialist experiment. Adopting the propensity of the Russian Imperial government (and of other modern European states in the nineteenth and twentieth centuries) to seek solutions to stubborn social and economic problems via government intervention, the Bolsheviks made the state an engine in the processes of modernization and social revolution. In this *étatist* spirit, the Bolshevik leadership formed the People's Commissariat of Agriculture of the Russian Republic (Narkomzem RSFSR) to push a peasantry that it considered a relic of the feudal era into the modern era. By the end of the decade, the Commissariat of Agriculture had become the country's largest commissariat, with over seventy thousand employees in Moscow and throughout the provinces. The Commissariat's Moscow headquarters aimed to establish a countrywide network with hundreds of local branches to offer agronomic aid, to educate farmers about modern techniques, to blanket the countryside with new equipment, and (to a very limited extent before 1929) to create large state and collective farms.

This story is perhaps even more striking as the case study of a state agency responsible for an extraordinary task. In the words of one Commissariat leader, the agency's mission was no less than to use the state "to organize the peasant in his entirety." This enormous undertaking, however, was for a variety of reasons entrusted to a cohort of employees about whom the Bolsheviks harbored distinctly ambivalent feelings. The vexing problem of cadres therefore is crucial to understanding key problems in the Bolshevik experience in the 1920s. The sudden success of the 1917 October Revolution created two major dilemmas for a party-state intent on establishing revolutionary institutions as vehicles for bringing new ideas to the peasantry: the social origins of its personnel and their political reliability. Who would build and staff the new state, especially in light of the very weak Communist presence outside the largest cities? Could the existing ministerial and administrative staffs in Moscow and the provinces be trusted? Which social groups' members belonged in specialist and administrative positions? The makeup of the Commissariat of Agriculture is especially revealing because of the questions raised by the prominent position of politically suspect "bourgeois specialists" and former sympathizers of the Socialist Revolutionary Party (SRs) in central offices and because of the governments' programs to recruit peasants into executive positions in Moscow and the provinces. Tracing the organization's experience casts light on the paradoxes of revolutionary institution building, the vulnerability of new Soviet agencies, and their susceptibility to attack by Stalin's supporters at the end of the decade. What can the nature of the state and its cadres tell us about the stability of the Soviet state administrative systems that were broken apart in 1929? Indeed, the upheavals we recognize as characteristic of 1929 took root a decade earlier in the labeling of large numbers of government employees as "hostile and alien," itself a consequence of a volatile mixture of modernization and class politics.

The Commissariat's planned "organization of the peasant" had many dimensions. Economically, the goal was to raise what Bolshevik leaders regarded as the very poor productivity of farming; to unleash the vast, unrealized productive potential of the countryside, and to address the simultaneous threat of severe grain shortages. With the introduction of the New Economic Policy (NEP) in March 1921, the Commissariat's personnel abandoned plans for the creation of a huge system of collective farms that the state had strived for briefly during the Civil War (1918–21).

Following the logic of the NEP (1921–29), Commissariat personnel provided technical and educational assistance to villagers who retained the right to choose their preferred type of land tenure and farm the land as they wished. Despite the change in method, the impulse to reorganize and "rationalize" traditional modes of farming remained powerful throughout the period. During the 1920s, agronomists and other technical personnel traveled to distant villages and tried to persuade peasants to abandon their "primitive" modes of production and embrace new techniques based on the latest science. Commissariat specialists strove to "bring light" to a "benighted" peasantry that they believed would not be able to shed its traditional ways and become modern in the ways that it farmed, worked, and thought without the help of science introduced from outside. In the eyes of most Bolsheviks, villagers were ignorant, economically backward, and culturally primitive.

The view among Russia's elite that peasants were dark and primitive was nothing new. Moreover, they believed traditional modes of farming hindered progress toward a rationally organized and productive economy. The peasantry, dispersed on tiny plots and living mostly at subsistence levels, was a far cry from the type of efficient, large-scale, highly productive farmers that many Bolsheviks envisioned. Nearly all land used for agricultural purposes was still tilled by peasants within the confines of traditional communes (95 percent of sown land in 1927). Soviet political leaders and scientists alike felt an urgent need to fix the agriculture "problem." Russian villages were starved for modern tools, machines, and draught animals. Farmers mostly organized their fields in the three-field and strip systems that Western European tillers had abandoned centuries earlier. Seven years of fighting on Russian territory during World War I and the Civil War left agriculture ravaged. Though production quickly improved in the several years following 1922, increases slowed in the second half of the 1920s. By 1928, some critical areas of output, deliveries of produce to market, and export still had not fully recovered to pre-war levels, creating anxiety among many Communist Party leaders. Equally important, in terms of the regime's powerful drive to catch and overtake the West economically, Soviet Russia was in even worse shape than before World War I. The industrial powers of Europe and the United States had moved farther ahead by comparison, having suffered far less in wartime than Russia. Production per capita in the industrialized Western economies was still growing at a more rapid rate than in the USSR; technological change was also leaping forward more quickly.[3] The Commissariat's tasks of managing the recovery of agricultural production, reshaping the farming practices of the peasantry, and managing the nationalized land fund were key components of Bolshevik efforts to extend the foundation for socialism to the countryside. As long as the productive capabilities of Western Europe (and North America) were used as the yardstick for comparison, however, the agricultural sector would remain a source of impatience and frustration.

Agriculture remained the heart of the economy in the 1920s, still providing almost half the national income, while industry contributed less than one quarter of the total.[4] The success of industrialization and, indeed, the entire socialist project depended upon the production of sufficient food and raw materials for the cities, for the army, and to export for hard currency. In the 1920s, most Bolsheviks believed that a relatively peaceful relationship with the peasantry was crucial for the new regime's stability. Efforts to build bridges to the farming population formed an important element in this search for stability and productivity. Over 90 percent of Communist Party members lived in cities, yet 85 percent of the population resided in the countryside. The village population was further separated from the regime by an enormous cultural gap, and the Bolsheviks were slow to set down roots and gain legitimacy among the mass of the peasantry. Despite the Party's ambitions, transforming the agricultural sector was not as easy as simply lecturing farmers or distributing new tools. A persistent difference in worldview separated the agricultural specialists, trained mostly in urban schools, from the villagers they were instructing.

The Commissariat of Agriculture was also charged with a challenging political mission: to create an organizational base in the countryside from which the state could try to establish relations with the peasantry. A high level of involvement in the rural economy demanded the creation of a gigantic, sprawling bureaucracy to grapple with what one Bolshevik official called "the most complicated, enormous, and disorganized affair" that the new regime faced.[5] Nevertheless, it was a central paradox of the young Soviet state (one that affected all branches of the government) that the Communists who embraced state-conceived solutions to intransigent socioeconomic problems were deeply mistrustful of bureaucracy in general and, more significantly, of their own government's apparatus in particular. Indeed, forced collectivization involved not just an attack by Stalin's group on the peasantry, but also an effort to destroy and recreate the state administration with the greatest degree of contact with the peasantry.

The evolution of tsarist administration in the last decades of the Old Regime provides a useful framework for conceptualizing the limitations of initial Soviet efforts at constructing a new state. Much like its tsarist precursors, the executive branch of the Soviet state comprised ministries that were responsible for particular niches of social and economic life. At the same time, they did not work completely in isolation from that society, but were grounded in the segments of society that they dominated. State institutions, like all bureaucracies, had their own political interests and constituencies and were shaped in part by them.

Each agency created its own internal, cultural world that helped to mold its actions in the political world.[6] Contemporaries called this *vedomstvennost'* (which might be defined as institutional self-sufficiency or autarky, but came to have the negative connotation "self-interest"), a phenomenon according to which the leaders of state agencies often acted in the interests of "their" organization, "their" staff, or "their" constituency, ignoring or contradicting the instructions of superiors or the concerns of peers in other institutions. The notion of vedomstvennost' is quite useful as a tool for examining the Soviet state in this period.[7]

A comparison of Soviet local government and tsarist administration also demonstrates similarities that were deeply troubling for the Bolshevik regime. Despite its reputation for stifling, overweening bureaucracy, tsarist Russia at the local level (like the Soviet state) was seriously "undergoverned," to use S. Frederick Starr's term.[8] Historians have emphasized the barriers that tsarist officials confronted in both reaching and controlling the mass of the rural population.[9] Scholars have also underlined the fear among tsarist and Soviet officials alike that underfunded and isolated provincial administrations were a breeding ground for disloyalty, "localism," corruption, and other challenges to central power and policies. Suspicion of the rapidly growing "third element" of doctors, teachers, agronomists, and other professionals, voiced by tsarist ministers and local officials during the final decades of the Old Regime, was echoed by some Communist Party servitors in the 1920s (and by the police) in their anxiety about the inordinate influence of non-Communist specialists in far-flung areas.[10]

To carry out the ambitious changes it envisioned, however, the Commissariat also faced serious challenges inside the ruling party itself. Politically, the agency found itself in a quandary, an unexpected byproduct of its uncomfortable role as the manager of peasant affairs in the proletarian dictatorship. Since the peasantry had seized (and the state subsequently had nationalized) nearly all state, private, and royal family land in 1917 and 1918, the Commissariat of Agriculture served the function, in essence, of a commissariat of the peasantry, a ministry representing a teeming "petty bourgeoisie" in the world's only country where private property in land had been permanently outlawed. The Commissariat's leadership took their assignment very seriously, openly stating that they believed that they represented, and would labor on behalf of, the economic interests of the peasantry. At the same time, the Commissariat's political leaders believed that protecting the interests of the farming population served the goals of the Revolution. The Commissariat argued that, in certain cases, the need to satisfy villagers in the short run surpassed the need to placate the minority of urban workers who comprised the Communists' principal social base. Indeed, the Commissariat advocated policies that increased the level of social differentiation among farmers. Stratification within villages—a direct consequence of Narkomzem's policies—would result in the creation of a class of well-to-do agriculturalists, traditionally condemned in Marxist literature, but upheld as models of innovation and productivity by Commissariat officials.

Before 1928, despite the guarded and wavering support of the majority of the party leadership for NEP concessions, the Commissariat found itself in an awkward political predicament. It was an institution that served as the advocate for a population considered by most Communists to remain stubbornly capitalist and if not latently hostile to the new ruling class, then at best indifferent to the proletariat's aspirations. The Commissariat's ideas and programs acted as lightning rods for criticism from many party members throughout the 1920s.

Nevertheless, some studies have downplayed the contradictions and internal tensions among party moderates at the time, while tending to overlook the political weaknesses of those who advocated a continuation of NEP policies. Stephen Cohen, for example, focuses on the ideas of one person, Nikolai Bukharin, often taking at face value the worldview propagated by Bukharin and the Right that held up "social harmony and class collaboration."[11] NEP measures toward the peasantry, though "gradualist" (at least relative to the bloody forced collectivization that came afterward), were not always "conciliatory,"[12] as indicated by severe restrictions on certain peasant preferences, such as households' separating from the commune. Even among moderates, there were persistent fixations on social class and notions of "alienness," restrictions on private property in land, and concerns with social control. The Communist Party was pervaded with widespread suspicion of spontaneous action among the population and the overriding belief that traditional peasant agriculture was dying out and (although there were disagreements about timing and method) must eventually be replaced with large-scale, collective production to reverse rural underdevelopment. The ever-present sense of urgency about "catching and overtaking" the West added to a sense of impatience with gradualist approaches.[13]

The Commissariat of Agriculture provides a revealing case study of the tribulations of an agency advocating for the economic interests of the petty bourgeoisie in a Marxist regime. It also presents a vivid arena for examining understudied elements of Bolshevik efforts to make concrete the rhetorical alliance, or *smychka*, between the urban regime, claiming to represent the proletariat, and the peasantry. In studies that investigate Bolshevik efforts to overcome the gap between city and countryside and to win the political and economic support of rural areas, little attention has been paid to programs that aspired to render the alliance physical by bringing peasants into key posts in government administration between 1921 and 1929. Nearly a decade of highly publicized programs to promote peasants into senior leadership positions in the central government had the Commissariat of Agriculture as a focal point. To encourage social support for the new regime among ordinary Russians, and as a critical element of the smychka, the Bolsheviks constructed a plan to place nonelites — "socially promoted cadres"—into various senior posts in the ministerial bureaucracy. Many commissariats took part hesitantly in ambitious projects intended to give farmers input and experience at the highest levels of national government.

The desirability of popular participation in the revolution and in government was central in Bolshevik political discourse. Yet the context for these promotion programs and their ideological goals has not been fully analyzed. Nor have historians explored the deeper implications for Bolshevik political culture and conceptualizations of the countryside. Programs to promote industrial workers "from the bench" into leading positions in the Soviet state have been thoroughly investigated; parallel programs for promoting peasants have not. With the availability of reports, correspondence, and statistical material in Soviet state and Communist Party archives, we now for the first time can form a complete picture of peasant promotion during this period.

The planning, execution, and reaction to programs to promote peasants between 1921 and 1929 provide insight into Bolshevik political and bureaucratic culture, the nature of post-revolutionary elites, and aspects of Bolshevik and intelligentsia perceptions of the rural population. The evolving politics of symbols and of class in the post-revolutionary situation are thus critical, as are the construction and fluid nature of social and professional identities and the political use of those identities. The Moscow offices of the Commissariat of Agriculture, then, provide a concrete location, a cultural world, within which a major goal of Soviet ideology—the mass participation of the lower classes in supervising and running the state—can be better understood.

Although some Bolsheviks regarded "bourgeois" groups as irredeemably counterrevolutionary, a "soft line" on cadre policy was embraced by many leaders, including those who headed administrations charged with the economic transformation of the country. Most leading Bolsheviks regarded bourgeois officials and scientists as reformable and potentially (or actually) loyal to Soviet power. Moreover, if efforts to camouflage one's social identity or one's past were endemic in this period of struggle over fluid class definitions, then the enormous Soviet state administration should be regarded as a place where compromised people could be sheltered and receive help reengineering their identities by, among other people, Communists desperate to staff the overburdened and understaffed agencies of state. In the face of growing criticism about the suspect social origins and political loyalties of their cadres in the mid-to-late 1920s, how did party leaders of state administrations attempt to defend those cadres, to shield them from attack or removal, and in many cases simply to hide them from view?

Local agricultural specialists functioned as an interface between the regime and the rural population. With their very difficult economic position under the NEP, many grew disillusioned and frustrated. Historians of the period have assumed that specialists seeking gradual change naturally opposed Stalinist promises of an explosive acceleration of industrial and rural development at the end of the 1920s.[14] To be sure, most top agricultural specialists in Moscow opposed collectivization policies as they were designed and implemented in 1928–29. But in the provinces, local specialists were, in fact, divided about plans to rapidly transform the Soviet countryside. Some local specialists definitely objected to plans for the accelerated collectivization of agriculture, fearing that it would create inefficiencies, disorganization, and a search for scapegoats amid chaos. Yet many non-Communist agrarian specialists, especially those living outside the big cities, showed enthusiasm for the rhetoric of accelerated modernization in 1928 and mid-1929, that is, before the massive collectivization drive became akin to Civil War in December 1929. This finding demonstrates the breadth of Stalinist appeals to professionals and specialists frustrated by many facets of NEP.

A major obstacle for scholars seeking to understand the role, worldview, and fate of specialists in the early Soviet period is the imbalance of studies of urban professionals at the expense of those working in rural areas. Generalizations about specialists are usually made on the basis of our knowledge of urban experts, especially engineers employed in heavy industry.[15] This focus on urban specialists in an agrarian country has created a blind spot. Based on these studies, historians of Soviet professions and of Soviet officialdom have largely come to a consensus that during the 1920s the privileges accessible to the Soviet functionary and specialist created expectations of a certain level of status and comfort among state bureaucrats. In the only collection of scholarly articles treating Russian officialdom that crosses the 1917 divide, Stephen Sternheimer summarizes the conventional wisdom. He argues that over the course of the 1920s, "seldom in Russian history had the lives and fortunes of those occupying lower-level posts in the outer reaches of the state's far-flung bureaucratic network so visibly improved." "Technicians and managers once again occupied comfortable and remunerative posts," he continues.[16] While it is true overall that later in the decade most types of specialists seem to have earned more than before the revolution, cultural and professional issues also affected professional self-esteem, outlook, and sense of mission. Certain strata in the bureaucracy, especially those associated with industry, the military, and the Communist Party, did enjoy relatively high salaries and expanded prestige in Soviet society. For employees of agricultural and land reform agencies, however, status, working conditions, and living standards remained poor in comparison with their urban-based colleagues. Reflecting their low status as professionals who were not highly valued in the NEP era, this gap affected the way that modernization plans were received by agrarian specialists in 1928–29. Poor conditions made some local specialists susceptible to radical solutions that would lift their salaries and prestige, value their skills, and offer them a role as the designer of a mechanized rural Russia, reorganized along scientific lines. Party leaders appealed to local specialists precisely on the grounds of elevating their positions, while lauding their expertise and "superior urban culture."

Historians have mostly neglected the importance of the Commissariat of Agriculture in their discussions of the 1920s, largely because until recently they have downplayed the importance of the state altogether. For years, historians and political scientists characterized Soviet state commissariats as nearly invisible, yet wholly obedient and homogenous, "transmission belts" between the Communist Party elite and the rest of the population, including the peasantry. Scholarship treating the Soviet state remained in the shadow of debates on the Communist Party's policy-making process and infighting at the highest levels. This preoccupation with an impersonal and nearly omnipotent Communist Party discouraged studies of the interaction between the decision-making elite and the governmental apparatus that was to implement the decisions.[17] In this view, the Commissariat of Agriculture was the loyal servant of the party leadership, as were all government agencies. In this conceptualization, the state was not and could not have been an autonomous actor with interests set apart from those of the party. A dearth of analysis of the Soviet state (as opposed to the Communist Party)—its culture, political face, and personalities—has resulted from a commonly drawn "totalitarian" portrait of a monolithic Communist Party and Soviet government that ruthlessly dominated a splintered and passive society. The state was considered the subordinate actor in the party-state, little more than an appendage of the party. By analyzing a critical part of the state as a complex interface between the urban Communist Party and the local village populations, this work challenges these assumptions. Commissariats embraced their role yet were frequently hindered by a party leadership suspicious both of the bulk of the alien nonparty government employees and of the capitalist peasantry. The ineffectiveness of such mediating bodies and the go-between specialists they employed laid the groundwork for the catastrophe of crash collectivization.

With few exceptions, scholars of Soviet history have only recently begun to recognize the central importance of the Soviet state and its officials (as distinct from the Communist Party organization) in the complicated revolutionary processes during the first dozen years after the October Revolution. From very early on, the Bolsheviks envisaged a critical role for the state administration as an "organizational weapon." Moshe Lewin, Roger Pethybridge, and others agree that the bureaucracy was a key tool in the Bolsheviks' ambitious projects for social and economic transformation. Yet, these scholars also emphasize that the bureaucracy was itself shaped by social forces beyond the party's control.[18] Investigation of the worldviews and political cultures of the early Soviet state is in its nascent stages. David Shearer, Peter Holquist, and Don K. Rowney have all made valuable contributions to our understanding of the critical role of the early Soviet state.[19]

The opening of Soviet state and Communist Party archives has allowed more comprehensive investigations into the dynamics of the early Soviet state machinery. A recent spate of archive-based histories examining aspects of the early Soviet state present new approaches, methods, and sources. Although they range widely in subject matter, these studies share an interest in the formative years of the Soviet state machinery.[20] My work pursues a number of the themes developed in this new scholarship, examining an ambitious project in state-directed transformation of a complex social reality. Each study explores a powerful faith, shared by specialists and political leaders alike, in the state as an instrument for overcoming what the intelligentsia regarded as Russia's persistent backwardness. Yet each ultimately highlights the limitations of social engineering in the Russian countryside, helping to demystify the catastrophe of 1928–30.

Although this book is neither an in-depth study of the Soviet peasantry nor a detailed discussion of their farming methods, the peculiarities of a post-revolutionary countryside prone to crop failure provide a backdrop. Moreover, while this study does not focus in detail on the processes of policy formation inside the party-state, it does examine a number of questions that were central to the way participants envisioned the future of the Soviet village.[21] Nor is this book a regional or local study, though such studies add to our growing understanding of provincial politics, society, and experience in this period.[22] In the final analysis, the Commissariat of Agriculture can be seen as a bellwether for the prospects of NEP. While NEP policies were in ascendance between 1923 and 1926, the Commissariat thrived, if uneasily; when the tide turned against NEP in 1927–28, the Commissariat found itself in deep trouble. Ultimately, the Commisariat's close identification with NEP policies and worldview left it vulnerable to attacks by NEP's many enemies. The regime's scapegoats of 1928–29—a government bureaucracy plagued with "alien" personnel, the "bourgeois" specialists and former sympathizers with anti-Bolshevik political parties, the "kulaks" and the policies that seemed to favor them, the "backwardness" of communal agriculture, the Communist Party's "Right deviation," the seemingly unbreakable cycle of crop failures and grain shortages, the relative gradualism in agrarian policy that seemed to block the Soviet Union's great power aspirations—all shared one thing in common: the People's Commissariat of Agriculture.

1

A False Start

The Birth and Early Activities of the People's Commissariat of Agriculture, 1917–1920

The Bolsheviks took power in October 1917 both promising and expecting to swiftly and completely restructure the tsarist state and reorganize rural life. They soon discovered just how difficult these missions would be. Obstacles to their goal of reshaping the Russian countryside—and the state apparatus they would use to remold it—were more intractable than the Bolsheviks first believed. Sophisticated and well-meaning state officials had been confounded for decades by the challenges of modernizing Russia's agrarian economy. Before October 1917, the Bolshevik Party had encouraged the breakdown of order in the countryside and the disintegration of the decrepit, bureaucratized apparatuses of the Old Regime and the Provisional Government. Immediately after taking power, however, Bolshevik leaders realized that they would have to protect or reconstitute much of the old administration in order to govern the country. During the chaotic first three years of the Revolution, the new government was pieced together spontaneously amidst social upheaval and war. Mistrusted tsarist-era officials were put to work, voluntarily or not, on behalf of Soviet power, side by side with impatient Bolshevik radicals. The result was frustrating for professional revolutionaries unschooled in the complexities of running a state. In the words of one Bolshevik, "Rank-and-file party members assumed leadership positions" in the newborn party-state. "But none of us had any experience. We had to learn our ABCs."[1]

This chapter on the years of revolution and Civil War (1917–20) briefly outlines several important themes explored in depth in the remainder of the study, which treats the years of the New Economic Policy (NEP) (1921–29), including issues surrounding the clash between two central Bolshevik ideals: overcoming rural backwardness and building socialism. The People's Commissariat of Agriculture (Narkomzem RSFSR) inherited the decades-old mission of modernizing peasant agriculture. In the first three years of Soviet power, Narkomzem attempted to manage the most extensive land reform in history, to ameliorate the poor productivity of peasant farming by reorganizing production to eradicate inefficiencies, to introduce modern technology, and to set up "socialist farms." Amid the social turmoil of the general post-revolutionary breakdown, how did the Bolsheviks manage to create the machinery of state? How did state interests competing for influence over the rural economy fare in their political struggles, and why? Focusing on the Commissariat of Agriculture, this chapter discusses the problems of state formation in the context of great disruption during the first three years of the new regime. Instead of disappearing, as revolutionaries had originally predicted, the Soviet state emerged larger and more coercive than the imperial state, just as Alexis de Tocqueville observed about republican France after the French Revolution.

During the Civil War, the Commissariat's staff was frustrated by a Bolshevik Party leadership that, in light of their struggle for survival, did not consider the recovery of agricultural production in the militarized economy a priority. Desperation bred improvisation as the Bolsheviks groped for whatever tools were handy. By various means, they recruited unpopular but experienced tsarist functionaries and specialists to staff their ministries in Moscow and in the provinces. Indeed, large chunks of the old regime's ministerial structures were simply dragged, renamed but essentially intact, across the revolutionary divide to serve the new regime. Within the Commissariat of Agriculture, many of these holdover experts quietly maintained a dedication to using the state to "rescue" what they regarded as an underproductive and largely ignorant village population from the medieval farming methods that had handicapped rural Russia for so long. From its establishment in October 1917 to the introduction of the NEP in March 1921, however, the new Commissariat of Agriculture and its local branches were marginalized in the new party-state as infant state organizations battled for scarce resources in an economy flattened by war and social chaos.

Land and Agriculture before 1917

Only in the context of the imperial government's inability to ameliorate rural conditions—and its obsession with rapidly increasing the productivity of the agrarian economy relative to Russia's industrial neighbors in Europe—can we fathom the agrarian situation the Bolsheviks inherited in October 1917. Before the Great War, Russian imperial agencies in charge of raising the productivity of peasant agriculture faced great difficulties in their self-appointed mission to overcome rural economic underdevelopment. Those agencies—including the

Ministry of Agriculture and the zemstvos—remained relatively poorly funded, organized, and staffed, despite the fact that nearly eight of ten inhabitants engaged in agriculture as their primary occupation.

The weak position of these agencies was particularly paradoxical since agriculture still provided twice as much of the national income than industry. Furthermore, the largest source of foreign trade income—over 70 percent—derived from the export of agricultural products.[2] Indeed, while Russia was the least industrially developed of the great European powers, it was the world's leading exporter of grains and many other agricultural resources before World War I. As a result of favorable weather and farmers' gradual (though uneven) adoption of improved technology, harvests increased between 1895 and 1913 by between 2.1 percent and 2.4 percent per year and yields were also gradually improving in the decades before the war. The Russian historian A. M. Anfimov, among others, has noted that these statistics mask weaknesses, however. Every year Russia exported a much larger proportion of its total harvest than other countries. An examination of production per capita demonstrates that Russia lagged behind the other major exporters, Canada, the United States, and Argentina. In other words, for Russia to maintain its high level of exports, domestic grain supplies had to suffer, and indeed consumption was relatively low.[3] The number of livestock per person, for example, declined for the empire as a whole and in the important Black Earth and Volga Regions in particular. In the Central Producer Region, a hub of agricultural production that suffered from endemic overpopulation, output of grain and sowings per capita in 1913 were lower than at the turn of the century.[4]

Agricultural specialists intent on the reconstruction of Russian peasant farming in the early twentieth century noted that the agricultural sector remained fragile in crucial respects. As political and scientific elites understood, agrarian Russia remained economically quite far behind its industrialized Western neighbors. Indeed, this *"relative* economic backwardness" (including a major technology lag) in comparison with more productive Western economies is what the historian Alfred J. Rieber has identified as one of Russia's "persistent conditions" that form a restrictive framework within which Russian political elites and reformers have had to shape policies for centuries and that have limited their choices.[5] Rieber points to a connected web of factors, including higher mortality rates, lower incomes, and a large technology gap in addition to "low crop yields and an underdeveloped commercial life caused by harsh climate, poor soil, and remote location from the world's major trade arteries" that left Russia at a comparative disadvantage to Western Europe. He goes on to note that impulses to radically reform the economy also posed great risks for the state, including the chance of popular rebellion, dependence on foreign powers, and dissatisfaction among local elites. At the turn of the twentieth century, growing international tensions rendered this relative backwardness even more alarming to Russia's leaders.

This discussion of Russia's relative economic underdevelopment should not be understood as an argument that the peasantry needed or deserved to be "civilized," "uplifted," or "mobilized" against their will for the purposes of increasing the total output of produce (or for other reasons), though some Russian politicians and agricultural specialists made this case.[6] Nor does this book argue that peasant culture was somehow barbaric or unworthy of respect, or that the peasantry behaved irrationally and was incapable of taking care of itself.[7]

Although agriculture provided much of the country's domestic income and foreign trade revenue, Russian output lagged badly behind its Western European neighbors' output throughout the late imperial and early Soviet era. On the eve of the war, Russian agricultural production per capita was on par with Spain and Serbia. Grain yields per hectare were only about one-third of yields from farms in Great Britain or Belgium, one-half of those in France or Germany, and barely one-quarter that of farms in Denmark or Netherlands.[8] These relative proportions remained essentially constant throughout the 1920s. With a less developed transportation infrastructure and industrial capacity than Western industrial nations, Russia's leaders might instead have compared the country's economic progress with that of Italy, Portugal, or the Habsburg Empire. Instead, befitting their self-image as a great power, Imperial (and, later, Soviet) leaders strove to match the performance of the economies of England, Germany, France, and the United States.[9]

On the eve of World War I, 139 million people lived in the empire, and Russia remained the most populous country in Europe. About 82 percent of them lived in the countryside. Ninety-seven percent of the rural population was classified as peasants.[10] Most agricultural production—nearly 90 percent—occurred on lands held by peasants rather than on large estates. Peasant farmers owned over 90 percent of the horses, cows, and pigs.[11] Output on the peasant holdings was poorer than that on the larger private holdings. Russia's farming population lived mostly in small settlements, few of which numbered more than two thousand people. The average size of Russia's villages was thirty to forty families (about two hundred people), but size varied widely. The household (*dvor*) was the basic unit in the village, and there were just over twenty-one million households in Russia in 1916.[12] The average peasant household was made up of 5.67 people in 1916, and the number of households was increasing. The growing number of households, and their smaller average size, worried officials dedicated to raising productivity, because smaller households on average produced less marketable surplus.

In accordance with peasant customary law, the household held the right to the land. The family owned property jointly. Most agricultural land worked by peasants was held in repartitional communes (the *mir* or *obshchina*). The commune had broad responsibility for deciding what was to be planted and when, as well as how land would be regularly redistributed among the member households.[13] The commune oversaw the use of meadows, pastures, forests, and land unsuitable for use. Farmers used some land, such as pasture, communally. Each household also had a garden plot *(usad'ba)* to grow vegetables for family use.

A distinguishing characteristic of agriculture in European Russia was the three-field fallow system of farming that prevailed on most communes. The three-field regime had been abandoned or was disappearing in nearly all of Europe by 1914 (especially its northern and western regions), but predominated in Russia until the 1929 collectivization of agriculture, particularly in the major grain-producing regions. Under this planting system, farmers divided the village fields into three parts. They sowed one field in the fall with wheat or rye; the second was planted in the spring with barley, rye, oats, or beans; and the third was fallow. Thus, at least one-third of the available arable land was unproductive in any given season as the soil was replenished with nutrients depleted by the previous crop. Indeed, agricultural specialists—and that part of educated society concerned with agrarian affairs—hated three-field farming (together with the commune itself) as an extremely inefficient, even medieval, relic in comparison with multifield or crop rotation systems that had brought rapidly growing yields and labor productivity to western European farms at that time.[14] (Of course, these areas of Europe also enjoyed superior soils and climate.)

Crop rotation, considered by experts to be one of the most important solutions to problems caused by three-field farming, was rare in Russia before World War I. In a crop rotation regime, rather than let a fallow field rest for a year, farmers would avoid soil exhaustion by alternating the sowing of various types of crops in order to replenish the soil's nutrients and preserve its fertility. In 1916, however, less than 2 percent of the total arable land in Russia was under crop rotation. It was practiced almost exclusively in the Central Industrial Region, the West, and the Northwest. In grain-growing regions, such as the Central Black Earth region, only 3 percent of arable land was under crop rotation.[15]

Communes further divided fields into sections that were again divided into long and widely dispersed strips (a phenomenon known as *cherespolositsa*) depending on the quality of the land. The commune distributed the scattered strips among the households, depending on need. From the peasant community's perspective, the distribution of farmland on this basis achieved a degree of equality in holdings allotted to each household; from the perspective of agricultural specialists, it sacrificed productivity and left farmers vulnerable to famine in the wake of major crop failures, which struck Russia in 1890–93, 1906–8, and 1910–11. In many regions, peasants' holdings, sometimes made up of dozens of strips, were scattered across large areas, a situation that drained the time and energy of farmers. The borders between strips alone took up 7 percent of all Russia's arable land, according to a study in the mid-1920s. The large quantity of strips created another barrier to increasing production, one that was often more serious—the distance between the household and strips in far outlying fields. Farmers spent a great deal of time traveling to remote parcels to sow, weed, fertilize, and reap the harvest of each strip.[16] Government specialists concentrated on diminishing the negative consequences of strip farming, such as the reduced ability to manure, the increased costs of production, and the difficulties inherent in transporting tools, animals, and harvests back and forth to the village.

In addition to railing against three-field and strip farming, agricultural specialists noted that Russian farming suffered from other idiosyncrasies long left behind in Western Europe, including primitive tools, seeds that were not properly chosen or cleaned, crops that were harvested late, and fields that were not tilled on time in the autumn. Compared to Western Europe, the introduction of technology to the Russian village was greatly delayed. According to a 1910 census, Russian peasants possessed ten million wooden plows as compared to only four million of the far superior iron plows.[17] Iron harrows were also scarce. Mechanized farming, including the use of threshing and reaping machines, was almost unheard of on peasant farms. Farmers still harvested with the sickle and scythe, and threshed with chains or the primitive hand-held flail. Russian peasants only rarely employed mineral or chemical fertilizers.

In most of the empire, the cultivation of technical crops also lagged. Technical crops, produced primarily for reprocessing by industry (and sometimes known as industrial crops), included plants grown for their oil, such as sunflower, flax, and hemp; those used for their fiber, such as cotton, flax, and hemp; sugar beets; and other nonfood crops such as tea, tobacco, and hops. Before the revolution, most such crops were grown on large private estates. Some, such as cotton, oil seed, and hemp, were grown primarily by individual peasants. Industrial crops comprised 4 percent of gross agricultural production before the war. Nonetheless, before 1914 Russia was one of Europe's leading exporters of industrial crops and their byproducts. In the Northwest, West, and Central Industrial Regions, for example, it was very profitable to grow flax (which would be spun into linen), and a large percentage of peasant households did so. The government exported over three million poods of flax fiber to Europe, satisfying more than 80 percent of the demand of European industry.[18]

Resource Shortages

Severe underfunding of state organizations dedicated to providing aid to peasant farmers created frustration among agricultural professionals eager to improve the efficiency of agriculture. A 1914 publication of GUZiZ (*Gosudarstvennoe upravlenie zemleustroistva i zemledeliia*, at that time the equivalent of the imperial Ministry of Agriculture) sounded a common complaint in assessing the reasons for Russian agriculture's poor performance: "Almost until the end of the last century, the population had not received agronomic aid in any serious measure, either from the government or from the local institutions [zemstvos], and was left in this regard almost completely to its own devices."[19] Indeed, before 1905, government spending on the technological modernization of peasant farming was minimal. Not until 1894, in the wake of the 1891–92 famine, was the first agriculture ministry (the Ministry for Agriculture and State Domains) even established. This birth date can be compared with the significantly earlier dates for the creation of separate agricultural ministries in Western states, particularly in France and Prussia (early in the nineteenth century), England (1860), and the United States (1862).[20] The tsarist government allocated several times more money for social control and police functions than for financial, agronomic, and educational assistance to the land-working population. The focus of the state's policies remained keeping the countryside under control rather than assisting it. The sharp, and long overdue, increase in spending during the Stolypin reforms of the final years before the war, a thirty-one-fold increase in the four years from 1908 to 1912, suggests desperation rather than commitment.

Agronomists argued that the resources provided to it by the Council of Ministers compared very unfavorably with the budgets of ministries of agriculture in Austria-Hungary and Prussia: "However large by their absolute measure, expenditures on land reorganization are relatively very small."[21] Moreover, agronomists noted in 1914 that most of this new money went to aid for the small minority of farmers who had separated from the commune during the Stolypin reforms, especially in the Ukraine and in the southern reaches of the empire. Concentrated mainly in the zemstvos, programs to assist the great majority of the communal Russian peasantry continued to be funded poorly, though total zemstvo budgets doubled between 1905 and 1914.[22] Indeed, complaints about state neglect of agronomic assistance to farmers were a common refrain among land officials and specialists between the 1891 famine and the collectivization of agriculture in 1929.

Agronomic Assistance

Pre-war agronomic aid efforts became the programmatic and institutional forerunners for the Soviet Commissariat of Agriculture's activities between 1921 and 1929. Soviet aid programs would follow many of the patterns established by the tsarist zemstvo agronomic aid network. A consequence of the state's paltry funding was that not until 1905 had local agronomic organizations begun to be established and joined formally in a network of *uchastkovye punkty*, local agronomic stations, the institutional equivalent of the American extension service offices.[23] This network became the key link in the zemstvo's agronomic aid system; by the final pre-war years, land reorganization and agronomic programs were being transferred by the government entirely out of the Ministry of Agriculture's hands into the jurisdiction of the zemstvos.[24] The typical agronomic point was attached to the uezd (district) zemstvo. It was headed by an agronomist who organized lectures, exhibitions, and reading circles while managing a model field, a small library of agronomic literature, and an equipment-lending station. The network of agronomic aid stations grew rapidly after 1905. In 1906 there were only 10 local agronomic organizations in 2 uezds, but by 1913, 1,447 had been established in 335 uezds. Despite the expansion, each agronomist was responsible for 100 or more communes and several thousand farms, an enormous territory that forced these specialists to devote the majority of their time to the nearest villages. Furthermore, most agronomists were concentrated only around Moscow and in the western borderlands.[25]

The mission of the agricultural assistance network was essentially educational and targeted the peasants who remained inside the confines of the commune. Zemstvo agronomists insisted on providing assistance to the communal peasantry, not exclusively to the consolidators, as the Stolypin reforms intended. Zemstvos tried to show that the productivity of peasant farming could be raised inside the parameters of the commune, not only on separated homesteads.[26] The Ministry of Agriculture, intent on implementing the Stolypin reforms' emphasis on "individualization"—that is, supporting individual farmers who had separated from the commune onto consolidated plots—thus conflicted with the zemstvos' desire to aid the communal peasantry.

By 1912, the agronomists' preferred method of increasing the productivity of communal agriculture was to locate the most innovative farmers, the risk-takers or "pioneers" in each village who were willing to listen to suggestions and ideas about new types of technology or practices and try them out on their own farms.[27] Neighboring peasants would then witness the positive results of innovations undertaken by the pioneers, and gradually an entire commune would elect to switch to more efficient practices. Agronomists were confident that within the commune at least some of the risk-taking peasants could farm productively and efficiently, in line with the agronomic principles they espoused. This approach of cultivating a "peasant elite" in each commune was later adopted by agronomists during the Soviet period and endorsed by the People's Commissariat of Agriculture.

It is important to note that agronomists were very skeptical of and often sharply critical of peasants' traditional modes of farming. They regarded their mission to be the education of farmers about new (i.e., better) ways of thinking about their own labor and land, while reducing farmers' dependence on "superstition." In fact, before the war many of these specialists made little progress in persuading peasants to adopt the farming practices they considered superior.[28] The agronomists were unsuccessful partly because of their own inexperience and youth. But a large part of the failure to persuade peasants must be ascribed to specialists' insensitivity to traditional peasant farming practices and lifestyle.

The Suspension of Agronomic Aid in World War I

Elements of Russia's World War I experience had a profound impact on agriculture in the countryside, which is briefly explored here. In light of Russia's major military setbacks, food shortages, and territorial losses almost from the beginning of the conflict in 1914, defending the motherland became the government's prime concern. Although rural overpopulation did provide some buffer against the effects of the drainage of labor into the army and harvests did not decline until 1916, the conflict nevertheless disrupted agriculture as people, supplies, and machines were redirected to the war effort.

The Ministry of Agriculture saw its role transformed, and this new role would dominate the ministry's activities for more than six years, throughout the period of the Great War, the Provisional Government, and the Civil War.[29] Rather than remaining an organization devoted to improving the technological level, organization, and output of agricultural production, the Ministry of Agriculture, now suddenly funded with all the resources it needed, was transformed into a branch of the army, responsible for procuring foodstuffs for the imperial army and the cities.[30] Similarly, zemstvos became part of the state infrastructure dedicated to supporting the war effort. In 1915, the Ministry of Agriculture introduced fixed prices for grain purchased by official procurement agencies.[31] In the agriculture ministry the new government established a chancellery of plenipotentiaries for purchasing grain *(glavnoupolnomochenyi po zakupke khleba)* and a section for collecting food supplies and fodder for the army. In 1915 the autocracy created the "Special Council for discussing and coordinating food supply," headed by Minister of Agriculture A. V. Krivoshein, who was removed as head of the Ministry of Agriculture in August 1915. The Ministry of Agriculture was ordered by the Council of Ministers to buy grain at fixed prices from peasants, landowners, or cooperatives. The government set low purchase prices that reduced incentives for peasants to sell to the state.[32] In light of the failure of this policy, in November 1916 the tsarist state established a grain levy.

Wartime prerogatives meant that the government suspended most of the ministry's (and the zemstvos') agronomic aid, educational and veterinary assistance, and land reorganization activities. Many agricultural specialists were drafted or became part of efforts to requisition grain, fodder, livestock, and other supplies for the army.[33] Agronomists were also asked to care for soldiers' families and supervise the rationing of foodstuffs. Many specialists resented these wartime measures. "Agronomists left in the rear were used in war management and gradually became alienated from their own duties" as large proportions of their time and energy were consumed by clerical and organizational duties they considered peripheral to their training and experience. Educational activities, so important for the long-term success of agronomic innovation among communal farmers, were cut back drastically. Some prominent agronomists including V. N. Vargin, former provincial agronomist of the Perm zemstvo, argued that specialists must be allowed to go back to their normal duties. Agronomists also understood that their activities requisitioning food often left them very unpopular with the peasant population. This unpopularity continued under the Provisional Government, when some agronomists on food committees were threatened, and even murdered, by peasants.[34]

A Precarious Transition: From Ministry to People's Commissariat (October 1917–January 1918)

When Nicholas II abdicated on March 2, 1917, the Provisional Government inherited the same complex of problems—economic, military, bureaucratic, urban, and agrarian—that toppled the tsar.[35] By adopting many of the same approaches as the imperial government, the Provisional Government established elements of continuity while ensuring its own failure. In the realm of the critical matter of food supply policy, on March 25 the Provisional Government instituted a grain monopoly. Farmers were ordered to turn over to the state all grain beyond a certain amount at a fixed price. Nevertheless, the state's administrative weakness in the provinces rendered it impossible to secure the food it needed.

On April 21, 1917, the Provisional Government created a hierarchy of "Land Committees" under the jurisdiction of the Ministry of Agriculture. The Main Land Committee was established in Petrograd and local branches were formed in each province and in most districts. These committees were charged with collecting data and making land reform proposals to the Constituent Assembly. It was in the Main Land Committee, together with the still-functioning *Departament zemledeliia*, that the major work on land reform was conducted between April and October, and here that the nation's leading agrarian specialists were gathered.

Although most of the personnel employed in the Imperial Ministry of Agriculture remained in place following the transfer of power, the Provisional Government replaced the top leaders in the tsarist ministries. After replacing the leadership, the new heads of the agriculture ministry formed commissions with sweeping powers that bypassed the regular bureaucratic channels in an effort to make substantial progress toward resolving the "agrarian problem." Special commissions to draft legislation on land reform and other pressing matters, located mostly in the Department of Agriculture, were formed to bypass the old ministry. In the Ministry of Agriculture alone, twenty-four different commissions were set up to scrutinize the details of land reform.[36] The sheer number of organizations naturally caused extensive conflicts in jurisdiction, not only among the three aforementioned categories of organization, but among the ministries themselves. For example, in the summer of 1917 five different ministries—food, agriculture, interior, finance, and war—which did not coordinate their assignments, all dealt with food questions. Imprecise, overlapping, and parallel jurisdictions limited the effectiveness of government efforts to contend with the quandaries plaguing agriculture and food supply.

The processes of the fragmentation of elites and society had led to a divided and impotent government, splintered political parties, and a peasantry that increasingly insulated itself from state intervention. The catastrophic and unpopular war effort that had so deeply eroded faith in the Romanov government among the civilian population and the elites also challenged popular faith in the Provisional Government. The policies of the Provisional Government on agrarian matters were undermined by political factors such as the weakness of the government, its inability to take concrete action, and the bureaucratic morass of competing administrations. The tsarist failure to address the issue of land reform left the Provisional Government with an impossible legacy, including increased peasant radicalization, a legacy of village distrust for the state, and rural collectivism and loyalty to indigenous institutions strengthened in the absence of local state authority.

The People's Commissariat: In the Beginning

Once the Provisional Government had been toppled, a new, symbolic language of revolution underscored the Bolsheviks' conviction that they were severing all ties with the discredited imperial past. After seizing power on October 25, 1917, one of the Bolshevik Party's very first measures was to establish a new executive branch of government, which they called the Council of People's Commissars *(Sovnarkom).*[37] With Lenin as its chair, the Council of People's Commissars replaced the Provisional Government's Council of Ministers, itself a structure inherited from the Old Regime. In Lenin's words, the very name Council of People's Commissars "smelled terribly of revolution."[38] In the same vein, the Bolsheviks considered the names People's Commissar and People's Commissariat to be symbols of a revolutionary new order. These new appellations replaced the terms minister and ministry, which were too closely associated with the corrupt administration of the Old Regime. Although the Provisional Government had used the term commissar to refer to some agents of central power posted in the provinces, the Great French Revolution clearly served as the new regime's inspiration. In the words of one eyewitness, the term people's commissars should "bear witness to the fact that the commissars were plenipotentiaries of the revolutionary people."[39] Officials also quickly replaced the tsarist term *departament* (department) with the more neutral (to the new rulers' ears) *upravlenie* (administration).

The People's Commissariat of Agriculture of the RSFSR was born of the same law that created the Council of People's Commissars. Unlike some commissariats, which were headed by an agency at the national level, the Commissariat of Agriculture was one of the so-called nonunited commissariats, for which separate commissariats were established in each republic.[40] The Council of People's Commissars did not establish an all-union ministry of agriculture. In fact, an all-union Commissariat of Agriculture was not created until the beginning of the forced collectivization drive in December 1929.

The primary features of the tsarist ministerial system had appeared between 1801 and 1835, and these structural parameters were inherited and largely preserved by the Bolshevik state builders. In 1802, Alexander I created a uniform ministerial structure that included the central ministries themselves, each with one head, the minister, and his deputies; an advisory council, or *kollegiia* (collegium), that served as a cabinet to the minister; a secretariat or chancellery; various specialized departments *(departamenty)* within the ministry that could be created and dismantled regularly as needs arose; and a hierarchy of provincial and subprovincial levels.[41] This system provided a large amount of flexibility and continuity, as the personnel and office staff complement could change frequently without disabling the ministry itself. It also enabled ministries to commit specialists to specific problems.[42] As Tocqueville, with his interest in continuity between regimes, would have expected, each Bolshevik commissariat borrowed from this basic structural pattern: people's commissar and his deputies, collegium, secretariat, specialized departments, and provincial sections.

The Narkomzem of the Russian Republic was the strongest of the republican commissariats of agriculture, and it served as the de facto all-union Commissariat, a fact befitting the Russocentric nature of the new government. The people's commissar represented the Commissariat in the Council of People's Commissars. Over the course of 1917 and 1918, provincial, district, and most volost' (rural district) soviets established a land section (*zemel'nyi otdel* or *zemotdel* for short). These were the departments within the soviet devoted to agricultural and land reform matters that served as local branch offices of the central Commissariat. By late 1918, the Commissariat of Agriculture was one of the largest state agencies in the country, with about 1,150 employees in its Moscow offices.[43]

Despite revolutionaries' aspirations to make a clean break with the past, the new leaders of the Commissariat inherited much across October's revolutionary divide. Among the legacies of the imperial Ministry of Agriculture *(Ministerstvo zemledeliia)* was the very name of the organization. The title of the Bolshevik agency, *Narodnyi komissariat zemledeliia* (literally, the People's Commissariat of Land Working) had a rather antiquated, nineteenth-century ring, and inaccurately reflected the scope of the agency's duties. The name *Narodnyi komissariat sel'skogo khoziaistva* (the Commissariat of the Village Economy, the other term used for agriculture) would more precisely have defined the organization's broadly conceived mission, which encompassed much more than just "land working." The Commissariat's assignments included the management of forestry, animal husbandry, veterinary medicine, land amelioration, and handicraft production. The appellation is a clear indication, however, of how closely land, the peasantry, and agriculture were tied together in the outlook of most Russian elites.

The Bolshevik Party immediately charged the Council of People's Commissars with purging each of the old ministerial apparatuses of "hostile" officials and transforming the ministry into an asset of the socialist regime.[44] In its original incarnation, Sovnarkom comprised fifteen people's commissariats, including agencies responsible for justice, social security, foreign affairs, war, trade, and so on. Most of the revolutionary government's ministerial structures—including the Commissariat of Agriculture—mimicked very closely those of their overthrown predecessors. The task of making old ministries work for the new regime was much more easily designed than accomplished, however. Much of the process of state formation in these first years is a story of frustrated ambitions, resistance among officials, and the hasty bypassing or co-opting of unruly or disorganized bureaucracies.

Foundations and Mission

The quickly evolving social and legal situation in the countryside during 1917 and early 1918 shaped the context in which the Commissariat of Agriculture tried to carry out its assignment. The Bolsheviks had inherited the food shortages and peasant rebellions that had plagued the tsarist and provisional governments. On October 25, 1917, as one of the new regime's first acts, the Second Congress of Soviets passed the Decree on Land, the first legislative cornerstone of the Bolsheviks' agenda for socializing rural Russia. The land decree forever abolished all private property in land, forbidding its rental, mortgage, purchase, and sale. The state confiscated all land from its owners without compensation. Land was controlled by "the people" and passed to the tenure of those who worked it.[45] Simultaneously, the law prohibited farmers to hire labor, thereby banning its "exploitation." The regime nationalized all mineral, forest, and water resources of importance, while local waterways and forests were transferred to peasant communal control under the regulation of local land committees and peasant soviets. The law stipulated that lands requiring intensive cultivation, such as estates containing orchards, vineyards, or cattle and horse farms, were not to be divided. Instead, they were to be taken over whole by the state or by peasant communes. Peasant communes were to divide land in an egalitarian way based on labor or consumption norms, and communes would periodically redistribute it, depending on the traditional determinants of population fluctuations and land fertility. The law gave peasants the right to choose the type of land tenure they wanted (excepting private property), whether communal, collective farm, or separated homesteads.

The second fundamental piece of land legislation, the Law on Socialization, was adopted by the All-Russian Central Executive Committee (VTsIK) on January 28, 1918.[46] The Law on Socialization contained passages that, more explicitly than the Land Decree, encouraged the creation of large collective and state farms (*kolkhozy* and *sovkhozy*), while reiterating the Land Decree's major points. In its most important article, the January law declared that the Socialist Revolutionary (SR)–dominated land committees no longer would oversee land redistribution, as the Land Decree had ordered. Instead, this task passed to the land sections of the soviets. On paper, the Bolsheviks controlled the soviets' land sections, though they were in reality largely beyond Moscow's influence.

In fact, these laws simply ratified ex post facto the massive, peasant-led "black repartition," which was the spontaneous communal redistribution of land that had been in progress for months across most of European Russia. The black repartition set the social stage on which the Commissariat undertook its tasks between 1917 and 1920. During the repartition, gentry and church lands were taken over and redistributed by the peasantry. In the years before World War I, the Stolypin land reforms had encouraged significant numbers of peasants in some regions to work the land outside the redistributional commune in consolidated plots. This land could be a *khutor*, a homestead in which all of a household's arable land (including fallow and household gardens) was concentrated in one place outside the village, or in an *otrub* that concentrated only plowed land in one place outside the village, but the farm buildings, house, and garden plot remained in the village. During the black repartition, however, nearly all the homesteads (*otruba* and *khutora*) created during the Stolypin reforms were reabsorbed by neighboring communes, and their lands redistributed among all the commune's families. Local state officials could do nothing to direct the spontaneous black repartition.

Narkomzem's activities—and indeed all the actions of the party-state in this period—must be discussed in the context of these upheavals of 1917–18. One of the Commissariat's primary and extraordinarily difficult tasks during these first three years (and, indeed, throughout the 1920s) was to reverse the regression in total agricultural output that resulted from the black repartition and wartime destruction.[47] Once rural inhabitants had seized the land and divided it among themselves, the Bolsheviks quickly understood that this massive land seizure was a mixed blessing. Despite the hopes of the peasantry and many revolutionaries, the wholesale redistribution of estate, church, state, and Romanov family land failed to solve the underlying problems that had beset the peasant economy for generations. Observers realized that the seizures did not eliminate land hunger, three-field farming, strip farming, or the large distances between strips. Indeed, the land redistributions further entrenched all these problems, since repartitional communes reabsorbed the separated homesteads, many of which had managed to establish crop rotation regimes and eliminate strips. Those households with too little land before the revolution generally received tiny additions, averaging about one-third to three-quarters *desiatina* per capita.[48] In fact, from the perspective of the Commissariat of Agriculture, an important negative consequence of the black repartition was a dramatic upsurge in subsistence farming. The peasantry sharply cut back surplus production intended for the market as "leveling" of landholding and draft animal ownership resulted from redistributions at the commune level.[49] The so-called middle peasantry *(seredniaki)* grew as a proportion of the rural population as extremes of poverty and wealth were reduced. The number of "wealthy" *(kulak)* and "poor" *(bedniak)* peasants decreased.[50] Large private farms that had produced for the internal market and for export before the October Revolution were also divided up among the communes' many households, further reducing production.[51] Bolshevik wartime requisitioning policies further exacerbated these tendencies toward leveling and subsistence farming.

In these difficult conditions, then, Sovnarkom charged the Commissariat of Agriculture with the formidable task of making the overwhelmed peasant economy productive again. This project involved several related activities that combined attempts to modernize the "backward" rural economy with efforts to "socialize" it. Sovnarkom set out three main assignments for the Commissariat (and its local land sections). The Commissariat was to provide agronomic aid to the small-farm economy; coordinate and oversee the distribution of seeds, equipment, tools, and expertise to the struggling peasantry; and carry out land reorganization *(zemleustroistvo)*, through which specialists would attempt to eliminate many aspects of traditional communal production that the Soviet government considered "ancient" and wasteful, including strip farming, the three-field fallow system, and the large distances between strips. Surveyors and agronomists also tried to introduce crop rotation. Importantly, and in a more utopian spirit, the state also intended for land organizers *(zemleustroiteli)* to organize and administer collective farms and state farms. Thus, the Commissariat of Agriculture's job was to help realize the Bolshevik vision of a productive and socialist countryside. During the brutal wartime conditions, these tasks were, for all intents and purposes, impossible to carry out as the regime directed nearly all its resources to winning the war.

The primary goal of land reorganization during the first half of the war (1918–mid 1919) was to organize socialist forms of production. Commissariat leaders were mainly charged with setting up state-sponsored collective farms. At the end of 1918, Lenin came out against the forced collectivization of agricultural production, which had made very little progress in any case. During the second half of the period (mid 1919–20), the party's new emphasis on conciliating the middle peasant (seredniak) dictated that, although collective farms were the ultimate goal, peasants must not be forced to join collectives, and traditional communal production would remain the basis of small-scale agricultural production. Although land reorganization personnel undertook many purely technical tasks (surveying, assessing land, measuring and marking boundaries), the project was not politically neutral in nature. The regime undertook to support a larger political and social agenda, in this case, the creation of socialist villages. Until 1920, the government legislated that the noncoercive, gradual creation of collective farms was one of Narkomzem's main assignments.

The Commissariat organized several types of production collectives during the Civil War, though the results were very limited. Three came under the general rubric of collective farms. First was the *kommuna*, the most collectivized form of production.[52] In the kommuna, all members shared all the production, housing, equipment, property, and animals. Kommuny attracted the poorest peasants, who would be guaranteed food and shelter and, since they had few possessions, would have to sacrifice little to the collective upon enrolling.[53] A less extreme alternative was the *artel'*, which was not well defined. The artel' usually was based on collective marketing of products, not collective production. Land was controlled jointly, though each household kept its own household plot. The most important farming implements and draft animals became the property of the artel'. Households received a share of the harvest based on the amount they contributed upon entry. The final type of collective production established by Commissariat land reorganizers in this period was the TOZ (association for the joint cultivation of land). These collectives were often artificial, existing only on paper. Usually all or part of the land of the TOZ was owned jointly and divided communally, but livestock and equipment (except for the largest farming implements) were maintained by individual families. The collective distributed income based on individual holdings.

Sovkhozy were set up on large former estates, monastery lands, or experimental fields. Land officials considered it inefficient to divide up estates that had been planted with crops that required intensive cultivation. Prime candidates for conversion into sovkhozy included estates containing orchards and large commercial gardens, or estates that grew crops in need of special technical expertise or equipment.[54] In addition, the regime created large-scale grain, meat, and milk "factories." Sovkhozy usually paid laborers a monthly wage, a feature that offended the sensibilities of many revolutionaries who opposed the use of hired labor.

Creating a People's Commissariat

How did the Commissariat's leaders try to organize the new agency to carry out their ambitious missions? The Commissariat's officials faced the daunting challenge of establishing their authority within the new Moscow government and among the peasantry in the villages of Soviet Russia. These were difficult ventures, since the institutions of state had to be created in conditions of widespread social chaos. Indeed, as one leading official later recalled, at first Narkomzem had no real program, possessing instead little more than a "central idea," to take over the tsarist ministerial apparatus and to write fundamental legislation.[55]

Not surprisingly, the Commissariat of Agriculture's first year was enveloped in the confusion that permeated the government. The dislocation caused by the World War (and later by the Civil War, which began in May 1918) as well as urban and rural unrest, greatly magnified the Commissariat's difficulties.[56] Moreover, just as in other state agencies, severe shortages of manpower and material resources hindered the establishment of an effectively functioning ministry. As Miliutin, the first chief of the Commissariat later recalled, during the first weeks "there was no centralized organization; all communications and all the work were conducted in Smolny," the Petrograd girls' school where Sovnarkom was headquartered. The "office" of the Commissariat consisted of exactly one table and two shelves set up in one corner of the single room that housed the Sovnarkom secretariat. Scarcity of (among other things) staff, paper, and even ink precluded all but the simplest work. The Commissariat's allotted credits were quickly exhausted paying minimal wages to a few secretaries who worked frantically for several bureaus simultaneously.[57]

On November 15, 1917, Sovnarkom decreed that each commissariat should take over the Petrograd offices of the ministry it had superseded and then begin operating with the remaining personnel of the old ministry. Coinciding with this takeover of the old ministry offices, however, was a short period of "sabotage," which is how the Bolsheviks labeled the passive and active resistance to the Bolshevik takeover by employees of the former Provisional Government's ministries. Government employees all over the country, fearful of the new leadership and encouraged by their unions, went on strike against the new regime. Many teachers, telegraph operators, and postal workers refused to work, as did white-collar workers in banks, municipal offices, and industrial enterprises. In the Ministry of Agriculture's offices, revolutionary leaders faced immediate boycott. Employees hid or destroyed maps, equipment, census reports, and statistics. Leading officials in every ministry made every effort to slow the communist takeover of the affairs of state, and this sabotage created bitterness toward "bourgeois specialists" that lingered among many Bolsheviks.[58] The Right Socialist Revolutionaries, who had long identified themselves as the "peasant party," also tried to interfere with Bolshevik control of the agriculture portfolio. Under the Provisional Government, they had controlled the Ministry of Agriculture (which had been in SR hands since April 1917) and the land committees, and they stridently opposed the Bolshevik seizure of power.[59] Right SR resistance and the brief strike by white-collar workers slightly hindered, but did not halt, the Bolshevik expulsion of most Right SRs from the Commissariat.

In mid-November 1917, after a period of negotiation, the Bolsheviks struck a deal whereby their allies of convenience, the Left SRs, would take charge of five commissariats. On November 17, the Left SRs, who had broken with the SR Party over the Bolshevik seizure of power, agreed to assume control of the Commissariat of Agriculture. Lazar Kolegaev became the new People's Commissar of Agriculture. Thus, the Commissariat's Bolsheviks began a short and uncomfortable period of "cohabitation" with the Left SRs.[60] Inevitably, both the Right SRs and the Bolsheviks attacked Kolegaev during his short tenure. In a Right SR newspaper, N. Ia. Bykhovskii lashed out at Kolegaev in an article entitled "The Destruction of the Ministry of Agriculture."[61] He denounced Kolegaev for dismantling the Land Committee's fifteen commissions and subcommissions, staffed by the country's leading agricultural experts, which for over a year had been drafting land reform proposals for the upcoming Constituent Assembly. Bykhovskii lamented that work on agrarian reform had continued unabated in the Land Committee through the tumultuous year 1917 only to be terminated in November by this "defector" from his own party. Now, he went on somberly, former Ministry of Agriculture buildings are deserted, and "silence reigns where until recently there has been life." Simultaneously, the Bolsheviks attacked Kolegaev from the Left for failing to make a clean break with the SR-dominated organizations of the Provisional Government.

The fact that the Bolsheviks granted the agriculture portfolio to the Left SRs further emphasized that land affairs were not among the communists' top priorities. Instead, the military, the secret police (Cheka), the Commissariat of Food Supply (Narkomprod), and the Bolshevik Party organization, each with its own extralegal and plenipotentiary prerogatives, would serve as the Bolsheviks' real instruments of power.

In March 1918, the Left SRs resigned from Sovnarkom, protesting the ratification by the Fourth Congress of Soviets of the Brest-Litovsk peace treaty with Germany. The Left SRs believed that the treaty conceded defeat by an imperialist aggressor. They also objected to several Bolshevik policies, including the forced requisitioning of farm produce by the food supply detachments (*prodotriady*), the class warfare preached by the Committee of Poor Peasants, and the policy of favoring collective agriculture.[62] (By summer the Left SRs and Bolsheviks would break off relations over the agrarian question.) Kolegaev's departure from Narkomzem in March allowed the Bolsheviks to consolidate their control over agricultural affairs.[63] The communists achieved control of the Commissariat of Agriculture several months later than most other branches of the economy.

For the first time since November 1917, a Bolshevik took over as People's Commissar of Agriculture. A. P. Sereda (1871–1933) served as chief until, like many government leaders, he collapsed from exhaustion at the end of the Civil War. Sereda brought Bolsheviks into the collegium, which was the cabinet of the people's commissar. The son of a railroad official, Sereda worked in zemstvos before the revolution. A Bolshevik of long standing, he entered the party in 1903. One source has him working as a zemstvo statistician, a notoriously radical profession, for close to twenty years before 1917. Like most Bolsheviks active in party life before World War I, he had been in and out of prison several times, convicted of various political crimes under the tsarist government. Sereda's three years as People's Commissar of Agriculture marked the high point of a largely uneventful party career.

Inheritances

Lacking a well-conceived plan, the Commissariat was more a product of improvisation in these early years. Skittishly and slowly, structures melded, often cracking apart again. The weakened remnants of the old regime stood side by side with the newly born, but still poorly established, institutions of the new order. A cohesive, long-term strategy was impossible to develop. This hodgepodge of structures was a result of the Left SR leadership's reasonable desire in the fall of 1917 and spring of 1918 to use the old ministerial machinery for the time being, rather than creating new institutions from scratch. The result, however, was confusion. The proliferation of overlapping organizations was a major contributor to the disordered state of affairs.

Upon his appointment as Secretary of the Commissariat, V. N. Meshcheriakov, one of the only high-ranking Bolsheviks in the Commissariat, dubbed Narkomzem "an SR nest" and an impenetrable "organizational mishmash." When Meshcheriakov wrote to People's Commissar Kolegaev begging for help in navigating the maze of overlapping sections, the commissar could only reply, "Right now no one knows how the Commissariat is organized."[64] He continued, "Almost nothing existed; everything had to be created anew."[65] In spite of his frustration—or perhaps because of it—Meshcheriakov greatly understated the degree to which the Bolsheviks borrowed from the old in creating the new.

In early 1918 three organizations with varied objectives operated nearly independently under the umbrella of Narkomzem.[66] All had roots in, and borrowed the bulk of their staffs from, pre-revolutionary agencies. The first set of institutional scaffolding absorbed by the new Commissariat included the official structures of the new organization, the People's Commissariat of Agriculture, especially the Current Land Policy Section (OTZP), which drafted policy and directed activities. This section became the core of the new Commissariat. Responsible for organizing and directing local land committees (and those soviet land sections that had been created by this time), OTZP drafted the 1918 Law on Socialization. The second hierarchy was the Provisional Government's Main Land Committee, which continued to work on land reform as a subdivision of Narkomzem, retaining its entire cohort of agricultural specialists. Its many commissions were headed by luminaries such as N. D. Kondrat'ev, N. P. Makarov, and others, many of whom had sympathized with non-Bolshevik parties in 1917 and before.[67]

The third organizational hierarchy was composed of the structures of the old Ministry of Agriculture itself. Significantly, the Bolshevik leadership temporarily left the former Ministry departamenty of agriculture and forestry intact. The Commissariat also preserved specialized sections that corresponded to various branches of the village economy. These specialized divisions, which had been key sections in the tsarist ministry, remained in place during the Civil War, though they were fairly inactive. During the Civil War, these holdover sections served as the home base for the bulk of the Commissariat's most important noncommunist specialists. When the war ended, they would emerge as the nerve center of the Commissariat.

The central administration of Narkomzem continued to be built in an ad hoc manner well into 1919, and legislation did not define formal structures, lines of authority, institutional responsibilities, or jurisdictions until at least that time. According to one eyewitness, ties among the three autonomous parts of the agricultural administration in those days were not institutionalized, but rather were based purely on haphazard and informal personal connections.[68]

Although the staff was able to accomplish a small portion of its tasks, Sovnarkom simply ignored or postponed the matter of establishing many of the Commissariat's operations. Indeed, most sections, including divisions dealing with agronomic aid, animal husbandry, experimental stations, and model farms, existed only on paper. The section for expanding the amount of territory under seed, for example, which was responsible for supplying farmers with quality agricultural equipment and seeds, had access neither to equipment nor to seeds.[69] Of the Commissariat's many divisions, only the Current Land Policy section worked relatively well during 1918. In other words, only that part of the Commissariat involved in designing policy functioned (even if weakly), not those involved with its implementation. Indeed, this phenomenon pervaded the nonmilitarized segments of the Soviet economy. More prosaically, part of the difficulty in establishing normal operations in the Commissariat of Agriculture in 1918 can be attributed to purely physical factors. In Moscow, the Commissariat's fifteen main divisions were spread over at least fifteen different buildings, "scattered and uneconomical." In the fall of 1918, Turchaninov was appointed to a committee charged with reorganizing the Commissariat. The course of his research took him all over Moscow searching for several of the offices.[70]

The Commissariat's weakness bred frustration among the more ambitious of its cadres, who saw the organization as a vehicle for immediately remaking rural Russia. Sections and subsections of Narkomzem sprang up like mushrooms to meet concrete crises as they attracted the attention of the collegium, then disappeared just as quickly. Narkomzem was more an "adhocracy" (in the words of Henry Mintzburg) than a real bureaucracy.[71] Under the circumstances, Meshcheriakov wrote in retrospect, "It was physically impossible to have a general plan."[72]

During 1918, the Commissariat leadership tried to operate in a more normalized way. The new leadership began to simplify or disband certain (but far from all) agencies closely tied to the Old Regime. They eliminated the overlapping jurisdictions of several organizations that had originally merged to form the Commissariat. Leaders formally liquidated two of the three former agricultural organizations. Nevertheless, although it abolished the Main Land Committee, for example, the Commissariat absorbed whole many of its subsections. Many sections of the old apparatus, Lenin reasoned, could adjust to the new order since their tasks were purely technical.[73] In the meantime, the collegium divided the former Departament zemledeliia of the old Ministry of Agriculture into three sections that would remain among the Commissariat's most critical for the next eleven years: those responsible for land working, experimental affairs, and education.

Party leaders quickly realized that the Soviet government had inherited, for better or worse, numerous structures and practices that were duplicates of the Provisional and imperial governments. Judging by an organizational chart alone, it would have appeared to the outside observer that the imperial Ministry and Bolshevik Commissariat were nearly identical. Nearly every section created by the Commissariat's new leadership had parallels in the ministries of the previous regimes. Directly descending from sections within the tsarist Ministry were Commissariat divisions devoted to agricultural aid, research and experimental stations, land reorganization, veterinary and forest affairs, land improvement, agricultural economics and statistics, and education, as well as technical matters such as accounting and bookkeeping.[74]

Furthermore, much of the bureaucratic practice and material culture remained the same. The Commissariat used many of the same paper forms as the agriculture ministries of the imperial and Provisional Governments. Sometimes the words "Ministry of Agriculture" were simply crossed out and "People's Commissariat" was scrawled above them, though busy officials usually had no time for such prettifying. The Ministry of Agriculture's seals appeared on official documents throughout the war years. The appellation "People's Commissariat of the Ministry of Agriculture" was even used at times in official correspondence through 1918. The bureaucratic language of the Imperial administrative machine also proved difficult to discard. Minutes of meetings were reported in the same way as the tsarist ministry: in the first column listed the issue "heard" (*slushali*); the second column recorded what the meeting resolved (*postanovili*). In classic Russian bureaucratic tradition, nearly every document had to be signed by two people.[75] A. G. Shlikhter, briefly the people's commissar of agriculture in November 1917, was disgusted by the ubiquitous presence of specialists trained in the tsarist period. On at least one occasion, he derogatorily referred to the Commissariat as "Narkom*zemstvo*." Such were the grotesque reminders for many Bolsheviks of the tsarist legacy in the new party-state. These continuities are not surprising; yet, for revolutionaries expecting radical change, they could be both shocking and disillusioning.

Moreover, much to their annoyance, revolutionaries-turned-officials began to realize that the business of tackling urgent problems often became swamped beneath what they called "vermicelli," the annoying minutiae of petty problems concerning staffing, budgets, and complaints that preoccupy any large bureaucracy. "Endless masses of unrelenting, whining requests" coursed though the bureaucracy, deluging the Commissariat's leadership.[76] Most Bolsheviks had long hated "bureaucracy," both in the concrete and in the abstract, and having taken over a gigantic, ungainly one, they were, on one hand, constantly provided with fresh reasons for their antipathy, and on the other, forced to try to tame the beast they had captured.

"Holdover" Cadres

The absorption of large sections of the old government apparatus meant that, more so than most other commissariats, the Commissariat of Agriculture employed large numbers of so-called holdovers, or technically trained experts and administrators who had worked in state offices before the revolution. (The holdovers will be discussed in detail in later chapters.) Narkomzem was not the only commissariat to retain a large number of holdovers in its Moscow headquarters. Nevertheless, the proportion of holdovers in the Commissariat of Agriculture was the highest total of any major economic agency. Suffice it to note here that at the end of 1918, holdover employees still comprised nearly 59 percent of all Narkomzem officials, compared with 23 percent in the Commissariat of Foreign Affairs, 46 percent in Internal Affairs, and 48 percent in the Supreme Council of the National Economy *(Vesenkha)*. The proportion remained essentially unchanged until the end of the Civil War, declining slowly over the course of NEP.[77] Most of these holdovers had served in upper or mid-level positions in the tsarist or Provisional Government ministries of agriculture or food supply.[78] Many of those employed in the Moscow offices were from the provincial zemstvo "third element"—agronomists, land reorganizers (the two largest agricultural specialties), statisticians, or economists. As one Narkomzem section director argued, the recovery of agriculture would be possible only with the large-scale participation of well-trained and experienced experts in agricultural and land sciences.[79] Experienced tsarist cadres proved to be valuable resources during this transitional stage, and they would remain essential to the Bolsheviks through the 1920s. Nevertheless, suspicion lingered among some of the party leadership and rank and file of potential "sabotage" by holdover technical specialists.

There are several explanations for the relatively high number of former tsarist officials in the Commissariat between 1917 and 1920. First, the Commissariat of Agriculture had a precursor in the imperial and Provisional governments. When the Commissariat of Agriculture absorbed sections of the old ministry, it was natural for ministry employees simply to stay in the same jobs, even to sit at the same desk in the same office, if the new bosses allowed. Moreover, despite its many tasks, Narkomzem was not a politically influential ministry. The directors of more politically sensitive institutions, such as the Commissariat of Foreign Affairs and the Commissariat of Nationalities, were more eager to evict the living remnants of the Old Regime. These agencies retained far fewer holdovers.[80] In addition, many of the Commissariat's functions were highly technical, and only persons with specialized training could handle them. Few Communist Party members had such advanced training.

Holdovers were a subset of the so-called *sluzhashchie* who comprised the great majority of the commissariat's personnel. This term referred to white-collar workers or "employees," as the term is most often translated, most of whom had occupied administrative, scientific, and technical positions before the revolution.[81] Many Bolsheviks questioned the loyalty of these white-collar employees, who were not classified either as peasants or as industrial workers. Most commissariats contained between 70 percent and 80 percent sluzhashchie throughout the 1920s.[82] Moreover, Narkomzem's cadres contained very few Bolshevik Party members. Of 1,150 staff members in late 1918, only 21 were members of the Bolshevik Party, a lower proportion than in any other commissariat.[83] Considering that in the first year after the October Revolution the ministerial bureaucracies drew heavily on Bolshevik Party officials for staff, it is revealing how few of these cadres ended up in Narkomzem. In late 1918, only 2 percent of the Commissariat's staff were party members, compared with about 9 percent at the Commissariat of Health, 10 percent at Internal Affairs, and almost 47 percent at Foreign Affairs.

The Dictatorship of Food Supply over Agriculture

The agriculture commissariat's activities between 1918 and 1920 cannot be discussed in isolation from the wartime conditions that affected every aspect of the economy and governance at the time. During the Civil War, the Bolsheviks subordinated the agronomic, veterinary, and land reorganization assignments of Narkomzem to the supply of the war effort, the feeding of the cities and the army, and the reconstruction of industry and transportation. The system of "war communism," as the measures of the wartime period were labeled after the conflict had ended (they were called "communism" during the war), kept the Commissariat on the periphery of economic life.[84] The regime nationalized nearly all enterprises of every size. To combat the overriding economic problem—the shortage of food—the party leadership instituted a grain monopoly, a so-called grain dictatorship under the Commissariat of Food Supply. The Provisional

Government had also decreed such a monopoly but had not been able to enforce it. Under the Bolsheviks' grain dictatorship, the free market in produce was abolished as local food brigades moved into villages and seized surpluses, which often were only enough for a household's survival, or which included seed for planting the following spring.

Although war communist agrarian policies were in some senses "emergency" measures intended to deal with the consequences of the crises facing the regime, they were by no means *exclusively* emergency measures. As late as the final months of 1920, the permanent outlawing of market transactions as "speculation," the eradication of private trade, the obligatory turning over of peasant harvests to the state, the notion that the village contained a stratum of exploiting capitalist kulaks who had to be controlled and weakened, the belief that ultimately agricultural production would have to be socialized, and the permanent hegemony of the working class in its relationship with the peasantry were all regarded as essential elements of the socialist economy and society that the Civil War was being waged to create.[85]

Along with the disruption wrought by war and rural upheaval, two other related factors explain why the Commissariat of Agriculture remained a neglected stepchild inside the party-state. Fierce power struggles among government agencies erupted, and there was a debilitating shortage of knowledgeable personnel, especially in the localities, despite the proportion of holdover staff. Interministerial conflict permeated the Soviet government during the war communism period (and later) as new agencies battled to secure their turf. As was the case inside the imperial government, interagency battles suffused every area of the economy, including transport, industry, and labor supply.[86] Moreover, like its imperial predecessors, the Soviet state apparatus was by no means free from internal conflict. During the war, the Commissariat was relatively impotent within the Council of People's Commissars. The forced requisition of food marginalized Narkomzem as an economic or political force. Compared with other state agencies involved in the agricultural economy, the Commissariat remained a weak competitor for power, resources, and personnel. The Commissariat's fragile position was directly related to the military and food-supply situation during the war. The regime's short-term need became the expropriation of agricultural production, superceding assistance to farmers or the modernization of their technique and methods of production.

The Commissariat of Agriculture's leadership was unhappy with its agency's political insignificance, which was reflected in its partial dismemberment by other, stronger economic ministries. In the first year, the jurisdiction of Narkomzem was regularly reduced as other agencies clipped off and digested a number of its departments and assignments. Two very powerful state economic administrations—the Commissariat of Food Supply and Vesenkha—did most of the clipping. Vesenkha's role as the economic supercommissariat allowed it wide latitude to consume the economic functions of other agencies. What is most interesting here is just how angrily Narkomzem's leaders expressed their frustration to Lenin and the Bolshevik leadership. Even four years later, when Meshcheriakov recalled his relations with the giant of the war communist economy, his fury was palpable. As he put it, the "imperialists at Vesenkha decided that Vesenkha alone was the economy; and [they] thereafter began systematically to gobble up piece after piece of Narkomzem."[87] An incensed Meshcheriakov complained angrily that the Commissariat of Agriculture had to waste valuable energy attempting to stave off takeover attempts—"amputations" as he put it—by "greedy" institutions. He concluded, "This pilfering ended in the complete defeat of the Central Commissariat of Agriculture."[88]

During the war, the party leadership considered the Commissariat of Agriculture's tasks just the first stage in a process, the ultimate goal of which was to provide food to the cities and the Red Army during the war. Two goals that were compatible in theory—to improve the productivity of peasant farming, and to supply urban areas and the military with food—fundamentally conflicted in practice. Seizures of surplus grain from the villages by Narkomprod's food brigades led peasant families to abruptly reduce the amount of land under seed, growing only enough to feed themselves. Narkomzem leaders protested heavy taxes on meat to the Central Committee, observing that "the food commissariat is writing decrees that force the peasant to slaughter his cattle" to sell meat to pay taxes.[89] The economist L. N. Litoshenko's later recollection of food supply brigades' wartime methods summarizes the combination of antipathy and moral outrage at the food supply commissariat's wantonness: "There is no statistic to calculate the endless quantity of tears, suffering, the deprivations of a last possession and of life itself which befell the unlucky sackmen [peasant grain traders] in the memorable winter of 1919–20. . . . In the Russian north, you cannot find one village where there were no victims of the food monopoly and of the primitive struggle for bread and life."[90] Amid a continual military crisis, the Politburo decided to provide the food supply commissariat all the work force, materials, and police authority it requested. This support often was provided at the expense of funding for the activities of the agriculture commissariat and other nonmilitary sectors.[91] Considering the wartime emergency, it is notable that Narkomzem's cadres, including its political leadership, were at times less than accommodating to the party's demands that the entire economy be bent to the task of winning the war. Meshcheriakov noted, for example, that Narkomzem was repeatedly foiled in its attempts to create a general all-Russian plan for distributing machine tools, seeds, and other goods. Narkomprod was not cooperative in establishing a plan. "All that is important to the food supply commissariat is to get more grain."[92]

In wartime, party leaders chose the food supply commissariat's no-nonsense methods of forced seizures and quick results over the Commissariat of Agriculture's approach of slowly encouraging increased production with agronomic education, land reorganization, and the distribution of tools and seeds. The regime regarded the former approach as absolutely necessary during the war, while the latter demanded time, patience, trained personnel, and a massive influx of equipment, staff, and seeds into the rural economy. Amidst a decimated economy, prolonged military actions, and devastated industry and transportation systems, the government lacked all these resources and could not count on obtaining them soon. Food supply brigades required hardened, dedicated loyalists, willing to employ violence against perceived class enemies to save the revolution. No technical training was necessary. With irony, Meshcheriakov labeled this state of affairs "the dictatorship of food supply over agriculture."[93] In 1920, a leading Narkomprod official urged the merging of the food and agriculture commissariats into a "Narzemprod," charging with condescension that the Commissariat of Agriculture was preoccupied with agronomy without due consideration of state needs. For its part Narkomzem simultaneously accused the food commissariat of ignoring the needs of agriculture.[94] The enmity between these institutional rivals lasted into the early 1920s, as leaders of both agencies continued to urge the suppression of the other.

Thus, heated infighting within the state apparatus began early, as agencies competed to define their roles—and to defend their institutional niches—within the framework of a suddenly nationalized and largely militarized economy. Amid the hostilities, the Commissariat of Agriculture was an organization under siege. During the war, sheer survival as an independent organization was perhaps its major achievement.

A People's Commissariat without Food Supply

In their efforts to strengthen their institution, the Commissariat's leaders faced two further, related obstacles: a critical shortage of staff, and their personnel's very difficult living conditions. In the provinces, land officials and specialists were few and far between. The lack of trained agronomists and surveyors rendered local agricultural assistance problematic. The Commissariat of Agriculture (like the Bolshevik Party generally) lacked specialists and managerial personnel familiar with agriculture and the village economy, especially posted to uezds and villages. Complaints about the shortage of agricultural specialists were common. The Narkomzem leadership insisted, to no avail, to the Central Committee and Sovnarkom that the agency needed two or three times more specialists than were available even for its minimum assignments. It is useful to contrast the number of people in Narkomprod's food requisitioning armies with the number of agricultural specialists. In December 1920, while there were fewer than ten thousand agricultural specialists in the country, there were more than sixty-two thousand members of the food armies.[95]

To some extent the shortage of experts was a legacy of the small number of schools for training agrarian technicians in the imperial period. As a result of the demand for specialists created by the Stolypin reforms, there was a huge leap in the number of agricultural specialists turned out by Russian schools between 1905 and 1914. The number of agronomists rose from five hundred to more than ten thousand.[96] Nevertheless, the number still lagged far behind what the Ministry of Agriculture and zemstvos considered necessary. By the eve of the revolution, only about fifteen thousand state employees in the agriculture sector possessed a higher or secondary education.[97]

Specialists who survived World War I and remained in Russia during the Civil War years witnessed the drastic worsening of living and working conditions of Moscow's Narkomzem staff. Of course, these conditions created problems for all but the most prosperous state agencies, not only for the Commissariat of Agriculture.[98] The chaos in which local experts worked did not abate. As the winter of 1919 approached, skyrocketing inflation made wages inadequate even for the bare necessities. Years later, N. Turchaninov, the head of the General Affairs subsection, recalled the extreme difficulties of the Commissariat's staff in Moscow. "In the dining rooms, kasha was considered the height of prosperity, and people fought over a scrap of bread, becoming enemies for life. . . . All the attention and thoughts of the majority of people at this time focused on questions of food." People clamored for jobs in Narkomzem in order to get their hands on the miserly rations and "meager social security" to which civil servants had access. They thereby temporarily eluded the brutal process of "natural selection" taking place on the streets.[99] Things did not begin to improve among Narkomzem's Moscow employees until 1920.

Some employees were able to shop their skills to other economic organizations, quitting Narkomzem to find better pay or working conditions. An official in the Central Finance Section complained that beginning in 1919 trained officials abandoned work because of inadequate material support. "Because of difficult work and insignificant salaries, employees flee from serving in the section. . . . It is essential to take measures toward improving the life of employees in terms of food and salary in order to stop the mass exodus of employees from the section. We cannot do constructive work without some security."[100]

An official pointed out the discrepancy between salaries and work conditions of Narkomzem staff and the employees of other, more prestigious organizations. "Officials are hungry, shoeless, and naked. They long to go where they have the opportunity to be fed and clothed. There are ministries and certain agencies where officials, and especially specialists and high-ranking white-collar employees, are given incomparably more salary than in Narkomzem. They also have food and everything needed for existence in satisfactory quantity and, in some places, in abundance. Narkomzem's officials are fleeing to those places."[101]

Low salaries, difficulty getting access to food, and equipment shortages often compelled surveyors and agronomists to leave their professions for jobs in other sectors of the economy. Some specialists joined construction enterprises.[102] Others returned to school to get further education, often in another field. Berzin pointed to the material insecurity in which surveyors and land reorganizers had to labor as the primary obstacle to the timely completion of land reorganization. Since they earned so little, surveyors had to secure other sources of income to supplement their "beggarly" budgets. Some used their skills to set up their own farms. Others became itinerant shepherds, venturing from household to household trying to find employment, reliant on villagers. One official observed, "morale is eroded when an *agent of the state is dependent* on that population to whom he goes *in the name of the state.*"[103]

Volost' land sections also faced shortages of properly operating equipment in spite of the state's efforts to supply it. The Saratov provincial land section was able to provide each agronomist with only one-quarter of a pencil and three or four pieces of paper to last for six months. Specialists had to use unreliable maps of communal land holdings that dated from as far back as the 1870s.[104] The job of Narkomzem officials was further complicated as the Army began requisitioning not only foodstuffs, but also horses, draft animals and, worst of all for local activities, trained personnel (often the most experienced) when the military situation deteriorated. Schools for training agrarian specialists were closed.[105] Experts died of war-related causes or emigrated. Many, of course, simply refused to work for the Bolsheviks, regarding the regime as corrupt or illegitimate.

Narkomzem also had to compete for specialists with other economic commissariats. The party believed that without a strong and effective food supply commissariat, the regime, together with society as a whole, would collapse. When the Army demobilized agricultural experts, as they did in late 1917/early 1918 (albeit temporarily) and again in 1920, the food supply commissariat usually snatched them up, with the Central Committee's approval.[106] During the war the Central Committee and Sovnarkom strengthened the food supply commissariat at the expense of other agencies. They shifted valuable workers from other organizations, including Narkomzem, to the food supply commissariat's jurisdiction. As Lenin put it in June 1918, "We decided to rob all commissariats to strengthen the commissariat of food supply in emergency fashion for two to three months, because otherwise we might die."[107]

The State Regulation of Agriculture

Just as the war was winding down, the party leadership endorsed a plan emanating from the Commissariat of Food Supply designed to assert more state control over the activities of peasant farmers in the name of combating the food crisis. In a series of articles in *Pravda* in September 1920, V. V. Osinskii, the deputy people's commissar of food supply, introduced a policy which he called *Gosregulirovanie sel'skogo khoziaistva*, or State Regulation of Agriculture. In December, a revised version of the policy was accepted by the Eighth All-Russian Congress of Soviets and later that month by Sovnarkom.

The state regulation plan was inspired in part by the catastrophic condition of agriculture in the waning months of the war, together with the realization among Bolsheviks that collective farms could not provide the answer to the crisis of production. Most of the party leadership had come to understand that the government could not afford to supply and maintain hundreds of scattered and poorly functioning collective farms. As Lenin understood well, growth in the number of these farms had stagnated. Those that continued to exist were not faring well, nor were they popular with the farming population. The hope that collective agriculture would appeal to a wide cross section of the peasantry in the near future was abandoned. The new plan would focus on forcing peasants to produce more within the confines of their traditional communes.

Collectivization was forced upon an unwilling peasantry early in the wartime period. The party and Narkomzem encouraged coercion and some land department personnel were ruthless. In December of 1918, however, Lenin had openly declared that the forced collectivization of agricultural production, a process that was supported by many personnel in the local soviets and Committees of the Poor, must stop.[108] Lenin declared that moving too quickly would alienate the middle peasant, needed by the Bolsheviks as an ally in the class struggle against the kulak. The middle peasant, Lenin insisted, must be convinced that the Bolsheviks were his benefactor and that joining a collective farm would be beneficial. The Narkomzem leadership endorsed Lenin's gradualist position. During the second half of the wartime period (mid 1919–late 1920), the party's new emphasis on conciliating the middle peasant dictated that peasants must not be forced to join collectives; rather, production by the household within the parameters of the traditional peasant commune should remain the basis of small-scale agricultural production.

Having made this plea for patience, however, Lenin conceded that in the long run, wide-scale collective production was the only vehicle by which Russia could escape its long-term agricultural crisis. Lenin asserted that ultimately peasant agriculture would have to be socialized, though this should be done without reliance on coercion. Narkomzem and the Bolshevik Party perceived and advanced collective farming as the ultimate ideal, at least for the long run. February 1919 represented the peak of the government's collectivist orientation. That month's statute "concerning socialist land reorganization and measures for the transition to soviet agriculture" declared that individual farming was dying out. The law gave agricultural collectives, including sovkhozy and cooperatives, priority in funding, technical assistance, and land allocation. Since the "unavoidable" transition to collective production was underway, such favoring of collectives was deemed an inevitability. "All forms of individual land tenure should be regarded as transitory and dying away," read the crucial passage.[109]

Thus, until 1920, the government legislated that the noncoercive creation of collective farms remain one of Narkomzem's main assignments.

The hope that collective agriculture would appeal to a wide cross-section of the peasantry in the near future was all but abandoned by the fall of 1920. The new "State Regulation" plan, which its designer Osinskii called a "Great Campaign in the village," would fall back upon certain elements of coercion, forcing peasants to produce more within the confines of their traditional communes.

Osinskii summarized his plan: "The principal factor in the socialist reconstruction of agriculture is the compulsory regulation of agricultural production as a whole. [This] regulation will penetrate deeper and deeper and will develop into state organization of production." A collegium member of the food supply commissariat argued that peasants were state employees who labored, after all, on state land.[110] The policy of state regulation stated that Narkomzem should set up a national sowing plan that would determine which field peasants should devote to which crops. Narkomzem offices in Moscow would pass the plans down to the provincial, then district, then volost' level. From the volost', each household would receive a quota detailing which crops, and in what quantity, it would produce for market. Sowing according to the quota would be compulsory, though each household would retain use of a small household plot for their own use. The primary goal was to compel farmers to plant fields that they had abandoned during the war years. Osinskii openly rejected Narkomzem's tactics of persuasion, calling the policy a "militarization" of agriculture that would entail "the transition away from agronomic volunteerism to state interference."[111] The policy also was intended to raise the quality of agricultural practices and raise average yields per acre. It focused on forcing villagers to adopt two farming practices: plowing fields in the fall for the spring sowing *(na ziab)* and plowing the fallow field in April instead of June. The coercion of peasants, completely without consultation, to farm in a certain way as a solution to grain shortages is an important feature of this period.[112]

The project was unsuccessful. Even had the gradual introduction of the New Economic Policy in 1921 not destroyed the premises upon which it was based, the plan was fundamentally unworkable. With the war abating such ideas found little support among the scientific and political leadership of the Commissariat of Agriculture. Most of the Narkomzem collegium and specialists viewed the plan on state regulation as foolhardy and overly ambitious state intervention. A program by which Moscow dictated quotas for twenty million peasant households, Narkomzem argued, could not possibly succeed. Indeed, agronomists had never attempted to force peasants to do anything, and doing so was not accepted agronomic practice. Narkomzem official Nikolai Bogdanov noted, for example, that forcing peasants to undertake these practices was "completely unrealizable both psychologically and technically." It was not laziness that prevented farmers from doing so in the first place, it was the shortage of livestock and time. Economic stimuli, not coercion, were truly necessary, Bogdanov argued.[113] Osinskii, on the other hand, had no patience for agronomists' fondness for long periods of education.

A Subculture of Expertise

During Narkomzem's wartime marginalization, several aspects of the organization's culture remained peripheral to the food requisitioning and establishment of collective farms that dominated the agency's agenda. What I call a subculture of expertise, touting the application of science rather than coercion to the problems of peasant agriculture, germinated beneath the dominant culture. With the end of the war and the launch of NEP, this subculture would emerge.

This subculture had its roots in the imperial agricultural ministries, particularly in the tsarist Department of Agriculture, where many of the Commissariat's most important holdover specialists had worked. The Department of Land Working, a division of the Ministry of Agriculture and State Domains, was where Russia's best specialists in the agronomic and veterinary sciences had been concentrated.[114] It served as the scientific research nucleus of the agriculture ministries, studying problems of the agricultural economy and then drafting legislation to accelerate the development of its various branches. Many tsarist ministries had established such *departamenty* as divisions to which they delegated the concrete work of data collection, statistical work, and other professional research.

Incubated in specialized agricultural agencies in the tsarist period, the Commissariat of Agriculture's subculture of expertise quietly matured amid the many specialized structural units established between 1918 and 1920. Despite enduring several reorganizations in this period, the Commissariat of Agriculture's structures retained several defining features that would become the foundation of the NEP-era organization. A law of June 10, 1919, for example, reorganized Narkomzem into four primary sections—Land Reorganization, Agriculture, Forestry, and General Affairs. Each was composed of several highly specialized subsections headed by a trained expert rather than a generalist administrator. Small subunits concentrated on specific agricultural questions. Leaders reasoned that an agronomic or sheep-breeding subsection of a provincial land section could be best run by someone with at least a minimum of practical experience and training.[115]

On one hand, this practice illustrates the growing specialization inside the Commissariat. What is more important, however, is that such an organizational scheme demonstrates the confidence of many—but not all—Bolsheviks that nonparty specialists could both professionally and loyally manage agricultural matters at the central and local levels. This conviction would become central to Bolshevik strategy beginning in 1921. Many party leaders recognized that, in light of the country's extraordinarily deep agricultural uncertainties, the regime needed experts both in the field and in administration. The principle represented an important change in approach from the imperial administration of agriculture, a situation in which generalist, nonspecialist bureaucrats supervised departments staffed by specialists. In the imperial administration, "experts were inferior both organizationally and socially," and were to be used only when called upon by their generalist bosses.[116]

From their perspective, some expert holdovers in the Commissariat of Agriculture believed that the revolution offered the chance to reorganize the administration of agriculture along these specialized (and ultimately more "progressive") lines. For many of the Commissariat's specialists the U.S. Department of Agriculture acted as a model. A 1919 publication of the Commissariat's Agricultural Scholarly Committee expressed glowing admiration for the scientific orientation of the U.S. Department of Agriculture and the leading role of its specialists.[117] The sentiments expressed in this publication represent a veritable manifesto of the subculture that would emerge strongly in 1921. The U.S. Department of Agriculture, the authors observed, "is divided into as many sections as there are specialties in agriculture. A specialist in the corresponding branch of agricultural knowledge leads each of these sections. Scientific establishments such as laboratories, offices, museums, and so on, are under their leadership. The Department of Agriculture annually publishes reports that clearly display its creative work. These publications are based entirely on the strictly scientific research of vital phenomena that Washington's Department of Agriculture undertakes." The "graphic example" of the U.S. Department of Agriculture, with its specialized subdivisions, was the model for the Commissariat of Agriculture's 1919 reorganization.

Russian specialists candidly displayed their admiration, indeed their envy, for the relative generosity with which the American government funded and supplied the U.S. Department of Agriculture. The authors contrasted this American largesse with the miserly allotments of Russian governments, past and present, since the current Commissariat and the tsarist Ministry were both woefully underfunded.[118] They also admired the "high cultural level" and agricultural literacy of American farmers, again contrasting them with Russian villagers. Russian experts also noted the good roads and railroads that linked the American department's branch offices with nearby cities. In a telling remark illustrating a view shared by many of the Commissariat's specialists, the publication notes that the Soviet Scholarly Committee hopes to see achieved what the American agency had accomplished: "Without exaggerating one can say that the Washington Department of Agriculture *recreated the methods of farming and enriched the country*" [emphasis mine], and these words can be taken as a mission statement for the Commissariat of Agriculture's specialists.

The authors declared openly that without generous state assistance, experimentation and other work in the agricultural sciences could not continue. Therefore, "the primary role in the creation of experimental matters in Russia belongs to the government. Without the state's help it cannot develop." Hidden during the wartime emphasis on food requisitioning and creating new types of collective production, a desire for the state to help specialists continue offering assistance to the communal peasantry lay just under the surface.

While acknowledging the extreme administrative frailty of their organization during the war, the authors pursued their comparison with the U.S. Department of Agriculture. In an obvious reference to the food supply commissariat's roving food brigades invested with extralegal powers, Narkomzem specialists complained that the People's Commissariat of Agriculture, like the American Department, "does not have at its disposal efficient plenipotentiaries." The American agency's "influence is based on *moral* interaction with the population. This interaction is manifested in spoken and press propaganda about scientific and practical ideas, by demonstration, and by extending broad assistance and advice to anyone who requests it." Narkomzem's specialists drew attention to their self-proclaimed moral authority, reminiscent of the traditions of the Russian intelligentsia. Like the leadership of the U.S. Department of Agriculture, they were convinced that success in increasing agricultural production could be achieved only through science and persuasion.

Yet, there was a major problem with this admiration of American achievement. Reaching the level of the American extension services was simply impossible considering the country's financial situation and competing prerogatives. Indeed, the ambition was almost guaranteed to engender disappointment. Constant comparisons of Soviet Russia to advanced western nations by Bolsheviks and experts alike created a structural frustration that would be difficult to overcome.

Alexis de Tocqueville wrote that "anyone who reads the letters that passed between the Intendants and their superiors or subordinates cannot fail to be struck by the family likeness between the government officials of the past and those of modern France." He added that not only the personnel and institutions, but even the internal bureaucratic terminology of the Old Regime was similar to that of post-revolutionary, republican France.[119] Despite their obsession with the French Revolution, Russia's revolutionary rulers had perhaps not read Tocqueville's cautionary tale about the persistence of the old-regime state. If they had, they might have learned quite a bit.

The Russian state during the nineteenth century was in many ways weak, administratively circumscribed, and understaffed. Typical of many land empires, it neglected provincial administration and distrusted its own personnel stationed outside the capitals. Nevertheless, Russia had grandiose aspirations of effecting a social revolution that would strengthen its geopolitical position.

Such great power ambitions emerged even stronger in 1917 with the new Soviet state, whose social modernization program was even more extravagant. Having inherited much of the social structure, administrative personnel, bureaucratic structures, and great power aspirations of old regime Russia, the Soviet leadership dreamed, as Tocqueville wrote of the French revolutionaries, of making "use of the central power . . . for shattering the whole social structure and rebuilding it on lines that seemed to them desirable."[120] Tocqueville could never have anticipated, however, that the new regime would add a volatile force to the mix—the drive to build a socialist countryside.

An investigation of the period between 1914 and 1920 raises several issues that form a backdrop for the rest of this study chronicling the dilemmas radiating from the Commissariat's efforts to peacefully "reorganize" the Soviet countryside in the 1920s. The foundation of the People's Commissariat of Agriculture was laid, often in unexpected ways, under the Old Regime and in the first years after the Bolshevik revolution of October 1917. The Commissariat inherited much across the revolutionary divide, despite the hopes of more idealistic Bolsheviks who expected a complete break with the discredited past.

Acting out of desperation during wartime, Russian governments relied on coercion to acquire agricultural produce to feed the cities and army. Historians have demonstrated elements of continuity between the Russian Imperial, Provisional Government, and Soviet Civil War policies regarding the problems of wartime food supply.[121] In all three cases and with varying degrees of success, the state implemented measures calling for the compulsory delivery of grain by peasant producers. Governments tended to regard the countryside instrumentally, as a producer of commodities to be turned over to the state for its use; the peasantry was the subject of state action. Agricultural assistance agencies were transformed into part of the wartime food procurement apparatus. Some leading officials in the Ministry of Agriculture embraced this new role.[122] Yet many agricultural specialists resented the new procurement duties, considering them to be detrimental to what they regarded as their real mission, to teach farmers to raise the productivity of communal agriculture. In each case, agricultural assistance programs were neglected in the interest of procuring foodstuffs. In wartime, the food procurement bureaucracies gained the upper hand; land and agriculture administrations were frustrated. During the early Bolshevik period, conflict between two methods of approaching the countryside was manifested in intense bureaucratic struggles between the Commissariat of Agriculture and the Commissariat of Food Supply.

The Soviet state was bequeathed a peasant economy composed of farmers entrenched in their communes, employing the traditional modes of organization, tools, and methods that Russian state modernizers had considered severely inefficient and unproductive. Although general agricultural output per capita slowly rose over the two decades before World War I, state officials remained concerned about lingering weaknesses in production relative to Western countries, which they attributed to a combination of rural overpopulation, soil exhaustion, poorly developed markets, ineffective technology, inefficient organization of farming, and the peasants' own stubbornness. In addition, Commissariat officials became heirs to a legacy of comparative economic backwardness, understanding that Russia occupied a relatively challenging position in the world, struggling to become an industrial power while lagging in important ways behind advanced Western economies. The Bolsheviks also inherited a sprawling ministerial apparatus, with most of its structures and much of its personnel intact.

This legacy was received in sharply contrasting ways. Pragmatists were pleased that experienced people could support the Commissariat's assignments. Some Bolsheviks, however, were hostile to the leftover personnel, almost none of whom were communists and many of whom had belonged to or sympathized with noncommunist political parties. It is one of the great paradoxes of the Bolshevik revolution that the new regime was fully committed to using the power of the state to oversee the massive reconstruction of the social and economic spheres, yet it remained at the same time deeply suspicious of the bureaucracy that lay at its disposal.

The roots of the agronomic aid effort were shallow thanks to underfunding and the brief period of time that agronomic aid programs fully functioned before the war. In times of crisis, a government could bypass them fairly easily, though they were never completely uprooted. During the Civil War, the Bolshevik Party marginalized efforts to rescue communal and individual (as opposed to state-organized collective) agriculture as they focused on the forced procurement of foodstuffs for supplying the army and cities. Within the Council of People's Commissars, Narkomzem occupied an ineffective position in relation to agencies that had been assigned more power and authority in the wartime economy, especially the food supply commissariat. Party leaders set aside the task of raising the productivity of the small peasantry through the distribution of tools, seeds, and agronomic knowledge in order to support the more immediate tasks of prevailing in the military struggle, acquiring food for soldiers and urban dwellers, and establishing a "communist" economy. As a result, the agriculture commissariat received minimal funding (most of which was dedicated to the nearly impossible task of establishing a network of socialist farms). And, not surprisingly, frustration built among professionals with aspirations to teach and transform the peasantry, both during World War I and the Civil War. After the Civil War, one official of the Commissariat of Agriculture recalled "the gaping abyss . . . , the unforgettable, incredible lack of harmony between the Commissariat's very diverse assignments and the workforce and money allocated to fulfill them."[123]

Rarely discussed by policymakers during the Civil War was any formulation of measures to assist with the overwhelming majority of the peasants who lived in traditional communes.[124] Many agricultural specialists regarded the impotence of Narkomzem during the war as an indication of the extent to which the Bolsheviks neglected assistance to the communal peasantry in this period. Although policy deemphasized the immediate, forcible establishment of collectives by the end of 1918, the gradual creation and maintenance of a collective farming sector remained a major assignment of Narkomzem until mid-1920. B. N. Knipovich, the leading Narkomzem statistician, noted that the establishment of collective farms was felt by the Commissariat's staff to be their "central task."[125] Indeed, as late as September 1920, Sereda sent a circular to provincial land departments scolding them for paying insufficient attention to setting up collective farms.[126] Referring to the 1917–20 period, Knipovich wrote in 1921: "Sometimes it is even pointed out that Narkomzem concentrated all its attention on creating collective farms and state farms, which occupy only 3 percent of the land, leaving the remaining 97 percent without attention."[127] Knipovich's words echo those of many pre-revolutionary agricultural specialists who despaired of the state's failure to devote adequate resources to modernizing communal farming. Similarly, reminiscent of agronomists during World War I, many agricultural specialists seem to have resented the agency's weakness and the regime's abandonment of agronomic aid efforts during the Civil War. Overall, the approach to the countryside during the 1914–20 period became an important and lasting legacy for the post–Civil War Commissariat of Agriculture. This wartime legacy was difficult to shed.

In spite of their marginalization during the war, the specialized subsections of the Commissariat that functioned poorly during the war demonstrated remarkable resilience, serving as the nerve center of the organization once the regime began to introduce NEP in March 1921. The end of the war and the gradual introduction of NEP provided reasons for new, if guarded, optimism to specialists in the shadow subculture of expertise, a subculture that would emerge stronger in 1921. NEP rhetoric would provide a new atmosphere of civil peace with the villages. The Commissariat would become an institutional foundation of the new—and problematic—political alliance (smychka) between the proletarian dictatorship and the peasantry.

Thus, the Commissariat of Agriculture's mission to cultivate a Soviet countryside in the 1920s–a mission much more complex and ambitious than that of tsarist agricultural aid programs–brought forth unexpected and powerful tensions and conflicts, as did NEP itself. The Commissariat serves as an example of the extraordinary challenges the new Soviet state faced as it attempted to come to terms with the great majority of the population. The fortunes of Narkomzem in the 1920s, in many ways the prototypical ministry in the state machinery, became a litmus test for the prospects of the NEP. As went the Commissariat of Agriculture in the 1920s, so went NEP.

2

A Struggle for Identity

The Uncertain Transition to the New Economic Policy, 1921–1923

Our apparatus is such an abomination.
V. I. Lenin, September 25, 1922

In 1921, in the wake of the savage Civil War, specialists in the Commissariat of Agriculture were, perhaps surprisingly, cautiously optimistic about the future of the devastated Soviet countryside. Late in that year, officials in the Commissariat's most crucial division, the Central Administration for Land Working (TsUZem), authored a small but revealing book. The slim volume served as a mission statement for an organization confronting novel challenges in the unstable peacetime conditions prevailing after the March 1921 introduction of NEP. TsUZem, known as "the brains of the country in the field of agriculture," titled the book *The Central Administration for Landworking in the Light of NEP*.[1] The title, with its metaphor of light so common to the progressive Russian intelligentsia, is revealing. For the Commissariat's specialists, the 1918–20 period, with its plummeting harvests, food requisitions, sharply declining area under seed, peasant suspicion of state activity, and state neglect of small-scale farming, was akin to the Dark Ages. By the end of the war, the agricultural situation was disastrous. The specter of a major famine hung over large parts of the country. In fact, the only parallel Commissariat officials could find in all of European history was the Thirty Years War of the seventeenth century. NEP, by contrast, promised to create conditions in which urban agents of the state could "bring light" to the village by applying the fruits of science to the ancient inefficiencies of the "uncultured" countryside. Even the Commissariat's publishing house was called The New Village. In its rhetoric, the Soviet government was committed to a new approach that would deliver renewal, progress, and the rationalization of production to the benighted Russian village.

During the war, much to the chagrin of the Commissariat of Agriculture's communist chiefs, the Commissariat of Food Supply's control of rural economic policy had rendered Narkomzem impoverished and nearly impotent, left in the shadows of political life at the beginning of the decade. The introduction of NEP, however, promised the prospect of increased budgets, elevated prestige, greater input on policy formation, the freedom to work without coercion, and a large dose of the respect that Commissariat officials craved (and that the specialists and staff of many other economic agencies were beginning to enjoy).[2]

Once NEP was launched, the Communist Party leadership committed itself to dedicating more staff and resources not only to the recovery of the collapsed agricultural sector, but ultimately to its restructuring along modern lines. The optimism that flows from the pages of the book reflects a faith that Russian agriculture, which communists and rural specialists alike had long considered so horribly backward, was finally on the verge of a new era. The critical element for the mission's success was the state's support of agricultural specialists in their efforts to spread their expertise among the farming population. One aspect of wartime policies that specialists did *not* reject was the notion that the state and its employees should play a critical role in reorganizing peasant farming along more efficient and productive lines. This emphasis on the state's role is reminiscent of the attitudes of certain Russian professionals and activists, dedicated to the country's economic progress, yet frustrated by the autocracy's stubborn exclusion of them from power. Many pre-war agricultural specialists were driven by a strong sense of mission to use their expertise to change society.[3]

With the introduction of NEP, the Commissariat set forth with new energy to, as they put it, "rescue" the Soviet countryside. Yet this mission was rife with contradictions and unexpected obstacles. The condition of the countryside, the post-war political culture of the Communist Party—much of which greeted NEP as a "retreat," if not an outright defeat—the wariness with which many communists regarded the "petty bourgeois" peasantry, and the weakness of many branches of the state itself, all hindered the Commissariat. As much as any other organization, the Commissariat lobbied for and carried out the gradualist policies of the smychka—the rhetorical alliance between peasantry and working class—that formed the heart of the 1920s' NEP. The Commissariat's institutional culture evolved, linking Bolsheviks and nonparty specialists who could agree on certain fundamental issues, including the need to use the tools of state to peacefully overcome what they considered rural underdevelopment and restore production. A subelite of pragmatic if ambitious specialists saw their leading positions in the economic administrations institutionalized. Nevertheless, before 1923, the Commissariat's personnel frequently saw their moderate approaches challenged both by a substantial lack of resources and by local party enthusiasts intent on applying the coercive lessons they had learned during the Civil War to the problems of rural transformation. At the same time, suspicion simmered among many Bolsheviks, especially at the local level, that noncommunist specialists and officials could not be trusted to manage the rural economy.

Moreover, throughout the 1920s the Commissariat of Agriculture's leaders would find themselves in a delicate political position. The agency became a veritable "Commissariat of the Peasantry" inside the "proletarian dictatorship" at a time when many Communist Party members still considered the interests of these groups antithetical. In 1921 and 1922, some party members grumbled that Narkomzem's policies strengthened the peasantry, and especially the wealthier peasantry, at the expense of the working class. An experiment to appoint a muzhik (peasant man) as chief of the Commissariat revealed a great deal about the nature and cultures of specialized economic agencies after the war. By the end of 1922, numerous crises of leadership and politics—together with the consequences of a horrific famine—shadowed attempts to rebuild rural Russia.

The State of the Countryside after the War

On the eve of NEP, the Soviet economy was in shambles. Hopes for a quick international revolution that would send assistance to revolutionary Russia were fading. The population of European Russia had declined 3.6 percent after seven years of war, epidemics, and emigration. In many areas, industrial production had dropped by an astonishing 75 percent. Coal output was at one-quarter of the 1913 level, electricity at one third. The production of steel and pig iron had plummeted to 3 percent of the pre-war level.[4]

Agricultural output experienced an equally chilling decline. By 1920, grain production was just over 50 percent of the 1909–13 average. The amount of land under seed, which had begun to decline in 1914–15 as a consequence of poorly conceived tsarist food policies, plummeted most sharply in the southeastern part of European Russia, an important grain-producing region. In 1921, fourteen million of the thirty-eight million acres of the area sown in European Russia failed to produce crops.[5] Livestock production in 1921 reached only 27 percent of the already sharply reduced 1917 level. Small livestock such as goats declined to 40 percent of the pre-war level, with the Central Producer Region and the North Caucuses the most seriously affected areas. Pig and sheep farming almost completely disappeared in the European part of the RSFSR. Organizing veterinary assistance to fight raging epidemics among livestock in the post-war conditions was extremely difficult. Purebred stock was nearly wiped out, as were milk cows, situations made worse by the mass consumption of these animals during a period of food shortages. Estimates agree that the number of horses dropped by 30 to 40 percent between 1916 and 1922. The large-scale death of draft animals in the first years of the 1920s kept the major grain producing areas of the South and Central Producer regions lagging behind their pre-war levels during the entire decade.[6]

The production of industrial crops such as sugar beets, cotton, and flax also suffered badly, especially in relation to grain production. Intensive production dropped; less progressive forms of extensive farming spread as villagers increasingly planted for subsistence rather than markets. For example, in 1921, cotton fabric was produced at less than 5 percent of prewar levels.[7] At the same time, the peasants' "black repartition" of farmland all but eliminated the farms run by two of the most productive segments of the rural economy—landlords and the wealthier farmers. Because large commercial estates were the source of industrial crops, their dissolution during 1917 and 1918 severely disrupted the output of products essential to the industrial economy.

In terms of landholding and livestock ownership, a widespread leveling of the rural population continued in most regions. The extremes of wealth and poverty were further smoothed out as the repartitional commune reabsorbed the homesteads of farmers who had separated onto khutors and otrubs.[8] The percentage of peasant households with no land dropped from about 11 percent to 7 percent of the total; those in the middle, with from one to four desiatins, increased from 58 percent to 72 percent; and households working more than four desiatins declined from 31 to 21 percent of the rural population. This leveling of land holding was partly responsible for the decrease in agricultural production as larger, more productive farms were divided into smaller ones that produced less. The wartime destruction of prime farmland and the sharp drop in the manufacture of agricultural tools also played large roles. As late as 1927, as much as 95 percent of agricultural land in the Russian Republic was still held in repartitional tenure and redistributed periodically. While the regular, voluntary redistributions of lands were considered by farmers to have beneficial consequences, especially in times of scarcity, state officials regarded this tradition with alarm since it splintered holdings into ever smaller and less productive parcels. With rare exceptions, the export of agricultural produce also came to a standstill during the 1920s. Indeed, by 1925, the USSR had become a net importer of animal products, including leathers and wool.[9]

This extraordinary rural disruption established the context within which Narkomzem's staff and Communist Party policymakers tried to plan the recovery of agriculture. Strip and three-field farming, low levels of fertilization, poor tools, and low literacy rates continued to be regarded by the country's political leadership and agricultural specialists as huge problems. In the minds of Commissariat leaders—and one is tempted to agree with them—the success of the entire economy, and ultimately the survival of the country, depended on the resurrection of the countryside. Convinced that Russian agriculture had been decimated by the war and set back decades from its already underdeveloped level, Narkomzem's personnel agreed with Lenin when he declared, "We know that in our devastated country the rural economy has been destroyed."[10]

The Introduction of NEP

It was in this environment of devastation that dramatic reversals in policies were forced upon the Soviet regime by circumstances that it did not welcome and could not control. The party leadership adopted NEP as a response to widespread and often violent dissatisfaction among sections of the peasantry rebellions in the armed forces (especially among the sailors at the Kronstadt naval base), and havoc wrought by the Civil War. The introduction of NEP was unexpected and bewildering inside the ranks of the Communist Party. Many people at all levels of the party strongly resisted the introduction of NEP policies.[11]

The government prepared for a long period of transformation to socialism in the countryside. As Lenin remarked pessimistically in March 1921, " To remold the farmer, to remold his entire psychology, will take generations."[12] Lenin expounded the general principles of NEP at the Tenth Party Congress, though in practice measures were introduced piecemeal in over one hundred different laws and decisions over the course of a year. Laws allowed and encouraged capitalist exchange. To restore the peasantry's deliveries of produce to the city and to encourage the replanting of abandoned fields, the government replaced forcible requisitioning with a tax in kind—a payment in food that equaled a certain percentage of their harvest. The peasants were allowed to sell on the re-legalized markets what remained of their produce after paying the tax. The tax in kind's burden on the peasantry initially equaled about half of the wartime delivery quotas. Lenin wrote in March 1921 that "the question of the replacement of requisitions with a tax in kind is primarily and essentially a political question . . . . We must not try to hide anything, but must say openly that the peasants are dissatisfied. . . . We must reckon with this and reexamine our policy."[13] The economy could not recover in the absence of the help, or at least the neutrality, of the peasantry.

The regime also gave peasants the right to choose their preferred form of land tenure. As a concession to budget constraints, to peasant dislike of collective farms, and in line with the emphasis on conciliating the "middle peasant," the government severely cut back funding for collective farms, continuing a process that had begun in 1919. Without state support, most collectives collapsed.

The tax in kind, however, was introduced too late to affect the sowing of the spring fields in 1921 and therefore could not immediately help increase supplies of seed and grain for 1921. Requisitions continued through the summer of 1921 and into the fall, and these methods still angered villagers and exacerbated the food situation. In some important grain-producing regions, including Western Siberia and Ukraine, introduction of the tax in kind was delayed.

Famine

Another cataclysm befell large swaths of the country during this period. As early as September 1920, Narkomzem published alarming reports in *Pravda* and *Izvestiia* warning of serious harvest failures and the possibility of starvation. The Narkomzem collegium warned at least as early as June 1921 that the famine would be worse than that caused by the disastrous 1891–92 crop failure. Crops were shriveling up in the fields. The harvest was tiny, and many farmers salvaged only enough food to feed their families for a matter of weeks.[14]

Two consecutive crop failures precipitated by drought marked the great famine of 1921–22. In the fall of 1921, between twenty and thirty million people, or upwards of one-third of the population of the RSFSR, lacked sufficient food.[15] The Volga, Urals, Ukraine, and Northern Caucuses were the hardest hit regions. Up to thirty million people suffered from the effects of malnutrition and disease, and at least three to four million people died.[16] American relief organizations still fed 10 million people a day as late as early 1923. Descriptions of life in the countryside pouring into Narkomzem's Moscow offices from the provinces were nightmarish—"critical," "catastrophic," "hopeless," "completely shattered."[17] Whole villages existed on poisonous "surrogate" breads, made from a combination of bark, weeds, grass, clay, and even ground bone. Instances of cannibalism were reported. Armies of beggars and starving migrants, having sold all their possessions, flocked to the cities in panic, then traveled from town to town desperately searching for food. Starving refugees camped along riverbanks, hoping to catch boats down the Volga to regions they believed had food. Hundreds of thousands of homeless children roamed the countryside, often committing crimes.[18] Typhus and cholera struck down hundreds of thousands and also spread by boat along the Volga. Children were especially prone to death from disease, and according to official figures over 7 million were starving in 1922.[19] Livestock was also decimated. Although deputy commissar of agriculture I. A. Teodorovich called the famine Russia's worst in fifty years, this was a gross understatement.[20] The working metaphor of Commissariat officials in late 1921 and 1922 was *apocalypse*.

We can only briefly summarize the causes of the famine. Famine in Russia was not unique to the Soviet period, of course. The countryside had been afflicted with dozens of major crop failures in the preceding centuries. The famine of 1921–22, however, was unusually extensive and resulted in vastly more victims than usual. Rainfall was very scarce in 1920, but the nadir of the drought came between April and June 1921 when the affected region experienced only 7 percent of its average precipitation.[21] Terrible heat and hot winds burned crops in the fields. Inadequate irrigation and a subsistence rural economy contributed to the severity of the disaster.

The extraordinary dislocation caused by the Great War and the Civil War was another major contributing factor. Imperial food policies during the Great

War created disincentives for peasants to plant crops beyond those needed for subsistence; sown area declined sharply during the war. Similar policies were implemented by the Bolsheviks during the Civil War, with similar results. The destruction of transportation and communications as a result of the Great War and the Civil War also placed enormous obstacles in the way of Bolsheviks' attempts to supply the famine zone with food and medicine. Not only railroads, but river barges as well had been destroyed in large numbers, and the factories that built and repaired them had also been ruined. Foreign blockades of Russian ports compounded the shortage of industrial goods of all kinds. The supply of farm implements and tools had fallen by three quarters or more during the World War and Civil War.[22] Widespread death of livestock resulted from the lack of fodder and wartime requisitioning of animals by Red and White armies alike. The drop in sown area during the war, in large part a direct result of the confiscation of farmers' food, seed, and animals, weakened a rural economy that could not provide a reserve in the event of crop failure. Fuel was also in very short supply. As a result, food often spoiled waiting in railroad cars for distribution.

Adding to the catastrophic situation, the Soviet state continued to requisition food in the Volga region into the summer of 1921, well after the war had ended and conditions in stricken areas had already become grave.[23] Lenin recognized that wartime policies had contributed to the famine, and he stated this at the Tenth Party Congress in March 1921. Karl Radek acknowledged that Civil War policies were a major factor in causing the famine, insisting that they had been "the price of victory over the imperialists and White Guards."[24]

"To Save and Strengthen Agriculture": An Evolving Mission in a New Environment

In Moscow, despite—or perhaps because of—the severity of the challenges before the Commissariat of Agriculture staff, they gained a newfound sense of self-importance and purpose once NEP began. This relative buoyancy is especially pronounced when contrasted with the demoralization that had existed in wartime. As one Commissariat official observed, spirits in the Commissariat had been lifted by early 1921. It had taken close to five years, but operations had finally become more active and businesslike. Divisions were organized more efficiently, the staff's quality improved, and its commitment to work intensified.[25]

One reason for the emergence of the Commissariat staff's more self-assured outlook was that state agencies that had previously attempted to appropriate all responsibility for the rural economy, such as Vesenkha and especially Narkomprod, rapidly lost power once the war ended. With the introduction of NEP, the Commissariat of Agriculture gained stature relative to these dual barons of the war communist economy, to which Narkomzem had lost every political battle in wartime. Although it remained an institutional competitor for another two years, Narkomprod was increasingly on the defensive as its raison d'etre began to evaporate in 1921–22.[26] The logic of NEP policies greatly eroded the food supply commissariat's position in the national economy and consequently in the political arena. A free market in grain left little need for a quasi-military agency that acquired grain for the state through nonmarket channels. The movement toward a money economy ordained the finance commissariat, not the food supply commissariat, as the national tax collector. In the localities food workers were the target of peasant violence, resulting in hundreds of deaths as villagers took revenge.[27]

Indeed, Narkomzem officials, sensing Narkomprod's vulnerability and unpopularity with farmers, unleashed an attack in the press and at party and soviet congresses. Throughout 1921–22, Narkomzem lobbied intensively, in open and closed forums, for a reduction in the amount of taxes peasants would have to pay, much to the chagrin of the Narkomprod leadership. Moreover, Sovnarkom had lowered the tax in kind by 1922, even for the well-off peasants, to just 10 percent of production. Narkomzem also alleged that Narkomprod's "harsh" requisitioning activities had exacerbated the effects of the crop failures. At the Eleventh Congress of Soviets local land workers laid out in detail the continuing excesses of requisitioning food brigades, charging that the brigades completely misunderstood their tasks.[28] The Commissariat of Agriculture further lobbied to have the tax in kind on meat canceled, since high taxes amid food shortages forced the peasants to slaughter their milk cows even though cattle were already terribly scarce.[29] One Narkomzem official went so far as to joke during a discussion of the need to control mice, locusts, and other creatures that destroyed crops, "Well, comrades, here I am reminded of the battle against pests. I think that the biggest pest of all is the food supply commissariat."[30] The comment was met with laughter by the delegates.

In a policy sure to irritate Narkomzem, by the summer of 1922 Narkomprod's representatives were already using its own predictions of a bumper harvest to argue for higher taxes on farmers and to push for increased exports of grain. In reply, the Commissariat of Agriculture warned that the harvest, in fact, would be smaller than many people expected.[31] Although yields per acre and total harvests were well above the extremely low levels of 1921, land officials argued that famine would again threaten if food supply and taxation policies were not managed properly. The Commissariat of Agriculture suspected that Narkomprod was exaggerating the total harvest as a way of collecting more tax in kind, often by coercive means, which Narkomzem rejected as an economic disincentive for farmers.[32] With higher taxes and exports, grain shortfalls could occur and starvation might again become a widespread phenomenon. These predictions turned out to be correct.

As early as August 1922, reports began appearing of starvation and the possibility of a new famine in the same areas as the 1921–22 catastrophe.[33] Resumed collection of taxes in kind, together with poor weather and the residual effects of the 1920–21 crop failures, created another crisis. Hunger was not as severe or widespread in 1923 as 1921–22, yet it was still very serious. Police reports document that hundreds of thousands, if not millions, of people suffered from shortages of food, ate surrogate breads, and migrated in panicked attempts to find sustenance.[34] Thousands starved or died of disease. Provinces in the Northwest, Central, Volga, and Southeast regions and parts of Ukraine again suffered from famine. Despite these grain shortages, the Soviet government exported more than forty-five million poods of grain in 1923. This apparently was done to gain capital to invest in industry and produce manufactures for peasants to purchase, thereby stimulating production of surplus grain.[35]

Suddenly on the defensive over the issues of taxation and food requisitioning in the late summer of 1922, the food supply commissariat's leaders argued that Narkomzem was unfairly "agitating" against their policies. The Narkomprod leadership responded with venom to what it considered to be scurrilous public calls for a reduction of its powers.[36] N. P. Briukhanov (Tsiurupa's successor as food supply commissar) alleged that his agency was the victim of a calculated campaign whose goal was the "withering away" of the agency.[37] Certainly, the Commissariat of Agriculture's specialist and political leadership hoped that their agency would be able to take advantage of the breach left in rural policy by Narkomprod's decline. Narkomzem's program and approach to rural development were more consistent with NEP's emphasis on free markets and persuasion. Narkomprod's demise was not exclusively a result of Narkomzem's campaign, of course. The food supply commissariat was the target of attacks from many directions, and it was officially disbanded in 1923–24. Narkomzem wasted no time in picking over the food commissariat's corpse. A memo circulated by the Commissariat's Moscow office to provincial land sections encouraging them to hire any agricultural specialists left unemployed by the food commissariat's timely disappearance.[38] Ultimately, Narkomzem's main competitor for supremacy over the agrarian economy was a victim of NEP.

Together with the Commissariat of Finance, Narkomzem was one of the main institutional proponents of NEP, Narkomprod of war communism. Indeed, the Commissariat of Agriculture leadership frequently defined its organizational mission and methods by directly contrasting them with their old foe, the food supply commissariat. In its mission to transform the countryside, Narkomzem was devoted to using persuasion, not coercion; the application of science, not military methods. NEP was more conducive to a scientific and educational approach to socioeconomic challenges. Narkomzem's attacks on the food supply commissariat helped the agency take advantage of the prevailing (if not unanimous or enthusiastic) sentiment among party elites that Civil War methods should be abandoned, at least for the short term. At the same time, contrasting its own activities with those of Narkomprod allowed the Commissariat of Agriculture's leadership to take the high ground, flaunting its superior moral authority as it advocated (with Lenin's encouragement) for the importance of technical expertise, scientific knowledge, and peaceful methods.

Smychka

In addition to its elevated position vis-à-vis the faltering food supply commissariat, Narkomzem's more optimistic outlook resulted from the fact that, with the gradual introduction of NEP, a more peaceful and cooperative relationship with the peasantry became a new priority in the party elite's rhetoric.[39] The party leadership deemed the recovery of agriculture to be one of the nation's most pressing goals. G. Krzhizhanovskii, head of the State Planning Commission (Gosplan), stated in November 1921 that his agency "considers agriculture the fundamental basis of the whole state economy."[40] The next month Mikhail I. Kalinin similarly argued that "the question of agriculture will be the cornerstone of our work; all remaining questions will depend upon its resolution."[41]

The goal of a strong alliance—smychka—between peasant and proletarian became a central tenet of the regime's peacetime relationship with the rural population. Various aspects of the smychka will be discussed below, but suffice it to say here that, with the cessation of wartime requisitions, the regime took a relatively "soft line" toward the peasantry, and Narkomzem's political and specialist leadership became a primary architect and defender of that line. The Commissariat gathered, interpreted, and distributed much of the data that supported the new party policies. Narkomzem's political and specialist leadership placed new emphasis on improving production within the communal structure, while tolerating individual homestead farming. The Commissariat distanced itself from the food requisitions and the emphasis (if waning after 1919) on setting up the collective farms of the war years, which had been very unpopular with the peasantry. The conclusion of a conference of Narkomzem personnel in June 1921 summarizes the Commissariat's new role: "Our land policy has changed. Earlier we assigned the most significance to forms of land usage. Now we assign the most importance to the mass lifting of the productive forces of peasant farming, relying on the equipment and means of production that the peasantry already possesses. The support and encouragement of socialist forms of agriculture are in the past; raising existing productive forces is in the present."[42] Charged with the challenge of persuading the farming population that the Soviet state had their interests in mind, Narkomzem's specialists and officials were a vital link for establishing peaceful relations with the peasant population. In many regions of the RSFSR, Commissariat of Agriculture emissaries were the only state representatives who actually traveled to the villages.

During the first part of NEP, the party assigned the Commissariat two formidable missions consistent with the goals of the new policies and the new political relations with the peasantry. The first was to rebuild the shattered agricultural economy, an assignment whose success would be measured in terms of total agricultural output, sown area, and marketed produce. The second task was to educate the peasantry about modern farming methods, in order to combat inefficiencies in agricultural technique.[43] In this period, the recovery of output took precedence over programs to educate farmers, although the tasks were linked.

It is important to emphasize that, following the traditions of Russian agronomy, specialists placed great stock in educational efforts. Based on their experience before the outbreak of World War I, they believed that if they could persuade some of the village's risk takers (often the most prosperous families in a village) to adopt new technologies and methods through the use of demonstrations, lectures, pamphlets, and other educational tools, then other peasants would follow when they witnessed the positive results. As a result, a new risk-taking peasant elite would emerge. Momentum for change would build in villages. Officials reasoned that instruction in the science of farming among the peasantry would lead to more efficient use of land and livestock, increased productivity, and larger yields. Positive change in peasants' economic behavior was considered a necessary precondition for cultural transformation. This approach indicates that specialists believed that many peasants were not wholly "irrational," even if they often farmed inefficiently. Rather, there was a faith among agricultural specialists that, once exposed to the proper information, correctly presented, peasants could and would gradually learn and adopt "better practices." In fact the entire Narkomzem approach to rural modernization was built precisely on this premise.[44]

In the face of scarce resources for education in these first two years of NEP, however, the Commissariat's activities were largely defined by the need to halt, and ultimately to reverse, the devastating decline in agricultural production. Actions to ameliorate the consequences of the famine and minimize the risk of recurrence dominated the agency's agenda. Measures included expanding the amount of cultivated area; supplying badly needed seeds, tools, machines, and livestock; defining boundaries between plots and communes; setting up rental points for loaning machines, equipment, and horses; and establishing breeding stations for cattle, horses, and oxen.[45] The Commissariat's specialists attempted to develop peasant agricultural technology and modes of production. Narkomzem encouraged the transition from three-field fallow to multifield crop rotation practices. Its personnel also tried to reduce the intermingling of strips and the problem of strips located far away from the village (*dal'nozemlia*), especially in the central, northern, and western areas where these phenomena were most pronounced. In some areas Narkomzem specialists gave special attention to the revival of industrial crops. In addition, the Commissariat initiated small-scale forays into veterinary assistance and land improvement work.[46] Because of the results of the famine, in addition to great shortages of staff, equipment, and money, the Commissariat in 1921 and 1922 necessarily had to focus efforts on quantitative rather than qualitative improvement in production. For example, officials urged peasants to expand the amount of land they planted, rather than immediately improve farming technique or organization. The famine necessarily reinforced the traditional peasant bias toward extensive rather than intensive agriculture, a bias which officials hoped to change in the long run. Thus, Moscow charged the agronomists, surveyors, and other specialists posted to land sections with stimulating the output of all types of agricultural produce while simultaneously lifting the general level of the peasantry's agronomic literacy by spreading knowledge that would enable farmers to improve output in the future.

The State's Role

In the wake of the war, officials understood their primary mission as nothing less than the rescue and remolding of peasant agriculture, albeit by using exclusively peaceful, noncoercive methods, while downplaying class distinctions. How would the Commissariat accomplish this extraordinary task, which nearly everyone agreed would take "decades, not years"?[47] The agency's leaders argued that the state, and in particular Narkomzem, should play a major interventionist role in managing and rebuilding the rural economy, and this remained a crucial tenet of the Commissariat's ethos throughout the decade.

The famine reinforced three central elements of an evolving Commissariat ideology. First, peasant farming on the whole was dangerously underdeveloped and remained perpetually on the brink of disaster. Second, most peasants were ignorant of the best ways to farm and would remain so without significant educational efforts undertaken by specialists (and funded generously by the state). Third, the state was compelled to intervene decisively to assist farmers and to create the conditions for agricultural recovery in the context of NEP policies. Importantly, these elements of the Commissariat ideology were ones that both Narkomzem's communist officials and its nonparty agricultural specialists could agree upon.

Among leading officials in the Commissariat, there was a shared belief that they had to lead the peasantry away from its "primitive" modes of production. Some officials blamed villagers' own inertia, passivity, and rejection of modern science for the famine. Thus, crop failures might be instructive for farmers in the long run since the catastrophe would give them tremendous incentive to adopt the modern techniques that agronomists had been preaching for years. As one land official wrote in 1922, "Death from famine is a motor for progress in Tsaritsyn Province." Another central Narkomzem official wrote, "The drought was not unexpected. There were warnings. But unfortunately the weak, poor, and still-dark peasantry could not prepare for it and were left with burnt-out fields and meadows." One dismayed observer wrote that superstitious peasants did not respond to their parched fields with science. "Instead of rationally managing their fields" they resorted to "praying and icons, or they bathe the rooster in the grain, or they tell fortunes in the fields at dusk"[48] Of course, one is left wondering just how peasants could have "rationally managed their fields" amid catastrophic weather conditions, overzealous requisitions, high taxes, a crippling lack of resources, and weak agricultural assistance agencies. Nevertheless, many Narkomzem and party officials understood the famine both as an opportunity to intervene and as proof that most peasants should not yet be left to their own devices. Narkomzem's personnel sometimes referred to themselves as the "only source of culture in the village," especially in light of severe cutbacks in funding for rural schools, and medical care in 1921–22.[49]

In October 1921, Bolshevik agricultural expert and Commissariat collegium member M. E. Shefler addressed the government's role in the agricultural economy, summarizing the view of the Commissariat's leadership. "It is absolutely impossible to imagine [peasant agriculture] *spontaneously* making advances in the future." The Russian village is "extremely backward, dark, deprived of adequate knowledge, [and] not accustomed to producing in a cultured way." He went on: "You hear people say every day that no regulation by the state is necessary now that NEP is here; [they say that] NEP is itself the regulator of the economy. In fact, of course, this is not so. Regulation by the state is the only way to save and strengthen agriculture. Just look at Siberia where huge expanses of land are either empty or irrationally sown. . . . Or look at the state of animal husbandry, so backward and disgusting. Powerful state intervention is needed to drain swamps, combat abandoned land . . . [and] restore territory afflicted by drought."[50]

The Commissariat's leadership insisted that under NEP conditions its role should not shrink but *grow* and grow sharply. An overriding theme was, in Shefler's words, "powerful state intervention" on the basis of education, persuasion, and science. Of course, balancing "powerful intervention" in village life with "peaceful persuasion" was a delicate task indeed for a Communist Party just emerging from a Civil War. In any case, as will be detailed below, the Commissariat's far-reaching aspirations to intercede decisively during the first two years of NEP greatly outstripped its modest abilities and scanty resources.

Among Commissariat of Agriculture officials, the commitment to increased activism thus coincided with the desire to "uplift" the agrarian sector. This conviction that peasant agriculture was on the whole, as Shefler put it, "extremely inefficient," and that the state must unleash an attack on its underdevelopment was an essential shared belief of Narkomzem's personnel. This was prevalent especially among the party members comprising the Commissariat's political leadership, but also among many nonparty specialists. In the words of one

Narkomzem collegium member, "Russian peasants farm so primitively and unsuccessfully (as in their grandfather's time) and they are so backward in their methods compared to profitable agriculture abroad" that efforts to improve peasant farming will practically have to start from scratch. Officials could provide dozens of examples of enduring, "decades-old if not centuries-old" irregularities in farming that needed to be "liquidated." The peasantry, according to the impatient Commissariat collegium member A. Mitrofanov, has become inert as a result of generations of stifling state guardianship. "No improvement of agriculture will be accomplished without a stubborn and decisive struggle with loafers," who, he made clear, comprise the majority of the rural population.[51] Mitrofanov urged a frontal assault on the "agronomic illiteracy of the peasantry. As long as the peasant works his earth a certain way, based only on how his grandfathers and great grandfathers worked it, the peasant will regard every suggestion for improving farming methods, no matter where the suggestion comes from, as an attempt to harm him. The peasant masses must understand the ruinous absurdity of holding on to grandfather's way of farming. They must come to understand, even if just a little bit, elementary information about which new scientific methods of working the soil and farming give the best results and exactly why they do so."[52]

Yet what is also critically important about this formulation of Mitrofanov, who was one of the least sympathetic of all Narkomzem's political leadership toward concessions to the peasantry, was that he believed that the peasants could "come to understand, even if just a little bit, elementary information" about modern techniques and technology. In other words, peasants' ability to learn how to farm better was accepted by leading officials in the land agencies and was seen as the way out of the country's agricultural mess. While this attitude is condescending toward the farming traditions of the Russian peasantry, it is not the same as believing that peasants were immutably irrational beings. This notion that peasants could and would change the way they farm for the better under the influence of good teachers and economic incentives lay at the heart of the Narkomzem approach to rural transformation.

In addition, one sees that for Mitrofanov the enemy in this equation is not the "kulak," but the lazy, the "loafer." This distinction is another key tenet of the Commissariat's understanding of rural modernization. An important feature of the Narkomzem approach to rural modernization is this emphasis on understanding that the village is divided not along class lines between the rich farmer and the poor farmer. Rather, the village can be seen as divided between the "lazy" peasants, who negatively influence their neighbors, and the "hard-working" peasants, who are to be encouraged and directed along the proper rails.

Inside the Bolshevik Party, many communists elevated the concern about peasant "agronomic illiteracy," which was common both among political and scientific elites, to a higher level. The adoption of NEP "concessions" to the peasantry was greeted with skepticism and confusion by most of the party leadership and the rank and file.[53] Some Bolsheviks continued to regard the peasantry as an irredeemably petty bourgeois and politically unreliable class that hindered society's progress toward socialism. Many party members suggested keeping the peasantry safely subordinated to the proletariat, who should control the Communist Party and the government in this unstable period. In an unpublished December 1921 letter to Lenin, for example, T. I. Sapronov expressed his fear that NEP would dangerously strengthen the peasantry: "It is no secret," he wrote with apprehension, "that with the new economic policy, the little peasant [*muzhichek*] will get stronger." He went on: "If there are two or three more years of good harvests (even one year will lift up the peasant), the peasant will demand his rights in questions of state construction, . . . will try to get the soviets in his hands, or will put forth the slogans of the Constituent Assembly."[54] This statement reflects a larger fear that the goals of the revolution would be swamped by a rejuvenated peasantry largely unsympathetic to Soviet power.

Rural producers, these skeptics feared, might attempt to blackmail Soviet power, to use their overwhelming numbers and control of the food supply to force political demands upon the party and the working class. Some disaffected communists questioned the party's NEP compromise with the "capitalist" proprietary peasantry; suspicion of the peasantry lay just beneath the surface. This suspicion did not disappear over the course of the 1920s, even as the party-line—and the People's Commissariat of Agriculture—became ever more tolerant of the capitalist peasantry. Narkomzem met resistance, especially at local levels, when it attempted to carry out the new policies.

The Civil War's Political Legacy inside the Commissariat

The end of the Civil War also forced Communist Party planners to attempt to reshape the economic commissariats into organizations that were more receptive to the opinions of specialists, more effectively organized, and in closer touch with their local branches. Lenin himself served as a major, if sometimes ambivalent, patron of non-Bolshevik specialists, urging that they be hired and protected.[55] Thanks to its large cadre of experts and its specialist-centered organizational structure, the People's Commissariat of Agriculture was, at least in principle, more prepared to make the transition to NEP than most state agencies emerging from the war.

The post-war ambitions of the state's leaders remained great. Dreams of overtaking the bourgeois economies never died, even as they admitted to themselves that world revolution was not on the horizon. But the government agencies charged with directing this socioeconomic transformation were in disarray. Indeed, a major theme of the immediate post-war period is the chasm between the aspirations of the party and the diminished ability of state structures to handle those challenges. In 1922, Lenin condemned the larger part of the ministerial system. "We have eighteen people's commissariats of which at least fifteen are of no use at all—efficient people's commissariats cannot be found anywhere, and I certainly hope that people will give this more of their attention."[56] All the economic commissariats faced these problems as they attempted to manufacture favorable conditions for the recovery of a wrecked post-war economy.

As was the case with many state agencies, the Commissariat of Agriculture entered the post-war environment burdened by "the legacy of war communism." Like all party and state organizations emerging from the war in early 1921, the Commissariat remained centralized, with a rigidly hierarchical structure. And like the local departments of all commissariats, land sections were still formally part of the executive committees of provincial, uezd, and volost' soviets. Before 1921, Moscow had rarely solicited the opinions of local land sections. Once the Moscow offices made a decision during the war, they passed it down the ladder to the province land sections. The provincial department would, at least in theory, hand the instruction down to the uezds, which then conveyed the decision to the volost' land sections. Sovkhozy, experimental stations, stables, nurseries, and the local land sections themselves all remained under direct control of the Moscow offices of Narkomzem. Local land sections had no legal jurisdiction over any agricultural establishments or enterprises in their areas.

Between 1921 and 1923, Sovnarkom reached the conclusion that the localities should play a "maximum role" in economic administration. One of Sovnarkom's paramount tasks became the decentralization of direct administration while maintaining the centralization of general management and planning. General direction, including policy making, was to remain the prerogative of the national economic agencies working on the basis of a unified, national economic plan. Agreeing with this principle, Narkomzem's leaders argued that overcentralization dampened local initiative and ultimately lowered the productivity of the rural sector overall. The land administration was, albeit gradually and with much confusion, reorganized accordingly. While the collegium fiercely defended its right to design specific land policies, Moscow transferred the responsibility for implementing most policies to provincial and uezd land officials. Direct administration of daily affairs became the priority of local branches. County, province, and volost' branch offices, the reasoning went, were better acquainted with local circumstances. They could fine-tune the general plan, exercise control over the activities of agencies under their supervision, and coordinate their work more rationally.[57] Moscow held on to responsibility only for planning and coordinating measures and for tallying the results of land sections' work.

Yet highly centralized and stiffly hierarchical organizations that discourage initiative and expect total compliance generally have difficulty adapting to changing circumstances. Centralization remained the rule in the commissariats during the first eighteen months of NEP, as they evolved only with great sluggishness. Investigators found that in practice decentralization did not succeed.[58]

Moreover, some land personnel simply remained reluctant to embrace the regime's new accommodation of the peasantry. A Commissariat publication stressed in late 1921, "Above all, every worker in the land organs must become imbued with the spirit and basic principles of the New Economic Policy."[59] Many communists, especially those posted to the provinces, still embraced a worldview that divided opposing sides into irreconcilable enemies. Most Bolsheviks had joined the Communist Party since October 1917. The mass of the party rank and file had received their political and ideological education in the cauldron of the Civil War, and this militarized worldview was difficult to modify. Deputy Commissar of Agriculture Osinskii complained in a May 11, 1921, letter to the Central Committee that many local communists were concerned that the abandonment of food requisitioning meant the gradual return to "bourgeois relations." Certain officials in Orel guberniia regarded all but the poorest peasants as "natural saboteurs in their relations toward Soviet power."[60] Though the number was shrinking, the belief persisted that the peasantry was a group to be immediately conquered, that the mission of the working class in rural Russia was to accomplish "political hegemony over the countryside."[61]

During the first two years of NEP, the Narkomzem leadership searched for a fresh group of cadres to staff an apparatus charged with tasks much different from those that it had pursued just a few months earlier, and these new cadres were expected to take a more "appropriate" approach to the peasantry.[62] Indeed, one reason why the Commissariat's leadership brought so many noncommunist, pre-revolutionary specialists back into local land sections in 1921–22 may have been to dilute the radicalism of the Commissariat's own local personnel. Many of the Civil War cohort simply never adapted to working in a Commissariat that had so thoroughly embraced concessions to the peasantry. As much as two years passed before many of these "enthusiasts" either fully embraced the new policy or quit the land administration outright. In the words of collegium member M. E. Shefler in November 1922, "The transition to NEP by the land organs has come late."[63]

A Usable (German) Past: Emerging from the Apocalypse

As the Soviet Republic struggled to rebuild after the Civil War, Narkomzem's leading specialists scoured the European past for an analogous situation to which they could compare Russia's devastating "period of decline." In the process, several elements of the Commissariat's new NEP-era ethos emerged quite clearly. The Central Administration for Land Working, the Commissariat's leading specialized division, put together a collection of articles under the direction of collegium member M. Shefler and the agronomist A. Teitel'. Thirteen of the Administration's leading nonparty specialists served on the editorial board.

In the volume, they posed the question: Had the rural economy of any Western country ever recovered from such a calamity? And if so, how? Specialists in the Administration found lessons in the example of the most catastrophic European conflagration before the Great War, the Thirty Years War (1613–1648).[64] The Thirty Years War reduced the population of the German states by 40 percent and caused untold losses in agricultural land, livestock, and commerce. By studying Germany in the decades after the Thirty Years War, Narkomzem's specialists tried to conceptualize a paradigm that took advantage of catastrophe as a springboard for development in agriculture. They noted that, compared to some of their Western European neighbors, German farmers in the wake of the Thirty Years War were relatively backward in terms of technology and the rational organization of their farms. Like the farms of Russian peasants, German production was based on communal land use with mandatory three-field farming, a very narrow range of sown grains, and communal cattle grazing in the post-harvest fields. As in Russia, population growth in the eighteenth century, together with the growing demand for grain, created incentives for farmers to increase the amount of sown land at the expense of pastures and meadows, which harmed production and decreased the amount of cattle and natural fertilizer. Compounded by insufficient roads and poor weather, these conditions led to frequent crop failures in the eighteenth century German states.

After a major famine in 1771–72, the real stars of the story entered the German stage. Not surprisingly, in the telling of these Narkomzem specialists the heroes who would pull the rural economy from the abyss were *agronomists* practicing their new science in the German countryside. With their help, German agriculture was transformed. The disappearance of famine in the German states (and in most of Europe) was coterminous with the appearance and application of the agronomic sciences. Commissariat specialists regarded the eighteenth-century German experience as a blueprint for creating an intensive, efficient Russian agriculture out of the traditionally extensive. In Germany, under the influence of agronomy and market forces, three-field farming began to give way to crop rotation. Yields rose because of improvements in livestock practices and the growth of fodder crops. Thanks to agronomists, harvests soared. Already by the beginning of the 19th century a "brilliant epoch in the development of agriculture had come into being" in the German states.[65]

This "brilliant epoch" in the history of science and agriculture, however, had passed Russia by. The authors argue that "the factors that brought Russia's agriculture to decline and crisis" in the pre-WWI decades were the same as those that afflicted Central Europe in the first half of the 18th century. Focusing on the Central Provinces of European Russia, they point out that Russia had the same "uncultured three-field system with its 'wild' fallow, cattle grazing on fields, and unvarying grain crops." In addition, peasants curtailed the area devoted to making hay and to pasture, reducing the number of cattle. In this distressed economic condition, Russia entered the European war and the Civil War and, after years of conflict on Russian territory, the small inroads Russia had made toward intensive farming were mostly eliminated and again replaced with subsistence agriculture. The Commissariat's specialists viewed the West's experience as instructive, a valuable lesson from which Russia's rulers did not learn.[66]

Nevertheless, this post-famine period could be both a period of dramatic growth in yields and a new epoch for the agricultural expert, when the knowledge of the agronomist would spread across Soviet Russia. The authors went on to advance a theme that specialists reiterated throughout the 1920s. Not only did farmers lack knowledge, but so did generalist officials in the state bureaucracy. Not only had the "agronomic illiteracy" of the farming population brought the countryside to this deplorable point, but the "weak literacy of the previous ruling circles" also made a major contribution. The authors scolded tsarist officials for "their very poor understanding of the history of the development of Western economic forms, where this development cycle was completed much earlier" than in Russia.[67] The state should grant trained and experienced specialists in the agricultural sciences, they argued implicitly, a greater role not only in the field, but also in designing the policies that would save Russian agriculture.

Though they did not say so openly, Narkomzem specialists also must have had in mind the current Soviet ruling circles when they alluded to ignorance among Russia's rulers. "Agronomic illiteracy," they surely knew, was at least as pronounced among the current Bolshevik leadership as it had been in the tsar's government. In later years, Narkomzem officials would frequently express similar frustration about the ignorance of most Communist Party leaders (not to mention the party rank and file and the peasantry itself) concerning agricultural matters. This ignorance among the political leadership, they would come to argue, could have catastrophic results.

New Leadership, the Brain Trust, and the Institutionalization of Expertise

Against the backdrop of rural catastrophe and the formation of a newly self-confident ideology that focused on using the state and its experts to achieve the salvation of Russian agriculture, the years 1921 and 1922 marked the beginning of struggles to remold Narkomzem's culture into a more specialist-centered one. The Commissariat's leadership aspired to create what Henry Mintzberg calls a "professional bureaucracy" that "modifies the principles of central control to allow greater autonomy to staff. . . ." Such an organization "is appropriate for dealing with relatively stable conditions where tasks are relatively complicated," and for a "professional organization where the people with key skills and abilities need a large measure of autonomy and discretion to be effective in their work."[68] The Commissariat of Agriculture was evolving into such an agency, as support from the top ranks of the Communist Party, new Commissariat leadership, and pivotal structural transformations combined to institutionalize a new culture.

As early as December 1920, a new emphasis on expertise and autonomy was evident, both in the field and in administration in Moscow. Increased efforts to attract specialists were not limited to Narkomzem, of course; the phenomenon was widespread throughout the state and economic administrations. During the first two years of NEP, Sovnarkom tried to transform the Commissariat of Agriculture from its Civil War incarnation into a specialist-centered ministry. If the food commissariat was the prototypical war communist economic agency, then Narkomzem became something of the model commissariat of NEP—and it would remain so until almost the end of the decade.

NEP wrought a fundamental change in state administration. This change can be seen in the switch from a "command-military" approach to rural transformation (epitomized by the food supply brigades) to one that emphasized persuasion and science (typified by the economic commissariats). In Narkomzem and elsewhere in the state apparatus, Lenin's Sovnarkom accelerated a cadre policy pursued only tentatively during the war. Commissariats avidly recruited "bourgeois specialists" and others with technical knowledge (but questionable social or political backgrounds) into all levels of state administration. Specialized knowledge, and practical experience applying that learning, reemerged as precious commodities in high demand. These specialists played a crucial role designing the state's agrarian policies in the 1920s.

Of course, many tens of thousands of the intelligentsia emigrated during the war or immediately thereafter. It was not particularly difficult to leave Soviet Russia in 1921–22, especially through the Caucasus, Finland, or the new Baltic states. Some specialists were exiled. Yet many thousands of noncommunist specialists voluntarily joined the Soviet government and economic administrations in some capacity. Many of these individuals had sympathized with non-Bolshevik left-wing parties, including the social democratic Mensheviks, SRs, and Kadets (constitutional democrats or liberals). Under pressure from Lenin, the Eleventh Party Congress in the spring of 1922 resolved that experts should be encouraged to work for Soviet power and must be protected from the antagonism of unfriendly party officials; party chiefs of administrations should consult even more frequently with specialists.

Mikhail Mikhailovich Glukhov is an example of a prominent specialist who served many years in the tsarist Ministry of Agriculture before choosing to work in the Commissariat of Agriculture. Glukhov began his career in 1903 as an assistant to a district zemstvo agronomist in Kazan'. After graduating with an advanced degree from a forestry institute, he joined the tsarist Ministry of Agriculture and worked there for five years, simultaneously publishing in scientific journals. Glukhov began work in Narkomzem in 1918 and between 1923 and 1928 was involved in its publishing house. The career of another specialist, A. V. Teitel', illustrates the presence of the pre-revolutionary third element at high levels of the Soviet ministry. Employed in land administration for twenty years before the revolution, Teitel's tenure included a fifteen-year stint as an agronomist in the Samara provincial zemstvo. When the zemstvos were liquidated in 1918, he transferred to the Bolshevized provincial land section. Teitel' never joined the Communist Party, yet in 1921 at the age of forty-seven he became the head of TsUZem, at that time the division of Narkomzem with the highest profile. Teitel' remained in leading positions in the Commissariat until 1928.[69]

Like most people's commissariats, Narkomzem experienced a change at the top once the war began winding down. In December 1920, People's Commissar Sereda, the person who had guided Narkomzem through the war communist years in the shadow of the food supply commissariat, was hospitalized for exhaustion. He officially stepped down, just weeks before the introduction of NEP, and soon was made a deputy commissar for Gosplan. The Commissariat of Agriculture had to work without an official people's commissar for an entire year after Sereda's resignation, including the first nine months of NEP.

New leadership oversaw the difficult transition in the Commissariat of Agriculture to a more specialist-centered organization. On January 4, 1921, Sovnarkom named V. V. Osinskii to the post of deputy people's commissar of agriculture.[70] He served as de facto people's commissar in the absence of an official chief until January 1923. Osinskii, whose real name was Valerian V. Obolenskii, was an Old Bolshevik, having joined the party in 1907. Descended from a poor branch of the famous aristocratic family, Osinskii was well educated, erudite, and fluent in several languages. He was also a member of the Central Committee, unlike the virtually unknown commissar Sereda. Lenin respected Osinskii's intelligence and dedication. In 1919–20, however, Osinskii had been a "Left communist" and a leader of the Democratic Centralist opposition group in the Central Committee. It is possible that Osinskii's oppositionist activities prevented Lenin from naming him the permanent people's commissar. In the fall of 1920, Osinskii had designed the policy of State Regulation of Agriculture during his brief tenure as deputy commissar of Narkomprod, and he brought these ideas to Narkomzem (together with many of his top advisors in the food supply commissariat's collegium). The introduction of NEP, however, soon led to the demise of the state regulation program, and the sowing committees were disbanded by the fall of 1921. Although he had serious reservations about NEP in its first months, Osinskii became an outspoken convert to the new policies soon thereafter. Indeed, it was Osinskii who coined the slogan that the party must embrace NEP "seriously and for a long time."

The December 1920 appointment to the collegium of forty-two-year-old I. A. Teodorovich was a landmark event in the reshaping of the Commissariat of Agriculture's post-war culture. The son of a chemist, Teodorovich joined the Social Democrats in 1896 at the age of seventeen. Like Osinskii, he was highly educated and well spoken. In late 1920, Sovnarkom transferred him to the agriculture commissariat from Narkomprod and charged him with recruiting specialists. The January Central Committee Plenum instructed the Narkomzem collegium to address "the wider and more systematic inclusion of specialists-agronomists" in the Commissariat of Agriculture's work.[71] Teodorovich became the Communist Party's leading patron of agricultural specialists, a position underappreciated by contemporaries and historians alike. Teodorovich acted as a linchpin for seven years, serving as a liaison between the premiere noncommunist agrarian specialists and the Communist Party elite. As Teodorovich correctly reminded Lenin later that year, "No one has done more than I have to ensure the maximum security of [the leading agricultural experts'] work."[72] Although Communist Party members held the majority of the very highest positions in the Commissariat hierarchy, most of the organization's abundant sections and divisions were staffed by nonparty specialists with higher agricultural education and several years of pre-revolutionary experience in state, zemstvo, or private enterprises. Fully 65 percent of the Commissariat's staff were specialists by late 1922. Many of these specialists had spent ten, twenty, or more years in provincial and central land work. Noncommunist specialists, including Teitel' and Nikolai D. Kondrat'ev, many of them holdovers from the Old Regime, directed most of the Commissariat's divisions in 1922. Indeed, many sections and subsections were still staffed entirely by experts with higher education or advanced technical training. Osinskii, and especially his deputy Teodorovich, oversaw the process by which specialists assumed more authority in the Commissariat. By 1922, these specialists enjoyed a great deal of autonomy in Narkomzem (as in other economic commissariats), and this situation persisted until 1928.

With the introduction of NEP, Narkomzem turned over to specialists much of the responsibility for forming strategies to revive Soviet Russia's moribund agricultural economy. Despite skepticism in some party circles about the sudden prominence of bourgeois specialists, the Moscow Commissariat took giant steps toward permanently institutionalizing the influence of its specialists with the creation of essential research and policy-design sections that became the brain trust of the organization. The collegium created a vital commission in March 1921.[73] The Commissariat of Agriculture's Planning Commission (more commonly known as Zemplan) employed hundreds of experts and undertook the drafting of perspective plans for the Commissariat.[74] Zemplan inherited, and continued, the very rich tradition of statistical research on the rural economy that zemstvo specialists had developed in the last decades of the Old Regime. Thousands of volumes of data on the peasant family household, the commune, land use, market mechanisms, and more were resources for Zemplan's specialists. Indeed, scholars who ended up in Zemplan had written some of the best agricultural studies before the revolution, and they would continue to do so during NEP.

Zemplan coordinated all the individual plans of the various branches of the Commissariat and represented Narkomzem and the interests of agriculture in Gosplan.[75] Compiling data about the condition of agriculture in the republic and drawing up the Commissariat's first plan, Zemplan became a central gathering point for the country's experts on agriculture.[76] Through Zemplan, the Commissariat of Agriculture maintained close ties with the leading agricultural research and training institutes, especially the Timiriazev Academy, where many of the Zemplan specialists had been trained and then taught until 1928. In May 1922 the collegium appointed Deputy Commissar Teodorovich as Zemplan's chief, a move that highlighted his predominance in the scientific and planning activities of the Commissariat.[77] It was Teodorovich, for example, who appointed the influential (and, in certain party circles, unpopular) scholar Nikolai D. Kondrat'ev as a leading member of Zemplan.[78]

Kondrat'ev was one of the most important of all the Commissariat specialists and one of the country's greatest specialists on the agrarian economy. Kondrat'ev is now renowned for his theory of "long cycles" of capitalist economies. Ultimately, this theory annoyed many Bolsheviks because it postulated periods of rises and declines of capitalism, which did not jibe with Marxist ideas about its imminent collapse.[79] A student of the famous Russian economist M. I. Tugan-Baranovskii, Kondrat'ev wrote about the regulation of the grain market during the war and revolution.[80] Born in 1892, he was just twenty-five years old, and a member of the SR Party, when he became the Minister of Food Supply for the Provisional Government during its final weeks in October 1917. He met the Bolshevik seizure of power negatively, believing that the Bolsheviks had no understanding of economics and the complexity of relationships inside the economy. Interested in questions of land reform, he resented the Bolsheviks' intense focus on class conflict, and their inclination to allow the dismantling of productive farms. Kondrat'ev began his break with the SR Party in 1919 over its methods of revolutionary insurgency and its "utopianism." He came to believe that the Bolshevik regime was not as unstable, nor as bad for the country, as he first believed.[81] Kondrat'ev resigned from the SR Party in February 1920. Later that year, Kondrat'ev became the head of the Commissariat's division of work on the agricultural economy and planning. Once in Narkomzem, Kondrat'ev became influential in the Commissariat. On economic questions, he represented Narkomzem in Sovnarkom, the Council of Labor and Defense (STO), and other state organs. During these years, Teodorovich was Kondrat'ev's sponsor and protector, and at times presented Kondrat'ev's reports in various economic forums.[82]

The First NEP Land Code

The 1922 Land Code of the RSFSR, which served as the legal foundation of the Soviet state's actions in its NEP-era relations with the land-working population, represented an uneasy compromise between the more radical factions of the Communist Party and the nonparty agrarian specialists.[83] The Land Code, formally called the Law on Toilers' Land Use *(Zakon o trudovom zemlepolzovanii)*, served as the foundation for land relations in the RSFSR until 1929. Over the course of several months, the code was drafted by a Narkomzem commission with twenty-five members, including many noncommunist scholars active in Zemplan and the Commissariat's other specialized divisions. Indeed, the lead author of the code was the former SR N. P. Rudin, a prime example of the kind of holdover specialist who populated Narkomzem's most important divisions.[84]

On May 22, 1922, the Commissariat commission announced the basic principles it had formulated. Importantly, the code reiterated that all land was the property of the socialist state, and the law placed that land under the control of the Commissariat of Agriculture. "The state is the only owner of the land," collegium member Pavel Mesiatsev repeated frequently in an article discussing the formulation of the Land Code.[85] "The land belongs to the government." Narkomzem took this notion of state ownership very seriously. As had been the case since October 1917, the purchase and sale of land was absolutely forbidden. Nevertheless, the code gave communes title to the land peasants worked, recognizing the holdings that they occupied on May 22, so long as the land was farmed by family labor. Guaranteeing farmers' tenure in their land in perpetuity, the code stipulated that this tenure could only be terminated if the family household dissolved itself or stopped farming entirely, or in the cases of migration or conviction for certain serious crimes.

The single most significant article in the Land Code guaranteed the land-working population the freedom to choose the type of land usage they preferred, as long as the land was worked by family labor. The code called this principle the "right to farm with one's own labor." Types of allowable tenure included communal-repartitional, collective farms, and consolidated homesteads. Importantly, the code stated no preference for any type of farming; there was no hint that collective farming was the most desirable. Lenin considered any aggressive move toward collectivization impractical, premature, and in violation of the spirit of NEP. The Narkomzem leadership (and the Land Code) wholly adopted Lenin's line. In addition, households could separate from the commune with the commune's consent, or without consent when there was a general redistribution, although the law did not actively encourage separations. The law allowed rural dwellers to grow any types of crops, raise any kind of animals, and erect any kind of structure they wished.[86] The terms "neutrality" (or "juridical neutrality") and "noninterference" were widely employed in the code (and mimicked in

Commissariat publications) to describe the state's guarantee of security of land tenure. Narkomzem's leadership described neutrality as "the lack of administrative interference, of violent compulsion no matter what."[87] The Commissariat leadership strongly supported this right of free choice and undertook extensive efforts to educate villagers on the details of the new code.

Taking a cue from a number of its land specialists, by early 1921 Narkomzem took the position that in certain circumstances and in certain locations the creation of a homestead separated from the commune—an otrub or khutor—was the best possible use of land. This new policy marked a reversal of wartime policies. A publication of the Central Administration of Land Working argued: "In the conditions of our farming economy—amid the shortage of grass seed and fertilizer, and amid the backwardness of peasant farming—the commune cannot always make the transition [to multifield farming]. Therefore, it is necessary to change the system of land use and switch to separated homesteads. This switch to homesteads is undoubtedly rational for the purpose of raising production." It would not be rational for collective farms to switch to consolidated homesteads, however, because this would mark a regression from a "more advanced" type of landholding.[88]

The stipulations written into the Land Code illustrate its restrictions, and they demonstrate the limits of the regime's willingness to appease peasant desires. In addition to permanently banning the purchase and sale of land, the code imposed limitations on the leasing of land and the hiring of labor, despite general agreement that these practices were covertly widespread in many areas of the country. Only the infirm and economically weak were allowed to lease land or hire extra hands, and then only during those parts of the planting or harvest season when extra help was necessary. On the other hand, many Commissariat officials and experts argued in this period that both the leasing of land and the hiring of labor were economically rational practices. They believed that the law should allow these traditions since the regime had irreversibly established the foundations for socialism by nationalizing land and banishing landlords from the village. Their efforts, however, met with resistance in the highest reaches of the party. Not until NEP's most liberal phase in 1924 were the leasing of land and the hiring of labor legalized.[89]

A class-neutral tone characterized the Commissariat's position during NEP, and is clearly reflected in the code itself. The rhetoric of rural class struggle and social stratification (or differentiation)—the competition between rich peasants (*kulaks*) and poor peasants (*bedniaki*)—was conspicuously absent in Narkomzem's corporate worldview, and the Land Code reflected this outlook. Indeed, social differentiation is not mentioned in the code. The Commissariat's mission to raise productivity would not be derailed by discriminating against the "well-off" (*zazhitochnye*) peasants—sober, hard-working farmers—as distinguished from the "genuine" kulaks who truly exploited their weaker neighbors.

(This distinction is discussed in chapter four.) Narkomzem downplayed the differentiation in the village that so obsessed many party observers searching for evidence of class struggle in the countryside. The Commissariat's policy of focusing its educational and modernization efforts on the most progressive stratum of the village population acted as a disincentive to stigmatizing the better-off peasantry. Indeed, Commissariat policies treated the well-off farmers as essential leaders in each village community. Professor N. Oganovskii called them the "progressive minority." Without progress among the group that officials considered the "vanguard"—the innovators and risk takers who would be most open to adopting positive change in agricultural methods and techniques—there could be no movement forward in the countryside.[90]

It should be noted that this encouragement of the leading stratum through offering freedom of choice in land tenure was the type of concession to rural capitalism that struck some in the party as downright antisocialist. For example, a comrade V. Karpinskii attacked Osinskii's formulation of the state's "neutrality" in the peasantry's land tenure preferences as a dangerous breed of "Soviet liberalism."[91] At least one communist among the Commissariat's leading group also regarded the Land Code's tolerance for freedom of choice in land tenure to be dangerously liberal; nevertheless, he lent his public support to the Commissariat's position and urged local land officials to do the same. The ambivalent position of Narkomzem collegium member Pavel Mesiatsev is representative of the attitude of some party members in land agencies about what must have seemed to be a regressive code that made concessions to individual farming. Eventually Mesiatsev supported the government's decision to approve the code, and made an effort (albeit half-hearted) to convince skeptical party members of the code's value: "The socialist direction of the land law cannot be doubted, even though it allows the individualization of farming to a large degree (the transition to homesteads). . . . It assumes as its basic task the creation of more suitable territorial and legal conditions for raising the productivity of 97 percent of agriculture [the communal peasantry]. *To work toward this goal is communist (although by appearances it does not seem to be communist).*"[92] Despite signs of foot dragging among some cadres, Commissariat leaders tried to rally the reluctant faithful at all levels of the bureaucracy around the agency's new mission.

Bringing Smychka Alive

As one element of the new approach to the peasantry at the beginning of NEP, the Land Code illustrates some of the tensions that accompanied concessions to farmers in this period of social and political confusion. The examples of Zemplan and the Land Code also highlight the coalescing of a new scientific-political elite in the Commissariat of Agriculture (and in other agencies) as communists began to act as patrons to nonparty specialists whose expertise was desperately needed even if their past political allegiances were suspect.

Another largely unknown but revealing dimension of the early NEP illustrates the contradictory impulses inherent in the party's efforts to simultaneously conciliate both specialists and villagers. Lenin and party personnel agencies created programs to place land-working peasants in visible positions in the Moscow offices of the people's commissariats. As we have seen, during these years the new regime attempted to create a smychka by improving relations with the peasantry. Rural-urban relations remained greatly strained by wartime requisitioning and the subsequent famine. The Soviet government's presence in the countryside was quite tenuous at the beginning of the decade when these programs were created. The Moscow headquarters of the people's commissariats enjoyed only intermittent contact with their own local branches. Moreover, these poorly funded and understaffed local offices still had little regular contact with the village. To bridge this gap, representatives from "the people" (narod) were placed into leading jobs in the people's commissariats.

Historians have highlighted the ambiguity in the Soviet use of class categories when discussing the peasantry and other groups.[93] The use of such categories as peasant, worker, and "white-collar" worker (sluzhashchii) were ascribed in a complicated and politicized way by government statisticians and investigators. The mutual incompatibility of Marxist class categories and preexisting estate (soslovie) categories obviously complicated matters. In the confusion of classlessness that followed the Civil War, the Bolsheviks felt an urgent need to "reclass" society, in part as a way of distinguishing between friends and enemies of the revolution.[94]

The party ideal, of course, was a state institution with most directors and specialists from the new ruling class—the proletariat and the poorest of the peasantry—the group most privileged in Bolshevik ideology.[95] Lenin's vision of constructing a state staffed (or at least supervised) by the laboring urban and rural masses clashed with the reality that nearly the only people qualified to work in economic administrations were members of the prerevolutionary intelligentsia and white-collar professions. Especially in light of the devastation of the working class in the world war and the Civil War, this desperate need for trained personnel meant that few (if any) agencies could come close to fulfilling the goal of broad representation in responsible positions by the working masses.

Amid all the bourgeois specialists, sluzhashchie, and other politically suspect individuals, Sovnarkom and the Central Committee ordered all commissariats to make vigorous efforts to dilute their ranks with industrial workers and, especially, with communists of working-class origin. The party leadership hoped to train large numbers of workers to take up the slack and to staff high-level posts in the central administrations. Pressure to fill high-level positions with representatives of the "common people" continued in 1921–22 and throughout the decade. There were serious problems, however. In addition to the losses of workers as casualties of war, the partial deurbanization of the cities as workers migrated back to the countryside resulted in a Communist Party that ruled in the name of a class greatly weakened by war.[96] The number of workers in the Commissariat of Agriculture climbed only very slowly during the 1920s. Even without the shortage of industrial workers, Narkomzem's interests and corporate identity, so obviously associated with the agrarian specialists and the peasantry, would not have attracted factory workers, who were more inclined to seek employment among their peers in a Communist Party, trade union, or industrial bureaucracy. The number of working-class officials remained among the smallest of any commissariat throughout the NEP period.[97]

Lenin decided that the People's Commissariat of Agriculture should also attempt to promote peasants into its Moscow offices, which employed about twenty-five hundred people by the end of 1921. Bolshevik leaders cited three related purposes for increasing the number of people of peasant origin working in responsible positions in the Soviet state. First, together with workers, they were eventually to replace the holdover specialists and administrators who continued numerically to dominate the state apparatus. This goal was consistent with Lenin's view, expressed most clearly in his 1917 essay, *State and Revolution*, that any cook could become a successful official. Lenin believed that increasing ordinary working people's representation in, and supervision of, the state apparatus would reduce the evils of "bureaucratism" in the government. He (incorrectly) ascribed the red tape, delays, and other forms of spreading bureaucratism to the mentality of holdover Tsarist functionaries. As one report noted, what most concerned some party leaders about these holdover specialists was that those with the greatest responsibility were the most likely to have been trained before the Revolution.[98] Diluting this old cohort with fresh blood from the laboring classes would initiate a much-needed revitalization of soviet administration. The effort to promote "peasants from the plow"—that is, those who still actively farmed—was the ideological equivalent of the more widespread policy of promoting "workers from the bench" (meaning people currently employed in industrial labor) into state and industrial administration.

Second, the Bolsheviks stated that they aimed to recruit representatives of the rural masses in order to learn from their life experience. Peasants from the plow would come to Moscow from the countryside and inform both the Commissariat of Agriculture's communist leadership (very few of whom had experienced village life first hand) and noncommunist specialists (nearly all of whom were urban-trained and urban-based middle-class professionals) not only about daily life in the village but about popular reactions to Bolshevik land, taxation, and agricultural aid policies. The promotion programs, therefore, would "be used for Narkomzem's work in establishing connections with the peasant masses."[99]

Finally, and perhaps most significant, rural people employed in leading positions in the state were to symbolize the smychka between the revolutionary proletarian state and the peasantry upon which NEP was based. Farmers, relocated to Moscow, would serve as living representatives of this peasant-proletarian partnership. The regime was eager to establish the legitimacy of the new party-state and to disseminate its message to a huge, mostly illiterate or semiliterate rural audience. The symbolic dimension of connecting with the masses, especially in view of the state's organizational weakness outside Moscow, took on crucial significance. Reaching out to farmers was made more urgent by party leaders' understanding that many peasants felt that the regime unjustly favored the working class legally, socially, and materially. As one Narkomzem official summarized the views of many villagers with whom he came into contact, "Peasants say that there is a big difference between the life of the worker and the life of the peasant. The rights of the peasants are limited. There is no trade union, no social insurance, and the Soviet regime does not pay as much attention to the peasant as to the worker. Thus, it turns out that earlier there were nobles, but now the workers are the privileged class."[100]

By including villagers in central and local administration, the party and the Commissariat broadened attempts to build bridges to the peasantry. The party leadership hoped that the visible presence of peasants in Moscow would demonstrate to the rural masses that their interests were represented at the highest levels of the government. The promotion programs reflect the Bolsheviks' awareness of the power of symbolic politics as one part of their effort to cement the legitimacy and authority of the weakly established communist order in rural Russia.

Within this context, on January 4, 1921, a Central Committee Plenum resolved to recruit more peasants into "responsible" positions in the Commissariat of Agriculture's Moscow headquarters.[101] In particular, the resolution stated, it would be desirable "to attract two or three practicing farmers as members of the collegium, and to elevate one to the post of people's commissar."[102] In the words of a Commissariat report, these new collegium members ideally should be not just peasants by social origin, but "peasants from the plow," "those who right up to the present have not broken their ties with agriculture."[103] These farmers would have no formal higher education, but rather would be promoted to leading posts on the basis of their life experience. As a circular emphasized, they "should not be white-collar workers (sluzhashchie) in soviets" but rather, by explicit contrast, "nonparty, truly experienced farmers. They should be sufficiently energetic, [and] sincerely in favor of Soviet power."[104]

Lenin wrote that he wanted Narkomzem to locate a "troika" of peasants. They would act as nonvoting members of the agriculture commissariat's collegium, having only a "consulting voice," and therefore fulfill a largely ceremonial function. They should be "old, Russian, land working peasant men, . . . (it would be very good if they were both nonparty and Christian). . . ."[105] In other words, Lenin hoped to recruit to the agriculture commissariat villagers who resembled village patriarchs, at least in the eyes of an urban-based party led mostly by intellectuals. All promotees in the 1920s would be men of Great Russian descent.

There was an almost mythic dimension to this construction of the appropriate peasant promotee for Moscow. He should *look* the part. This prototypical peasant had his roots in the realist art and literature of the 1860s and 1870s—bearded, mature, hands gnarled and face weathered by arduous labor in the fields, espousing folk wisdom, simple yet profound.[106] He more resembled an icon than an official or leader, much like the model revolutionary of Paris that appeared on broadsides and crockery in 1793 wearing trousers, an open shirt, a short jacket, boots, and a liberty cap over long, uncombed hair.[107] Bolsheviks created an archetypal peasant promotee depicted in the propaganda art of the early 1920s as muscular and bearded, carrying a scythe, and dressed in his bast shoes, peasant blouse, and homespun pants.[108]

With these first steps in 1921 and 1922 began a constant feature of social promotion throughout the decade. Peasant promotees should have a certain presence, to appeal to the broad peasant masses, but not yet any real power. In almost every case, the peasants actually promoted into responsible positions in the Commissariat of Agriculture—there were a total of about forty over the course of eight years—did not remain in the Commissariat for more than a short time before being reassigned or sent back to the countryside, a pattern that continued throughout the 1920s.[109] The first three promotees brought into the collegium each lasted only a few months.

"He Knows the Soul of the Muzhik": The Peculiar Case of People's Commissar Iakovenko

These patterns were embodied in the most revealing promotion experience of the early years of NEP, one that placed a peasant (muzhik) at the top of the People's Commissariat of Agriculture. Correspondence indicates that it was Lenin's idea to appoint a peasant as People's Commissar, and he pushed the idea strongly in early 1921.[110] The Central Committee discussed the notion as early as January 1921. Nearly a year passed before a peasant commissar was chosen, perhaps reflecting Moscow's heightened suspicion of villagers' motives in the wake of the Antonov peasant uprisings and the Kronstadt rebellion. It was not until December 1921 (in the midst of the famine) that Deputy Commissar of Agriculture I. A. Teodorovich wrote to Lenin that he had found the ideal candidate for the post of people's commissar.[111] Thirty-two-year-old Vasilii Grigorevich Iakovenko was a native of Teodorovich's home county—Kansk uezd in Eniseisk province in western Siberia—and had farmed as "a middle peasant" until 1911.

He had fought in the Imperial army from 1914 to 1918 and joined the Bolshevik Party in July of 1917. Appointed chairman of a volost' executive committee immediately after the October Revolution, Iakovenko quickly earned impeccable Civil War credentials battling Kolchak's armies as a partisan chief in west-central Siberia. From 1920 he had served as chairman of the Kansk county soviet executive committee.[112] Sovnarkom confirmed Iakovenko as the new People's Commissar of Agriculture in January 1922.

How does a farmer in Western Siberia get promoted to Minister of Agriculture of the world's largest country? In the fifth year of the Revolution, Iakovenko was the first people's commissar of peasant descent. With one exception, the various leaders of other commissariats (thirty-five or so in the preceding five years) had been born into middle-class or upper-class families.[113] In a confidential unpublished letter of introduction to the Central Committee, Teodorovich related why he was so impressed with Iakovenko.[114] He believed that Iakovenko could help to win the allegiance of the peasantry to Soviet power. All villagers in the region where Iakovenko served as chief of the soviet were "calm." This tranquility resulted from Iakovenko's "great authority among the peasantry." Iakovenko's power to tame the countryside, Teodorovich apparently felt, could be magnified by placing Iakovenko at the head of the national ministry most actively involved in peasant life.[115]

In his description of Iakovenko's place in village life, Teodorovich expressed a degree of mystery about the rural "other" that was typical of Russian urban elites. Iakovenko, he wrote, with his "blood ties to the village," will help us to understand the motivations of rural dwellers because "he knows the soul of the peasant."[116] Precisely how Teodorovich believed the soul of the peasant differed from, for example, the soul of the bureaucrat is not clear from this letter. In any case, the "soul of the peasant" idea was tied to Teodorovich's conception of village life and the ancient traditions of rural Russia. He believed that a complete understanding of the peasant soul was accessible only to a man of the soil, a man who, as he described Iakovenko, was "in love with the land." Iakovenko, he stressed, was intimately acquainted with "peasant *byt*," or daily life, which, Teodorovich correctly implied, was foreign to most Bolsheviks.

Furthermore, Iakovenko looked like a peasant, and his appearance was a priority in the minds of Teodorovich, Lenin, and Bolshevik publicists. Teodorovich described him as "massive and powerful" looking, a "full-bearded man from the plow."[117] A journalist for *Izvestiia*, the government newspaper, searching after his first encounter with Iakovenko for an adjective to describe the new commissar's countenance, could come up with only one: "his appearance—peasantlike (*krest'ianskii*)."[118]

Teodorovich went on to maintain that Iakovenko's first-hand knowledge of peasant mentality could also be put to use by the Commissariat of Agriculture and the Soviet state: his familiarity with village life "can be very subtly used by the Narkomzem apparatus for any agricultural campaign. Wherever and whenever he appears among the peasantry, 'such' a peasant will help get done what is necessary." The emphasis here is less on the Bolsheviks' using Iakovenko to learn about rural life than it is on social control, on finding ways to keep the countryside calm and cooperative, and, when necessary, easily mobilized for actions such as sowing and harvest campaigns or tax gathering.

Iakovenko also should be able to take advantage of promotees' anticipated authority among other peasants, Teodorovich argued. By virtue of their rather simplistic conception of the cultural homogeneity of the Russian peasantry, many leading Bolsheviks assumed that the authority of a peasant promotee was universal in the countryside simply by virtue of the fact that he was "from the peasantry" *(iz krest'ianstva)*. In other words, a peasant who commanded the respect of his region in Western Siberia should also be able to earn the reverence of the rural population on the Volga, and in Vladivostok, and in the entire country.

Immediately after the appointment of the new commissar, Lenin confided to Iakovenko that "there is much truth in the complaints of the muzhik. But he'll speak this truth only to you or another peasant whom he considers one of his own. He'll hide this truth from our institutional bureaucrats."[119] This conviction that the new commissar, with his folksy language, could serve as a bridge—a living, breathing link in the smychka—between an unstable, unpopular, urban-based communist government and a peasantry traditionally skeptical of state authority, was central in the minds of the Bolsheviks who chose him. The men involved in Iakovenko's appointment appear to have been guided by a new variation on the "Tsar myth." They understood that the peasantry, over the decades and centuries, had become accustomed to the untrustworthiness of central and local bureaucrats. Iakovenko could be set up as a sympathetic figure to whom villagers could appeal over the heads of corrupt or indifferent local functionaries. Inside government and party circles Iakovenko was known as the "peasant people's commissar" (*krest'ianskii narkom* or *muzhitskii narkom*), as Lenin and Teodorovich both referred to him, and as an article in *Izvestiia* introduced him.[120] This language permanently branded him as an outsider in the bureaucracy and party. One can hardly imagine a similar prefix for a leading Bolshevik from any other social group. The petty bourgeois commissar? The son-of-a-noble commissar?

Iakovenko's ascension to Minister of Agriculture would, of course, have been inconceivable before the collapse of the Romanov dynasty. In this sense, his appointment signified a revolutionary break with the patterns of social mobility in the Imperial government. For the first time a peasant was elevated into the Moscow elite. Nevertheless, although the Commissariat of Agriculture publicly portrayed him as its leader, it is clear that Iakovenko played a largely symbolic role both in the agency and in the Soviet government as a whole, and he does not appear to have contributed to decision making. He rarely wrote for the press. During his tenure, key correspondence from Central Committee agencies and the Council of People's Commissars was usually addressed to his deputies, bypassing the People's Commissar himself.[121] In mid-1922, six months into Iakovenko's tenure, three of the Commissariat's collegium members formed a secret "shock group" to try to formulate a plan for resolving the series of organizational and fiscal crises the Commissariat was enduring. Remarkably, they did not invite People's Commissar Iakovenko to participate.

The exclusion of Iakovenko from an active role was likely a result of his lack of sophistication in this specialist milieu. The photograph of the new commissar and his collegium that appeared in the press illustrates his peculiar position. Iakovenko sits behind a desk in traditional dress, gripping a pen. He sports a beard and appears startled and out of place among the rest of the Commissariat leadership who stand by his side, mostly smiling intellectuals attired in European-style suits, neatly trimmed goatees, and pince-nez's. Available material indicates that Commissariat officials isolated and ignored Iakovenko. Although he was literate, he wrote at an elementary level that specialists in the Commissariat may have found simplistic.[122] The rare executive advice he managed to dispense to officials, such as "every land worker should take the Land Code in his hand and study it like his own five fingers," may have struck some experts in this extremely class conscious society, sharply divided along rural/urban lines, as facile, if not foolish.[123]

Much of the Communist Party leadership of the agriculture commissariat agreed with this evaluation of People's Commissar Iakovenko. The Commissariat's leadership—political and scientific—throughout the decade viewed promotees of village origin as little more than tokens who presented an obstacle to accomplishing the real mission of the organization, which was not to act as a vehicle for peasant participation in central government but to rescue Russian agriculture, to rebuild it along modern lines.[124] This skepticism toward peasant promotees persisted throughout the promotion campaigns of the 1920s.

Furthermore, the ministerial structures in the last three decades of the Old Regime had become organized around specialized, economic tasks. This growing specialization produced ministries that employed highly trained experts in key positions—a kind of technocratic subelite, as Rowney puts it—rather than the generalist-administrator and politicians of previous eras.[125] Daniel Orlovsky has also demonstrated "a qualitative and quantitative increase in the autonomy and influence of those specialized sectors of the ministerial bureaucracy directly responsible for the economy" in the years leading up to the revolution.[126] This is not to argue that nonparty specialists suddenly gained full power in a Bolshevik ministry. Rather, the point is that apart from the political, cultural, and social factors presented here, there were long-standing *structural* sources of resistance to the introduction of untrained peasants into powerful positions in the Commissariat of Agriculture (and every other Soviet ministry) in the 1920s.[127]

Persistent Problems—Money and Cadres

During the tenure of the "peasant people's commissar" in 1922, the newly self-confident political and scientific leaders of the Commissariat of Agriculture used the Communist Party's emphasis on the peaceful recovery of the rural economy and the simultaneous eclipse of the food supply commissariat to underscore their contention that Narkomzem deserved both more respect and increased resources.[128] Nevertheless, during the first two years of NEP, the Narkomzem leadership fought for financial resources largely without success. Of course, in these years the RSFSR, bankrupted by war and economic collapse, barely sustained a budget at all. Every sphere of the economy, including industry, the cities, and transportation, was in urgent need of investment. In its struggles to garner as large a piece of the small budget pie as possible in 1921–22, the Commissariat's leadership tried to convince state finance agencies that their organization needed allotments sufficient to support the active role it planned in the countryside. Acting commissar Osinskii called these lobbying efforts "the battle for the budget."[129]

Commissariat officials constantly complained, for example, that there were too few officials available who possessed any knowledge of agriculture to fill the needs of the new bureaucracy. Narkomzem's leadership was never satisfied with the quantity of specialists in its administrations, despite its constant lobbying. The number of agricultural experts dropped sharply after October 1917, due to huge losses caused by emigration, deaths from a variety of causes during the Civil War, the disruption of education between 1914 and 1921, and the refusal of many specialists to work for the Soviet regime. Acting Commissar Osinskii complained at the Ninth Congress of Soviets in December 1921 that the number of specialists in the country was "entirely inadequate" to support a peasant population of around 100 million.[130] By the Commissariat's calculations, famine-plagued Saratov province alone suffered a shortage of some six thousand experts.

The desperate shortage of cadres is one example of how the ambitious goals of Narkomzem did not correspond to its paltry budget. The Narkomzem party leadership took every opportunity to insist to Gosplan and the Commissariat of Finance that the Commissariat both needed and deserved much more money, especially for salaries.[131] Nevertheless, in the midst of the agrarian disaster of 1921 and 1922, Narkomzem (along with the Commissariat of Education) remained one of the most poorly funded commissariats. As of late 1921, Narkomzem's budget ranked sixth among all commissariats.[132] Osinskii lamented that despite its vital assignments, "The Commissariat must carry on a stubborn struggle to secure elementary conditions for existence and work."[133] Amid the flood of rhetoric about the importance of agriculture, money was not forthcoming. "The lack of resources this year has blocked the work of Narkomzem at every step. The

Germans call this . . . 'Plenty of sympathy, but not a kopeck.' Narkomzem needs deeds, not words."[134] The Commissariat leadership explicitly tied the issue of funding to its mission to "bring light" to the village. One leader predicted that "darkness will remain in the countryside for many years if Central organs . . . do not allocate sufficient attention to the material situation of land workers, who are now abandoning the village. This, comrades, is collapse. There are regions where agronomic forces are completely lacking."[135] In May 1922, the Commissariat's collegium privately discussed which of the agency's sections would have to be shut down if Sovnarkom failed to provide sufficient funds.[136]

During eighteen months beginning in the summer of 1921, the Commissariat's public statements evoked the image of catastrophe—past, present, and future. In an article begging for increased credits for agriculture, a leading statistician lamented, "The last eight years have destroyed our agriculture."[137] The famine of 1921–22 served as a constant backdrop for the arguments of Commissariat officials as the crop failures brought the plight of agriculture to the attention of party leaders. Commissariat officials summoned memories of the 1891–92 famine and the tsarist government's failure to address the problem aggressively. They warned that the tsar's mistakes must not be repeated. Just as in 1891–92, specialists drew attention to the deadly combination of bad weather, technical underdevelopment, and government neglect. There could be no better evidence for the need for Narkomzem's activities and funding than the famine. In his report to the Ninth Congress of Soviets in December 1921, Osinskii first lamented the Commissariat's shortage of funds, then immediately moved to discuss the Commissariat's "heroic" famine relief efforts. His message was clear: shortages of funds and personnel would exacerbate the effects of the crop failures, and without substantial increases, disaster would strike again.[138]

A further source of financial problems emerged when the government instituted the practice of *khozraschet*, or commercial accounting, in all state agencies in 1922–23.[139] Commercial accounting required that many of the Commissariat of Agriculture's operations, previously funded by the state budget, suddenly had to become self-supporting. Some branches saw funding evaporate completely. Local land agencies that had provided services to the farming population free of charge—services such as surveying, lending equipment, dispensing advice, and so on—would have to begin charging fees for them. The Commissariat protested bitterly against the commercial accounting policy as both unrealistic and likely to discourage farmers from seeking assistance. For many enterprises in the Narkomzem system, commercial accounting was an unmitigated disaster. Enterprises that Narkomzem transferred to commercial accounting complained of the enormous strain of such a system. Land sections had to find new sources of funding. Experimental stations, breeding stations, and seed farms reasonably argued that they had little or nothing of value to sell or barter, and therefore had no way to produce revenue for supporting themselves. Most simply closed down under intense financial pressure.[140]

The principle of decentralization that was so popular in 1922–23 was deficient to the extent that it relocated the center of gravity for commissariats' operations to local departments, even as their staffs and budgets were significantly reduced.[141] Layoffs disrupted central and local departments. Because Moscow's goal was a higher proportion of specialists in local agencies, secretarial and support personnel were the prime targets of the staff reductions, but the firing of support staff had unexpected consequences, forcing the re-allocation of specialists' time to clerical work. Worse yet, the Commissariat of Finance implemented the policy so suddenly that many local agencies had to make drastic cuts at a moment's notice. Between 1921 and 1924 the number of employees working at experimental stations in the RSFSR plummeted from 16,345 to 3,317. Of the latter figure, fewer than 700 had specialized scientific training, down from 3,400 just two years earlier.[142]

In 1922 correspondence with the Central Committee Secretariat, Narkomzem's leaders complained that "the difference [in the budget] between the amount asked for and the amount received is depressing." Miserly allotments "threaten even the most crying needs of agriculture and forestry. . . . In important areas, the budget of Narkomzem has been cut cruelly. . . . The reduction in staff demanded by the extreme slashing of our budgets is already sometimes directly reflected in productive work."[143] A November 1922 investigation by an outside agency supported the Commissariat's position: "In part, the insignificance of [Narkomzem's] accomplishments is explained by the lack of resources dedicated to improving the Commissariat of Agriculture's work. It is imperative that [the resources] be significantly strengthened."[144] Thus, despite their intentions, in the second half of 1922 the Commissariat's personnel still lacked the resources and staff to see through ambitious plans to transform agriculture, and they were bitterly disappointed with this weakness.

Backlash: Specialists as Targets

A critical shortage of resources, however, was not the only factor that damaged the Commissariat's ability to fulfill its aspirations. At the same time that specialists' influence was institutionalized in the Commissariat's many divisions, a number of the Commissariat's leading experts came under intense negative scrutiny from hostile outsiders in the party and the secret police. Controversies in the summer and fall of 1922 damaged the Commissariat's standing and upset the agency's equilibrium, already skewed by its unsatisfactory budget and staffing situation. The period between May and the end of the year was a time of great pressure inside Narkomzem. Incidents involving the country's leading agrarian experts illustrate the uncertain parameters of policies in agriculture, as well as the continuing vulnerability of the non-Bolshevik intelligentsia, during the first eighteen months of NEP.

The "SR Threat"

Magnifying the Bolsheviks' concern over the shortage of communists in the state bureaucracies, several people who had been sympathetic to non-Bolshevik political parties were scattered throughout the state administration. Former Socialist Revolutionaries, Mensheviks, and Kadets were especially prevalent in economic agencies such as Vesenkha, the industrial trusts, Gosplan, and the commissariats of finance, internal trade, and agriculture. Former members of non-Bolshevik political parties were also influential in the Academy of Sciences, and they held high-profile positions on the editorial boards of prominent economic journals.[145]

In the 1920s, Narkomzem enjoyed a reputation for harboring a significant contingent of former members of, or those sympathetic to, the SR Party. In the 1920s a number of leading specialists in the Moscow Commissariat had been prominent SRs or had identified with their policies before and during 1917. The presence of such sympathizers is not surprising since the SRs controlled the Ministry of Agriculture and the Main Land Committee (and their local branches) under the Provisional Government. These state administrations had served as something of a magnet for educated persons interested in addressing the countryside's underdevelopment. During the Civil War many of these SR sympathizers either simply remained in their jobs, or they rejoined state administration when it appeared that the Bolsheviks had moved a long way toward accommodating SR policies in 1921–22. Specialists with international reputations before the Revolution who were willing to work for the Soviet government in the Commissariat of Agriculture in the 1920s included the "neo-narodnik" former SR scholars A. V. Chaianov, N. P. Makarov, A. N. Chelintsev, and A. L. Vainshtein, the former Kadets Kondrat'ev and N. P. Oganovskii and many others. These "Narkomzem professors" were concentrated in the Commissariat's most important divisions, especially Zemplan and the Village Economy Administration *(Upravlenie sel'skim khoziastvom)*.[146]

Much about the SRs concerned the Bolsheviks. The SRs had won most of the peasant vote to the Constituent Assembly in national elections, had openly taken up arms against the Reds in the Civil War, and, the Bolsheviks believed, had encouraged peasant uprisings against the Soviet regime at least as late as 1921. In February 1922, forty-seven SRs were arrested, and between June and August of 1922 the regime put the remnants of the SR Party on trial. In fact, there is no evidence that former SRs posed a real threat to Soviet power in the 1920s. Certainly, Narkomzem's communist leadership believed that the SRs' contribution to creating policy in Moscow (and implementing it locally) was more valuable than their previous political affiliations. The Commissariat's leaders were, therefore, willing to disregard previous allegiances and support former SRs as politically loyal.[147]

More than the relatively few (if inordinately influential) former SR sympathizers in Moscow, it was the SR presence in the localities that most worried party watchdogs, who were concerned that certain pressing issues—especially taxation, drought, famine, high prices for industrial goods, and the perception of preferences for industrial workers—angered the rural population. Some Bolsheviks suspected, and these fears were clearly exaggerated, that local land administrations were an ideal forum from which SRs could covertly urge the peasantry or certain strata within it to resist Soviet power. Because of the chaotic state of record keeping during the Civil War, it is difficult to determine just who comprised the local land administrations between 1918 and 1921. Nevertheless, in the early to mid-1920s, many complaints surfaced about a significant SR presence in the local land administration, especially in the Central Agricultural, Volga, and Southeast regions that were the SRs' traditional strongholds. Reports from the secret police continued to discuss purported SR activity well into the 1920s.[148] To concerned Bolsheviks, the term SR was defined very broadly, meaning not just party membership, but also an alleged affiliation, or simply even sympathy. Local communists feared that agricultural specialists whose declared political affiliation was nonparty in fact were now, or had been, SR sympathizers.

Why did many former SR sympathizers end up working for Bolshevik agricultural agencies? In the context of Narkomzem's expanded mission during NEP, several explanations should be considered. First, between 1921 and 1928, the Bolsheviks' policies toward the peasantry harmonized very closely with SR land policy. In the words of one person with close ties to the specialists, the regime's perceived "retreat from utopianism to a realistic policy allowed for a more optimistic view of the possibility for Russia's economic development."[149] Significant areas of overlap between SR perspectives and Bolshevik land policy included the emphasis on the free selling of surpluses, the encouragement of increased production within the commune and cooperatives, the abandonment of most collective farms and sovkhozy. Many SRs believed that the Bolsheviks were conceding that the SRs had been correct all along, at least with regard to land policy. Moreover, most specialists who remained in Soviet Russia were, in the final analysis, concerned with rebuilding the economy, regardless of political affiliation.[150] By 1921–22, it became clear to those unsympathetic with the Bolsheviks that Soviet power would not be overthrown soon. They felt obliged to attempt to help revive the economy. In the words of the editor N. V. Valentinov, much of the intelligentsia came to the conclusion that "not wanting to be left outside life, there was no other road except to honestly and with good conscience work together with Soviet power." Many believed that "contact with the democratic and socialist intelligentsia, working in the Soviet economy, would to some degree favorably influence the psychology of communist power, help its democratization, move it away from the persistent, crude formula 'dictatorship of the party.'" "We will infect them with our *kulturnost'*," as one stated.[151]

Second, a flood of administrative and specialist personnel searching for jobs poured into the land administration after the conclusion of the Civil War in late 1920 and early 1921. This helps to explain the large quantity not just of SRs, but also of holdover personnel from tsarist administrations. Once hostilities had ended, Narkomzem and its local branches, desperate for individuals knowledgeable about agricultural matters (especially in the midst of the famine), appear to have hired almost anyone with minimum qualifications. During an eighteen-month period beginning in late 1920, Narkomzem's Moscow offices nearly tripled in size (from 1100 to 2900) as personnel were pressed into service to combat the effects of the crop failures. Local land agencies underwent a similar expansion. Committees responsible for verifying credentials frequently did background checks only several months after an individual was hired, if at all, and there was no reliable way to verify the political sympathies of the new recruits. In the face of pressure to set up agricultural development programs, local administrations had their hands full simply trying to verify educational qualifications and work experience, which were much easier to check than class background or prior political allegiance.[152]

Unwanted Scrutiny

With a reputation for harboring political undesirables, especially SRs, Narkomzem found itself the focus of several incidents that damaged the organization's standing in the spring and summer of 1922. This burst of action coincided with the arrest and exile of 160 prominent intellectuals, non-Bolshevik socialists, and university administrators in July 1922.[153] Several non-Marxist Narkomzem scholars, many of whom had previously supported the SRs or Kadets, authored articles that angered Lenin. In May 1922, Lenin was outraged by an article cowritten by A. L. Vainshtein and Oganovskii that appeared in the May 6 edition of Narkomzem's internal journal *Sel'sko-khoziaistvennaia zhizn'*.[154] The article took issue with the March 17 decree "On the United Tax in Kind on Agricultural Produce for 1922–23." The two authors suggested instituting a money tax, lowering the total amount to be collected, abolishing progressive taxation, and reducing benefits for poorer peasants. Lenin denounced both the writing and the publication of these ideas. He instructed the Orgburo (Organizational Bureau) to investigate the editorial board and "to take steps to prevent such inadmissible editing of *Sel'sko-khoziaistvennaia zhizn'* from recurring in the future." On May 11 (just two weeks before Lenin's first stroke), the Politburo reprimanded the Narkomzem collegium. Lenin wrote to Osinskii shortly thereafter insisting that the editor of the journal, A. N. Morosanov, be removed from his post and urging that Vainshtein and Oganovskii be placed under special surveillance.[155] Finally, he accused the Commissariat's communist leadership of having "fallen victim" to these experts, "who are most likely Right SRs." Lenin's fears of political disloyalty were portentous, as was his sensitivity about the former party affiliations of leading agricultural specialists.[156]

After several weeks of attention, the Politburo actually closed down *Sel'skokhoziaistvennaia zhizn'* for these infractions on June 1, 1922, and the periodical did not recommence publication until November with a new editorial board. For five months Narkomzem's Moscow headquarters had no internal journal to distribute to its thousands of local officials. This breach of communications further damaged the Commissariat's already fragile connections with the local land sections with which Moscow was desperately trying to establish lines of communication in the midst of the famine.

A second incident brought the Commissariat's leadership more undesired attention, this time from the Central Committee Secretariat. In June 1922, New Village, the publishing division of the Commissariat of Agriculture, issued *O zemle (On Land)*, a collection of articles by specialists in Narkomzem's Land Improvement and Reorganization Administration. Some of the articles advocated the establishment of small-scale homesteads and supported the leasing of land and the hiring of labor. Most contained notably non-Marxist analysis of the agrarian situation. The collection came to the attention of General Secretary Stalin, whose assistant testily wrote to Teodorovich: "Comrade Stalin requests that he urgently be informed who takes responsibility for the content of articles published in the Commissariat of Agriculture collection *O zemle*, and how the Soviet character of the articles in the collection was guaranteed."[157] This note served notice that the General Secretary was reading their publications with some degree of dissatisfaction. Stalin implied, in fact, that the collection was insufficiently Soviet in character, an unwelcome charge. Stalin's reaction to Teodorovich's brief and factual response is unknown.

A more significant blow to the organization came in the late summer and early fall of 1922 when the GPU (the Main Political Administration, which replaced the Cheka in February 1922 and assumed its responsibility for internal security) arrested several of the Commissariat's leading specialists. Among those apprehended were N.D. Kondrat'ev, L. N. Yurovskii, Rybnikov, and Oganovskii (the former Kadet who had just been censured in connection with the *Sel'skokhoziaistvennaia zhizn'* incident). The arrests continued from July to mid-October. Kondrat'ev was arrested on August 17, 1922, after a meeting of Zemplan in which he had just delivered a report. He had recently testified at the trial of the SRs; his arrest came just a few days after its conclusion.[158] The symbolism inherent in the arrest of the organization's leading specialists as they emerged from a meeting of the brain trust could not have been lost on the Commissariat leadership, and it surely sent shock waves through the organization. Zemplan, which earlier in 1922 had been meeting more frequently than the Narkomzem collegium itself, did not convene at all during the month of September.

The arrested specialists were sentenced to prison, where some spent several weeks. Kondrat'ev, Yurovskii, and Rybnikov all appeared on lists of intellectuals to be exiled from the country. After the specialists had been sentenced, Teodorovich, Osinskii, and Shefler pled for the experts' release and their restoration to their former positions. Within a few months, the sentences were reduced or annulled and the scholars were allowed to remain in the country.[159] Despite these controversies, specialists remained in key leadership and administrative posts in Narkomzem. Indeed, by the fall of 1922 the arrested specialists returned to their posts.

These incidents illustrate both the persistent suspicion of "bourgeois specialists" in certain party circles, and the resilience of those experts during NEP. Expertise had been institutionalized in the Commissariat and all over the government, yet, despite their positions, specialists were still the targets of various types of harassment during the following years.

The low point of the Commissariat's political fortunes was reached in the autumn of 1922 when the agency was forced to submit to outside oversight. The controversies of the summer of 1922, divided leadership, and agencywide disorganization led Lenin to assign deputy Sovnarkom chair A.D. Tsiurupa to monitor the Commissariat.[160] An investigation in the fall of 1922 pounded home the depressing conclusions that the leadership already understood: the institution that was to be the vehicle for this grandiose, activist mission was politically weak, out of touch with its branch offices, and desperately short of specialists. Very little coordination had been achieved between the activities of the central Commissariat and its branch offices. Indeed, reports and correspondence for this period shows that Moscow had little idea what local land sections were doing, or even who comprised their leadership and staff. In the words of a damning 1922 report, Narkomzem still did not have an accurate count of the number of its specialists, never mind their locations or qualifications. In some provinces—Tambov, for example—the agricultural and land reform administration simply stopped functioning for several years after the war. The transfer of most aspects of administration from Moscow to underfunded local land sections as part of a general decentralization program was no panacea for these problems and, indeed, compounded frustration. Until 1923, the Commissariat remained more a conglomeration of multiple, nearly independent parts under a single umbrella than a united agency. In the words of the investigation's final report: "Everyone agrees that the Commissariat of Agriculture is sick and must be healed."[161]

As controversy swept over the organization in the summer, another crisis of leadership was brewing. The "peasant commissar" Iakovenko had taken over the Commissariat during the famine. Serving in Moscow, he felt himself isolated from his home region, unable to help in their time of need. Iakovenko complained that his desperate comrades from the countryside were leveling terrible accusations against him. They claimed that he lived in the lap of luxury in his fancy official apartment in the big city, ignoring his comrades while they and their families suffered from hunger back home.[162] Iakovenko clearly felt tortured by the charge that he was turning into just another bureaucrat. The famine may have ruined any chance Iakovenko had of winning over the peasantry, since many farmers blamed Moscow for the disaster. Furthermore, Iakovenko was powerless to protect the Commissariat specialists who had been subject to censure and arrest during his tenure.

As early as August 1922, Iakovenko sent a note to Lenin (who forwarded it to Stalin) implying dissatisfaction with his position as the head *"chinovnik"* (bureaucrat) of the Commissariat of Agriculture. By November, the search for a new people's commissar was underway. Within a few months, the Central Committee transferred Iakovenko out of an utterly disorganized Commissariat of Agriculture.

Within the context of central insecurity and weakness, a new emphasis on a peaceful partnership between city and countryside, and a new mission to employ its tools to elevate the productivity of the rural sector while building bridges between the new regime and the peasantry, Narkomzem (and the regime itself) emerged from the Civil War with enormous ambitions. An institutional subculture that had begun to develop during the war emerged with the introduction of NEP. Between late 1920 and the end of 1922, a new guiding ideology emerged, and it was ultimately embraced by both the specialist and (after some hesitation) the political leadership of the Commissariat. The defining characteristic of the ideology was the drive to modernize a benighted countryside to the level of the Western states that both specialists and party leaders envied. This would be done through the state-sponsored application of science to the reorganization of communal and individual-homestead farming. The state was to play a very active role in providing the tools of self-improvement—knowledge and technology—to the peasantry. The achievements of science were to be brought to the village by the agents of the Commissariat of Agriculture, who would show farmers how to mechanize production and eliminate inefficiencies. Narkomzem officials downplayed concern among many communists of growing social differentiation—a "kulak threat"—in the village as insignificant for the long-term development of the peasant economy. In the Commissariat's view, villagers, irrespective of social position, should be encouraged to embrace the new approach to rural reconstruction. The military methods of the Civil War years, with their physical and fiscal coercion, were to be replaced with persuasion, education, and an emphasis on economic incentives.

A rapidly evolving economic, social, and political environment should have secured the foundation upon which the agriculture commissariat would gradually become a more powerful political force. As a 1922 Gosplan report remarked: "Narkomzem is one of the most important commissariats. It is called upon to manage agriculture, the basis of all soviet construction."[163] The introduction of the tax-in-kind and the gradual liquidation of the food supply commissariat should have served as endorsements of Narkomzem's approach to the countryside. With confidence at the beginning of NEP, Narkomzem launched an effort to revive production and to enlighten the peasantry. The mission affirmed Narkomzem's "specialist" ethos. Using Rowney's definition of technocracy as an organization dedicated to solving social problems through a bureaucracy staffed primarily by educated specialists, Narkomzem was an early Soviet prototype.[164] Once the war ended, the Commissariat could proceed much farther toward becoming what many of its specialists had envisioned during the war: a well-funded organization with a vital educational and economic mission. During the first twenty-four months of NEP, the primary influence of experts, almost none of whom were communists, became institutionalized, and the worldview of these experts dominated the outlook of the organization until 1928.

This drive to "uplift" and "modernize" rural Russia served to unite communists and noncommunists alike. Even sympathizers of the Socialist Revolution Party, many of whom joined (or rejoined) the land administration in 1921, could appreciate the state's effort to render the commune more productive and to raise the rural standard of living. In this early period, certain attitudes coalesced as part of the organization's culture: science can solve social problems, and the state should help experts use this mastery of the agricultural sciences to strongly influence policy formation. This specialized culture began to permeate the party leadership of Narkomzem. Like some of their counterparts in other economic commissariats, Bolshevik leaders of Narkomzem made every effort to protect the professional autonomy of their experts.

Nevertheless, during the first two years of NEP, the "light" that Narkomzem's specialists expected would emanate from new, "pro-peasant" policies did not shine as brightly as they had anticipated. Troubling contradictions emerged that would reappear in various guises throughout the decade. Once NEP was launched, the Commissariat's specialist and political leadership expected a great deal from the party's promise to revive and remake agriculture. Amid financial crisis, however, the state continued to pump its scarce resources into sectors of the economy party leaders considered more essential for constructing a basis for socialism, especially industry and transportation. In the meantime, suspicion simmered among many Bolsheviks not only that certain social groups could not be trusted, but that political enemies might be employed inside the state apparatus *itself*, often in the guise of nonparty specialists, and often disguised or protected by their party superiors. Others accused the new specialists, most of whom had pre-revolutionary land experience and many of whom had sympathized with the SRs before the revolution, of possessing an "alien ideology."[165] The mid-1922 burst of attacks on Narkomzem cadres demonstrated the organization's vulnerability. Its close association both with nonparty "bourgeois" specialists and with the more "progressive" vanguard strata of the "capitalist" peasantry made the Commissariat a target for those skeptical of concessions to the peasantry.

Meanwhile, programs to promote common farmers into visible positions in the state and economic agencies embodied another contradiction, as peasants who came to Moscow were often stereotyped and excluded from power. In the political-specialist milieu of Narkomzem, peasants had no real status apart from the symbolic. The tenure of Iakovenko, the "peasant people's commissar," points up elements of early Soviet political culture, as both political leaders and specialists resisted the presence of "peasants" in their midst. Farmers were the *subjects* of Commissariat action, not themselves the designers of those policies.

It was in this extraordinary context that, in early 1923, the Central Committee assigned Alexander Petrovich Smirnov the challenging task of "curing" the organization responsible for "curing" agriculture.

3 "Too Many Comrades Misunderstand the Countryside"

A Commissariat Comes of Age, 1923–1927

In the wake of the great famine of 1921–22, the mid-1920s provide a fruitful setting for examining the regime's evolving political and institutional cultures. The Communist Party in some senses began to turn against itself—and against the state apparatus that was supposed to carry out its decisions. In the aftermath of the crises that beset the agency in the first years of the decade, the Commissariat of Agriculture offers an opportunity to analyze the increasingly divisive and contradictory issues of class, expertise, social stigma, and the masking of identities— all of which generated a great deal of conflict within the revolutionary regime. An investigation of these issues points to sources of instability that shaped the path of the revolution in the 1920s (and beyond). The Commissariat of Agriculture's particular culture and political face increased the chances that it would remain under a cloud of suspicion among those in the party elite and rank-and-file membership impatient with NEP's concessions to a "capitalist" peasantry. Indeed, Narkomzem, committed to the country's slowly "growing into socialism," was precisely the kind of commissariat despised by NEP's numerous enemies. As designers of the party Right's "soft line" toward the countryside, the Commissariat had to defend itself from charges that it was excessively solicitous of both the bourgeois specialist and the kulak, charges that became more common in this period between 1923 and 1926.

The evidence indicates that the relationship between party and state was not simply one of subordination and superordination. Rather, much interaction occurred, involving negotiation between powerful interests and individuals whose loyalties were often difficult to discern. Concerning cadre policy, for example, the state did not blindly implement the party's decrees without question. Government agencies at times acted with a significant degree of autonomy, and they fought hard to maintain that autonomy. Chiefs of commissariats maintained quite a bit of power and latitude in matters of personnel policy, a fact that has not been sufficiently documented by historians. The new People's Commissar Alexander P. Smirnov and his associates in Narkomzem exemplify a certain phenomenon. They were communist leaders of a government commissariat, torn between allegiance to their party and loyalty to their organization and its constituency. Having embraced the interests of their agency and personnel, they defended these interests, sometimes directly contradicting the wishes of party superiors and investigators.

During this period, the Commissariat's leaders developed numerous strategies to combat interference by outsiders in its internal matters, especially concerning cadres. They shielded their personnel from attacks by cadre hawks (located mostly in bureaucratic oversight agencies) eager to "purify" the state apparatus that many communists suspected of covert hostility to Soviet power. Skillfully deployed by Narkomzem's party chiefs, these defensive tactics were quite often effective. Many communist heads of government organizations argued that nonparty experts' unhindered input was crucial for running the economy. Narkomzem leaders derided party comrades for ignoring the needs of agriculture. By frequently chastising communists for their ignorance about the village, the Commissariat's leadership argued that the agency should serve as a mediator between the regime and the rural masses. They insisted that only by taking into account their understanding of the social and economic life of the village could central policies be correctly formulated and locally implemented. During Smirnov's tenure (1923–28), this was a powerful and, for the time being, effective argument.

The difficulties facing the agency that inserted itself between the communist party and the country's villagers highlight important phenomena. Indeed, the agency's tribulations cast glaring light on both the strengths and the weaknesses of the New Economic Policy, while raising grave doubts about its prospects.

Enter Smirnov

The Commissariat was in a chaotic state when the Central Committee appointed forty-five-year-old Alexander Petrovich Smirnov to serve as Deputy Commissar of Agriculture in the fall of 1922, transferring him from his position as deputy commissar of the collapsing food supply commissariat. In a matter of months, he would replace the ineffective people's commissar Iakovenko. As Smirnov took over Narkomzem in the spring of 1923, the international situation gave the agency's mission a new urgency. A cloud of pessimism about the prospects for successful international revolution hung over the Communist

Party of the Soviet Union. It was becoming disappointingly clear that sporadic revolts in industrial Europe would not soon establish new socialist states to come to the aid of the Soviet revolution. A large dose of demoralization settled into the party's ranks. Hopes faded for assistance from abroad as capitalism appeared to be firmly entrenched. Party leaders struggled to come to terms with the unpleasant fact that at least for the near future they would have to build a socialist society without the help and resources of sympathetic, industrially advanced European states. Thus, the extraordinary challenge of spreading socialism to the countryside—expanding its productive capacity, securing the political reliability of its population, increasing its ability to produce the resources necessary for industrialization—became an even more critical issue for the party leadership to resolve.

The Comissariat that Smirnov took over may have been in turmoil in 1922 and early 1923, but it was also enormous. With more than thirty thousand employees in central and local offices (not including another forty thousand or so forestry personnel), the People's Commissariat of Agriculture was the largest of the Soviet Union's thirteen commissariats by the mid-1920s.[1] Most commissariats, by contrast, employed between four thousand and twelve thousand people (see table 3-1). To look ahead for a moment, by 1927 Narkomzem had grown to the point that it employed nearly one of every five employees in the entire commissarial bureaucracy,[2] and fully one-third of the RSFSR's ministerial bureaucracy.[3] Although party inspectors attempted to reduce the size of state agencies amid fears of a ballooning bureaucracy throughout the 1920s, Narkomzem continued to grow as a consequence of the regime's intensified determination to resolve the "agrarian problem." This expansion was manifested in the creation of a sprawling network of local agronomic, veterinary, and land reorganization stations. Between 1925 and 1928, the land administration managed to grow by more than sixty-six hundred people, by far the largest increase of any commissariat in the period. While the staff of the ministerial system as a whole shrank by 10 percent, the contingent of people involved in land work increased by almost 19 percent.[4]

In March 1923, Smirnov became the chief of this enormous organization, over which he presided until the early spring of 1928. Over the course of the next five years, he would come to personify the Commissariat of Agriculture. Osinskii departed the Commissariat soon after Smirnov's appointment, having served as de facto people's commissar for nearly two years. The "peasant commissar" Iakovenko moved to a position of relative tranquility as head of the People's Commissariat of Social Security.

By all accounts, the Commissariat was in serious disarray when Smirnov arrived on the scene.[5] The ministry, a pillar of efforts to construct a "partnership" between city and village, was hindered by a "number of defects," as one inspector observed with a generous dose of understatement.[6] Weak leadership, waves

TABLE 3-1 Total number of central and local staffs of the people's commissariats, 1925 and 1928 (ranked by size)

Date	Commissariat	Central staff	Local staff[a]	Total	Total as % of all commissariat staff
1/1/25	Finance	4,900	57,300	62,200	24.8
	Internal Affairs	1,046	35,889	36,936	14.7
	Agriculture	**2,424**	**32,959**	**35,383**	**14.1**
	Statistical	1,506	9,747	11,263	4.5
	Vesenkha	4,262	6,537	10,799	4.3
	Health	970	9,632	10,602	4.3
	Education	—	—	9,100	3.6
	Ways/Commun	—	—	9,094	3.6
	Trade	—	—	8,284	3.4
	Labor	—	—	5,732	2.3
	Justice	—	—	5,695	2.3
	Post/Telegraph	—	—	5,008	2.0
	Rabkrin	—	—	4,314	1.7
	Soc. Security	—	—	2,530	1.0
	Foreign Affairs	—	—	1,187	0.5
1/1/28	**Agriculture**	**2336**	**39,100**	**42,016**	**18.7**
	Finance	3822	35,316	39,820	17.7
	Internal Affairs	730	35,109	35,839	16.0
	Statistical	4,009	14,606	18,615	8.3
	Health	1,020	8,916	10,753	4.8
	Vesenkha	—	—	8,351	3.7
	Education	—	—	8,206	3.6
	Ways/Commun	—	—	8,163	3.6
	Labor	—	—	6,977	3.1
	Justice	—	—	6,832	3.0
	Trade	—	—	5,323	2.5
	Rabkrin	—	—	3,439	1.5
	Post/Telegraph	—	—	2,617	1.2
	Social Security	—	—	1,783	0.8
	Foreign Affairs	—	—	729	0.3

Source: Tsentral'noe Statisticheskoe Upravlenie SSSR, *Gosudarstvennyi apparat SSSR, 1924–1928 gg.* (Moscow, 1929), 16, 104–5.

[a] Local staff includes guberniia, oblast', okrug, and uezd officials. Does not include raion or village soviets.

of arrests in the summer and fall of 1922, and a lack of structure and coherence had all served to diminish the agency's stature and effectiveness. Moreover, a full six years after the Bolshevik revolution, the government still had not passed basic legislation defining either the Commissariat's specific role or the responsibilities of its many constituent parts.

Smirnov had cut his teeth during the Civil War serving in the Commissariat of Food Supply, first as a plenipotentiary to Saratov and Samara provinces, and from 1919 as a collegium member and then deputy commissar of food supply.[7] Apparently with the food brigades' reputation for discipline, ruthlessness, and results as a major consideration, Sovnarkom assigned Smirnov to the agriculture commissariat to try to hammer the struggling organization into shape. Smirnov's appointment resulted from the Politburo's belief that strong, reliable one-man rule in the Commissariat was needed to oversee its reorganization and revitalization. It appears that Sovnarkom ordered Smirnov to inject some of the food supply commissariat's legendary no-nonsense culture into the floundering Narkomzem apparatus in order to instill vigor and efficiency. Indeed, Smirnov explicitly distinguished himself from the previous leaders of the organization. Thus, a self-styled disciplinarian emerging from a quasi-military bastion now headed this highly specialized, but quite disorganized, agency. Yet, it soon appeared that the Commissariat of Agriculture would transform Smirnov as much as he would change the organization.

Smirnov, who often referred to himself in the third person, was described by friends and foes alike as practical, direct, and short tempered. Not one to mince words, Smirnov, whose nickname in the party was Foma, was irritable and prone to sarcastic outbursts. The cause of this testiness likely was an illness of unknown origin that caused him to suffer from frequent and debilitating headaches, leaving him bedridden for weeks and even months at a time. Smirnov was also considered to be a dedicated worker who was utterly devoted to the Bolshevik party, having spent twenty years in party work by the time of his appointment to Narkomzem in 1923 (plus another six years with the Social Democrats before Lenin created the Bolshevik Party in 1903).

Smirnov was not among the very leading group in the Bolshevik Party; rather he served in what might be called the second tier. Nevertheless, he held key positions in the state and party apparatus throughout the 1920s, most prominently as a member of the Central Committee. In 1924 Smirnov became a member of the Orgburo of the Central Committee, the powerful commission in charge of high-level party personnel appointments. The following year he was appointed deputy chairman of Sovnarkom RSFSR. In fact, he held five high-ranking party positions simultaneously by the mid-1920s. His standing as an Old Bolshevik certainly gave him more authority in the party and government than the token muzhik commissar Iakovenko, or the petulant oppositionist Osinskii, who had managed to find himself on Lenin's bad side with surprising regularity. In terms of the political authority of its leader, then, Narkomzem was suddenly in a much better position than it had been before 1923.

When he assumed the post of people's commissar in the spring of 1923, Smirnov brought a number of his most trusted colleagues from the quickly disintegrating food supply commissariat. Throughout the 1920s, Smirnov retained a fierce loyalty to comrades from his old organization.[8] Most notably, Smirnov immediately named A. I. Sviderskii to be one of his deputy commissars. Smirnov's choice of Sviderskii as one of his two closest lieutenants illustrates his determination to improve the Commissariat's operations immediately. Sviderskii had served in Narkomprod during the Civil War and had been a trusted colleague of food supply commissar A. D. Tsiurupa during their years in land work and in social democratic circles in Ufa.[9] Later, as head of the agriculture and food supply section of the Workers and Peasant's Inspectorate in 1922 and early 1923, Sviderskii had led a series of painstaking and highly critical investigations of Narkomzem's operations. Sviderskii possessed the experience of the *revizor* (an inspector general), and brought his skills to bear on the muddle that he and Smirnov found upon arrival in the Commissariat of Agriculture.

In a decision that would have great significance, Smirnov left Ivan A. Teodorovich in place as his second deputy commissar, a post that Teodorovich had occupied since December 1920. As the party's leading patron of noncommunist specialists on the rural economy, Teodorovich remained a vital presence during the entire period of NEP.[10] The Soviet Union's best remaining agrarian experts, most of whom he had personally recruited to Narkomzem in 1920–21, continued to serve under Teodorovich's supervision in Zemplan and in Narkomzem's specialized divisions.

Smirnov's ascension marked a new stage in the life of Narkomzem as he managed to guide it from its legacy as a weak, poorly coordinated, and isolated agency to a much more respected national force. By absorbing the views of his deputies and noncommunist specialist subordinates with whom he was in constant contact, he clearly defined the agency's mission. Smirnov also benefited from a climate inside the upper reaches of the party that was presently, if uneasily, favorable to the policies, claims, and world view of the Commissariat of Agriculture.

To Discipline and Protect

As Narkomzem's new strongman, Smirnov immediately flexed his muscles. In one of his first official acts as deputy commissar in late 1922, he fired off a circular to the chiefs of all provincial land administrations.[11] Smirnov used a combination of threats and promises to gain the support, or at least the respect and attention, of local land bosses. Still wedded to the exhortative military rhetoric so common in the heyday of the food supply brigades, he urged land workers to achieve "decisive successes on the agricultural recovery front." He ordered provincial organizations to maintain the "closest possible relationship with uezd land sections" and personally to take responsibility for their work. Moscow would not tolerate "separatism" in the work of provincial land sections. It must have appeared to many Commissariat officials that Smirnov's appointment foreshadowed a return to the Civil War style of exhortation and military-style mobilization and methods.[12] In fact, the vehemence of his threats belied his weak ability to force employees outside Moscow to do his bidding.

Similarly, Smirnov's first published editorial after his promotion to people's commissar, which appeared in the Narkomzem internal weekly *Sel'sko-khoziastvennaia zhizn'* in May 1923, took a severe line toward the bureaucracy he now headed.[13] Smirnov made it clear that, although his long-term goal was the recovery of agricultural production, and ultimately its mechanization and socialization, the first step toward fulfilling that mission was the injection of order and rigor into the Commissariat. "The first condition for the success of our work is discipline in the land apparatus from top to bottom." Smirnov displayed his soft spot for infantry imagery by emphasizing that he wanted to create "an army of land workers." The irony of relying upon military metaphors during a period that the party regarded as "a retreat" was lost on Smirnov, if not on those whom he was trying to mobilize.

In this first communication with Commissariat employees, one can see everything that Smirnov and his party superiors believed was wrong with the Narkomzem apparatus, and, indeed, with a great deal of state administration across the country. He notes the shattered relations between Moscow and the localities that breed "separatism," the absence of personal responsibility among officials, and agricultural personnel's vulnerability at the hands of local communist party chiefs. While rhetoric in the period emphasized the notion of decentralization, Moscow in reality regarded strengthened central control over provincial administration as a precondition for effective government.

Smirnov launched a campaign (and there is no other word to describe the vehemence and intensity of his efforts) to strengthen the nearly moribund land administration all over the RSFSR. Indeed, he was a much more effective advocate for the interests of agricultural administration than anyone had been previously. A key part of his program was quickly to locate a cohort of experienced, well-trained specialists in agriculture and land affairs. As early as May 1921, Lenin had tried to counter many local party secretaries' misgivings about the growing number of appointments of noncommunist personnel to posts in local administrations. He maintained that there were thousands of loyal and honest noncommunist experts whom the party could (and already did) profitably recruit to work for Soviet power.[14] Despite Lenin's instructions, the attitude of many local party secretaries and soviet executive committee chiefs toward Commissariat personnel in the localities reflected an antiexpert mentality.

Indeed, it was not the tsarist-era holdovers in the capital who most captured the attention of those concerned about the potentially unreliable nature of the apparatus; more anxiety was generated by the high percentage of holdovers in the periphery, where Soviet power had been much slower to set roots.[15] The statistics paint an impressive picture. By 1923, a full six years after the Revolution, and following two years of almost unrestricted hiring based less on loyalty to Soviet power than on requisite education or previous experience, the proportion of specialists who were holdovers had actually increased from the wartime figure, to 63 percent. In 1923, among the country's 15,000 agricultural specialists, the average length of service was eleven years.[16] In 1926, about 60 percent of local (*uchastkovye*) agronomists had worked in tsarist land administration and 40 percent of this group had worked for five years or longer before the revolution.[17] Indeed, local party officials frequently complained about the political untrustworthiness—either genuine, or, more often, potential—of specialist personnel, particularly those with the greatest contact with the villages. As a report by the Penza provincial land administration put it in 1925, "The shortage of specialists for work in the land organs and the weak preparation of the majority of the current contingent of specialists, especially those working in the localities, has raised the question of the political complexion of all specialists working in land organs."[18] A report from Gomel' province highlights this attitude. The secretary of the provincial party committee complained, "We are convinced that [the provincial land section] has mightily, mightily sinned, [and] that it does not have a good picture of what is happening in the localities. In the provincial land section, the policy itself is incorrect. The real bosses were not the communists sitting there but specialists of doubtful character."[19]

Narkomzem's cadres were often a target of such antispecialist sentiment, which affected the local staffs of numerous commissariats. Local communists often harbored a deeper hostility to nonparty specialists and officials than the generally more tolerant Moscow cadres did. On October 16, 1924, in an attempt to curb the phenomenon, the Politburo (probably at the initiative of Rykov) distributed to all provincial party committees a circular entitled "On the verification of personnel in state agencies."[20] The Politburo ordered provincial party committees immediately to halt the purging of local branches of People's Commissariats that had been occurring without the permission of the Central Committee. "The mass purge, occurring now in a number of places," the circular states, "is inefficient and gives undesirable results, disorganizing the work of the agencies.... The government apparatus cannot employ only party workers, an insignificant number of whom work in soviet agencies. Nor can it employ only nonparty workers and peasants. For the most part, the state apparatus employs the so-called intelligentsia and elements belonging to other classes. These elements are often entirely alien to us, but at present, the state apparatus still cannot get by without them.... [We] consider it utterly pointless to carry out a mass purge of the state apparatus at this moment."

In this context, provincial and uezd party secretaries commonly tried to remove or transfer experienced land section officials without the Commissariat's approval. The archives show that these removals without permission remained a sore point for the Commissariat leadership until 1926. Despite the pleas of the Narkomzem leadership, the party Central Committee did little to discourage the frequent firing of allegedly "doubtful characters." For years there was little the Narkomzem leadership could do to combat the dismissal, even the arrest, of its local cadres.[21]

Smirnov denounced the practice, making the issue the centerpiece of his campaign to fortify Narkomzem's provincial and uezd presence. Anyone who attempted to fire or transfer employees of the land administration without central permission was to be reported immediately to the provincial party committee and the Moscow Commissariat headquarters. Angered by the destabilizing turnover of local personnel, the new commissar indicated that establishing stability of tenure for the land administrations' local leadership and top specialists had become an absolute priority. Smirnov insisted on placing the power to appoint and transfer local personnel solely in the hands of the Moscow Commissariat of Agriculture.

Smirnov sent his first letter protesting local interference in cadre selection to the Central Committee in December 1922. Over the course of the next four years, the Narkomzem leadership forwarded at least seven more letters on this theme, increasingly vehement in tone, to the highest communist party bodies.[22] These letters decried the "epidemic of poaching," as experienced province-level land section chiefs were being replaced with unqualified, "poor workers" who were "completely unknown to Narkomzem." The Moscow Commissariat of Agriculture usually learned about the replacements only accidentally, weeks and even months after the fact. Correspondence documents more than forty unauthorized replacements and transfers, most of which came after the Politburo's initial warning. The activities of overzealous local party secretaries, the Commissariat's leaders wrote, have caused Narkomzem's work in the localities to suffer. Indeed, work has become "paralyzed" in many places.

Under pressure from the Commissariat of Agriculture, a memo was circulated to all provincial and oblast' party committees in June 1923, above the signature of Central Committee secretary Viacheslav Molotov.[23] The circular reminded communist officials that the revival of agriculture was "extremely important as the basis for the recovery of the nation's economy, the foundation of industrial development, and a pillar of the state budget." Recovery was possible only if local party workers paid attention to land work and if the local land apparatus was strong. This initial, rather tepidly worded circular had little effect, and Narkomzem's complaints did not abate. In December 1923, Smirnov pointed out that provincial and uezd soviet executive committee presidia rarely invited the heads of land sections to meetings.[24] Such slights "can be explained only by an inadequate consciousness" of agriculture's importance in the work of the soviet administration. Letters from Narkomzem's leaders reflected a specialist ethos. They argued that the intricacy of land workers' assignments mandated that the chief of a land section needed at least a year to become familiar with his tasks and the particularities of a given region. Yet, more than half of all chiefs and their deputies had spent less than a year in their current position. The Commissariat also maintained that the flurry of substitutions also meant that local land section chiefs did not have time to establish their authority among the farming population before they were shipped out. For the farming population, land sections were becoming just one of the many arbitrary and anonymous local bureaucracies, and the chief of the land section had become another faceless *khoziain* (boss).

After several years of insisting, Narkomzem appeared to have won the battle for the stability of local cadres. By 1927, the situation had greatly improved from Narkomzem's perspective. There were no unauthorized replacements that year, and the Commissariat declared victory.[25] Smirnov bragged that Narkomzem's local officials had become immune to outside interference. This stability was a crucial achievement for the agricultural administration, but one that was short-lived. The "victory" would come just when the Central Committee was becoming more dissatisfied with Narkomzem as an organization.

Turning Our Face to Agriculture? Competition for Autonomy and Power

The larger political stage upon which the Commissariat acted influenced its peculiar position in political life. Debates about the future of the countryside were part of a larger political struggle between the party's Right wing and the Trotskyists (otherwise known as the Left Opposition). On most issues, Narkomzem's leadership was firmly part of the Right wing of the party leadership. In fact, Smirnov, influenced by the leading specialists in the organization, especially Nikolai P. Oganovskii, N. P. Makarov, and Nikolai D. Kondrat'ev, was a leading advocate for many of the principles that comprised the heart of the post–Civil War policies toward the countryside. The party's most important Rightists included Aleksei I. Rykov, deputy chair of Sovnarkom between 1922 and 1924 and Sovnarkom chair after Lenin's death in 1924; Feliks E. Dzerzhinskii, head of the Cheka/(O)GPU and chief of Vesenkha; Nikolai Bukharin, head of the Comintern and editor of the Party newspaper *Pravda*; and Mikhail Tomskii, chairman of the trade unions. Josef Stalin was also a prominent Rightist until 1927.

The Left, led by Lev Trotsky and Evgenii Preobrazhenskii, advocated a more substantial investment in heavy industry. They believed that socialism would not truly be achieved until help came from advanced revolutionary regimes abroad. The economist Preobrazhenskii called for "primitive socialist accumulation," a stage analogous to "primitive capitalist accumulation" in the early stages of Western industrialization, during which time early capitalists extracted surplus capital from the labor of the proletariat. In NEP conditions, he argued, the state would have to turn the terms of trade against the peasant majority by setting the prices of agricultural products artificially low while prices for manufactures would be set high. The Left frankly stated that in the short term the state would have to exploit peasants through price manipulation and high taxation in order to produce the surplus capital for investment in a socialist industrial base in the USSR. The Right was quite hostile to the forced industrial tempos that the Left encouraged.

A common fear of a possible military coup d'etat by Trotsky unified a number of more moderate Bolsheviks into the Right wing, which comprised the majority in the party leadership until Trotsky's political defeat in late 1927 and his exile in January 1928. The Right wing attacked the Trotskyist Left, accusing it of insufficient sensitivity to the peasant question (among other things). Tarring the Left with the accusations that it underestimated the importance of the peasantry was useful to the Right in the political struggle. The Central Committee's "Face to the Countryside!" *(Litsom k derevne!)* campaign helped the anti-Trotsky majority by proffering a slogan that highlighted the Left's "incorrect" position on the peasant question.[26] Meanwhile, concern about Trotsky's alleged Bonapartist ambitions, his confrontational approach toward the peasantry, and his apparently aggressive "permanent revolution" policy distracted Rightists away from Stalin's accumulation of great power inside the party apparatus and his growing influence within the secret police.

Finally, an amorphous fear of peasant rebellion, which could be incited perhaps by another famine, ran through the majority leadership and informed its actions and policy decisions. The Right wing was worried that the implementation of Trotsky's "inflammatory" policies toward the peasantry might spark rural uprisings. In the mid-1920s, a continuing belief that peasant rebellion could remove the party from power encouraged the Right to preserve the conciliatory measures toward the countryside that lay at the heart of NEP.

If Smirnov's campaign to acquire a degree of control over the appointment and firing of local personnel reveals a concern among some local party members about the increasing prominence of noncommunist specialists, Smirnov's struggle to gain respect for land officials among local communists exposes part of a paradox that bedeviled rural officials during the 1920s. On one hand, Commissariat officials were convinced that their role in the recovery of the economy was both vital and irreplaceable. Russia was an agrarian country for which agriculture would remain the backbone of the economy far into the future, even given the regime's aspirations to industrialize. The Commissariat's leadership repeated this idea endlessly. Commissariat specialists and administrators therefore considered the modernization of inefficient agricultural production and the enlightenment of the village as crucial tasks that the party leadership should value and fund generously. At the same time, however, an urgent need to rebuild the nation's industrial base, cities, and transportation networks during the 1920s meant that the regime diverted resources from the countryside. In the midst of tight budgets and far-reaching economic reconstruction imperatives, the regime's priorities did not include funneling large amounts of money into salaries for rural officials, large credits for local land sections, or tools and machinery for farmers.

Nevertheless, for a short time in the mid-1920s, Commissariat of Agriculture leaders were relatively pleased with the thrust of state policy, the agency's budget, and the degree of respect the Commissariat earned in national forums. This satisfaction was, of course, in marked contrast to perceptions inside the Commissariat in 1921–22 that the organization was being treated shabbily. Judging by the frequent adoption of its proposals and its prominence at party and soviet congresses, the summit of Commissariat influence began early in 1924 and lasted for about eighteen months.

This period coincided with the "Face to the Countryside" campaign, which was launched in the summer of 1924 and publicly celebrated by the Commissariat. Three major developments precipitated the new policy. The first was the closing of the price "scissors" in favor of agriculture at the end of 1923, a decision that Narkomzem strongly favored.[27] More importantly, a partial crop failure in the middle Volga region, the Northern Caucasus, and eastern Ukraine sparked fears of another famine while contributing to a sense among the party majority that the countryside needed an expanded investment of resources. As reports of the crop failure reached Moscow, Smirnov wrote that rumors about the end of the world were spreading among villagers. "The peasantry in the famine regions has lost hopes for the harvest. Their mood is one of panic, not because it is clear that the harvest is finished, but because of their memories of the horrors of the famine of 1921–22."[28] Also that summer, a series of peasant uprisings in Georgia, which were put down by the Red Army, added to a sense that much of the Soviet peasantry was greatly dissatisfied with Soviet power.[29]

In the wake of the scissors crisis, a resolution of the Thirteenth Party Conference embraced Narkomzem's positions on a number of crucial issues. The resolution stated that "our party should . . . in appraising any step it takes, never forget or for a moment fail to take into account the prevailing importance of peasant agriculture."[30] It further called for an extension of short-term rural credit, a reduced tax burden for the village, and stepped-up grain exports.[31] Chairman of Sovnarkom Rykov noted in *Pravda* that the Conference marked the first time that a discussion of agriculture had been the lead item in a party resolution.[32] At the Eleventh RSFSR Congress of Soviets in January 1924, the Narkomzem representative was the first to present a report, and discussion of its contents lasted the entire second day.[33] With pride bordering on glee, *Sel'skokhoziaistvennaia zhizn'* reported the prominence the Congress gave to the Commissariat's speech.

The Fourteenth Party Conference in April 1925 and the Fourteenth Congress in December 1925 represent the high-water mark not only for the Commissariat of Agriculture, but also for the Right wing in general. The party's adoption of policies in 1925 that Narkomzem had long advocated, including granting peasants the right to hire labor and lease land under certain circumstances, gave rise to a newfound confidence among the Commissariat's representatives. In 1925, collegium member M. I. Latsis boldly declared that the tasks of Narkomzem were so important that it should be allotted a budget larger than any other commissariat. That year Narkomzem asked the finance commissariat for twice the salary allotment and almost double the operational budget of the year before.[34] Unlike previous years, the financial organs considered these requests seriously and nearly fulfilled them in full.

This relative prominence did not last long, however, before Narkomzem again complained of being a poor cousin inside the Soviet government, as it had been in 1921–23. Only during the "Face to the Countryside" campaign in 1924–25 was the Commissariat's leadership even partially satisfied with the agency's financial allotments. Indeed, the budget struggles that Narkomzem had waged with the financial organs from 1921 to 1923 continued every year throughout the twenties. As Smirnov wrote to the Politburo in 1924, "It turns out that far from everyone understands that to stand with 'faces to the countryside' means to stand with our face to agriculture, which we cannot revive with agronomists and veterinarians" who are grossly underpaid.[35] In a letter to the party's Central Control Commission (TsKK or CCC), Smirnov accused the finance and labor commissariats of "wretchedly" handling the allotments for salaries. The system of credit allocations to commissariats was "ugly and scandalously irrational."[36] Smirnov suggested that the entire wage fund be divided among all the people's commissariats more "justly" and "correctly." Not surprisingly, the Commissariat of Finance rejected the suggestion out of hand.[37] The slogan "Face to the Countryside!" with its promise of greater consideration of the needs of rural administration and of the countryside in general, mocked Narkomzem's aspirations. Commissariat officials sometimes mentioned the slogan with sarcasm. Leading party and state agencies did not meet their raised expectations. In a spring 1925 letter urging greater funds for credit to small farmers, Smirnov himself chided the Politburo, asserting that "practically speaking this summer the policy 'face to the countryside' will come to nothing."[38] Some land officials even ridiculed the regime for turning its "ass to the countryside."[39]

Commissariat leaders negatively compared current funding to prerevolutionary expenditures on agriculture. By 1926–27, the Soviet government spent about 70 percent more on agriculture than the Imperial government had earmarked in 1913. Yet, by contrast, the spending on industry rose about 700 percent relative to the imperial government's investment.[40] Narkomzem's resources were never impressive compared to the proportion of the budget being poured into industry. In 1924, Deputy Commissar Sviderskii noted that the state spent seven million gold rubles on agricultural education in Russia in 1913, as compared with only one-and-a-half million at present.[41] As the Commissariat scholar N. P. Makarov noted in 1927, the budget for agriculture was smaller per farm than it had been in 1913.[42] After peaking in 1924–25, the Commissariat's budget declined by 26 percent in 1926–27, from 128 million rubles to 95 million rubles, and its proportion of the total budget fell from 3.3 percent to 2.1 percent.[43]

Although salaries in the land administration rose slowly after 1925, the wage fund of Narkomzem remained among the lowest of any commissariat throughout the 1920s. The pay of agricultural specialists and cadres was miserly in comparison to specialists with comparable training employed in industry and transport.[44] The Commissariat of Agriculture's 1923–24 report to the RSFSR Congress of Soviets insisted that "the material welfare of agro-personnel is extremely inadequate. . . . Such a level of pay, of course, cannot create normal conditions for work and does not enable the development of the necessary initiative and creativity."[45] Furthermore, poor pay in the land administration repelled Communist Party members, an elite who could be somewhat selective about the jobs they chose. As Deputy Commissar of Agriculture A. I. Sviderskii pointed out in July 1924, land agencies "faced difficulties in getting party members to work in Narkomzem when land workers are poorly paid."[46]

It is striking that budget complaints from the beginning and end of the decade are nearly identical, indicating little improvement as the 1920s progressed. The Face to the Countryside campaign saw a significant, if brief, improvement in the salaries of central and local personnel. But by 1926, agricultural experts were again objecting that they were faring poorly in relation to specialists in other branches of the economy. Indeed, the average wages of the central staff ranked last among six economic commissariats from 1925–26 to 1927–28, having hovered near or at the bottom in the first half of the decade.[47]

Relatively low salaries led to high turnover of cadres. The great shortage of qualified people created enormous demand for skilled workers, who sold their labor on the free market. Smirnov wrote to the Politburo, "Because of low salaries, the best employees are running away." In a preliminary draft of the letter, he had added, "Only those who cannot find work in other agencies remain. It is becoming increasingly difficult to keep even those who quietly carry the burden by virtue of their love for their work. . . . If this is the way things are with *experienced* employees, there's no point in discussing the *new* ones."[48]

The Politics of Expertise

Low salaries and budget struggles were hardly the organization's only major challenges in this period. The Commissariat of Agriculture's leaders found themselves in an awkward political position throughout the 1920s. Commissariat policies, intended to increase incentives for the middle peasants *(seredniaki)* and especially the "well-off" (*zazhitochnye*) to produce more, in a more efficient and intensive manner, remained controversial and unpopular with some party members (see chapter four). The Commissariat of Agriculture's position as an agency with close contact to farmers prompted suspicion of collaboration with untrustworthy villagers against the interests of the proletariat. Issues of class were explosive, as many party loyalists viewed the interests of the peasantry and those of the proletariat as fundamentally antithetical, both economically and politically.

In fact, the Commissariat's advocacy of policies that stimulated production among the wealthier, or "more progressive," stratum of peasants earned its political and specialist leadership a reputation throughout the decade as having "pro-kulak" leanings. The finer points of Narkomzem's position were lost on many communists, especially but not exclusively the followers of Trotsky. At a closed meeting of the Central Committee Plenum in 1924, for example, Smirnov alluded to the Commissariat's situation. Politburo member Zinov'ev, Smirnov notes, had asked him to make a presentation on the Commissariat's activities: "Somehow in conversation [Zinov'ev] mentioned that a number of comrades claim that the Commissariat of Agriculture is biased in favor of the kulak. He asked if this were true. I told him it is not true. Unfortunately, comrades do not pay enough attention to agriculture and to Narkomzem's work."[49] Smirnov's statement illustrates his sensitivity to charges of collusion with the kulaks, a group viewed by all Bolsheviks as an enemy of socialism.

At this plenum meeting, Smirnov displayed an important dimension of his strategy as leader of a virtual "ministry of the peasantry" in a country ruled by a party whose goals were clearly urban and industrial. After his accusation that comrades were insufficiently attentive to the needs of agriculture, Commissar Smirnov proceeded to give an excruciatingly detailed speech, filled with dense statistics covering every aspect of land affairs and the rural economy. Such a speech was hardly conducive to attracting his comrades to focus "on agriculture and on Narkomzem's work."

This technique of using specialized scientific knowledge as a cudgel against his critics ignorant of the complexities of the agricultural economy, remained one of Smirnov's favorite political and polemical tools. I call this phenomenon the politics of expertise, a strategy by which the people's commissar and his assistants attempted to gain political advantage by laying claim to the exclusive mastery of a huge and complex body of specialized information. By so doing, they staked claim to stewardship over a sphere of the economy, in this case land affairs and agriculture. These were areas that the entire Communist Party had to admit were of vital importance for economic recovery and, ultimately, for political stability. Smirnov could use this expertise as a shield against criticism by "comrades who ignore agriculture" or "comrades who do not pay sufficient attention to land affairs," to quote two of his favorite phrases. In June 1925, for example, Smirnov wrote to Molotov with a variation on the familiar theme of the party leadership's failure to consider the needs of agriculture properly: "I cannot explain this persistent scorn for the interests of agriculture."[50]

On most issues, Smirnov sympathized with the Party's Right wing, struggling against the group of Trotsky and Preobrazhenskii supporters who argued in favor of more rapid industrialization. Smirnov, however, did not direct his politics of expertise solely against the Left. Rather, he was convinced that the Communist Party leadership did not understand the problems facing rural Russia and, therefore, frequently made policy errors. Underlying the politics of expertise was a fundamental assumption: Narkomzem's cadres—and especially Smirnov himself—understood the problems of agriculture and land affairs; almost no one else in the party did, regardless of factional affiliation.

In Defense of Specialists

In this context, the personnel of the Commissariat of Agriculture endured a variety of attacks between 1923 and 1926. What was the nature of these attacks and what were the Commissariat leaders' strategies for defending their specialists and officials? The answers expose strained relationships between the Commissariat and sections of the party elite, and between the Commissariat and state control agencies.

This discussion of instances of attempted intervention in the Commissariat's activities is not intended to imply that the Commissariat was constantly under siege from hostile outsiders. Whereas no organization is free from tension (including social and political tension), most of the daily business of Narkomzem's cadres went unhindered by the vagaries of outside interference. Indeed, as we have seen, Sovnarkom and the Commissariat's party leadership had institutionalized the ubiquitous influence of noncommunist agricultural specialists in Narkomzem. Despite negative pressure from some quarters, nonparty specialists were largely running the Soviet economy well into the twenties. As long as the Central Committee supported the policies of NEP, the Commissariat could be fairly confident that its extensive employment and protection of leading bourgeois specialists would be safeguarded. Nevertheless, the phenomenon of specialist baiting and taunting was present throughout the state and economic apparatuses. The Commissariat of Agriculture was replete with specialists with "suspicious" backgrounds, and the prominence of nonparty experts in administration generated a discernible hostility among some in the party. This was the case even during "High NEP," between 1923 and 1926. Although during much of this period the policies that Narkomzem espoused were in favor, it was also an era of political volatility. Narkomzem came under pressure from Trotskyists and Left radicals, unhappy with the policy of accommodating the more prosperous peasants. The slow pace of efforts to "proletarianize" agricultural production frustrated many supporters of Trotsky. In their view, this lackadaisical pace was reflected in the paltry allocation of resources to collective farms and in the official policy of appeasing the well-off and middle peasants. The Commissariat was also attacked by anti-intellectual radicals, mistrustful of the power of noncommunist specialists in the economy and the presence of "alien elements" in senior positions.

Historians have shown that many noncommunist economic specialists, especially those who worked in industry, trade, and finance, were shielded by leading party figures who acted as their patrons in the 1920s.[51] In many cases, these protectors were party chiefs within the commissariats. Some of these patrons are well known, including Sergo Ordzhonikidze when he served as People's Commissar of Heavy Industry, Feliks Dzerzhinskii in his capacity as chairman of Vesenkha (which was in charge of all large-scale industry and employed many former Mensheviks in leading posts), and Valerii I. Mezhlauk when he presided over Vesenkha. According to an eyewitness, Dzerzhinskii, for example, reacted to any attacks on Vesenkha's cadres "with a sharpness that was almost vicious."[52] Aleksei Rykov, head of the Council of People's Commissars, acted as a powerful defender of specialists in the ministerial system. However, historians have not adequately recognized the patrons of the Soviet Union's talented nonparty agricultural specialists. Alexander P. Smirnov and his deputy Ivan A. Teodorovich stand out in this respect. Nor have scholars discussed the issue in the context of social stigmatization.

If Smirnov's guiding metaphor at the beginning of his tenure in 1923 was that of the military officer restoring order to an undisciplined brigade, he quickly changed roles. He never abandoned his authoritarian leadership style, expecting loyalty and obedience from cadres. Yet within a year of his appointment, Smirnov had undergone something of a transformation, viewing himself the leader of a contingent of experts, protecting their right to work calmly on extremely complex and important problems, and encouraging their initiative. He came to envision himself less as a commanding officer and more as the head of an academic department or institute—a professor, as he began to call himself on occasion—responsible for ensuring the ability of his colleagues to do their scientific work in peace.[53]

The Investigations of 1924

Two campaigns intended to trim the size and improve the quality of the state apparatus reached the Commissariat of Agriculture in 1924. The first was a review of the land agency's Communist Party contingent in the spring, and the second was a general investigation and "cleansing" of the entire state apparatus in the autumn. Narkomzem's reaction to both staff reviews illustrates Smirnov's conviction that protecting the Commissariat's cadres—on one hand, his assistants and deputies, and on the other hand, his precious cohort of specialists—was an utter necessity.

Some background on the powerful organization that supervised these investigations sets the stage. In 1922 and 1923, Lenin made plans to revive, streamline, and "rationalize" the bloated bureaucracy, including a reconfiguration of an agency that would become both central in campaigns to fight "bureaucratism" and an important political actor in the 1920s. In particular, Lenin drew up a blueprint for reforming the Commissariat of Workers' and Peasants' Inspectorate (NKRKI), or Rabkrin.[54] This agency would become one of Narkomzem's leading antagonists throughout the decade. Rabkrin was made responsible for supervising the commissarial and government bureaucracies. The TsKK, created in 1920 as a department of the Secretariat, served as Rabkrin's party equivalent for supervising and investigating "failings" in the Communist Party apparatus. Lenin wrote that Rabkrin's heavily bureaucratized cohort of twelve thousand employees must be reduced to several hundred of the country's very best experts on administration. On Lenin's recommendation, the two agencies merged in 1923 to form a juggernaut, Rabkrin-TsKK. The combined agency was charged with training and supervising officials in efficient work methods at all levels of the state and party apparatuses. As Leonard Schapiro put it, Rabkrin "soon became a commissariat above all the commissariats, the eye of the party inside the whole administrative machine."[55] Until April 1922, Stalin headed Rabkrin, which he used as one of his power bases. During his tenure as chief of Rabkrin, Stalin came in for scathing criticism by Lenin, who lashed out at him for his agency's tendency to focus its attention only on organizational and human defects without proposing serious solutions.[56] Nevertheless, Rabkrin became a superbureaucracy that itself was the source of political intrigue throughout the 1920s. Lenin's prescription for what Daniel Orlovsky has called "overcoming bureaucracy with bureaucracy," especially with an agency that possessed what amounted to extraordinary powers, was profoundly flawed and had long-standing repercussions.[57]

Rabkrin announced in April 1924 that it would soon begin reviewing the Commissariat of Agriculture's entire cohort of party members, with the participation of the Moscow city party organization. This review was part of the general verification of the credentials and qualifications of all members of the Communist Party with an eye toward jettisoning the incompetent, the deceitful, and the disloyal. Like most other commissariats in the ministerial system, only a tiny proportion of Narkomzem's staff was party members. Following the example of the Red Army during the Civil War, when party watchdogs closely observed former tsarist officers who had agreed to work for the Bolsheviks, party leaders created a system of dual control in the economic commissariats. Communists were posted to monitor nonparty experts for political obedience. Party personnel offices made sure that communists occupied the key administrative positions, though it is clear that they often only nominally supervised the professionals under their watch. These posts were the so-called nomenklatura positions—members of the collegium (the commissar's advisory board comprised mostly the heads of divisions and the top specialists) and the heads of the major administrative divisions. In the lower ranks, however, the situation was very different, among specialists in particular. Considering the virtual absence of party members with any knowledge of agriculture, the idea of placing party members at the head of the Commissariat's many smaller sections was "utopian," as Commissar Smirnov asserted without a trace of irony in 1924.[58] Noncommunist experts outnumbered communists by about ten to one throughout the 1920s. Even by the end of the decade, on the eve of the collectivization, these percentages for the Moscow offices had changed little.[59]

The weak communist presence stemmed in part from the vigorous actions of Smirnov himself, who insisted on accepting people to fill leading posts only if they possessed relevant scientific or administrative skills. Few communist candidates fit the profile. Smirnov fought hard for this principle, writing to the TsKK that despite his best efforts to locate specialists on agriculture within party ranks, very few existed.[60] As a result, between January 1924 and January 1927, the Communist contingent in the central Commissariat of Agriculture actually decreased, albeit slightly, to just over 10 percent. Amidst a renewed antibureaucracy campaign in the first half of 1927, representation jumped to 14.4 percent, still the lowest for any of the ten commissariats for which there is data.[61]

The 1924 investigations of the Commissariat's party personnel, therefore, had major repercussions. Rabkrin's conclusions stunned Smirnov, who lay in bed convalescing from his recurring illness in Sukhumi on the Black Sea coast when he was handed a telegram containing news of the final report. Despite Smirnov's plea to delay final decisions until his recovery, Rabkrin forwarded

Table 3-2
Central commissariats: Average yearly increase, party representation, 1924-1927

Commissariat	% annual increase in CPSU members
Agriculture	1.1
Finance, USSR	1.5
Foreign Affairs	2.3
Justice	2.6
Labor, RSFSR	3.3
Trade	4.1
Vesenkha	4.3
Transport	4.6

Source: *Piatnadtsatyi s"ezd VKP(b), dekabr' 1927 goda, stenograficheskii otchet* (Moscow, 1961), 1: 446–47.

him their disturbing conclusions: many of the commissariat's most prominent communists were simply unfit for work in that agency. Indeed, investigators ordered that fully one-third of the Commissariat's communists be removed from their positions, many of whom directed divisions with large cohorts of noncommunist experts.[62] Investigators had found several of the Commissariat's leading Bolsheviks guilty of transgressions against the party.

Most remarkably, Rabkrin recommended that Smirnov's deputy, the Old Bolshevik I. A. Teodorovich, be reprimanded and transferred to another, unspecified, agency.[63] Rabkrin made this recommendation even though Teodorovich was one of the Communist Party's very few genuine experts on agriculture. Teodorovich was accused of failing to pay his party dues on time. He also "frequently fell ill," a charge especially unlikely to win over the ailing People's Commissar. On these frivolous grounds, Rabkrin ordered that Teodorovich, whose tenure as a Social Democrat officially dated to 1895, be ejected from Narkomzem. More than anyone, Teodorovich had overseen the institutionalization of expertise as chief of Zemplan and as the leading recruiter of bourgeois experts into the Commissariat's many specialized divisions. However, the deputy commissar had earned a reputation as a patron of nonparty specialists who was oversolicitous of their opinions. The information used against Teodorovich most likely had its source in Narkomzem's quite hostile Communist Party cell.

When Smirnov heard of the decision, he immediately contacted General Secretary Stalin to protest the action.[64] Smirnov cabled that the recommendation that he be deprived of his most knowledgeable communist deputy was "insane." How, he asked, could the Rabkrin commission decide to expel almost one-third of Narkomzem's communists? How could Rabkrin choose to remove persons as irreplaceable as Teodorovich and two other current or former col-

TABLE 3-3
Communist Party members and candidate members in central Commissariats, July 1927

Commissariat	Total staff	Number of communists	% of communists
Agriculture	1538	221	14.4
Finance, RSFSR	563	96	17.0
Interior	410	72	17.8
Finance, USSR	1040	189	18.2
Vesenkha, USSR	2034	422	20.2
Transport	1599	350	22.0
Justice	295	60	22.4
Trade, USSR	1090	265	24.3
Labor, RSFSR	136	38	28.0

Source: Piatnadtsatyi s"ezd VKP(b), dekabr' 1927 goda, stenograficheskii otchet (Moscow, 1961), 1: 446–47.

legium members from a commissariat in desperate need of qualified party members?[65] Smirnov's appeal triumphed. Teodorovich's transfer was canceled, but Narkomzem's troubles were far from over.

Alien and Hostile Elements

Two months after the audit of party members in the spring of 1924, a general review of the noncommunist personnel of the state apparatus reached Narkomzem. On June 30, 1924, the party TsKK ordered Rabkrin to begin research into the Commissariat of Agriculture in preparation for a *proverka lichnogo sostava*, or staff credentials inspection, which was to examine every state agency. The full review, this time of nonparty cadres, took place in September and October.[66] This process represented the beginning of Rabkrin's stepped-up interest in the social background of noncommunist cadres in the state apparatus. The period 1923–24 was a time when the party Secretariat attempted to assume ever more control over appointments not just of the top level of the apparatus, but increasingly of nonparty personnel.

The commission brought together several key party agencies. Each had a degree of responsibility for ensuring the quality of cadres in the state apparatus, and each remained a thorn in Narkomzem's side until 1929. This 1924 verification commission was chaired by the communist party cell located inside Narkomzem (headed at this time by Vinogradov). The party cell had established a consistently hostile position toward the Commissariat leadership once Smirnov took over in 1923. The joint Rabkrin-TsKK also participated as the agency responsible for the proper behavior and professional activity of party members. (Although the TsKK had merged with Rabkrin in 1923, the TsKK remained responsible for investigating party comrades, while Rabkrin still handled the government bureaucracies.) Furthermore, Narkomzem's branch of Uchraspred, the Central Committee's influential personnel records and allocation department, participated as the agency responsible for collecting the biographical and career data on these nonparty cadres. Uchraspred worked very closely with Rabkrin in these "credentials reviews."[67]

Meanwhile, the Orgburo oversaw personnel appointments pertaining to the top party layer in government and economic administrations. In 1923–24, elite appointments gained a new level of political significance as part of the anti-Trotsky campaign. The Twelfth Party Congress resolved that the party had responsibility for choosing not only the nomenklatura, but also nonparty members. Trotsky's supporters were expelled from the state apparatus under the supervision of Stalin's associates, Molotov and Kaganovich. The Central Committee, through Uchraspred, claimed the right to approve not only the leading party stratum in each state institution, but also noncommunist specialists in responsible posts. The Orgburo recognized that many nonparty cadres were completely loyal to Soviet power, but asserted that this loyalty must be verified by commissions similar to the one that reviewed Narkomzem's cadres in the fall of 1924.

Indeed, by the early 1920s, Narkomzem gave Rabkrin plenty of grist for its mill. The Commissariat's officials included former White Army officers, gentry (*dvoriane*, both landed and nonlanded),[68] priests and their children, and others who had been considered deadly enemies of the communist regime during the Civil War but who possessed urgently needed experience or expertise. To the inspectors in Rabkrin and Orgraspred, Narkomzem's numbers were conspicuous, at times scandalous, even in a state administration that was full of tsarist-era holdovers in professional positions.[69] Both these agencies charged that the Commissariat's leadership was insufficiently attentive to staffing integrity, and they constantly pressured Narkomzem to remove holdovers on the basis of their perceived unreliability. It is in these inspection agencies that we see the strongest reflection of the belief among many party members that one's past determined one's political outlook.

In the summer of 1924, the members of the Rabkrin commission were to check not only all Narkomzem officials' qualifications, but also their "social origin and relationship to Soviet power." In the process, Rabkrin tried to separate the wheat from the chaff. The commission especially targeted the two brain trusts of the Commissariat, Zemplan and the Agriculture Administration, where the critical mass of Narkomzem's senior specialists was located.[70] Of approximately two thousand staffers in Moscow, Rabkrin recommended that hundreds be transferred or removed. Narkomzem objected to the removal of approximately 290 of these employees.

Upon the completion of the inspection, Nikolai M. Shvernik, chief of the Rabkrin agriculture and food supply inspectorate, summarized his findings in a blistering letter to Smirnov.[71] Shvernik began by acknowledging that as the agency in charge of the recovery of the vast and wounded agricultural sector, Narkomzem was one of the most important of the country's commissariats. Nevertheless, he followed with a scathing eleven-page indictment of the Commissariat's Moscow personnel. "Soviet land policy," he wrote, "must be carried out by an apparatus [the Commissariat of Agriculture] that has not grasped the tasks and ideas of Soviet construction in the countryside. It is riddled with elements that are alien and even hostile to Soviet power." Shvernik pointed to the "weak communist contingent . . . not only among specialists but also among the leadership." He decried the presence in the Moscow commissariat offices of many former estate owners and nobles, and pointed out that hardly more than one percent of its staff were peasants or workers by social origin. Administrators as well as specialists frequently had prior experience in the pre-Revolutionary bureaucracy.[72] Excluding lower service and secretarial personnel, Narkomzem employed twice as many former gentry and nobles as workers and peasants combined.[73] Shvernik pointed out that any former nobles and landed gentry took mid- and low-level positions in land administration (in part because they were in grave need of an income). One senior bookkeeper in Narkomzem's agricultural division had noble parents, had graduated from a seminary, had carried "important responsibilities in a religious institution," and had served as a vice director in the tsarist Ministry of Education.[74] A deputy in the Commissariat's Administration of Land Reorganization had led a strike by Ministry of Agriculture personnel against the new Bolshevik government in 1917. "The Commissariat of Agriculture is working with weak human material," Shvernik maintained as he dredged up example after example of similarly suspect cadres.

These were remarkable charges from a top official in the oversight agency. Not only did Narkomzem's cadres demonstrate "hostility" to Bolshevik power, they did not understand the new regime's mission or guiding principles. Shvernik wrote with disdain of the "enormous influence" of nonparty experts. He correctly observed that, because they held prominent posts, nonparty specialists were able to choose freely the contingent of employees under them, surrounding themselves with still more aliens. He concluded, "It is obvious that the majority of [Narkomzem's] personnel is completely unsuitable both socially and politically." To further cleanse the Commissariat of "hostile elements," Shvernik suggested that another special Rabkrin commission be established.

In response to Shvernik's letter and in further correspondence with Rabkrin, the TsKK, and the Politburo, Commissar Smirnov laid out his rebuttal. He focused on the key issues of the quality of his personnel, their political complexion, and his hiring practices. Smirnov first acknowledged that, of course, it would be desirable if more Bolsheviks occupied visible positions in the Commissariat. He pointed out that he had worked hard to increase the percentage of communists in leadership posts since he took the helm. Nevertheless, he repeated, very few Bolsheviks possessed practical agrarian experience, and Smirnov insisted that only people with the requisite service and educational qualifications were acceptable to fill central positions. He further accused Shvernik of interfering in the Commissariat's complicated internal business, insisting that only the Narkomzem leadership was equipped to make decisions about the cadres who would rebuild Soviet agriculture.[75]

To Shvernik's suggestion that an extraordinary commission be established for purging the Narkomzem apparatus of "aliens," Smirnov responded that this was completely unnecessary and "even harmful" and would "introduce unnecessary ballyhoo and nervousness" into Narkomzem. Smirnov always insisted on making the final decision regarding appointments. For example, he was one of several heads of state agencies who resisted the mandatory creation within the Commissariat of a branch of Uchraspred, which would have had input in personnel selection.[76] The hiring of top-level employees, he declared, had occurred "always with my direct participation and my personal review of every candidacy.

This is the only possible way." Smirnov went on to pledge that the final cleansing of the apparatus would be completed by January 1, 1925. *He* would carry it out, however, and on his own terms.

Within several months, Rabkrin, not satisfied with Narkomzem's self-policing efforts, conducted another review of Narkomzem's staff. The conclusions were highly critical once again. Rabkrin established a commission, again chaired by the secretary of Narkomzem's party cell—an enemy of Smirnov and the Commissariat's specialists—to audit the Commissariat's cadres. Once again, Smirnov resisted angrily. Smirnov wrote to Rykov, complaining that Rabkrin's investigations fixated on inadequacies rather than making good-faith suggestions for improving the state apparatus. This sentiment, as Smirnov and Rykov surely knew, precisely echoed Lenin's critiques of Rabkrin in his 1923 article, "Better Fewer but Better."[77] Rykov, himself a patron of specialists, surely sympathized. Smirnov further complained that these repeated investigations intolerably delayed decisions about staffing. Rabkrin had overstepped its jurisdiction with this review. With insight that presaged Rabkrin's attempts to take over the economic commissariats in 1927–29, Smirnov argued that the relationship between the supervisory agencies (such as Rabkrin) and economic apparatuses must be strictly defined.[78] In other words, the government must sharply curtail the intervention of Rabkrin into the activities of specialized state ministries.

Despite his many criticisms of the labyrinthine network of committees that comprised the apparatus, Smirnov was skilled at using the system of these commissions to his and his organization's advantage. He insisted, for instance, that proposals to reduce the size of the Commissariat staff be dragged through several government commissions. When it suited Narkomzem's purposes, Smirnov delayed sending requested materials to commissions on cadres. He also objected to the language of resolutions and insisted that they be rewritten repeatedly. He refused to send representatives to meetings, claiming that his overworked staff could not spare a body. Smirnov's stalling tactics drew a sharp response from Rabkrin. On February 16, 1925, an inspector sent a letter to Shvernik.[79] He complained that the Commissariat of Agriculture's repeated refusals to implement several of Rabkrin's suggestions "prove yet again the strong opposition to our work on improving the apparatus that this agency is putting forth. . . . This poses a serious danger to the measures that have been carried out and to all subsequent measures concerning Narkomzem. I consider it necessary and proper to place the issue of the relationship of Narkomzem and Rabkrin on the agenda of the Presidium of the Central Control Commission."[80] Smirnov's "strong opposition" was real. Smirnov reiterated that Rabkrin must conduct relations only with him personally, not with his deputies or other subordinate personnel. Smirnov would brook no interference. (Similarly antagonistic correspondence between Rabkrin and Smirnov on the matter of personnel continued as late as December

1927, when Rabkrin again angrily accused Smirnov of lying about layoffs he was supposed to have made.[81])

Specialist-Baiting in the Press

Between 1924 and 1927, Smirnov also felt compelled to shield his agency's prominent specialists from attacks in the press. An example is an April 1925 article written by Iurii Larin containing a critique of Narkomzem's hiring of two prominent agrarian specialists. A Central Committee member who fancied himself an expert on agrarian issues, Larin was also a political patron of the Agrarian Marxists, who regularly attacked the Commissariat's agricultural specialists in the press. The Agrarian Marxists, on whose behalf Larin wrote, comprised a group of young Marxist scholars and students whose institutional base was the Agriculture Department of the Communist Academy.[82] In their journal, *Na agrarnom fronte*, they focused on questions of rural sociology, especially social differentiation, but also social structure, interclass and interfamilial conflict, and the use of hired labor.

Larin's article was provoked by the return to Moscow from Berlin in 1925 of the important scholars A. N. Chelintsev and N. P. Makarov, who had left Soviet Russia soon after the Revolution. After the arrests of Narkomzem scholars in the summer and fall of 1922, Narkomzem's leadership again aggressively courted specialists. For example, in a 1923 letter to the Politburo, Feliks Dzerzhinskii opined that, based on his experience in the transport commissariat, those specialists who remained in Russia after the war were "the worst, without initiative and without character. . . . They work [only] to survive." Fortunately, he went on, "not a few" specialists who had fled to Berlin were eager to come back to the RSFSR.[83] The GPU, in concert with the economic commissariats, tried to attract émigré specialists back to the USSR.

In fact, the year 1925 marks a significant point in the relationship between the Soviet regime and the nonparty specialists. The agrarian laws of 1925, which guaranteed peasants the right to lease land and hire labor and reaffirmed the right to choose one's preferred type of land tenure, received especially positive reaction from many agrarian experts. As expressed by N. V. Valentinov, the deputy editor of a Vesenkha journal and a friend to many nonparty specialists, "The overwhelming mass of nonparty specialists [who chose to remain in the USSR] considered that capitalism was finished forever, that the restoration of previous social relations was impossible, and that it was necessary to live and work in the new order that had appeared with the hope that it would become more democratic."[84] They believed that the Bolsheviks had abandoned their "utopianism" of the Civil War years. Much more inclined to be supportive of the Right than the Left, specialists were pleased with slogans calling for civil peace rather than civil war. There was also an element of patriotism, as they came to believe that there was no alternative but government service for those who wished to serve their country. An optimistic hope that the current Soviet leaders would allow the USSR to evolve toward something permanently more in line with their own views and approaches is essential for understanding the close working relationship between specialists and sympathetic Bolsheviks. Both specialists and Bolsheviks wanted to rebuild Russia, to raise productivity.

In this context, Makarov and Chelintsev decided in 1925 to return to Soviet Russia. Persuaded by Smirnov and deputy commissar Teodorovich to leave Germany to work in Narkomzem, these famous scholars created a stir upon their arrival. Makarov and Chelintsev were publicly accused by Larin of sympathizing with the Socialist Revolutionary Party.[85] Smirnov replied to Larin in a letter to the TsKK Presidium. Larin, known in the party for his sarcastic wit and penchant for hyperbole, had pressed the TsKK to investigate the reappearance in Moscow of Chelintsev and Makarov and, in particular, Teodorovich's role in hiring them. Smirnov was not amused. In answering the charges, Smirnov addressed the type of complaints often lodged against Narkomzem.[86] The letter contains the arguments he frequently had to make in defense of "his" specialists and "his" organization.

Commissar Smirnov started by lamenting the lack of understanding among communists of the village economy, a situation that he considered sadly ironic in a country of land-working peasants. After taking over as Commissar of Agriculture in 1923, Smirnov wrote, he made vigorous attempts to locate specialists on agriculture within the party ranks, but this search was unsuccessful. There simply were no communist specialists to replace the "bourgeois" experts. Having established his comrades' ignorance on agrarian questions, he went on sarcastically, making fun of the Agrarian Marxist journal *On the Agrarian Front*: "Nevertheless, a lack of knowledge has not prevented many of our party theoreticians and economists from considering themselves experts on every 'front,' including the babbling front." Theoreticians like Larin, Smirnov charged, are demagogues who are unqualified to resolve the practical questions of the village. Those who (inaccurately) consider themselves experts in agriculture, Smirnov taunted, should be sent to Narkomzem for some practical experience. The Commissariat leadership often used this tactic, arguing that the polemics of "mere theorists" could not reconcile the concrete problems of economic restructuring.[87]

Upon locating Chelintsev and Makarov in Germany, Smirnov continues, "I did not ask them to confess their voluntary and involuntary sins." Instead, "I asked them if, in the future, they would work honestly on behalf of Soviet power." He contends that Larin's article is nothing more than specialist baiting that interferes with the Commissariat of Agriculture's work. Furthermore, this brand of specialist baiting is extremely dangerous because "the attacks are cloaked" in specious "general discussions of Marxism's applicability in agriculture." Defending the use of specialists in sensitive positions, Smirnov cites the military, where "many former counterrevolutionaries now work for us in building the Red Army." The Red Army was the example of success most often employed by Commissariat chiefs. Soviet Generals Brussilov and Tukhachevsky were, after all, two of the tsarist army's greatest commanders. Of course, the very idea that an individual could become, in Smirnov's words, a "former counterrevolutionary" was unacceptable to many Bolsheviks who believed in the enduring, permanent hostility to Soviet power of certain irredeemable social "elements." Smirnov here also reveals his sensitivity to the insinuation that Narkomzem's agrarian policies are somehow not Marxist. After all, he could not deny that most of the people who designed and implemented those policies were not Marxists.

Yet in this confrontation, another aspect of Soviet bureaucratic and political culture is visible. Smirnov had closely bound himself with the Commissariat's personnel and policies. In defending himself privately to the TsKK against Larin's accusations in *Pravda*, he wrote angrily that the article was not only an attack on Kondrat'ev, but on Narkomzem, and also a personal attack on Smirnov himself. "I think that amid all this fantasizing, comrade Larin is not so stupid as to fail to understand the consequences of the publication of an article like this. He should understand (and I am convinced that he understands perfectly) that the appearance in the press of such an article would discredit not only me, as a member of the Government, having offered these specialists well-known guarantees about their work here (a fact which is also well known abroad, of course). But he [also] knew that this would have consequences for all our work. He understands that because of the article not only the specialists (who, Larin claims, 'direct' agricultural work) would be discredited, but also that a situation would be created for me and other Commissariat leaders in which further work in the Commissariat of Agriculture would hardly be possible."[88] Without him, he claims, the Commissariat could not function.[89]

Smirnov threatened to resign over this incident, citing his inability to work amid petty interference from outsiders. In the end, Smirnov won this confrontation. Chelintsev, Makarov, and Kondrat'ev kept their positions in Zemplan and served there until 1928, though not without controversy.[90]

Losing Revolutionary Perspective: The Party Cell Attacks for the First Time

Still another source of specialist baiting was situated inside the Commissariat itself, and was fed by a particularly combustible combination of factors. Narkomzem's own party cell offered a bountiful, if tainted, supply of accusations against the Commissariat leadership. Conflicts between the leaders of people's commissariats and their party cells were not uncommon in the 1920s, especially in the specialized socioeconomic ministries, with their large contingent of noncommunist experts. Narkomzem's relationship with its cell was not exceptional in that sense. Dissatisfied members of the Commissariat of Agriculture party cell enthusiastically provided much of the compromising evidence to Rabkrin inspectors for their nearly annual (1924, 1925, 1927, 1928, 1929) investigations and attempted cleansings of the Commissariat's staff.

It is difficult to judge the accuracy of pointed accusations made by disgruntled Narkomzem party cell members. Additional evidence indicates, however, that some of the phenomena denounced in a furious December 1925 letter were indeed correct. This remarkable letter was signed by the members of the bureau of the Narkomzem Party and written by its chief, a certain comrade Taranenko. Addressed to General Secretary Stalin, the virulent nineteen-page letter contained a sweeping indictment of Smirnov's reliance on nonparty specialists, his leadership style, and the work environment he created.[91] The accusations contained therein were so inflammatory that they sparked a five-month-long investigation by the TsKK of the "Affair of the Narkomzem Party Cell." Documents produced by the investigation provide us with unique insights into culture and conflict inside a people's commissariat at the height of NEP.[92]

The letter complains that the communist leadership in the organization has sold out to duplicitous, untrustworthy, noncommunist specialists. Party cell chief Taranenko alleges that while he was overly solicitous of these "alien" experts, Smirnov was simultaneously showing tremendous condescension to the party cell, going so far as to squelch the results of several elections for party cell chief. Smirnov finds any excuse to kick cell leaders out of the organization. The previous cell chief was "exiled" to Tbilisi, and Smirnov transferred the cell secretary, a certain Bol'shakov, to Siberia. Furthermore, Smirnov and his circle view all criticism of their leadership as personal insults. He is intolerant of dissension, and this has led to feelings of isolation, demoralization, and meekness among the party cell members. In fact, the letter asserts, the great majority of communists in the Commissariat have absolutely no influence, either in the organization as a whole or in those parts of the agency where they work. Instead, certain nonparty specialists have almost unlimited plenipotentiary authority. The letter echoes an apprehension commonly expressed by dissatisfied communists during NEP. In the words of one Uchraspred inspector, "If we do not take radical curative measures, the promotion of communists is doomed to failure and the nonparty spider web will be spun ever wider."[93] Indeed, Narkomzem's party cell leaders sensed vermin crawling all around them. Resentful of the fact that their input was rarely solicited, they envied the status and special benefits of the specialists—especially salary bonuses and preferred housing—which Smirnov protected and enhanced.

The letter proceeds to charge that Smirnov insists that he is responsible only to the Central Committee. Heads of Narkomzem's specialized administrations simply ignore the party cell requests to meet with them. "Extreme centralization of responsibility leads to absolute irresponsibility, arbitrariness, bureaucratism"—in a word, it causes vedomstvennost', or institutional self-interest.[94] Smirnov and his circle of advisors, all of whom had "lost their revolutionary perspective," refuse to listen to the party cell. "His assistants and his assistants' assistants" also ignore the cell's opinions. Instead, Smirnov surrounds himself with people whom he calls "trustworthy people": old friends such as A. I. Sviderskii, whom he brought over from the food supply commissariat, as well as "dishonest" specialists whom "he trusts blindly." Party cell leader Taranenko goes on to accuse Smirnov of bringing to Narkomzem the style of leadership he practiced in Commissariat of Food Supply during the war. "Demagoguery" and "monstrous centralism" are the results. He overburdens employees as urgent tasks are piled one upon the other, disrupting the regular assignments of the apparatus. "It may have been acceptable to work this way in the food supply commissariat during the war, but not now in the Commissariat of Agriculture."[95]

Smirnov, as was typical, issued a blanket denial of all charges, asserting that the accusations were irresponsible and false. The party TsKK, after an investigation, backed Smirnov and censured the party cell, branding two of its leaders "Trotskyists."[96] The TsKK mildly upbraided Smirnov only for his poor communication with the cell, but this confrontation left a bitter legacy. In 1928–29, the cell would play an active role in the purge of the Commissariat staff.

In Defense of Alien Elements

How did the Commissariat's Party leadership fight on many fronts to retain its skilled personnel in the face of criticism from several sources? The Commissariat of Agriculture's leadership strove to protect the employees they regarded as indispensable, regardless of social or political background. They actively pursued strategies for protecting those cadres from attacks.[97] It is important to note that, even in defending his staff, Smirnov used the prevailing class language and rhetoric of the revolution. He never argued that the very concept of social aliens was incorrect or absurd. Rather, he contended that he had reduced the numbers of social aliens in his organization to acceptable levels, or that the category "alien" should include only a small number of his employees. In other instances, he made the case that the potentially negative influence of aliens somehow had been neutralized in his organization.

Narkomzem's strategies can be grouped loosely into several categories. First, as we have seen in our discussion of Narkomzem's resistance to the Rabkrin-TsKK 1924–25 verifications of credentials, Smirnov insisted on complete control over determining whether his cadres were loyal. He asserted that most individuals who were compromised in the eyes of Rabkrin inspectors (and the Party cell) were in fact loyal to Soviet power. In fact, he found that they were nearly all dependable. Their allegiance to the new regime was genuine, despite their less-than-pure career paths or previous sympathies with discredited political parties. Like many Bolsheviks (including Lenin), Smirnov placed great faith in the ability of a "correctly" organized commissariat to harness the skills and expertise of all types of people, as long as they were not actively counterrevolutionary. The influence of past political allegiances and social origins were diminished in an organization with properly institutionalized lines of authority, a well-structured hierarchy, and strong leadership.

When inspectors requested data on the class background of its personnel, the Commissariat used another strategy. Narkomzem would simply hide or mask alien personnel in vague or obfuscating categories. Statisticians in the Commissariat's administrative-financial division concealed, or at least cast in the best possible light, data about those who might be suspected of disloyalty. Smirnov and his associates played down this information even while accepting Rabkrin's premises that objectively desirable and undesirable class categories existed. For example, Narkomzem's personnel offices used the class category "other" or "various" (prochie) well into the 1920s, apparently to avert the gaze of inspectors from possible aliens. As much as possible, statisticians avoided employing pejorative and explosive class categories such as noble, estate owner (pomeshchik), and townsperson (meshchane) to describe their own cadres. Of course, the porousness of these categories and the blurred boundaries among them means that "other" was a perfectly reasonable way to classify many of these people. Nevertheless, as would be expected, Rabkrin inspectors drew the worst possible inferences from the Commissariat's dissembling. A December 1924 Rabkrin letter to the TsKK noted that the Commissariat categorized an extraordinary 86.6 percent of all staff as "other"! Investigators quickly brought this anomaly to Narkomzem's attention. Nevertheless, a Rabkrin inspector noted eighteen months later that 56 percent of the staff was still listed in Commissariat reports as "from 'various estates and classes.'" He noted dryly, "One must infer that this group contains a significant percentage of alien elements."[98] Indeed, it was in its relations with Rabkrin-TsKK that Narkomzem leaders became most sophisticated in their methods. Correspondence between the two agencies resembles a game of cat and mouse. Still, efforts to divert or disguise often backfired, simply inviting increased scrutiny.

Statistical subterfuge failed to halt the cadre hawks' demands that the Commissariat rid itself of aliens. When the Commissariat leadership was forced to expel cadres, its approach was two-tiered. The leadership seems to have been willing to dispense with some social aliens ceremoniously, but only those who worked in the lowest level positions in the Commissariat. To use a chess metaphor, leaders sacrificed a few pawns in order to save the kings and queens. In the 1924–25 verifications of personnel, for example, the Commissariat complied with demands to eject dozens of people because of their social origin, their pre-Revolutionary employment position, or their parents' occupation.[99]

Nonetheless, the Commissariat leadership rarely removed officials and senior specialists in positions of authority. Instead, they allowed the purge commission to expel clerks, chauffeurs, bookkeepers, and other token personnel with questionable social or political backgrounds. For example, a certain G. Ivanov-Rozhdestvenskii, a bookkeeper in the Administrative-Financial division, was fired as a "former big bureaucrat." V. N. Zhemochkina, a clerk in the forest administration, lost her job because her father was a "former merchant."[100] Narkomzem sacrificed "former" people almost exclusively from these more easily replaceable occupations.

Another more theatrical approach seems to have been designed to satisfy purists while protecting the most valuable of the Commissariat's alien personnel. Under pressure from Rabkrin, the Narkomzem leadership waged highly publicized campaigns against those relatively few cadres who came from the most offensive groups, regardless of their position in the apparatus.[101] Inspectors even found—and jettisoned—a hated tsarist land captain (*zemskii nachal'nik*).[102] But former estate owners were especially visible targets, and the Commissariat launched a loud campaign to evict them from the agricultural administration all over the country. Between 1924 and 1926, Narkomzem expelled at least 160 former landlords in the network of land agencies. Many of them had been first unmasked and denounced in the national or local press as elements "with a psychology that is harmful to land work."[103] In *Pravda*, Smirnov triumphantly attacked a certain Graf Bot who worked in the Agriculture Administration.[104] The 1924 verification commission fired a certain Obodovskii, the head of the subsection for organizing the resettlement land fund. He was exposed "as a former landowner—an element hostile to Soviet power." Similarly, three men were removed from their posts as horse specialists for being former estate owners.[105] Thus, in the spring of 1926, Smirnov could brag to Rabkrin that the central offices of Narkomzem had been (with one exception) cleansed of former estate owners.[106]

The category pomeshchik itself had hazy boundaries. Sviderskii could argue to the TsKK that one employee whom the party cell labeled a landowner was, in fact, a "peasant, though well off," who worked his family's land with the help of his fourteen children. The fact that in 1926 leading communists were still arguing over the definition of the terms landowner and peasant is itself revealing of the contested nature of class ascription and the resulting fluidity of categories and identities.

Narkomzem banished most estate owners without a fight in order to protect the large numbers of indispensable personnel who came from slightly less heinous categories. Employees from these less inflammatory groups included people from nonlanded noble families, former White officers or soldiers, people who had lived in occupied White territory during the Civil War, former SRs and former clergy, and the children of all the above. For example, a large percentage of the staff of the state hippodromes and stables was former White or tsarist army cavalry officers. As one official pointed out, children of clergy who did not choose the priesthood often became veterinarians, a profession in desperately short supply.[107] Discrimination against entire classes of employees because of social origin or parents' background would disqualify huge numbers of capable and potentially loyal people from aiding the Soviet government in achieving its economic goals.

A final tactic that Narkomzem pursued entailed the demotion of specialists with suspect backgrounds to putatively nonleadership positions. In 1923–24, each of the Commissariat's four functional administrations was headed by a nonparty specialist with extensive experience either in the zemstvo system or in the tsarist agricultural ministry. For example, the chief of the statistics subsection of the Agriculture Administration was dropped in rank in 1924. G. I. Mikhailov had two strikes against him: not only was he a "former White officer," but he had also been an SR. Rabkrin wanted to expel him, but Narkomzem protested. In the end, although the Commissariat took away his title as chief of the subsection, Mikhailov remained in the same office as a "senior specialist." In these years, noncommunist heads of divisions were downgraded to "assistant" all over the government apparatus.[108] These men were "demoted" to the ranks of assistant director of their administrations, beneath newly appointed party specialists. The influence of nonparty experts was still clearly felt, however, as the thrust of policies did not change. Not surprisingly, party chiefs, generally without training in agricultural matters, still relied heavily on the advice of their expert assistants.

The Commissariat seems to have won on this issue once the dust settled. In spite of all the noise and paperwork produced by assorted verification commissions, little change beyond the cosmetic was made in Narkomzem's staff. Judging by the data on social composition cited above, the Commissariat's ploys appear to have been mostly successful at least until 1928. Rabkrin, on the other hand, was hardly content with the results.[109]

Sheila Fitzpatrick has written that "the immediate political thrust of the new rulers' interest in class was to find out who should be stigmatized as a bourgeois class enemy, on the one hand, and who should be trusted and rewarded as a proletarian ally, on the other."[110] Public attacks on members of the pre-revolutionary exploiting classes also served to legitimize the regime in the eyes of the peasants and workers whom the regime claimed as its constituency. To be sure, stigmatization and reward were central to Bolshevik cadre policy, yet the application of labels was quite complicated and contested in practice. In the state administration, where the prerogative to govern was enormous, and where agencies had deep social roots in the society they administered, this stigmatization took on unexpected nuances as it was tempered by social and bureaucratic reality. Fitzpatrick points out that "the class identities of a very large number of Soviet citizens were both contestable and contested in the 1920s" and shows that "evasive strategies" were taken by the stigmatized.

This study moves further, to point out that government agencies actually actively conspired with their suspect personnel to shield them from cadre hawks and to disguise or bury social origins and previous political affiliations. The Bolsheviks were not monolithic on the question of the relationship between one's class origins and the ability to serve Soviet power. The notion, popularized by Lenin himself, that many suspect people could overcome their past and serve the goals of Soviet power became a key tool for party leaders of state agencies desperate to fill thousands of positions. This ability to use people with compromised pasts was especially possible inside the confines of a properly structured, communist-led organization, Smirnov felt. In some agencies, leaders minimized stigmas to the point where a person with a questionable background could comfortably work, resting easy that he or she was protected by the Commissariat's leading Bolsheviks.

Only in the context of the agency's sense of mission, together with the great shortage of available personnel, can we understand the Commissariat's motivation to divert attention from its cadres' background. The tremendous challenges inherent in fulfilling what Narkomzem's political leadership viewed as an urgent assignment—the exceptional challenge of dragging underdeveloped rural Russia from its perpetual poverty and ignorance—tempered concerns about alienness.

The Peasant Commissar, Revisited

While the Commissariat faced pressure because of its contingent of bourgeois specialists, it was also pushed by Rabkrin and Party personnel agencies to promote villagers into responsible positions. In 1922, many social, political, and cultural conflicts within the Commissariat had surrounded the appointment of Iakovenko, the muzhik people's commissar. In the Smirnov years, pressure to hire common villagers created friction in the Moscow offices of Narkomzem, while casting new light on the internal dynamics of the agency that promised to transform the countryside.[111]

Several months before Iakovenko's official departure from Narkomzem (and Smirnov's appointment) in early 1923, people in party personnel agencies began prospecting for a new commissar of agriculture. The focus of the search from the start was again to locate someone who could carry the banner of "peasant people's commissar." This new search reinforces many of the conclusions drawn from Iakovenko's short tenure.

The first name recommended by Narkomzem's collegium was Civil War hero S. M. Budyennyi, known as the Peasant-General. Despite the support of many of Stalin's circle, K. Ye. Voroshilov opposed Budyennyi. (By 1923, Stalin already controlled most high-level personnel appointments.) On what grounds? As he wrote to Stalin on February 1, 1923, Budyennyi was "too much a *peasant*, disproportionately popular and extremely sly." Although Voroshilov may have been expressing a degree of jealousy at Budyennyi's fame, his reaction also represents larger dimensions of Bolshevik political culture at the time. Budyennyi was a man who seemed to be too close to the peasantry. Voroshilov clearly expressed many Bolsheviks' fear that the party's grip on power was still uncertain in rural Russia when he stated his concern that Budyennyi would side with the peasantry in case of a "serious clash of interests" with the proletariat.[112] In the future, counterrevolutionary forces might count on Budyennyi as their "peasant *vozhd*'" (charismatic leader) to head a mass anti-Soviet movement. "To throw Budyennyi into the peasant-land abyss [Narkomzem] in these conditions would be crazy." Budyennyi's candidacy crashed on the rocks of his reputation as the popular peasant military figure, considered a threat to a regime still quite insecure about its own position, especially outside the cities.[113]

"Ia sam muzhik": A. P. *Smirnov and the Political Use of Identity*

In the wake of the failure of Iakovenko's tenure and the early death of the Budyennyi candidacy, a peasant of a very different kind took over the Commissariat in 1923. One could regard both Smirnov and his predecessor Iakovenko as archetypes of leading Soviet officials in the early revolutionary period. The contrasts between the two, however, illustrate important dimensions of evolving Soviet political and institutional culture. The cases of these two peasant commissars further illustrate the assertion of scholars that "the Russian Revolution had a profound impact on social roles and identities," often in unexpected ways.[114]

In contrast to Iakovenko, who joined the Bolshevik Party only in 1917, Smirnov had been a socialist activist for close to thirty years. What is of special interest about Smirnov is that despite the fact that he had not lived in his native village in Tver Province for a full twenty-five years (having migrated to Moscow as a fifteen-year-old to work in the Morozov textile factory), he took pains to broadcast that he was the son of a poor peasant.[115] Indeed, Smirnov's peasant roots were a critical component of the persona that he adopted as chief of the Commissariat of Agriculture. Smirnov often stated that he had grown up in extreme poverty in a village, the son of poor peasants who had themselves been serfs. He used these roots to his political advantage.[116] Smirnov repeated that his village background, plus his long tenure as a dedicated communist, made him particularly well suited for the post of commissar of agriculture. Pamphlets and newspaper articles directed toward the village reader referred to him, as they had to Iakovenko, as a peasant, a sympathetic leader in Moscow who would understand the needs of the rural population and influence Moscow's policy accordingly. The title of a short biography, "From Peasant Hut to the Post of People's Commissar of Agriculture," reflects his eagerness to advertise his origins.[117] At a 1924 Moscow meeting with noncommunist villagers, for example, he implored his audience to trust and to confide in him. "As an old comrade and peasant [muzhik], I simply want to get advice from you about how we can work better."[118] Smirnov's glorification of his modest background reflected the concern of many Bolsheviks that they be recognized as coming from humble origins.[119] But there were other reasons to cultivate this persona.

How, for example, did Smirnov, a self-styled man of the people, react to the intense pressure from party inspectors to appoint peasant promotees to top posts in his Commissariat? A 1925 incident is indicative of Smirnov's skill at manipulating his own identity for a variety of political purposes. In that year, the Central Committee's personnel department repeatedly urged Smirnov to find three peasant promotees and place them into high-ranking positions in the Commissariat of Agriculture, one as deputy people's commissar and two as deputy chiefs of divisions. Smirnov wrote back that he "categorically opposed" a mandatory quota of such positions. The reasons for his opposition illustrate both a new kind of politics and a new kind of politician in the early Soviet period. "I myself am a *muzhik*," he insisted. "In this situation my deputy should not be a peasant just taken from the village, even from the plow, but an educated, fully developed [and experienced] person who can easily orient himself to our work."[120]

This example points out a basic distinction in most Bolsheviks' understanding of the peasantry. When determining suitability for service in the central state apparatus, Bolsheviks distinguished between two types of peasants: Smirnov represents one, Iakovenko the other. Smirnov was a "conscious" (*soznatel'nyi*) peasant aware of political subtleties, thoughtful, and immersed in urban culture. Iakovenko on the other hand was a "spontaneous" (*stikhiinyi*) villager, presumed to be ignorant, culturally backward, and politically illiterate. Smirnov contrasted his own life experiences with those of his predecessor Iakovenko and of the peasant promotees whom, in his view, overly idealistic party personnel chiefs were trying to foist upon him. Smirnov had been born in the village, but he had left; he had obtained a political education, and done so in Social Democratic factory reading circles, in the revolutionary underground, in exile and in prison, leading the "stormy life of the underground revolutionary worker."[121] He had learned organizing skills in revolutionary cells, then in the Red Army, and at the head of food supply brigades during the Civil War. Smirnov was no "gullible" peasant.

Smirnov further argued that the Commissariat of Agriculture is a "very complex organization with enormously intricate, specialized tasks."[122] Smirnov's depiction of the "intricacy" and "complexity" of the Commissariat's technical assignments was a leitmotif, repeated constantly to poorly informed outsiders who would meddle in the affairs of "his" agency.[123] Especially adamant about any attempts to interfere with his power over personnel decisions, Smirnov insisted that only specialists with education and experience were prepared to do these jobs, not raw peasants. As proof that it took specialists to carry out these assignments properly, he argued that the peasant promotees currently working in the Commissariat were disoriented. "Those peasant employees whom I have recruited to the central apparatus . . . are beginning to feel a lot of stress. Examples have already surfaced of [promotees] trying to leave work in the Commissariat of Agriculture, a result of . . . undertaking complicated questions."

The case of peasant promotees in the early Soviet period serves as an example of fluid post-revolutionary social identities and conceptions of legitimacy in the revolutionary state bureaucracy. Smirnov made claims to be from the peasantry but not currently a peasant; he ascribed to himself all the positive qualities and shed the negative. He had not lived in the village for over two decades, yet he still referred to himself as a peasant. At the same time, Smirnov used his own background as a poor villager—his constructed persona—as another way to control personnel appointments and as a shield against bringing "underdeveloped" peasants into his organization.

Peasant Promotion in the Smirnov Era

Between 1923 and 1927, as had been the case in the first years of the New Economic Policy, the Central Committee reiterated its conviction that the Commissariat of Agriculture needed aggressively to locate suitable peasant candidates and eventually promote them into "responsible, leadership positions." Nevertheless, staff of peasant origin remained extremely scarce in the Commissariat's Moscow offices throughout the 1920s, despite clamorous promotion campaigns. While peasant representation rose very sharply in the province and county-level land administration beginning in 1923, this did not occur at the center. The number of peasant promotees in the central Commissariat of Agriculture remained very low even in comparison with commissariats that had little contact with the countryside. As late as the year 1927, only five peasant promotees were transferred to Moscow (in a central organization with approximately two thousand people), and just six followed the next year, despite constant pressure by party inspectors. This persistent scarcity of promoted cadres irritated party and Rabkrin inspectors who were impatiently pushing for higher numbers in central state agencies. And just as in 1921–22, the "peasants" whom the commissariat did promote later in the decade were "not from the plow"—farming was not their primary occupation.

In 1924, for example, the Commissariat brought in the forty-six-year-old K. D. Savchenko to serve in the collegium, where he worked until 1928. Savchenko was the Commissariat's major promotee success story in the 1920s. He was very large in stature, with an imposing beard. He became the most visible of the Commissariat's promotees, pictured in the press with a visiting delegation of Mexican peasants or lecturing vigorously at the opening of the First Exhibition of Peasant Horses. He had been a party member since 1898, having participated in illicit Social Democratic groups and serving jail time for his political activities before the 1917 revolutions. Yet, when he was asked to report his social origin on his application form Savchenko replied that he was a worker, a blacksmith by specialty. How can we explain this discrepancy? Savchenko probably understood that he had a whole menu of identities to select from, depending on his audience.[124] Having spent the first several years of his life in the village, he could call himself a peasant by social origin. He eventually learned the trade of blacksmith and could thereby identify himself as proletarian. Having worked as an employee in a local soviet in 1917, he was a sluzhashchii, or white collar official, by social position. Each of these identities could serve his interests in some capacity in the USSR in the 1920s. Savchenko the worker would have privileged access to party membership, to higher education, and to employment in certain industrial enterprises. Savchenko the official might receive preferential rations. Savchenko the peasant was eligible for promotion to a highly visible and prestigious position in the collegium of a key national ministry, and subsequent quasi-celebrity status (though he may not have actively sought out this last benefit). Savchenko provides another example of a person who capitalized on the ability to manipulate one's identity.[125]

Sheila Fitzpatrick has discussed the "conscious creation of class identities" as a way that Soviet citizens could "mask" or disguise an undesirable past. Yet, peasant promotees often masked desirable pasts. In other words, they chose to identify themselves as peasants when their life experience—in industry, in the army, or in soviet administration—gave them the right and the opportunity to claim proletarian identity. Further, the examples in this book show how people in prominent positions could take on peasant identities in place of giving "real" peasants power in the state. The state colluded with individuals to create identities, often for political purposes.

Although Savchenko was a Communist Party member, none of the other promotees were. Promoted peasants were not typical of the village population. According to brief biographies contained in the files of party personnel agencies, almost all had either worked in local soviets or served in the Red Army, or both, and thus had broken to some degree from the village and its traditions. All were literate (one "writes very well for a peasant"). The adjectives most commonly used by party personnel inspectors to describe prospective peasant promotees included sober, calm, restrained, and honest. They "love to work."[126] Such descriptions implied that the "average" peasant's character was deficient in all these areas. Negative stereotypes like these were never far from the surface.

Smirnov ordered that the few promotees recruited into the Commissariat of

Agriculture be closely supervised to make sure that they did their jobs in a professional fashion. In June 1924, Smirnov instructed the heads of the Commissariat's divisions to keep close watch on the promotees in their sections, reiterating the idea that the peasants had a long way to go before becoming trustworthy, "developed" comrades.[127] He urged section chiefs to try to educate the raw recruits, to help in the process of transforming them into responsible administrators. "We must assign one of the most responsible party workers in the Commissariat for continuous, uninterrupted supervision of the promotees." "Protect them from any possible harmful, unprofessional deviations and teach them to be serious, devoted to duty, . . . disciplined comrades, contributing to the broadest widening of their horizons. . . ." Again, the implication is that peasant promotees arriving in Moscow might be undisciplined, immature, narrow-minded, and prone to unprofessional behavior if not kept in check. Throughout the twenties, much of the Commissariat's specialist and communist leadership took a dim view of the inexperienced, "undeveloped" peasants working in their ranks.

Complaints of Peasant Recruits

In mid-1926, a farmer by the name of Tselinov expressed his hope that the highest levels of the Soviet government would someday be replete with peasant promotees making decisions about matters pertaining to the countryside. Unlike the bureaucrats with whom farmers most often came into contact, a peasant promotee would know village life intimately and would help to smooth relations and hasten understanding between the new regime and village Russia by acting as a kind of cultural go-between. "It would be very good if peasants promoted from the plow stood at the helm of our government," Tselinov declared. "Take a peasant who has worked seventeen years with a wooden plow, who knows our life, who knows our poverty. It is impossible even to imagine that he would do anything bad to us."

Nevertheless, for their part, promotees complained that they were neglected and ignored by their bosses, and that communists and noncommunist specialists alike resisted their assumption of important responsibilities. They reported in interviews that "we sit for years and do not know what the Commissariat wants from us, or for what purpose we are sitting here." They were excluded from important meetings. An inspector wrote, "They were not used for work that they desired, they did not participate in the compilation and discussion of plans. The discussion of many questions of interest to the promotees was carried on without their participation."[128] Promotees complained that they stayed in the same peripheral jobs, passing the time for many years until they "turned into a run-of-the-mill Soviet bureaucrat."[129] In short, they focused on the sharp contrast between the prominent positions and influence that the Commissariat had promised them and (with a handful of exceptions) the menial jobs they were given.[130] Some Narkomzem section heads simply placed promoted peasants in so-called temporary positions, which remained outside the nomenklatura system that provided job security and privileges. The agriculture Commissariat's leadership instead assigned most promotees jobs as inspectors or instructors. These positions involved taking excursions to rural areas to investigate local conditions and then reporting to Moscow. Such assignments, in principle, would take advantage of the promotees' reputed authority among other villagers, who would candidly report their concerns to their fellow peasants. Unfortunately, very little money was available for such excursions to the provinces. As a result, peasants employed as inspectors and instructors had little to do.

It is clear that party leaders and nonparty specialists alike were complicit in placing obstacles in the way of promotees, though often with different motives. The Commissariat's party cell, for example, offered promotees little or no help. Rabkrin investigators charged that this was true for all party members in the Commissariat, whose activity was "aimed not at promotion [of peasants] but at moving certain employees (members of the party) up the service ladder."[131] In 1928, the Moscow Party Committee asked the chiefs of the Commissariat's five divisions (all of whom were party members) to supply a list of posts that peasant promotees could occupy. Despite repeated reminders, only one of the five division chiefs ever replied.

The Culture of the Commissariat of Agriculture: "Peasant Promotees Are Not Specialists"

Smirnov and the specialists in the Commissariat insisted on hiring qualified people to assume the available posts because, they argued, their mission was of the utmost seriousness. They considered their scientific activities part of a life-or-death struggle to rebuild peasant agriculture on a new basis. They wanted to avert catastrophes such as the horrific famine of 1921–22 and the widespread crop failures of 1924, and they were confident that only the Commissariat of Agriculture—if properly funded and staffed—could do so. The Commissariat leadership believed that the zealots at the party personnel agencies and Rabkrin who insisted on the use of peasant promotees in crucial positions had not grasped the Commissariat's extraordinary crusade.

A confidential 1924 letter written by Vladimir I. Senin, the head of the Agriculture Administration, the most essential of the Commissariat's divisions, makes this point.[132] In the midst of a catastrophic drought affecting much of the middle Volga and eastern Black Earth regions, party personnel hawks had ordered Smirnov to appoint more peasants to responsible posts. Senin knew that conditions among the farming population in the afflicted areas were desperate. Thousands of villagers were spontaneously migrating south or west to the Kuban or Siberia. Peasants were selling their cattle to pay for grain, and the resulting oversupply drove down the price for meat. Some villagers consumed their milk cows, or ate "swans and other surrogate foods."[133] Amid this chaos, Senin protested, "I cannot put peasant promotees in administrative positions. . . . I cannot release a specialist on fertilizer or a specialist on machines in order to bring a peasant promotee into his place. . . . Peasants are not specialists. But a whole series of our sections are comprised completely of specialists, and we cannot get rid of a single one." He reiterates that only he and other experts working in the state apparatus can solve Russia's enormous agricultural problems. Senin's frustration is evident: "This is an enormous task. We are trying to rebuild one-hundred thousand peasant farms [that have suffered most seriously from the effects of the recent drought], but in the meantime we have to argue about some five or six people for whom we should secure work." This statement suggests the defining characteristics of professionals: on one hand, their sense of exclusivity, uniqueness, and differentiation from the mass of the population; on the other, their belief that only they can find solutions to intractable social, economic, and technical problems.

As one Rabkrin report charged, people like Senin "deliberately frighten peasant promotees with the difficulty and responsibility of work in the state apparatus." Certainly, the accusation was true.[134] Many experts genuinely believed that their enterprise determined the fates of millions of people. They felt that inexperienced peasants and their party patrons alike needed to understand this. The clash between a fundamental Bolshevik ideal of mass participation in government and the professional ideology that only the implementation of their principles and plans could save Russia is exposed here. Specialists argued that only people like themselves—not inexperienced peasants or proletarians from the bench, and not party outsiders—could possibly grasp the complicated scientific nature of their work and of Russian agriculture. They used these arguments to deflect the introduction of the working masses into their cohort. One sees here a peculiar conjunction of a radically democratic and inclusive ideology at a moment when economic and reconstruction imperatives were paramount.

Thus, Smirnov used the Marxist political language of consciousness to resist hiring promotees in the name of participation, while specialists used the professional language of competence, skills, disdain for the uneducated, and commitment to the national interest to do the same. These languages overlapped and reinforced each other.

Smirnov and the Commissariat's other party leaders energetically supported the autonomy of their specialists. Commissariat officials tried to preclude interference by people whom they considered naive, overzealous ideologues—"babblers," in Smirnov's words.[135] In effect, Smirnov urged the party elite to stick to its own job—setting the general line on policy—as Narkomzem strove to achieve its mission—securing the recovery of agriculture. The communist leadership, together with the professionals in the Commissariat, emphasized that the responsibilities of the Commissariat demanded expertise of a certain type, scientific knowledge beyond life experience. This knowledge was simply not to be found among people fresh from the village, no matter how long they had farmed, regardless of their authority among peasants in their region, and irrespective of service in the Red Army or a local soviet.

Professors from the Plow

In the period between the end of Iakovenko's brief reign as people's commissar and the end of Smirnov's tenure in the spring of 1928, the ideal of the "peasant from the plow" as Commissariat official was displaced or, more accurately, underwent a metamorphosis into a new blend of pre-revolutionary and post-revolutionary forms. Social and professional identities were mixed and shifting in unprecedented directions in this revolutionary cultural world. A 1924 exchange between Smirnov, the self-described "peasant people's commissar," and Kondrat'ev, one of the country's most influential specialists on the rural economy, illustrates this phenomenon. At a meeting of Zemplan about eight months after Iakovenko had been removed, both the communist Smirnov and Kondrat'ev, the well-credentialed bourgeois expert, identified themselves as "professors from the plow."[136] The "professor from the plow," an amalgamation of social and professional identities, became the new ideal for the Commissariat's specialist and party leadership in this bureaucracy.

For a specialist like Kondrat'ev, a man who called himself the son of a peasant, a claim of familiarity with farming and village life was a way to legitimize his expertise beyond book-bound scholarship. Here we have an internationally renowned expert on the village economy, the author of dozens of articles and books, having earned advanced degrees and made numerous research trips abroad—all this and still claiming to be from the plow. The specialist, gaining power and stature in the ministerial bureaucracy, especially in the last two decades of the tsarist regime, met the peasant, the man of the earth in whose name, in part, the Revolution was waged. For the muzhik-communist Smirnov, in order to contrast his village childhood with his present stature, the title "professor from the plow" indicated a degree of knowledge and sophistication, of consciousness beyond that of the rural population that the Commissariat was trying to lift out of its ignorance and poverty. This new Soviet hybrid combined in one person the expertise of the specialist with the peasant's understanding of farming and the concrete realities of the village. Practicing farmers themselves, of course, could be safely excluded from this new formulation. Clearly the professor, and not the plow, was the more essential part of this construction.

The appearance of the professor-from-the-plow archetype also demonstrates a process of adaptation, as specialists with suspect backgrounds began to reshape their own identities to conform to Bolshevik expectations and to avoid the scrutiny of cadre hawks, eager to cleanse the state of "bourgeois elements." At the same time, the Bolsheviks adapted to their desperate need for expertise in order to build the state and economy. Peasants were not really needed for this project, at least not among the Moscow designers of the new countryside.

The initial, uncertain years of the New Economic Policy reinforced lessons learned during the Civil War about the debilitating results of weak leadership, disorganization, and a poorly developed and isolated network of branch offices in the periphery. The Commissariat's leaders labored to strengthen their arm of the state, using every tool at their disposal; not just financial and organizational means but political and symbolic weapons as well, including struggles over definitions and categories of analysis. Under the new commissar Smirnov, Narkomzem became a formidable organization. Between 1923 and 1926, the Commissariat designed and implemented the agricultural policies that were the centerpiece of NEP. In 1924–25, Narkomzem achieved the pinnacle of its influence in the government. In these two years, the budget reached its highest level, the policies for which it had lobbied for three years were in place, and its reports gained center stage at national congresses of Soviets and the Communist Party. The Commissariat also retained a significant degree of control over personnel appointments as it battled powerful institutional interests (especially Rabkrin and the party secretariat under Stalin). This time in the sun would be short lived, however, partly because Narkomzem's interests were so obviously connected to two groups that were increasingly considered as pariahs and scapegoats—the agricultural specialists and the better-off sections of the peasantry. Over the course of the 1920s, most of the Commissariat's cadres remained decidedly nonproletarian and noncommunist in character. They often appeared tainted in the eyes of party hard-liners who were extremely suspicious of many categories of employees on social or political grounds. Much of Narkomzem's personnel was considered untrustworthy by virtue of having served in the tsarist civil service or having supported the SRs.

Assuming control at Narkomzem in the spring of 1923, commissar Smirnov soon began to identify himself with the agency that he headed. His rapid change in outlook is striking. Smirnov went from a disciplinarian, sent by Sovnarkom to clean up a gigantic mess at the Commissariat, to its leading advocate. This transformation was a result of the exceptional challenges inherent in the arduous technical and cultural missions that greeted him. Smirnov's identification of himself with the Commissariat of Agriculture illustrates an important phenomenon, known pejoratively in Soviet bureaucracies as vedomstvennost', or institutional self-interest. Vedomstvennost' was something of a Soviet four-letter word. At times, Smirnov considered the interests of the Commissariat and himself as its chief to be more urgent than the needs of the Communist Party. Not uncommon among chiefs of state agencies in the 1920s, there was no shortage of vedomstvennost' in the Soviet government.

After taking his new position, Smirnov quickly realized that, in order to fulfill his assignments, his organization desperately needed expertise of a type that few party members possessed. Like the heads of other people's commissariats, Smirnov insisted that if he were to make this bureaucracy effective, oversight agencies must desist from meddling in Narkomzem's affairs, especially concerning cadre selection. Smirnov urged party chiefs to follow existing instructions that prohibited local party secretaries from interfering with land work, and from replacing qualified specialists with ill-equipped political appointees. Smirnov wanted the party to allow the state apparatus to do its job without petty interference. The responsibilities of the Commissariat demanded a great deal of expertise, Smirnov emphasized, which simply was not to be found inside the Communist Party. Narkomzem's staff keenly felt the separation between the state and party apparatuses and the diminution of the former's influence.

By the late 1920s, land administration had deep roots in the Russian society with which it interacted. This was especially the case for the two alien groups—the specialists, many of whom were sluzhashchie and even holdovers from tsarist administration, and the peasantry. Yet in the 1920s, the party leaders needed the cooperation of both groups in order to preserve the revolution: the specialists for their indispensable expertise and the peasants for the food and industrial raw materials that they produced. The state's unexpected need for their requisite skills meant that the directors of central and local agencies had to be less selective about pre-Revolutionary experience or political affiliations when hiring, especially when recruiting specialists. Throughout the 1920s, Narkomzem's bosses also allowed local agencies to hire without regard for a potential employee's social affiliations or even pre-revolutionary political loyalty. One could say that although certain party inspectors were obsessed with pre-revolutionary social and political origins, Narkomzem was obsessed with qualifications, with staffing its network of three thousand branch offices and aid stations with people who had both proper education and experience. This tolerance for those considered to be social and political pariahs in some party circles, typical of many state agencies with assignments demanding technical expertise, made Narkomzem an obvious target for the waves of purging that would crash across the state apparatus in 1928–29.

As the programs to promote peasants into the top ranks of the Commissariat leadership demonstrated, the professional values of specialists—a sense of exclusivity, the overriding superiority of formal education over personal life experience, dedication to mission and service—were shared by the party leadership of the commissariats. In the central ministerial bureaucracy, party chiefs and specialists collaborated on strategies for limiting peasant promotees' access to responsible positions. The peculiar bureaucratic culture of specialized economic institutions in the 1920s, sustained by an ideology of technological modernization, worked against the hiring of peasants (or in some agencies, against the hiring of workers). Catherine Merridale has shown that many working class promotees from factories recruited to industrial administration simply "were absorbed into the culture prevailing in the host institution," and did not refresh the organization with new attitudes and ideas.[137] In the Commissariat of Agriculture, this absorption did not and, perhaps, could not occur. Peasants could not easily be accommodated by the culture of the Commissariat of Agriculture, nor were the professional specialists and party leadership inclined to help them adapt. Either given nothing to do or assigned the most menial labor, they were marginalized to peripheral posts, jobs that peasants "could handle," most notably holding meetings with other peasants.

Much of the Moscow specialist and party elite believed that they were acting in the best interests of the Russian village and felt that they fully understood the life experience of the peasants. Nevertheless, in the 1920s, the self-perception of agricultural specialists as a superior caste was strengthened, ironically, by the introduction of peasants into their midst. Specialists' ideas about the superiority of agronomic expertise relative to villagers' "organic" knowledge acquired through "life experience" served to reinforce specialists' own self-image. The reaction inside the Commissariat to promotion programs provides evidence of a reossification of bureaucratic culture, as once again the top bureaucratic and specialist elite comprised a stratum of their own, resisting outsiders from the lower classes.

In a November 1924 letter to the Central Committee, People's Commissar of Agriculture Smirnov noted that many communists currently believe that agriculture, having moved along the road to recovery more quickly than industry, "no longer needs special patronage." Smirnov strongly disagreed: "Such opinions are wrong." [138] Smirnov obviously considered "his" organization to be that special patron for the interests of agriculture, and he never gave up that sense of guardianship, almost to the level of ownership, over the agrarian economy. Moreover, he viewed himself as Narkomzem's guardian and as the protector of its cadres, just as he saw the organization as a whole to be the savior of Soviet agriculture in this difficult period of transition.

NEP's official, if uneasy, toleration for concessions to peasants and to bourgeois specialists paved the way for a figure like Smirnov. Ironically, in 1923 Smirnov was assigned to strengthen a weak, disorganized, and poorly funded Narkomzem apparatus, yet his very success was partly responsible for his downfall and for the ultimate dismantling of the Commissariat. Perhaps the best indication of Smirnov's success in securing freedom from interference is the fact that the Commissariat of Agriculture RSFSR was incapacitated during the collectivization drive. As Narkomzem grew stronger, its enemies became more determined. The Commissariat's tolerance for undesirables made Narkomzem an obvious target for purging and decapitation in 1928–29. One could argue that the ability of Narkomzem's party leaders to protect a cohort of competent but "unreliable" cadres from removal in the mid-1920s was one of the factors that eventually sealed its fate at the hands of Stalin's circle.

Narkomzem's policies toward the countryside were another source of controversy. Ultimately, the policies and world view that the Commissariat embraced had important consequences. A close examination of the Commissariat's vision for a modern, productive and collectivist countryside brought to the surface a number of the tensions inherent to NEP, and to the Soviet leadership's efforts at building socialism in agrarian Russia.

4
Socialism in One Countryside

Architects of a New Rural Russia, 1923–1926

Small Steps and Great Strides

Whenever his collegium gathered for its regular meeting in building number 5/8 on Moscow's *Staraia ploshchad'*, People's Commissar of Agriculture Alexander P. Smirnov always reserved the last word for himself. He enjoyed summarizing the arguments of the others present and then expounding his own point of view. The collegium's secretary duly recorded verbatim the comments of the People's Commissar, circulated them to the agency's various departments, and filed away a copy in the Commissariat archive.

At the meeting of June 6, 1925, Smirnov sat surrounded by his deputies, I. A. Teodorovich and A. I. Sviderskii, the heads of the Commissariat's many specialized divisions, and the Commissariat's leading experts, including N. D. Kondrat'ev and N. P. Makarov. After each speaker had presented his report, Smirnov summed up his perspective on the progress of rural Russia in the revolution's eighth year. His remarks on this day embody his outlook during NEP: a combination of pragmatism about the country's present difficult situation, commitment to using peaceful methods in transforming the countryside, a focus on "enlightening" farmers via persuasion about the most efficient modes of farming; frustration with the persistent "backwardness" of Soviet agriculture and farmers relative to Western countries; and optimism that socialism would eventually develop and be solidified in the countryside. "We live in a poor peasant country," Smirnov told the experts and members of his collegium gathered around the table. "Small-scale peasant farming is still undertaken in rudimentary forms and has taken only the first steps to move forward."[1]

Rather than dwell on the negative, however, he jumped to his dream of a brighter future for rural Russia. Smirnov ruminated, "In the future our country's development will take gigantic strides." In this private forum he admitted that, although he felt that Soviet Russia was starting from a barren foundation, he harbored grand aspirations for the creation of a countryside that was technically sophisticated, highly productive, and socialist; one whose agrarian economy would surpass those of the Western countries. At the same time, noncoercive methods including education, technical assistance, and the demonstration of new methods must be peacefully employed to persuade the peasantry to participate in the reconstruction of the countryside. Russia would have to move ahead "not with the stick, but on economic grounds, on the basis of coordinated teaching, on the basis of persuasion."[2] Once the state reached the peasants and persuaded them to adopt the proper ways to farm, Smirnov forsaw "that as soon as all the power of the laboring masses themselves has matured, the development of the country will jump forward with great strides."

Smirnov's comments echo mainstream Bolshevik attitudes toward the countryside at the time. In an address before a congress of land officials in 1926, Rykov, chairman of Sovnarkom, highlighted the extraordinarily ambitious economic and sociocultural goals that the Bolshevik party charged Narkomzem with a key role in achieving. He congratulated his audience of Commissariat officials and specialists for making strides on the path toward "conquering ignorance and backwardness" in the countryside, as "science enters every pore of our economy." With the help of the Soviet state, and the land administration in particular, Rykov predicted that the socialist regime will "organize a human society in which there will be no poverty and no ignorance."[3] Indeed, Smirnov, like his political ally and fellow Rightist Rykov, set his sights extremely high, despite the extraordinary natural and economic obstacles Soviet agriculture faced, including the short growing season, poor soils and climate, underdeveloped markets and infrastructure, a dilapidated transportation system, and a large technology lag. As he told his collegium, "Our task is to organize the peasant completely."[4] Or as Rabkrin put it the following year, the Commissariat of Agriculture was responsible for "the mass reorganization of peasant farming."[5]

There are several dimensions to the Commissariat's efforts to "invent a Soviet countryside" between 1923 and 1927. Substantial tensions are evident in this vision of a recreated Soviet countryside during NEP—containing a population no longer "ignorant," "inert," mired in poverty and "cultural backwardness"—as expressed by the ministry most responsible for carrying it out in the period of High NEP. In this period, the Commissariat's leadership formulated a strategy, albeit contradictory, for bringing its ideas to life, a strategy it considered consistent with building socialism in the agrarian USSR. The Commissariat's leaders insisted that this agency—with its Moscow general staff composed of the country's greatest agrarian experts commanding a sprawling and growing network of local assistance branches—was capable of designing and carrying out this program. In spite of this confidence, the Commissariat's agenda for uplifting rural Russia posed troubling questions with implications that proved very difficult for Communist Party leaders to resolve, questions that forced party and Commissariat leaders to wrestle with three often-conflicting agendas: economic development, the building of socialism, and the state's ability to maintain control over the countryside. Indeed, the Commissariat's leadership did not always reap what it thought it had sown.

The exploration of the nature of the Commissariat's efforts at social and economic transformation during the mid-twenties begins with an examination of the condition of rural Russia between 1923 and 1927. Later in the chapter, we scrutinize the Commissariat's image of what a socialist countryside should look like and how the village could travel the road to that ideal. Although this book will not recount the well-described "industrialization debates" that divided the leadership of the Communist Party in the mid-1920s, these debates and the political struggles swirling around them form the backdrop for any discussion of the twenties.[6] The Commissariat of Agriculture's contributions to the discussion of issues at the national level affected the development of rural society and economy. During this period Narkomzem played an underappreciated role in shaping the debate on several important socioeconomic questions involving class, production, state power, and social control. A number of the elements of this view—modernization, collectivism, limitations on some manifestations of peasant spontaneity, and the Commissariat's own institutional interest—were inextricably linked, in ways that cast light on important facets of NEP political culture. The dilemmas inherent to the party-state's approach to the countryside in the 1920s cannot be understood without discussing all of these elements as a connected package with implications that were not always obvious to the participants.

An Agrarian Nation Emerging from Crisis

Sovnarkom gave A. P. Smirnov two major assignments when he was selected to take the helm of the People's Commissariat of Agriculture in the spring of 1923. Smirnov was relatively successful in the first task, to rebuild and then to defend the Commissariat apparatus that he inherited. His second objective was to help draft, promote, and discharge the agricultural reconstruction policies of the New Economic Policy.

Disputes involving Narkomzem in these years were closely linked to the industrialization debates. These debates in turn were intimately tied to political battles among party elites between the pro-NEP majority (the Rights), and the Left Opposition. These debates must be understood in the context of the collapse of the possibility of international revolution coming to the Soviet Union's assistance soon. The Right seized on one of Lenin's final articles, "On Cooperation," written in January 1923 but not published until May 1923, a few weeks after Smirnov assumed the helm at Narkomzem. In this piece, Lenin wrote that the USSR possessed everything necessary for building socialism, including a dictatorship of the proletariat, a union with the peasantry and leadership of them by the proletariat, and a cooperative network. He argued that the entire peasantry could be attracted to cooperatives within "ten to twenty years." The Rights focused on a phrase in his article that insisted on the need for "objective economic preconditions for building socialism," which meant, in fact, economic and technical preconditions. They repeated Lenin's message that "we must move ahead immeasurably, endlessly more slowly than we had dreamed."[7]

The Commissariat of Agriculture's political leadership, in harmony with the majority in the Politburo and Central Committee, reviled Trotsky and his followers, nearly always siding with the Rights in the economic debates between 1923 and 1928. For their part, Left Oppositionists were skeptical that it was possible to build socialism in these backward conditions, at the "tortoise pace" that the Right advocated. Conversely, Narkomzem officials earned the enmity of Trotsky and his followers on matters relating to the "kulak threat," collective farming, and the tempo of industrialization. Indeed, Commissariat researchers (together with those from the Commissariat of Finance and the Central Statistical Administration) supplied the NEP majority with much of the data it needed to formulate and defend its policies. As long as the Politburo supported NEP, the Commissariat leadership tended to win its battles.

The Rural Context: Uneven Recovery after Famine

By most measures, agricultural production moved ahead strongly between the 1922 famine year and 1926. Nevertheless, in several critical areas of production and the delivery of produce to market the Soviet Union had not regained its pre-war levels by 1927. (Russia's pre-war levels, of course, had already been low relative to the West.) Commissariat officials and party leaders were disappointed and concerned with these weaknesses.[8]

Overall, the 1920s were marked by growth in agricultural output. After 1922, rapid recovery can be observed in many areas of the country and many branches of agriculture. If we compare 1927–28 to the disastrous famine year 1922, the improvement is striking. In this five-year period, gross sown area increased by 45 percent, the area under cereals increased by about 40 percent, and gross agricultural production jumped by almost 40 percent. In fact, when one considers gross agricultural production, in 1926–27 and 1927–28 the levels exceeded the 1909–13 averages by 5 to 6 percent.[9] Output of potatoes and vegetables, industrial crops, and total livestock all significantly exceeded the pre-war averages.

TABLE 4-1
Annual yield and gross harvest of grains, 1913–1929

Year	Yield (centner/hectare)[a]	Gross harvest (million centners)
1913	8.1	765.0
1909–13 (annual average)	6.9	651.8
1917	6.4	545.6
1918	6.0	495.3
1919	6.2	504.5
1920	5.7	451.9
1921	5.0	362.6
1922	7.6	503.1
1923	7.2	565.9
1924	6.2	514.0
1925	8.3	724.6
1926	8.2	768.3
1927	7.6	723.0
1928	7.9	733.2
1929	7.5	717.4
1924–28 (annual average)	7.6	692.6
1925–29 (annual average)	7.9	733.3

Source: V. P. Danilov, *Sovetskaia dokolkhoznaia derevnia*, 284.
[a] A *centner* is a measure of weight equal to 50 kilograms. A hectare is a measurement of distance equal to slightly less than a *desiatina*, or about 2.6 acres.

Thus by some important measurements, agricultural production had recovered to, and even exceeded, pre-war levels by 1926–27 (see table 4-1).

Even these achievements in the areas of sown territory and total production, however, were tempered by other factors. The gross figures mask variations by region and by sector. Although some areas leaped ahead of their pre-war levels, the major grain-producing regions in the South and the Central Black Earth region, crucial to both the internal and external markets, lagged behind those areas. The delayed recovery in these regions was a result of the widespread death of draft animals during the 1921 and 1924 droughts. Additionally, when the gross numbers are adjusted for large population increases in rural areas, sown area in 1927 had reached only 91.4 percent of the pre-war figure.[10] Less grain was produced both in terms of volume and per capita after the war than before. More alarming for the regime, two key indicators—exports and the amount of produce farmers sold at market—still lagged behind the pre-war results. Shortfalls in these areas—in other words, in produce that made it into the government's silos, for the government's use—created much anxiety within the Soviet leadership. As late as 1926–27, the amount of agricultural produce that the USSR sold abroad was still only 33 to 42 percent of the pre-war level.[11] Figures for the years 1922–25 were even worse. Grain exports posed a particular problem considering the small quantity the regime could sell abroad, even after the relatively good harvests of 1925 and 1926. (Narkomzem was a major advocate for the export of agricultural products.) The elimination of large commercial farms, the disappearance of the larger, more profitable peasant farms after the 1917–18 land redistributions, and government price policies that acted as a disincentive to produce, all reduced collections by state agencies and subsequently cut into the exports of major cereals.

In addition, as late as 1927, the total amount of harvested grain that reached markets still had not recovered. The total proportion of gross marketed production dropped from 22 percent before the war to 17 percent in 1926–27. The average quantity of cereals produced for market between 1923 and 1927 was less than half of that for the five pre-war years. The decline in marketed wheat was somewhat smaller but still about a third. The quantity of marketed potatoes, meat, and sugar beets also dropped.[12] Between 1918 and 1929, marketed produce never reached pre-war levels, even before the unbalanced price policies of 1927. Furthermore, the quantity of marketed raw materials for industry also fell by about 9 percent between 1913 and 1926–27.[13]

Finally, while Soviet agriculture was more productive than Asian countries such as India and China, yields of grains per hectare in the USSR still lagged badly behind the industrialized European economies. The average yield of wheat, rye, and barley still amounted to only one quarter to one half of farms in most western countries (see table 4-2).[14] The very large gap between Soviet and western production was of great concern both to Communist Party leaders and noncommunist economists, agronomists, and other agrarian experts. Amid the indisputable progress on a number of fronts, weaknesses in critical areas persisted.

The Commissariat leadership believed strongly that its actions and policies were essential for lifting agriculture from the edge of the precipice. As they understood from the 1921–23 famine and the major crop failure of 1924, another poor harvest would set back the cause of agricultural development and have profoundly negative consequences for Soviet power.

A Vision for Rural Russia

The Farmer's Ten Commandments

Narkomzem's leadership tried to impress upon its specialists who traveled to the village the paramount importance of their role in rural transformation, as well as a larger sense of what was at stake for the country. Narkomzem's instructions to its locally posted specialists displayed a combination of pragmatism with an almost missionary idealism. In a moment we will discuss the practical strategies specialists followed when attempting to reorganize villagers' modes of farming.

TABLE 4-2
Yield of wheat in European countries, 1925–1928
(in hundreds of kilograms per hectare)

Country	1925	1926	1927	1928
Denmark	33.1	23.4	23.1	32.6
Belgium	26.7	24.3	28.0	28.4
Holland	28.4	28.0	23.6	33.3
United Kingdom	22.9	20.8	22.0	22.9
Sweden	25.6	21.8	18.8	22.9
Switzerland	22.5	21.3	21.8	22.5
Germany	20.7	16.2	18.8	22.3
Finland	16.5	16.0	16.2	14.7
France	16.0	12.0	14.2	14.6
Austria	14.8	12.7	15.9	16.9
Bulgaria	13.2	10.7	12.0	11.8
Italy	13.9	12.2	10.8	12.5
Rumania	8.6	9.1	8.5	9.8
USSR	8.3	7.9	6.6[a]	7.1[a]

Source: League of Nations, Economic and Financial Section, *International Statistical Year-book 1926* (Geneva, 1927), 38-39; also the *Year-book* of 1927 (Geneva, 1928), 1928 (Geneva, 1929), and 1929 (Geneva, 1930).
[a]Includes "Asian" territories

First, we will briefly examine what specialists called "agro-propaganda," which included teaching courses, giving lectures, showing films, and having conversations. In their discussions of the principles of agro-propaganda, one sees specialists' hope about the ability of peasants to adopt new ways of thinking about their land and labor. As one Narkomzem publication put it, when teaching young peasants, the agronomist "should take part in raising peasant children in the spirit of agricultural knowledge and skills. At some point in school they had to study God's law. Now, those hours [of studying God's law] must be replaced with the teaching of the rudiments of the natural sciences as they are connected with agricultural knowledge.... Such teaching has to be provided systematically. The ten commandments of the farmer must be written down and hung on the school walls in the place of God's commandments.... They must be studied and memorized, just as the commandments of God's law were memorized in their time."[15]

This hope that peasants would replace the Ten Commandments with the commandments of agronomic science represents the specialists at their most optimistic. The Commissariat also attempted to persuade its specialists of the importance of their work for the country as a whole. The labor of the agronomist or veterinarian "increased the country's internal resources in very concrete ways" and "strengthened its international position." Thus, the Moscow headquarters had a dual educational mission not only to bring knowledge to farmers, but to persuade its own specialists of the tremendous significance of their actions in the village, and to imbue in them persistence, vehemence, strength of purpose, and commitment to the cause of strengthening the national economy. In the absence of large budgets for local specialists, together with their difficult working conditions, this kind of exhortative language was often all Moscow had to offer them.

Toward an Efficient Commune

In the tradition of the zemstvos' agronomic aid programs, the Commissariat's measures to raise production focused on the communal peasantry, rather than the small minority who had broken away from the commune, or the even smaller group of peasants that chose to work on collective or state farms. Like the NEP-era agronomic aid program, this approach to agricultural improvements had been popularized on the eve of World War I. At that time, most Russian agronomists had come to believe that agricultural improvements were more likely to bear fruit when introduced within the confines of the commune, rather than on the consolidated plots favored by the Stolypin reforms. Specialists, together with many officials, came to believe that the dispersal of the most innovative, daring farmers out of the communes and onto consolidated plots might have actually slowed the spread of agronomic knowledge among the farming population.[16]

The repartitional commune had emerged strengthened from the World War, the dual revolutions of 1917, and the Civil War. Although Bolsheviks were split on its long-term desirability, the commune remained by far the most widespread form of land tenure in the countryside. In 1927, peasants still held at least 97 percent of agricultural land in the RSFSR in repartitional tenure.[17] In that year, 222 million of 233 million hectares in the RSFSR were farmed inside the repartitional commune. Collective farms controlled only two million hectares, as did otrubs, while khutors occupied 6 million hectares.

There was a great deal of variation in the way that the commune regulated land holding, based on regional, economic, and geographic factors.[18] In light of space restrictions, however, we cannot address all these variations here. All communes shared the strip system with open fields. Additionally, in all communes the land was held in common, but not worked in common, by the commune's households.[19]

Rationalization and Intensification of Production

The Commissariat leadership, for a number of reasons, remained intent that the peasant commune must be preserved, at least for the near term. In this context, the Commissariat's local specialists undertook two major categories of efforts to increase communal production: rationalization and intensification. By rationalization of production, agricultural specialists meant the application of scientific farming organization and methods to communal agricultural production. At heart, rationalization meant eliminating what specialists saw as inefficiencies in the way that peasants organized their communal farming. Local experts were to apply agronomic science to the lands of the communal peasantry. These measures were to be introduced by land reorganizers, surveyors, and especially agronomists, and carried out by the peasants themselves. Rationalization was a critical dimension of what the Commissariat called the "cultural reconstruction of peasant farming."[20]

It is important to note that when agricultural specialists observed that some peasants farmed "irrationally," they generally meant that farmers were using available resources inefficiently, not that they lacked intellectual capacity or potential. While many specialists certainly believed that too many peasants were overly influenced by superstition, religion, and an unscientific world view, their concept of rationalization was more an economic or organizational principle: a plan (often idealized and based on ideal-type Western models) to best organize production to spur maximum output with the available capital, labor, and land.[21]

Specialists usually tried to persuade farmers to begin with relatively simple changes to production methods that would, by themselves, have a major impact on yields. Such changes included reducing the numbers of strips (which numbered in the dozens for many households) and cutting down the distance of those strips from the dwelling;[22] widening very narrow strips to ease the use of machinery; tilling fields in the fall for the spring sowing; and tilling fallow fields in April instead of June. Agronomists cited studies showing that these latter two techniques had the potential by themselves to raise yields by 50 percent to 100 percent for a given household.[23]

Difficult and expensive measures also fell under the rubric of rationalizing production. These included improving the quality of cattle through proper breeding and feeding, and changing grazing regimes by, for example, introducing new kinds of grasses. The latter was a prerequisite for making the transition from the three-field fallow system to crop rotation.

In the mid-1920s, crop rotation or multifield farming was rare in Russia, although the amount of territory farmed under these regimes was increasing somewhat. Despite a substantial assault by agronomic aid organizations before the European war, the three-field (or open-field) system predominated in Russia throughout the 1920s, especially in the major grain-producing regions.[24] In these areas, farmers used the three-field system almost exclusively. In the Central Black Earth region, for example, only 3 percent of arable land was cultivated using crop rotation. In other cereal-producing regions in 1924, such as the North Caucuses, the Lower and Middle Volga and Siberia, the totals were even smaller. In that year, multifield rotation had been adopted on only about 7 percent of the Russian Republic's sown area. (This figure nevertheless represented a significant jump from the 1916 figure, which totaled less than 2 percent.[25]) Multifield farming was undertaken almost exclusively in areas such as the Central Industrial Region, the West, and the Northwest. In these regions, peasants grew specialized industrial crops, including flax, sugar beets, and tobacco, which required more intensive cultivation. Many separated homesteads in these regions, gearing themselves to local market conditions, converted to multifield farming and planted potatoes and clover.[26]

From the farmers' perspective, however, there were a number of serious obstacles to successfully making the transition to multifield farming. Villages needed easy access to customers who would buy the large quantities of root crops such as the sugar beets and potatoes they would now be producing as an integral element of the crop rotation regime. Yet in much of the country, access to buyers did not exist because there were simply not enough factories that needed the types of crops produced in this system. In addition, multifield farming required a good deal more time for farmers to cultivate the labor-intensive root crops. Farmers would also need to shoulder the increased burden of taking care of livestock as the common grazing of cattle on the fallow field would be abolished.[27] The conversion to the multifield regime also often demanded that peasants reduce their sowings of rye, the stalks of which families used as a fuel source in the winter. In light of the larger amount of labor required of farmers in the multifield regime, farmers would have to hire extra hands to perform various seasonal tasks. Soviet law, however, outlawed the hiring of labor before 1924, and when it was finally legalized, albeit briefly, it was very expensive for the average household. Shortage of seeds for fodder grasses, especially clover, was another major obstacle for farmers who did want to convert to crop rotation.[28]

Moreover, these economic and technical hurdles to switching to crop rotation do not take into account the great shortage of personnel qualified to assist farmers in making the transition. Despite the government's urging that peasants abandon three-field farming, there were simply too few specialists with sufficient training and integrity to aid peasants who chose to do so. Some peasants complained that local agricultural specialists demanded bribes for timely help. Many hundreds of letters from peasants complaining about indifferent, inefficient, and inebriated local officials poured into Narkomzem's Moscow offices. One report examining a year's worth of peasant letters concluded that "provincial and uezd land administrations are hiding criminals" who should be turned over to prosecutors.[29] Of course, most officials were not corrupt or alcoholic.

Nevertheless, Narkomzem's optimistic blueprint for rural rationalization was tempered by difficult local realities.

Another trend that alarmed the Commissariat officials interested in improving farming methods was the phenomenon of the splintering *(droblenie)* of communal households. There were just over twenty-one million households in the USSR in 1916. By 1927, the number of households had increased by nearly 15 percent, to perhaps twenty-four million.[30] This increase reflected the division of tiny parcels of land into even smaller parcels (and the consequent further narrowing of strips), which occurred at a rate of 2.3 percent per year between 1920 and 1923. This rate significantly surpassed the pre-war figure of 1.7 percent per year.[31] In the RSFSR, the number of households grew by 414 thousand per year between 1923 and 1927, in part a result of population pressures, and partly a result of young families' increasing desire to set up their own households apart from their parents. This growing number, and the consequent rural unemployment and poverty, worried government leaders already concerned about the productivity of the rural sector.[32] At the same time, the size of the average peasant household itself declined from 5.67 people in 1916 to 5.1 in 1927. As a result, the countryside witnessed rising numbers of smaller family farms with fewer workers and animals, and less equipment per farm. These smaller units were typically less productive and could not market as large a proportion of their produce. Narkomzem opposed frequent communal land distributions, though they did so without effect. Most villagers in grain-producing regions chose to redistribute land for the purpose of equalizing their holdings, and did so fairly often, just as they favored the commune as their preferred means of organizing their farming.

In terms of rationalization, progress was made during the 1920s in a number of areas. By 1927, early fallow was raised in 25 percent of winter fields, and fall tilling of the spring fields was occurring on about a third of all arable land.[33] By 1928, the total amount of arable land under multifield cultivation reached 41 percent in the Central Industrial Region and 33 percent in the North Caucuses and the Northwest. For the entire RSFSR the total was approximately 17 percent of sown area.[34] The major cereal producing regions, however, still lagged badly behind these averages. Still, these figures marked significant change.

The second type of improvement to communal farming—the intensification of production—required large-scale capital investment into a farming economy that the Narkomzem leadership considered "technically still extraordinarily backward."[35] The Commissariat's specialists argued that an essential precondition for the revitalization of rural Russia was an influx of machines, tools, and chemical fertilizers that would enable the transition to "superior" forms of farming. Villagers could then switch from extensive modes of farming, which concentrated on growing cereals, to intensive and more diversified regimes that (depending on the region) centered on significantly expanding dairy farming and the production of industrial crops, goals that would take many years to reach.[36] Raising productivity by way of intensification did not require an increase in the amount of land worked, nor in the quantity of labor in the village. Instead, specialists encouraged peasants to produce more with the land and labor they currently possessed by providing the village with improved means of production. They hoped that the purchase of livestock or equipment would enable farmers to overcome the lack of incentive to reinvest profits into their farms.

As late as 1926–27, the average amount of capital per farm in the RSFSR had dropped sharply since 1913. The total value of existing livestock, buildings, tools, and machines on the average farm had fallen. For Commissariat of Agriculture planners concerned with reversing that trend, draft animals were the first priority.[37] They believed that the recovery of livestock farming was crucial to the revival of the agricultural sector as a whole. Quantities of livestock in the RSFSR declined steeply between 1916 and 1922, when the number of draft animals fell by a third.[38] In 1925, 30 percent of farms still had no horses; in some regions, the figure was as high as 60 percent.[39] During the black repartition, peasants had confiscated and redistributed the estate owners' animals, including their purebred stock, which state officials tried in vain to preserve for further breeding. Many other animals had died because of "famine" and war. The Central Producer Region was the worst affected area. The drop in the output of manure, used as a fertilizer in the almost total absence of chemical fertilizers, was also a critical problem in the village. The Commissariat tried to provide farmers with better horses and livestock, either through direct supply or, more commonly, by providing credit. Indeed, the number of animals began to recover in 1923 and significantly surpassed the prewar level by 1928.[40]

The industrial crops that specialists tried to convince peasants to cultivate had also fared badly during the wars. Because these crops were grown almost exclusively on large estates, the dissolution of such estates during and after 1917 severely reduced sowings. Nevertheless, the sown area dedicated to industrial crops recovered to pre-war levels as early as 1922, almost doubling between 1913 and 1929.[41] The total production of technical crops recovered as early as 1925, and after two poor years in 1926 and 1927, advanced to 23 percent above the 1913 level.[42] Nevertheless, from a farmer's point of view, without nearby markets that served industry, the processes involved with the production of industrial crops could be extremely time consuming and costly without adequate payoff.

Another essential step in the process of intensification was increasing the supply of tools and machines, high-quality seeds and seed drills for planting them, mineral fertilizers, and building materials for silos, barns, and other structures. Metal equipment and machines were relatively rare in the pre-war village. The level of technology was very limited until the latter half of the 1920s, at which point mechanization seems to have rapidly accelerated. The so-called famine of machine supply during the world war and Civil War created a voracious need by 1921.[43] By 1923–24, the sale of machines reached only 30 percent of the prewar level. Shortages caused prices for machines to reach significantly higher levels than before the war. Nearly one-half of all plows in use as late as 1924 were still the primitive wooden variety.

The government could urge peasants to use more machines in their production processes, but in the absence of supply, it could only sow frustration and skepticism among them. Farmers complained that seeds were supplied inconsistently, delivered late, or promised and never supplied. One peasant observed that the sorted seeds on the agronomists' farms had only improved the harvest by 5 percent. For all his trouble and investment of labor, the payoff was too small in his region.[44] State supply agencies often sold machines of poor quality, and prices were high. From the perspective of villagers, since the average peasant household was still farming only four to six desiatins of arable land, investment in new equipment was beyond the budgets of most families, even those households most willing to innovate. Intensification was very expensive, even when the state subsidized prices. Certain types of machines were in high demand, including metal plows, which most peasants took to as soon as they were tried. Nevertheless, machinery was very difficult for peasants to acquire, especially in the Central Black Earth region, where only 7.5 percent of households owned any machinery at all, and the Lower Volga, where 12.5 percent did so.[45]

By the late 1920s, however, significant improvement had been made in some areas of supply. As of 1928, the wooden plow, or *sokha*, had been almost completely replaced with the metal plow; only about 10 percent of arable land was still turned over with the sokha. In addition, the supply of mineral fertilizers had recovered and surpassed the pre-war levels by about 50 percent.[46] Nevertheless, Narkomzem emphasized that significant deficits remained in the level of agricultural technology. Narkomzem specialists focused on significant pockets of rural underdevelopment that persisted in the Soviet Union throughout the twenties. They noted that, by the end of the decade, although most plowing was done with metal plows, 31 percent of households in the RSFSR still did not own their own plow; they were forced to rent from cooperative rental points or, more often, from neighbors.[47] Three-quarters of Russian peasants still did their sowing by hand, while over 40 percent of households continued to reap with scythes or sickles and to thresh by hand. Twenty-eight percent of households were still without draft livestock of any kind.

The Shape of the Soviet Countryside

While Commissariat personnel attempted to encourage the intensification and rationalization of communal production at the village level, the Commissariat's leadership also argued that, in the NEP environment, national policies must support and reinforce the Commissariat's efforts. The state must maximize market incentives by creating favorable credit and price policies to stimulate peasant production. A market for raw materials and manufactured goods must be developed so that peasants would have something to buy with the profits drawn from their farming operations. The Commissariat's arguments generally stemmed from an understanding of its mission as the major organization in charge of land and the rural economy in an agrarian country. This perspective shaped its identity as the architect, builder, and regulator of an agrarian economy undergoing a very gradual transformation to an industrial economy. An analysis of certain of the most significant issues will illustrate the Commissariat's vision for a modern, socialist countryside. A number of controversial issues—including the role of collective farms, the extent of rural social differentiation, the definition of the term kulak, and the place of the peasant commune (obshchina) in the Soviet republic—were both closely related and hotly disputed.

The Commissariat leadership's interpretation of rural socioeconomic realities was undergirded by the outlooks of agency specialists, located largely in Zemplan. On policy toward the village, Zemplan became a brain trust of the party's Right wing, providing a great deal of research about the countryside. Zemplan's interpretation of this research tended to support the Right's more gradualist, geneticist approach toward the transformation of the rural economy. Much of the statistical and anecdotal evidence (the latter came from agricultural specialists in the field) that lent credence to the Right's understanding of peasant psychology, attitudes toward the state, and economic behavior originated in the Commissariat of Agriculture. Besides the scholarly and statistical work of researchers, the leaders of Narkomzem received reports on rural opinion from its own local officials and specialists who worked in direct contact with the peasantry (as opposed to the very thin and widely dispersed network of rural party cells), from letters to periodicals serving the village population, and from the police. Stressing the notion that it was the defender of the interests of agriculture, the Commissariat's relatively pragmatic and gradualist approach was reinforced by the anecdotal evidence they received. Information confirmed that at least certain segments of the peasantry craved a generous supply of credit, tools, draft animals, seeds, machines, and advice on how to best use them.

Other views of the Commissariat's leadership were reinforced by the gist of reports that they received from the village—that the specter of social differentiation was not regarded as a serious issue among most villagers; that it was the better-off stratum of the peasantry that was most interested in heeding specialists' advice; that heavy-handed interference by local party officials or the police frightened the more innovative farmers in the village; and that farmers were more likely to increase output if their taxes were kept relatively low and simple. The Commissariat's political and scientific leadership believed that data from the countryside confirmed that they should pursue a policy that encouraged production by creating the conditions in which initiative and increased output would be rewarded, rather than an "extractionist" policy based on high taxes and lower fixed purchase prices for agricultural goods relative to industrial products. Despite shifts at the national level, certain continuities remained in the agriculture commissariat's policies between 1921 and 1928.

The Desertion of Collective Farms

The Commissariat was also a strong advocate of the creation of agricultural cooperatives, and hoped that villagers would utilize them. In 1926, over eight million farms participated in some type of cooperative. The most important type was the consumer cooperative, which provided discounted goods to villagers. According to Danilov's figures, by 1927 one-third of peasant households in the USSR participated in consumer cooperatives, and 50 percent made use of them by 1929. Over half the value of goods purchased in villages was obtained in cooperative stores.[48] Agricultural service cooperatives were another important variation. They provided farm machinery, credit, and marketing opportunities. Through this type of cooperative, a farmer could rent farm implements for milling grains or processing food such as oil, fruit, and vegetables. In addition, most credit obtained by farmers came through agricultural credit cooperatives. In October 1927, there were 28,700 of these agricultural service cooperatives in the RSFSR, comprising 44.5 percent of the total of cooperatives (64,573). Ninety percent of farmers who participated in cooperatives belonged to this type. Legislation limited membership and influence in cooperatives by farmers who were defined as kulaks, while encouraging the poorest to participate. Poor and middle peasants comprised the majority of agricultural cooperative members in 1927. Simple production cooperatives spun off from these co-ops, and eventually some adopted large-scale production methods.

Party leaders since Lenin had hoped that production, credit, and sales cooperatives would be a step along the road to collectivization. Nevertheless, most Narkomzem specialists and officials in this period remained skeptical that large socialist farms could succeed in the conditions prevailing at the time. Between 1921 and 1927, the Communist Party devoted little in the way of resources to the construction of production cooperatives, including collective farms (kolkhozy) or state farms (sovkhozy), or even to the maintenance of those few that had been built during the Civil War. Collective farms were virtually abandoned in this period.[49] All Bolsheviks, however, including the Right wing, agreed that ultimately the party-state would have to create a great network of large, highly mechanized, socialist farms, which would modernize agricultural production permanently, whether this process took five or fifty years. Questions of timing and method divided communists. No one, however, anticipated the kind of massive, bloody war against the peasantry that Stalinist collectivization became.

Few peasants were interested in joining collective farms. According to numerous sources, farmers typically regarded collective farms as a waste of land, and many villagers openly derided those who did join.[50] The sovkhozy were supposed to serve as model farms that would show neighboring peasants how to farm in the most efficient and scientific ways. Yet, for a variety of reasons, most peasants despised them. In 1924, Feliks Dzerzhinskii, chief of the OGPU, observed that "peasants are extremely hostile to sovkhozy (as a result of land hunger)." A certain peasant Golubkov informed Narkomzem that in a sovkhoz near him, at least fourteen of seventeen horses had died thanks to the incompetence of the organizers, and only three of forty cows had survived. He reported that the sovkhoz was so incompetently organized that no peasant would ever follow its example, no matter how much the government spent on it.[51]

By drastically reducing funding after 1921, the government forced collective farms to fend for themselves without state subsidies. The surviving collective farms occupied only 0.6 percent of sown land in 1927; state farms occupied just 1.1 percent.[52] The number of collective farms decreased overall between 1924 and 1927. At the end of 1927, around 22,000 collective farms occupied only 1.5 percent of all land in the RSFSR, on which lived perhaps 1 million people, about 1 percent of the village population.[53] Most officially existed to facilitate the joint ownership of equipment, 3,500 were intended for land improvement, and 1,880 were dedicated to cattle breeding. Collective farms received almost no agronomic assistance from Commissariat specialists. The small and inactive Narkomzem department responsible for collective farms shriveled on the vine. Similarly, the party left sovkhozy to their own devices. By 1921, the Commissariat's leaders had decided that state farms could not serve as the basis upon which the regime would supply the cities and factory towns with food. Soon thereafter reports poured into Moscow about the terrible condition of most state farms. The OGPU verified the deterioratiation of surviving sovkhozy.[54] In the mid-twenties about twelve hundred state farms remained in the Russian Republic, according to Narkomzem data.[55]

Smirnov agreed that the time was not right to devote a great deal of state resources to creating collective farms. He certainly did not anticipate, nor would he have supported, the forced and immediate collectivization of the peasantry. Smirnov believed in the superiority of collective farming over communal, but he also felt that the time to make this transition on a large scale would come only some time in the future. Conditions had not yet ripened for even beginning the process of building any model collectives that would serve as examples for those peasants who were inclined to dedicate themselves voluntarily to joining collective farming units. Narkomzem's 1924 agricultural plan was predicated on the notion that small-scale farming would form the overwhelming majority of agricultural output into the foreseeable future.[56] As Smirnov put it in 1925, "I have put this question [of collectives] on the back burner for tactical reasons. I believe that we should give two or three years in order to gradually overcome all that is old, all the sick remnants of the past, in order to get down to the organization of healthy farms that will become exemplary model farms."[57] The following year he sounded an even more pessimistic note: "It will take decades to bring peasant farming to the proper level. Why fool ourselves?"

In Defense of Kulaks? The Quagmire of Rural Class Struggle and Categories

In light of Narkomzem leaders' understanding that villagers were unlikely to welcome collective farms soon, together with Commissariat efforts to improve the productivity of communal farming, the question of rural social stratification took on great significance in the agency's outlook. Commissariat officials and specialists remained generally united in their view of socioeconomic stratification in the village, even as they downplayed the degree of differentiation.[58] Commisariat policy makers and specialists before 1928 were not concerned that a powerful stratum of kulaks was growing, either as a political or an economic force. In Narkomzem's view, "capitalist" exploitation of poor peasants by kulaks was not a widespread phenomenon.[59] Nor did kulaks dominate the commune, as some critics charged. Nor would allowing peasants the right to lease land (a right upon which Narkomzem insisted) create kulaks.[60] Beginning in the fall of 1923, the Narkomzem position on differentiation was reflected in official policy and discourse, reflecting the Right's desire to downplay the level of rural differentiation.

The Commissariat's foil in this debate was the group of Agrarian Marxist scholars. The Agrarian Marxists were allied with the Left Opposition critics of the Central Committee majority (especially Preobrazhensky and Trotsky), with whom the Commissariat leadership waged polemical battles. Focusing on what they perceived as the rapidly accelerating class struggle in the village, the Agrarian Marxists saw growing social differentiation and economic exploitation among peasants. Beginning in 1925, Agrarian Marxists attacked Narkomzem's view, gathering and publicizing statistics that emphasized a growing threat posed by social stratification in the countryside. They denounced Narkomzem's policies, which, they alleged, favored kulaks. In 1925, for example, the Agrarian Marxist A. Gaister accused Smirnov of "attempting to legalize the kulak by denying his existence."[61]

Deputy Commissar of Agriculture Sviderskii wrote to Molotov on this theme in the spring of 1925. Molotov served as head of the Committee on Work in the Countryside, which was attached to the Central Committee. After acknowledging that economic differentiation was occurring and would occur more markedly in the future, Sviderskii asserted that "your point of view does not contradict ours, but we (Narkomzem) would say more strongly: Differentiation still has not taken such form and degree to the point that we must *now* build *all* our tactics deriving exclusively from differentiation."[62]

For their part, Narkomzem officials believed that most socioeconomic distinctions had been erased in the post-revolutionary countryside. Extremes of wealth and poverty—the numbers of the wealthiest and poorest peasants—were greatly reduced by the black repartition. As a result of this leveling, the so-called middle peasants, seredniaki, comprised the overwhelming majority in the countryside. The Commissariat's officials believed that middle peasants "should be at the center of the state's attention and should serve as the main lever in the recovery and development of agriculture. All measures of a mass character should be aimed at their needs and interests."[63]

Despite this rhetoric about the middle peasant, however, it was the upper strata of the middle peasantry that most benefited from the policies that Narkomzem advocated. A Zemplan report illustrates the emphasis officials put in the innovators and risk-takers in any commune: "Do not forget that in any movement forward there is a vanguard, a progressive stratum that is the most energetic, adaptable, and diligent. In many measures aimed at awakening initiative among the agricultural population, the state will have to rely first of all on the stronger strata *[naibolee sil'nyi sloi]*. The state should allow them room to use their initiative, while ensuring that they do not take advantage of the more disadvantaged population."[64]

As for the poor peasants, "special attention" must be paid to the weakest agricultural producers. "Serious study must be made of the reasons for their frailty and backwardness."[65] Although under political pressure that began in 1926 the Commissariat made a somewhat more concerted effort to create programs geared toward the rural poor, until then Narkomzem sent out a clear message to its local personnel: in current conditions the state will take energetic measures to encourage the middle and well off, while paying less attention to the needs of the poor. Commissariat policy held that helping better-off farmers was both economically healthy and socially progressive (so long as the farmers did not separate from the commune). Commissariat officials argued that providing incentives would increase the proportion and total amount of grain brought to market. By arguing that very few genuine kulaks remained in the countryside, the Narkomzem leadership justified policies directed toward encouraging the village vanguard.

Of course, the Soviet state must wage a "merciless struggle" against those few kulaks who remained, Smirnov acknowledged. Nevertheless, his narrow definition of kulak rendered him hard pressed to find many.[66] The kulak, by Smirnov's definition, was a conscious exploiter of weaker groups. Often he was a village businessman who hired workers so that he could live off the labor of others. Alternatively, the kulak might be a usurer, lending money to the poor and middle peasants at exorbitant, even "ungodly" rates, enslaving his poorer neighbors.⁶⁷ Debates over the total number of kulaks were waged in many party forums as well as among statisticians. Most observers agreed that kulaks comprised between 2 percent and 5 percent of the rural population. This proportion represented a steep decline in the pre-war figure of perhaps 15 percent.⁶⁸ In Smirnov's view, without property in land, the pre-revolutionary type of kulak had no economic base from which to exploit his neighbors.⁶⁹

Smirnov distinguished between those few genuine kulaks and a stratum of well-off peasants: "I am a great defender of the strong *(krepkii)* farmer but not of kulak farming."⁷⁰ Smirnov valued the "well-off" *(zazhitochnyi)* and "strong laboring peasant" *(krepkii trudovoi muzhik)*, using these terms to refer to those who were economically above average but still counted among the middle peasants.⁷¹ Well-off farmers were sober and hard working. They tried to strengthen their own production by means of capital investment including livestock, equipment, mineral fertilizers, machines, and better seed. These well-off farmers did not exploit labor, since they hired help only when needed on a temporary basis, around harvest time, for example.⁷² Smirnov argued that the state should undermine the power of kulaks through taxation, vigilant punishment of labor code violations, and the supply of abundant, low-interest credit to the poor to reduce their dependence on usurers. The Soviet state should offer incentives for the well-off peasants to rationalize and intensify operations through the application of new technology and methods. In maintaining that such policies would raise the economic level of agriculture as a whole, the Commissariat argued that the country needed a peasantry that could accumulate capital to provide a market for industrial goods.⁷³

There was, however, a critical problem with this formulation. Many villagers worried that they would be labeled kulaks if they did invest in improvements for their farms.⁷⁴ If peasants who accepted the teachings of agricultural specialists were penalized for their adoption of more efficient techniques and new technology, then the Commissariat's actions would be completely undermined. This is another reason why Commissariat officials and agronomists argued strongly for the use of the category "well-off" to describe productive farming households, while rarely using the term kulak. Locally, party and soviet officials often smeared relatively successful peasants with the dreaded kulak label, and then applied punitive tax assessments.⁷⁵ Farmers who owned more than one horse or who bought advanced agricultural machinery, for example, could be stigmatized as kulaks. Strong farmers could be deprived of civil rights and the right to participate in credit cooperatives. Many farmers were concerned about the government's conflicting agendas. As one peasant put it in 1925, "You agronomists come and tell us to have four cows instead of two. But as soon as we do, local power comes and considers us kulaks. Confusion in the definition of who is a kulak and who is strong [krepkii] must be resolved before you can even talk about the intensification of agriculture."⁷⁶ Similarly, communal farmers who wished to switch to multifield farming would often have to hire helpers to assist with the more labor-intensive nature of the tasks in that farming regime. Yet the use of outside labor indicated to many party activists that a farmer was a kulak. Among the stronger middle peasants, anxiety verging on panic plagued those afraid of being labeled kulaks by local officials.[77] Smirnov expanded on this theme at the October 1924 Central Committee Plenum, touching on the discrimination toward farmers who had been identified as kulaks: "It is not clear what is meant by kulak. There are instances where a peasant with two cows is called a kulak with all the associations that accompany the label, though he does not trade, does not rent, and works on his five *desiatiny* with his family. We must wage a struggle with kulak price exploitation but not at the cost of ruining the growth of production. . . . There is not the kind of growth in the number of kulaks that would justify all this noise."[78] To be sure, Narkomzem's agricultural modernization programs absolutely depended on the principle that peasants could improve the productivity of their farms *without penalty*.

Another unexpected result of Narkomzem's approach was that many poorer peasants came to believe that Narkomzem was more interested in helping the kulaks than the poor folk. From the point of view of the poorer peasants and the landless peasant laborers (the *batraks*), the emphasis on village vanguard meant that the poor received little. A peasant Chugunov noted that since his home province of Penza was overpopulated, short on land, and impoverished, plans to help the well-off truly benefited only a small minority. Agronomists "mostly serve the kulaks, and not the real peasant farmer." Observing that the well-off were often favored with the best equipment, one letter to Narkomzem complained that specialists "bend to the pressure of the zazhitochnyi element in the village."[79] Although agronomists could argue that in the long run this strategy of focusing on the most prosperous villagers would benefit all, many peasants were not persuaded.[80] The new "wager on the strong" seemed to alienate many of the weak, who resented Soviet government's apparent abandonment of the downtrodden mass in whose name the regime spoke.

Moreover, by 1923 Narkomzem officials were aware that their policies on rural differentiation were opposed by what they called "the remnants of war communism." The Agrarian Marxists launched their first attack with the publication of the Commissariat's *Fundamentals of the Perspective Plan for the Development of Agriculture and Forestry* in 1924.[81] The Commissariat also came under increasing attack from the Left Opposition for offering too much help to wealthy villagers and not enough to the poor. Trotsky accused Smirnov of carrying out policies that catered to kulaks at the expense of the working class and the poor peasantry. The opposition platform at the Fourteenth Party Congress derided the "openly Right tendency" of Smirnov, Kalinin, Rykov, and other party moderates. Trotsky argued that Smirnov and Narkomzem worked from a "kulak point of view," employing a "vulgar theoretical revision of Leninism" that minimized social differentiation in the countryside, and "followed precisely the example of the Populists."[82] Smirnov replied, as usual, with barely restrained contempt: "The accusation that we did not notice that the kulak was exploiting the poor and that we allowed this to occur is stupidity and demographic trifles. . . . This noise about the kulak is based on inaccurate figures and calculations."[83]

The Right wing, including Bukharin and Rykov, embraced the Commissariat of Agriculture's analysis. Narkomzem's experience provides concrete evidence of the deep roots of the Right in the state apparatus. Largely on the strength of his ideas about the relative complexity of rural sociology, Smirnov won a reputation as a leading Rightist thinker on the issue of the peasantry. Historians have not recognized the role of Smirnov, with the help of Teodorovich and the leading specialists of Zemplan, in formulating the NEP majority's approach to the kulak question. Apart from Trotsky's supporters referred to above, one contemporary who did note Smirnov's influence was Nikolai Vladislavovich Vol'skii, deputy editor of a Vesenkha journal in the 1920s. Vol'skii, who wrote under the pseudonym N. V. Valentinov, counted Smirnov among the four major leaders of Right communism, together with Bukharin, Rykov, and Dzerzhinskii. Vol'skii correctly asserted that although few outsiders knew of him (he was neither a Politburo member like Bukharin and Rykov, nor the famous head of the Cheka/GPU), "ideas developed by Smirnov as early as 1924 anticipated much of what Bukharin and Rykov later said," especially with regard to the Right's views on the peasantry. "His contribution to the doctrine of right communism must be considered indisputable. . . . To those who lived in the USSR then and were in touch with what went on behind the scenes, the role of this individual is well known for working out the doctrine of Right communism, particularly its attitude toward the peasantry and to agriculture. . . . Smirnov truly devoted much effort to attempting to enforce within the Party a correct view of the well-off [zazhitochnyi], laboring peasantry." [84]

Thus, we should point out here that Smirnov was trying to modify the accepted, oversimplified categories into which peasants fell—poor, middle, and rich—and that he was one of the first Bolsheviks to do so in a sustained and systematic way. Smirnov deserves credit for refusing to accept the vague and simplistic categories of rural class analysis commonly used in the party. In trying to reduce perceptions that a major kulak threat existed, he tried to minimize the number of peasants who could be labeled as kulaks. One is tempted to be sympathetic with this effort on Smirnov's part.

However—and this was a key shortcoming not only in his thinking but in the strategy of the entire Right wing—he did acknowledge that kulaks existed in the Soviet countryside. To be sure, he stressed that there were not many of them, and he argued that their influence was much less than some Bolsheviks asserted. Nevertheless, in Smirnov's view, where "genuinely exploiting" kulaks had free rein to take advantage of their weak neighbors, they caused true harm and had to be stopped. Although he always rejected the use of violence or coercion against kulaks, Smirnov alleged that in relatively rare cases there existed malicious exploitation by kulaks.[85] The editor Valentinov's observations seem pertinent here: "In sum, Smirnov saw no bloodsucking kulak in the village, but, afraid of accusations that he was concealing the kulak and denying 'the canon of differentiation,' he pretended that he saw the bloodsuckers as well."[86] Valentinov observed that the Rights were afraid of denying (and in fact could not deny) the Marxist notion that social stratification, and therefore class struggle, must exist among the rural population.[87] Once they publicly accepted not only that differentiation existed among the peasantry, but also that there was a stratum—albeit very small—of exploiting kulaks that might pose a threat to the revolution, they had willingly endorsed a great, fatal illusion. The real problem was only partially that the Right used the category "kulak;" more troubling was that they admitted that kulaks were or genuinely could become a counterrevolutionary "threat" to the achievement of socialism, even if they argued that the threat was very minor at that time.

One can compare Smirnov's struggle to walk this thin rhetorical tightrope to Dzerzhinskii's own distinction between the economically very useful "honest trader" and the altogether harmful "speculator" or "parasitical trading element." On the one hand, Dzerzhinskii, one of the most prominent Rightists, pointed out accurately and reasonably at the July 1926 Central Committee Plenum: "It is unfortunate that we have people in the government [who are] afraid of the prosperity of the village. But how can we industrialize the country if we think about the prosperity of the country with fear?"[88] Yet, at the same time, he wrote of his concern that "speculators" were swamping the Soviet Union's urban areas: "We must do everything possible to free our cities from the hundreds of thousands of parasitical-speculator elements."[89] The problem was that, as the historian Alan Ball has pointed out, "the concept of speculation" could be applied "to ban nearly all private trade, if [the government] chose."[90] Moreover, regular police sweeps of the cities and villages to arrest "speculators" and entrepreneurs (known as Nepmen) most likely reinforced in peasants' own minds that the party-state was in practice less tolerant of "capitalist elements" than Rightist rhetoric about NEP would allow. In Dzerzhinskii's mind there was a very sharp distinction—and yet for the civilian population a perilously thin line—between the beneficial and indispensable "traders" and the revolution-destroying "parasites."

One might further speculate about the degree to which the GPU's reports on the countryside influenced Smirnov's concern about the existence of a counterrevolutionary (though very small) and strengthening (albeit very slowly) kulak class. Police reports typically made no distinction between kulak and well-off farmers. Instead, they often compressed the two categories into kulak-zazhitochnyi. This conflation of categories uprooted with one fell swoop the distinction so carefully planted by Smirnov and Narkomzem in the minds of communist officials in Moscow and the localities. The GPU, with its huge police network and special authority in the party, and under the direction of a leading Rightist, planted the seeds of suspicion of a potentially very dangerous kulak threat. For example, the OGPU viewed the crop failure of 1924 as fertile soil upon which "kulak influence" could grow in the village, just as Narkomzem was downplaying the same threat.[91]

This book argues that as Narkomzem went, so went NEP, both as a political system and as a strategy for building socialism. The tensions inherent in NEP were reflected starkly in the Commissariat of Agriculture. The Commissariat's position on the kulak, which was essentially the Right's position, contained a fatal flaw. While it properly downplayed the kulak threat, pointing out that the demonization of so many peasants would spell doom for the Right's program toward the countryside, the admission under political pressure from the Left (and likely under pressure from the observations of the GPU in its reports) that the region was faced with a kulak danger, even if currently latent, helped to undermine the Right's position.

"Master of the Land": The Commissariat and the Commune

The Commissariat's views on differentiation reveal crucial elements of a strategy for modernizing the countryside that included specialists' development of a village elite, a nucleus of strong and creative well-off peasants who would ignite the productive potential of the village. Similarly, Narkomzem approaches toward the commune (known officially as "the land society") highlight the Commissariat leadership's official understanding of the location where that modernization process must occur given the absence of a strong collective farming sector. This focus on the commune also highlights the limits of the Commissariat's willingness to accommodate the peasants' own perspectives or preferences.

In the view of the Commissariat leadership, the commune was, on one hand, a temporary laboratory, something of a way station for the introduction of technological and organizational improvements in farming during this transition period that would inevitably lead to advanced socialist forms of production. On the other hand, the commune also remained an incubator of collectivist sentiments among a stubbornly individualistic population. In the Commissariat's view, the commune could serve a triple function in these turbulent times when Soviet power was still weak in the countryside: as an essential institution to accelerate modernization, socialization, and the state's social control in the countryside. Finally, and not unrelated to the previous three functions, the agency leadership found that the persistence of the commune was also very much in Narkomzem's institutional interest.[92]

The Rural Soviet Alternative

After the seizure of power, the new regime attempted to transfer many of the administrative functions of the commune to the new rural soviets *(sel'sovety)*—the official administrative organ of the new regime in the village. In addition to their administrative role, the soviets were intended to drum up support for the new regime among the peasantry. Nevertheless, rural inhabitants before collectivization were almost always more devoted to their commune than to the local village soviet, despite party efforts to win peasant allegiance for the soviets.[93] The village soviets garnered little respect among the peasantry, much to the frustration of many Bolsheviks. At an Orgburo session in July 1927, a frustrated comrade Sulimov affirmed that, in most places, the rural soviet enjoys less authority than the commune.[94] As proof he noted that although the local population rarely participates in meetings of the village soviet, all members of the village soviet go to gatherings of the commune. This was natural, he observed, since the communal meeting decides the matters most relevant to the village population, including land reorganization, veterinary matters, and forest issues. The village soviet, meanwhile, wastes time passing resolutions on international affairs and other matters irrelevant to farmers. Sulimov noted that during his travels in the Urals 70 percent of the people he talked to told him that the *skhod* (gathering of heads of households) was viewed as an authority superior to the village soviet. For Sulimov, this created a "distorted situation" in which "the village soviet carries out the decisions of the village gathering, not the other way around."[95]

Local party committees complained that in many areas the village soviets were utterly dormant and could not be counted on. The presence of communists in the village soviet network was negligible. Indeed, simply finding people to work in village soviets, with their tiny budgets, could be extraordinarily difficult. A party inspector in Penza, for example, noted that in the Il'minokoi village soviet (Bol'sheviasokoi volost') local authorities for some time searched for a volunteer to serve as chair. No one would agree to hold the position. They finally came to the decision that whoever came tardy to the next meeting would "earn" the honor. In another locality, the members of the soviet spun the official seal on the table; whomever the seal pointed to when it stopped spinning was named chair.[96]

An incident from Penza province further illustrates the unreliability of some village authorities in the eyes of a frustrated Communist Party leadership. On the day in January 1924 that Lenin's body was interred in the Kremlin wall, some rural soviet officials staged a ceremony of their own. First, they threw "an enormous, drunken party." As comrade Orlov, Secretary of the Penza provincial Communist Party Committee, personally reported to Stalin, Molotov, and the rest of the Orgburo, these village authorities drank until they were thoroughly inebriated. They then yanked one of the ubiquitous portraits of Lenin from the wall of a government building. After hammering together a makeshift coffin, these representatives of Soviet power in the countryside dropped the painting in the coffin, nailed down the lid, lowered Vladimir Il'ich into a freshly dug grave, and buried it. After the "service," they continued their bacchanalian celebration late into the night. "This is the kind of thing we have to deal with," Secretary Orlov concluded dryly.[97]

In Defense of the Commune: Narkomzem's Notion of the Commune's Role

In the absence of either a strong government presence or a serious collective farm sector, the commune remained a vital institution in rural social, economic, and juridical life as an organ of local self-government. The elimination of the zemstvos and landlords had given the commune the opportunity to expand its purview well beyond what imperial law had allowed. As was to be expected in conditions of weak central control, the customs embodied in the commune, given new vitality by the 1917-18 agrarian revolution, continued to govern village life.[98] Communes continued to redistribute their lands regularly, generally every three to five years. The 1922 Land Code had assigned the commune equal standing with all other forms of land tenure, including the collective farm and the separated homestead. Article 51 of the Land Code gave the village gathering the right to resolve questions involving the commune as a whole, such as land tenure, land reorganization, separations, timing for field work, and the types of crops to be grown.[99] Until 1928, legislation recognized the commune as possessing legal authority and administrative responsibilities in the village, although it was not always clear what these responsibilities were.

In these circumstances (which were expected to continue, at least in the near future), the Commissariat of Agriculture's leadership defended the existence of a strong commune as the fundamental institution of the village. The commune played an absolutely central role in the Commissariat's vision of the new countryside. Many Bolsheviks, however, believed that the commune was obsolete, a relic of feudalism that prevented the modernization of agriculture. The commune, some critics argued, slowed the progress of agriculture, since it usually preserved what many specialists considered inefficiencies such as the strip system, three-field farming, and the frequent redistributions of land. Separated homesteads, by way of contrast, nearly always abandoned them.[100]

Despite such opposition, the commune nevertheless played a special role in the Commissariat leadership's conception of the path to the socialist future. Smirnov maintained that the commune was the form of land use from which peasants could most easily make the transition to collectivized production. Yet this transition could be made only when the time was right. For Smirnov, an efficient and productive commune that had undergone rationalization measures and that had access to advanced technology represented the superior type of land working in the conditions that existed in this transition period. Nearly all the Commissariat's efforts in the localities were therefore directed toward improving farming techniques within the confines of the commune, rather than accelerating its demise. Kondrat'ev, the chief author of the 1924 Perspective Plan and Narkomzem's most important specialist, also asserted that the Commissariat should influence peasants toward choosing the commune as the best way to organize their farming. He argued that although it is transitional at the present moment, it is also the most "progressive" type of land use.[101]

There were certainly elements of the ways that peasants traditionally organized their farms inside the commune that Smirnov disliked and tried to control. Narkomzem tied the issue of the preservation of the commune to the economic question of the stability of peasant land-holding patterns. In December 1926 Smirnov warned General Secretary Stalin that the continued splintering of households into smaller units, together with the subsequent weakening of the commune, was having very adverse consequences for the rural economy.[102] Smirnov denounced the "frequent and unregulated communal division of land [and] the abnormally high-pressured process of redistributions of peasant holdings among family members." As families divided, the growth in the number of households damaged "initiative among the peasant population to invest money into their land and improve and intensify farming." Narkomzem proposed legislation to limit the splintering of households, but it does not seem to have made any difference in practice.[103]

Perhaps the most revealing way to examine the agency's insistence upon the commune's utility is to analyze a moment when the Commissariat leadership believed that the commune was seriously threatened as the central institution in the village. During debates over new land legislation in the summer of 1926, a commission under Sovnarkom USSR drafted legislation that would have minimized the importance of the commune by instead recognizing the family household (dvor) and cooperatives as the fundamental legal entities (or "land users") in the countryside. Narkomzem's political and specialist leadership strongly disagreed with Sovnarkom USSR on this issue, and they submitted a counterproposal.[104] This proposal asserted that the commune was the form of land working which most closely resembled the collective farm, and therefore was more appropriate to this transition period. Commissariat officials argued that the commune, and not the much smaller household, should continue to be legally recognized as the "principle landholder" in the countryside (though "certain changes would have to be made in its structure"). Membership in a commune should be mandatory for all peasants, including landless rural laborers.[105]

Smirnov preferred that the commune remain the legally recognized holder of land for several reasons. First, the commune satisfied the state's need for an institution through which the government could attempt to exert a degree of social control over the mass of the peasantry.[106] The Commissariat's leadership viewed the commune as a key institutional bulwark for maintaining the status quo social order in rural Russia. Deputy Commissar of Agriculture Sviderskii argued that to eliminate the commune as the landholder in the eyes of the law would "have the further result of depriving the state of the *intermediary organization* through which it now conducts the regulation of rural economic relations, and comes face to face with twenty-four million *dispersed* peasant households."[107]

Of equal importance, the Commissariat leadership was also concerned that the specter of private property could return if the commune were weakened. The commune represented "one of the foundations of the nationalization of land," in Sviderskii's words.[108] Indeed, a prime motivation for the Commissariat's communist leaders was the conviction that the communal regulation of land holding provided defense against individual land ownership until the transition to socialism had been completed. In a July 1926 letter to Sovnarkom Chair Rykov, Smirnov stated his fierce opposition to Sovnarkom USSR's draft land law, which would have designated the household as the basic landholder or "subject of land law."[109] Such a proposal would have unexpected and disastrous consequences, Smirnov believed. He argued that this legislation threatened a giant step backwards toward private property in land and therefore represented a major retreat. If the government both elevated the legal importance of the household and diminished the commune's place in the law, peasants would be more likely to abandon the commune for separated homesteads.[110] Smirnov argued that making the family household the fundamental land-holding unit in the village, while simultaneously stretching the period during which a farmer had the right to unlimited land use, would accelerate the spontaneous and highly undesirable cultivation in the peasantry of property consciousness. He feared creating "illusions" about private property in peasants' minds. As Smirnov put it, "Exploitation lies in the petty bourgeois nature of individual peasant farming," thereby equating exploitation and petty bourgeois tendencies with peasant agriculture.[111] The commune served to rein in these harmful property instincts.

Separated Homesteads

As the discussion of the proposed 1926 land legislation demonstrates, the Commissariat's emphasis on maintaining the commune begat a largely negative attitude toward farmers who wished to break away from the commune and form separated homesteads. Many observers of the countryside, and especially researchers in Rabkrin, argued that the state should help peasants leave the commune, since it was the enclosed homestead that offered the best soil for farmers to make the transition to collective working of the land on a large scale.[112] Furthermore, many critics argued that the commune preserved the superiority of rich peasants over the poor and that it allowed the kulak to dominate the rural soviet as well.[113]

In some regions of the Russian Republic, millions of peasants had decided to form consolidated holdings—both khutors and otrubs—and they occupied a significant part of the sown territory. In certain areas, especially in the Western provinces, large numbers of peasants chose to work their land outside the strip system and the redistributional commune.[114] Some elected to form a khutor, a consolidated holding with its dwelling and arable land (including fallow and household gardens) moved to a spot outside the communal lands. Other farmers set up an otrub, concentrating only the plowed land in one place outside the village, while the farm buildings, house, and garden plot remained in the village. The Stolypin land reforms, of course, had encouraged peasants to undertake this type of farming (and especially encouraged the creation of khutors), but the 1917 revolutions and the mass redistribution of land that accompanied them had effectively reversed the Stolypin reforms in most areas. Communes had reabsorbed and redistributed the lands that peasants had consolidated. By the end of the Civil War, homesteads existed in significant numbers only in Smolensk, Vitebsk, and Belorussia.

After the 1922 Land Code confirmed farmers' right to choose whichever type of land tenure they preferred, however, farmers in certain areas embraced the homestead. Indeed, in a few regions, homesteads became more popular than they had been in 1916. In 1925 in Smolensk, for example, 33.5 percent of all households farmed in khutors or otrubs, a jump from 16.9 percent in 1916. In Leningrad province in 1925 the figure was about 24 percent, and in Tver it was 25 percent. In 1922, over one half of all land being converted to homesteads was located in the Western region. Peasants, however, almost never separated from their communes in the producing regions of central Russia, the Caucasus, and the Urals.[115] In those regions, peasants decided to stay within the commune for a number of reasons, including the expense of moving; shortages of land, water, forests, and meadows; the desire for safety in case of natural disaster; and the wish to stay close to one's neighbors.

Before mid-1923, Narkomzem officially exercised a good deal of flexibility in questions of land tenure, although laws made it easier for peasants to join collective farms than to separate onto homesteads. Commissariat instructions stated that the principles of noninterference and freedom of choice in land-use decisions should guide specialists' actions. Until 1923, Narkomzem's position was that farming on individual homesteads was a better form of tenure for making the transition to intensive farming, which would in turn produce more surpluses for market while employing excess rural labor.[116] Commissariat publications argued that, especially in the West and Northwest, it was entirely rational for many farmers to separate from the commune during this transitional period. As late as 1925, Narkomzem's Perspective Plan allowed that in these regions homesteads made the most sense. The legalization and revitalization of internal markets made the movement to homesteads logical for many peasants, and in 1922 the government anticipated that this process would actually accelerate.[117]

After Smirnov became Commissar of Agriculture in March 1923, however, the percentage of land converted into homesteads in the RSFSR dropped sharply, a reflection of his strong personal antipathy toward khutors and otrubs. Smirnov considered consolidated plots to be a form of land holding that represented a significant step away from socialist farming. In the earlier discussion of Smirnov's favoring of the "strong peasant," one cannot help but hear the echoes of Stolypin's "wager on the strong." But the critical difference is that Smirnov believed that the strong laboring peasant must remain inside the commune. The strong peasant should produce more, but within a structure the state finds administratively useful.

Differences of opinion on this issue existed within the Commissariat, focusing mainly on the question of region. In early 1924, collegium member M. Latsis noted that "in putting together the Land Code [of 1922], we gave the population freedom of choice in land use. [We told them] if you want to live in the commune—live there; if you want to separate onto homesteads—separate; if you want to manage an artel' or a kommuna—manage it. But do not interfere with others switching to more progressive forms of farming. This is the only limitation."[118] A resolution drafted by the Third All-Russian Congress of Land Organs in 1926 pointedly called for enforcing the Land Code's freedom of choice in land tenure. The Congress insisted that officials not "place administrative obstacles before the population in the selection of any particular form (communal, khutor, otrub, etc.)."[119] Many believed that in some regions homesteads represented a "more rational organization of agriculture."[120] Zemplan experts still argued that peasants in the West and Northwest should be allowed to establish homesteads wherever their creation was economically rational. A Professor Khauke argued at a March 11, 1927, Zemplan session that limiting homesteads in these areas would make no sense, because peasants were eagerly setting them up on their own, even without the assistance of land reorganizers.[121] Such language pointed to the tension between the desires of Moscow's political leadership and some specialists who viewed positively the higher yields, greater productivity, and potential for a more intensified regime that consolidated holdings offered.

Indeed, Smirnov's position on separation from the commune represented an important difference with other leaders of the Right wing, who insisted that administrative obstacles not be placed in the way of peasants who wanted to leave the commune. Despite the Land Code's guarantee of freedom to choose one's form of land tenure, and the government's consistent affirmation of this right, Smirnov's Narkomzem quickly took steps to discourage separation from the commune.[122] Smirnov believed that homesteads were only temporarily useful, and only in certain regions where they had traditionally existed. After two or three years, they would become an "extraordinary hindrance" as the village developed along the lines of cooperative and collectivist forms of land use.[123] As Smirnov put it in October 1924, "Collectivization is, practically speaking, the only way to resolve the agricultural crisis. [It will] move splintered production toward long-term, unchanging development along the path to the organization of mass production. Indeed, in splintered individual [homestead] farming we are able to see only the growth of the strong at the expense of the weak, the movement ahead of some at the cost of the ruin of others. Nowhere does the productive process move as slowly and painfully, and with such squandering of effort and resources, as in individual agriculture."[124] (It is important to emphasize here that when party members spoke of collectivization in this period, they did not have in mind the violence of Stalin's forced collectivization; rather they envisioned a gradual, peaceful, and voluntary creation of large, productive farms.) Smirnov argued that in this period when agriculture would progress toward the collectivization of agriculture (albeit extremely slowly), the government should discourage types of farming that marked a "retreat to individualism."[125] To allow the creation of homesteads would be a concession to the petty bourgeois spontaneity of the muzhik.[126] Smirnov understood that this policy would sacrifice some productivity in the short term, but he believed that ultimately the long-term benefits of discouraging separations outweighed these small losses.

Smirnov believed that peasants who had previously separated would eventually have to be reintegrated into the commune; this would be an expensive and time-consuming process. The government could dedicate extensive agronomic efforts to improving communal organization of agriculture and land holding and eliminating its most flagrant inefficiencies; in contrast, it would be nearly impossible as a practical matter to apply improvements to individual, separated farms. More importantly, Smirnov held that the commune's collectivist mentality had to be preserved in order to better prepare the peasant to participate in cooperatives and, eventually, to join collective farms. When separators reintegrated, this protosocialist mentality would be reimposed and reabsorbed by the recently returned farmer. As Smirnov wrote in November 1924, "We must move along the line of improving the commune.... In land use, it is extremely important to preserve all the social [i.e., collectivist] experience developed in our—albeit bad—commune."[127]

Narkomzem used financial means to discourage the creation of homesteads. In June 1923 the Commissariat established a scale of payments by which land reorganization personnel charged much more to set up an enclosed farm than to establish a kolkhoz. Credit was also more difficult to obtain for cash-strapped peasants who wanted to set up khutors.[128] In October 1924, Narkomzem circulated an instruction to land sections stating that the Commissariat opposed homestead consolidations: "Active measures should be taken to stop further transfers to fully enclosed farms. The population should be attracted to other forms of land holding from which transfer to collective farming would be less difficult." The Commissariat urged local land personnel to keep in mind that the ultimate goal of land reorganization was the conversion of the peasantry to collective farming.[129] In that year, the proportion of khutors established by land reorganizers fell from 13.2 percent to 3.1 percent, according to official statistics.[130] That proportion kept dropping until 1928, by which time the Commissariat's land reorganizers were setting up almost no homesteads. It is important to emphasize, however, that Smirnov never expressed the desire to reincorporate peasants forcibly into the commune or into state or collective farms. Clearly, Smirnov did not envision the large-scale collectivization of agriculture any time soon.

Despite Smirnov's personal antipathy toward separated homesteads, Narkomzem as an organization sent mixed messages to its local officials on the issue of separations. Conflict resulted from the dichotomy between Smirnov's long-term goal of establishing a socialist countryside based on collective farms and the more immediate goal of boosting output. Thus, at the same time that Smirnov voiced his personal opposition to the creation of khutors and otrubs, and the Commissariat issued instructions severely limiting their establishment, legislation continued to allow specialists to set up homesteads where the population demanded them. Certainly, land reorganizers created homesteads much more frequently than they established collective farms until 1927, even with the disincentives Narkomzem established. The creation of khutors was still legal, though officially discouraged, until 1928.

The End of Narkomzem?

During this period, Smirnov apparently feared that certain unnamed forces were working to undermine "his" Commissariat, and in his anxiety one sees yet another dimension of Narkomzem's embrace of the commune. The commissar's apprehension was expressed explicitly in a July 1926 letter to Rykov.[131] In the letter Smirnov strongly opposed the passage of the earlier-mentioned legislation proposed by Sovnarkom USSR that would have greatly augmented the legal standing of the family household (dvor) relative to the commune. Such legislation, he suspected, would spawn a mass movement of peasants out of the commune and onto separated farms, permanently weakening the institution of the commune. Smirnov feared two potential consequences of the process: first, the development of property consciousness among villagers—and perhaps even the legalization of private property in land—and, ultimately, the slow death of the Commissariat of Agriculture.

Smirnov emphasized that during the tsarist period there existed multiple categories of land overseen by many different agencies. The Revolution had successfully curtailed this "chaos" of private interests, which had been detrimental to state interests. All land was now in a "unified state land fund," and all of it was under Narkomzem's supervision.[132] Allowing the disintegration of the commune, however, would threaten all that. "If you destroy the commune, you destroy Narkomzem as the director of the land fund. Politically, the course is perfectly clear. Once the course has been taken towards property in land, even if furtively, Narkomzem with its many sections will not be necessary as the organizer of agricultural production on the lands of the nationalized land fund, located in temporary tenure [by the peasantry]."[133] Smirnov seems to have believed that every acre of land settled as a separated homestead, and thereby cut away from the commune, was an acre lost from the Commissariat's direct control. He appears to have determined the strength of his organization in part by calculating the total acreage of land controlled by the commune, and therefore under Narkomzem's supervision in the national fund. When the organization's position was threatened, Smirnov seems to have ignored the fact that the Commissariat's assignments concerned increasing production and improving economic conditions, which applied to homesteads as much as to the commune. Thus, the retention of the commune became a key element of Narkomzem's institutional interest.

In effect, Smirnov had equated the interests of the revolution with those of his organization, arguing that unnamed forces were simultaneously conspiring to undermine both the greater goals of October and his Commissariat. By this time, Smirnov appears to have come to believe that his agency's power in the Soviet economy stemmed directly from the Commissariat's jurisdiction and sphere of economic influence: the larger the organization's area of management, the greater its power. As one Commissariat official viewed the matter, the October Revolution had forever annulled the principle of private land ownership. This annulment rendered the Commissariat of Agriculture the country's only "master of the land" *(khoziain zemli)*. The government, through Narkomzem, allows laborers the right to use land, not to own it. The supervision and regulation of economic activity carried out on the land is concentrated in the hands of the Commissariat of Agriculture.[134]

Having served as deputy commissar of the food commissariat in 1922, Smirnov observed from inside that agency's path to dissolution. By 1926, Smirnov seems to have feared that Narkomzem might face the same fate that his former agency had met a few years earlier. He worried that with increased enclosure of land, and with murmurings about private property in land, the Commissariat's mission would gradually disappear, or at least suffer severe limitation. Smirnov echoed the food supply commissariat's frantic 1922 petitions to the Central Committee (see chapter two) expressing concern that with the coming of NEP the organization's raison d'être was being whittled away. For

Narkomzem, proposals to reduce the legal stature of the commune may have seemed equivalent to the introduction of the tax in kind and the abolition of requisitioning for the Commissariat of Food Supply in 1921–22: they presaged an institutional death on the horizon. It was becoming increasingly clear that under Smirnov's tenure Narkomzem had become akin to a "Commissariat of the *Communal* Peasantry." If the commune were weakened, either by a mass movement by the peasantry onto consolidated homesteads or onto collective farms (as would happen in 1929), Narkomzem's institutional power and status would be greatly threatened. In fact, by 1926, the Commissariat of Agriculture RSFSR's effective demise was indeed approaching. No one in the organization, however, could have anticipated the circumstances.

In the Commissariat's positions on collective farming, downplaying the kulak threat, the village soviet, the role of the commune, and enclosed farms, one discerns an uneasy balancing act, one that emerged from the collision of the agency's many missions. Among these were the fostering of rural economic development, especially the modernization of technique and the production of a surplus; the furthering of a new kind of collectivism among the peasantry that would help limit the "instinctual individualism" of much of the rural population and the survival and prosperity of Narkomzem itself.

The NEP was the party leadership's effort at economic and social reconciliation with the broad mass of the peasantry. Architect of the party's soft line toward the peasantry during NEP, the Commissariat of Agriculture designed approaches toward rural modernization that the party tentatively supported during the period of the High NEP.

A. P. Smirnov remained devoted to NEP principles of noncoercion throughout his tenure as people's commissar. Smirnov had a Rightist inclination in some senses. He dedicated himself to promoting policies that would give farmers incentive to boost production and embraced freedom of choice in land tenure. In other ways, however, Smirnov was less firmly dedicated to concessions to the peasantry, and this is particularly evident in his animosity toward separated homesteads and his related concern about means of maintaining control over the rural population. In certain cases, such as the peasants' disregard for local soviet and party authorities and his downplaying of rural differentiation, the Commissariat made concessions to what he understood to be peasants' allegiances. But in many other areas, including his complete rejection of private property in land, his attempts to forbid frequent land repartitions, and the strong discouragement of villagers' breaking away from the commune onto homesteads, Smirnov rejected peasant spontaneity and focused on ways to limit their actions and push them toward socialism when the time became right, at some time in the not-yet-foreseeable future. In this a conflict emerges among party

Rightists: their goals of relatively peaceful, gradualist modernization, rising living standards, "enlightenment," and (eventually) socialism sometimes clashed with some peasants' resistance to these goals in favor of independence from state authority, individualism, egalitarian farming, and the maintenance of folkways.

Smirnov believed that the transition to socialism would be hastened if the commune, with its collective land-working traditions, were maintained until the preconditions for the establishment of large collective farms were in place. His vision for a socialist USSR included the mandatory preservation, for as long as necessary, of the commune as the most collectivist economic and social form of land tenure. These ideas were reinforced by and merged with a political and institutional interest as well. Smirnov began to identify the success of the Revolution with the success of his institution and, ultimately, of himself. Narkomzem's leaders made every effort to preserve and enhance the agency's political position, and its limited power in the economy, by defending its institutional role as the master of the national land fund in the transition period. He insisted that the Commissariat maintain complete control over the nation's land fund. Any trace of movement away from the nationalization of land challenged that role. Any hint of private property in land threatened to end Narkomzem's monopoly over the control, supervision, and distribution of the country's land. Private property therefore posed a tremendous political threat to the Commissariat's institutional interests. This was a brand of institutional self-interest (vedomstvennost') at its most mature.

From the perspective of the great majority of the peasantry, however, their farming most certainly did not need to be "completely organized" by the Soviet state. From the farmers' point of view, their local economies had adapted to natural and market conditions in times of tremendous social, political, and economic upheaval. It functioned for the most part in a well-coordinated way born of an internal logic and rationality. The emissaries sent by the state to persuade farmers to change their modes of production very often (though not always) did not understand the rural economy or traditional ways of farming. Some specialists who had the closest contact with farmers were aware of the clash inherent in the state's effort to "uplift," "transform," and ultimately to "socialize" peasant farming. Yet there is also evidence that agronomists often did not sufficiently understand the difficulties farmers faced in adopting new systems of agriculture, which led to frustration from both parties.

Between 1923 and 1926, most of Narkomzem's positions on major policy issues held sway, albeit tenuously, inside the top ranks of the party. Already by 1925–26, however, Narkomzem and the Right would begin losing battles over economic and political issues. The Politburo majority reset the political course toward a more rapid industrialization process at the expense of agriculture. Antikulak legislation followed, which Narkomzem vehemently opposed.[135] The 1925 and 1926 harvests were fairly good, but low state purchase prices and a confusing array of purchasing agencies kept the total amount of marketed grain relatively low. The government had to cancel plans for increased grain exports, not without rancor against peasant producers and their defenders. Measures were implemented restricting wealthier households, primarily through increased taxation and restrictions on credits. Policies intended to protect the poor peasantry from exploitation made it more difficult to hire labor. A retrenchment against NEP inside the party began to gain momentum, and, consequently, the Commisariat of Agriculture remained on the defensive for the rest of the decade. The NEP consensus was crumbling not only among key segments of the party leadership, but also among some officials and specialists posted in the provinces.

5 Professional Identity and the Vision of the Modern Soviet Countryside

Local Agricultural Specialists, 1927–1929

It is important to examine the challenges that local specialists faced in actually carrying out the rationalization and intensification of farming promoted by the Commissariat. The evidence indicates that specialists encountered great difficulties—many of their own creation—implementing these measures. A number of major obstacles stood in the way of provincial experts and officials who hoped to transform peasant farming during NEP. Moreover, growing frustration with a local soviet and party authorities, with their own working conditions, and with a worldview and culture of the farming population had an important impact on the way specialists perceived NEP. Ultimately these frustrations led to ambivalence and disillusionment for some about NEP's promise. As a result, support among locally posted rural specialists, who were an important constituency for NEP's economic incentives to raise the productivity of farming, began to erode in significant ways by the end of the decade. Some of the specialists who entered the era with such optimism about the prospects for NEP began to question whether its approaches to rural modernization could resolve the fundamental problems of the countryside.

Historians have assumed that agricultural specialists at all levels of the Soviet state bureaucracy, well-trained and dedicated to "objective science," would have enthusiastically embraced NEP's conciliation of rural Russia and reject Stalinist ideas as unsound.[1] Scholars have taken for granted that, with the highly publicized denunciations and arrests of renowned agricultural experts such as A. V. Chaianov and N. D. Kondrat'ev in 1928–30, local specialists were either forced out of their positions or simply quit in disgust. Agricultural specialists, almost none of whom belonged to the Communist Party, are supposed to have followed the lead of Chaianov and Kondrat'ev and sneered at Stalinist plans as unscientific. The pre-1991 work of Soviet historians tended to reinforce this view. "Bourgeois specialists" at all levels of the land administration opposed collectivization, so the official story went, and this was reflected in the 1928–31 campaign to "unmask" and uproot enemies within the state bureaucracy.[2]

For a variety of reasons, many specialists who were employed in the Commissariat of Agriculture in local administration became quite dissatisfied with the government's strategies for modernization in the countryside and its relationship with the village population during the 1920s. Why did some rural nonparty specialists become disillusioned with NEP? Why were some open to radical proposals to reorder the Soviet countryside on the eve of collectivization?[3] And how did the Stalinist regime attempt to draw them into its grander reconstruction plans? An examination of the state of the agronomists' profession at the end of the 1920s—especially working conditions, attitudes toward the countryside, and other elements of the local experience—helps one begin to grasp these phenomena. Approximately ten thousand engineers possessed some level of higher education in the USSR in 1928. Yet, about twenty thousand agricultural specialists, including agronomists, land surveyors, veterinarians, and forest specialists, also had some specialized education. Nearly all case studies in revolutionary institution building in the 1920s treat the industrial bureaucracies, but not the very different dynamics of the young rural administrations.[4] Investigations of the lives, outlooks, and professional identities of those staffing rural bureaucracies in the waning years of NEP are needed to lend balance and nuance to a consideration of the eve of the Soviet Great Leap Forward.

The evidence discussed here takes us to mid-1929 and does not examine agricultural specialists' roles in or understanding of the full-scale assault on the peasantry, with its de-kulakization, deportations, famine, and extraordinary bloodshed that began in December 1929. The participation of local specialists in that episode still awaits a historian. Here we look at how local specialists viewed their roles in NEP society and how some understood the promises of rural modernization and mechanization as they were discussed between late 1927 and mid-1929, on the eve of Stalin's declaration of the immediate and total collectivization of the peasantry. During the greater part of the 1920s, the Commissariat was still not encouraging the creation of collective farms.[5] Rather than strive for the establishment of kolkhozy, the Commissariat's personnel during NEP concentrated on providing technical and educational assistance to the communal peasantry. In this period, collective farms were relatively quite small, with rarely more than a few hundred people each, although by late 1927 party policymakers were beginning to discuss the accelerated creation of large numbers of huge, mechanized collective farms that would be organized around cooperative machine and tractor columns.

Although the rural specialists stationed outside Moscow—those twenty thousand or so who worked under the auspices of the People's Commissariat of Agriculture—were a diverse lot, they shared certain elements of a worldview in the 1920s. First, they were certain that their role in the recovery of the national economy was especially vital. In 1928, nearly one half of national income still came from agriculture. Russia was a country in which, it seemed, small-scale agriculture would remain the backbone of the economy far into the future. Specialists insisted that the modernization of agricultural production and the simultaneous enlightenment of the village were extraordinarily valuable tasks. They considered themselves scientific and economic workers, not simply cultural ones like teachers, and therefore crucial to national reconstruction. As one agronomist declared in 1926, "Agricultural work is the most important of the economic functions" of local soviet organs.[6] Reviving the rural economy, he insisted in a widely shared view, is more vital than road building, education, tax collection, or medical service. The fact that there was a great shortage of agronomists to serve the huge peasant population added a sense of urgency to their mission.

The specialists' ultimate goal was to shift agriculture permanently to a more planned and rational foundation through the widespread application of the most advanced achievements of science.[7] This effort meant transforming the unplanned, spontaneous, seemingly chaotic nature of peasant agriculture through the introduction into the countryside of mechanization and the latest agronomic teaching about fertilizers, land organization, livestock management, seeds, and so on. Specialists believed that the state should play a major role in that transformation, and they were therefore part of a Russian intelligentsia tradition that emphasized the state's ability and, indeed, obligation to undertake social and economic modernization. Moreover, they demanded recognition of the value of their type of expertise and of their activities in this direction, recognition that was not forthcoming during NEP.

The party-state felt urgency to rebuild the nation's industrial base, urban infrastructure, and transportation networks, all of which had been wrecked during World War I and the Civil War. This situation served to block recognition of professionals who worked to revive the rural economy. The state's meager resources were diverted from the countryside. The regime's priorities had always been urban and industrial, even when NEP included economic policies intended to assist the rural economy. In some ways, the regime had essentially left the countryside to its own devices. The paltry proportion of the state budget allocated to rural areas, especially before 1926, demonstrates underfunding not just for the agricultural sector, but also for health care, education, and other state-provided services.[8] Rural specialists had reason to resent this abandonment, because it affected their salaries, status, and work environment.

The Working and Living Conditions of Agrarian Specialists

Rural officials believed that Moscow's neglect of the countryside was reflected in their poor pay. The salaries of agricultural specialists were miserly in comparison with specialists with similar training employed in industry and transport.[9] Rural specialists were acutely aware of this disparity and voiced their resentment openly. Some local specialists were even forced to find creative, if humiliating, means of raising money. A number of agronomists worked as shepherds, and some went begging door-to-door. One agronomist's assistant taught reading and writing to peasant children in order to scrape by.[10] Such behavior diminished the status of rural professionals in their own eyes and in those of the rural population. The example of pre-Revolutionary village schoolteachers, "grubbing for their salaries before the local zemstvo," is analogous here.[11] By 1927 and continuing until the end of the decade, agricultural specialists strenuously objected to the fact that they were faring poorly relative to specialists in other branches of the economy.[12] And this shortfall relative to their peers in other sectors of the economy made all the difference. The issue of relatively low salaries was framed by agricultural specialists themselves as a great insult to their professional self-esteem.

The fact that the Commissariat's local specialists found their living and working standards unbearable is reflected in the enormous turnover of its personnel, what Commissariat of Agriculture officials lamented as an "exodus." Employees fled from the land administration to other economic agencies where their skills were better rewarded. Tempted by promises of higher wages, better apartments, and greater prestige, officials and specialists marketed their skills to the highest bidder.[13] Most left to work in other economic agencies, such as transportation and especially industry, where they received from two to five times the salary they drew in agricultural work. Highly educated workers in Narkomzem received only as much as clerks in some other organizations, and some staff were even willing to take secretarial jobs in industrial enterprises. In addition to higher pay, the prestige associated with industry was much greater in the "proletarian dictatorship," headed by a party that called itself the representative of the working class.

Although experts sometimes quit the profession entirely, choosing to work in better-paid and more distinguished occupations, agricultural specialists more often would bounce around in land work from region to region, searching for better conditions, peddling their skills to specialist-starved local governments. Narkomzem used derisive if theatrical terms for people who capitalized on these conditions: they were "touring performers" (*gastrolery*) or "Flying Dutchmen" (*letuchshie gollandtsy*).[14] Agronomists who remained in the same district for two years were considered "old men."[15] One specialist who took advantage of this situation serves as an example.[16] According to the Commissariat's weekly journal in 1928, this man scoured the national press responding to some of the many advertisements inviting surveyors to specialist-poor land sections. He sent applications to several places but only accepted offers where he could haggle for travel expenses and better wages. In this way "this touring performer circled practically the entire USSR," finding employment in Odessa, Kharkov, the Caucasus, Archangel, Tver, Perm, Omsk, Biisk, Blagoveshchensk, Kustanai, and Samarkand. He never spent more than six months in any one place because he could always find a land section desperate for experienced surveyors and was willing to outbid for their scarce services.

The most pronounced exodus of specialists occurred at the lowest level of the agrarian aid network, the three thousand or so aid stations created in the 1920s. In 1928, a study of Kostroma province undertaken by Rabkrin showed that the one factor that most hindered agronomic work was the extraordinary turnover of personnel. In 1924–25, 35 percent of all agronomists hired that year for the local aid network left their jobs. The figure shot up to 75 percent in 1925–26. And a remarkable four of every five agronomists hired by Kostroma aid stations in 1928 quit the same year.[17] The report asserted that this problem was no less pronounced among district agronomists. To counteract this trend, in 1928 Narkomzem began awarding financial retention bonuses to specialists who remained in their jobs for one year.[18]

Very difficult work conditions were another major cause of the extraordinary turnover of agricultural personnel. Woefully inadequate transportation, equipment, and housing were part of daily life for provincial officialdom. Agronomists asked for "the elementary means of production: a horse for travel, a very modest apartment (preferably one with both basic heating and lighting), a modest amount of space for the aid station."[19] These basics were by no means guaranteed for the overwhelming majority of local specialists throughout the 1920s, despite repeated instructions to local officials from the Council of People's Commissars (Sovnarkom) and Central Executive Committee (TsIK).[20] The absence of funds for transportation was especially troubling since the average local agronomist was responsible for eighty-eight villages and four to five thousand farms. Only 40 percent of district agronomic stations possessed a horse for the use of its specialists.[21]

Agronomists complained that "we work more with our legs than with our head," an embarrassing statement for a scientist struggling for status. The lack of apartments was considered an especially egregious indignity. In some cases, the local executive committee would take the space allotted to the agronomic aid point and rent it out for more profitable purposes when the agronomist took an extended trip to villages in the region. Instances are recorded of agronomists returning from their excursions only to find that local executive committee chairmen were using these spaces as bakeries, stores, or wine shops.[22] Another agronomist was fired when, after a laborer drove a cart on the experimental station's field ruining an entire year's worth of work, he angrily called the driver a "klutz." The executive committee removed him for "insulting the proletariat."[23]

Moreover, most agricultural specialists seem to have greatly disliked the rural setting in which they worked. It is striking that Russian rural specialists trained to work among the peasantry with the goal of improving the quality of farming frequently were intolerant both of farmers and their milieu. Naturally, most officials and specialists were posted outside the big cities in small towns or villages.[24] Despite the occasional passage of apparently unenforceable legislation intended to improve the lot of local agricultural personnel, most of them desperately schemed to remain in a city, especially Moscow or St. Petersburg. This yearning to remain in urban areas can be documented for the entire decade in numerous sources, both published and archival.[25] Reluctance to live in the countryside even extended to the graduates of the country's most prestigious agricultural institute, Moscow's Timiriazev Academy, at which the Soviet Union's internationally renowned agrarian experts served as instructors. Indeed, the issue reached the Politburo, where at a 1925 session a speaker remarked that recent graduates of the Academy simply refused to accept appointments to the localities.[26] In 1927, a Rabkrin inspector confirmed that students fresh from the agricultural departments of technical institutes did everything they could to stay in the center.[27] Barring an appointment to a position in Moscow or Leningrad, they would take jobs in the capitals as "statisticians, accountants, salesmen, ticket takers, etc."[28] In 1928 and 1929, reports of refusal to accept postings outside the big cities became even more common. Lezhnev-Finkovskii, the head of Narkomzem's agronomic section, told the Fourth Congress of Land Workers in frustration in 1929, "Many agronomists do not want to go to the village at all," and their refusal has become a "mass phenomenon."[29] The more education an agronomist possessed, the less likely he or she was to accept an appointment in the provinces. Narkomzem reinforced this pattern by posting the most promising graduates to positions in the large cities or to coveted posts in experimental stations while punishing the weaker students (and disciplining its own unsatisfactory employees) by sending them to jobs in rural areas. A posting outside of the cities was commonly known as "internal exile."

A feeling of antipathy between specialists and the mass of the peasantry could be mutual. This is not to say that all specialists failed to connect with the peasantry. Still, many peasants apparently did not value the agronomists' rare appearances among them. Peasants often either entirely refused to listen to experts' lectures, or rejected their advice (and even their authority to dispense advice) out of hand. One should note that by 1928–29 peasant rejection of agronomists might have been moderating, as specialists began to report that farmers—especially the innovators and the "well-off"—were becoming more interested in listening to their suggestions and trying them out. Yet it is also clear that many agronomists simply gave up on the rural population, having come to believe that in too many villages virtually no one was listening. Typical of this sort of complaint was one Saratov agronomist's observation that few peasants attended his talks. When they did, they were "dispassionate" and sometimes declared, "I myself am an agronomist. For ages I have been working the soil and I know how to run my own farm." When visiting experimental farms, "peasants usually announce that if *they* had such machines and resources their own fields would produce harvests no worse than the demonstrator fields" that agronomists had planted to exhibit the latest techniques.[30] Other peasants regarded specialists—especially young ones—as impractical or unskilled. A peasant from Vladimir province complained that as soon as a young agronomist arrived in the village, he began "chasing girls," causing his work to suffer.[31]

Fundamental clashes between urban and rural cultures were at the heart of the relationship between specialist and villager. Peasants' adherence to traditional methods of farming, and to what agronomists considered irrational folkways and superstitions, clearly aggravated many agronomists, some of whom over the course of the 1920s became disillusioned with the refusal of the "unenlightened" peasant masses to accept their teachings. The continuing belief that much of the peasantry was "agronomically illiterate" was pervasive among specialists, and, indeed, represented an essential dimension of their worldview.[32] One agronomist, a certain I. Galkin, cited a litany of peasant superstitions that undermined his work, including belief in the so-called rebirth of grain (for example, that wheat can turn into rye or that wheat seeds can give birth to rye plants); the idea that agronomists can control the weather; and the use of folk remedies to treat sick animals (such as treating cattle's stomach ailments with a mixture of urine and swill). For Galkin, the most frustrating was the belief that the three-field system had been ordained by God and represented the Holy Trinity. The persistence of this belief rendered infinitely more difficult the process of persuading a community to switch to multifield farming. All of these practices, he asserts, should "provoke horror in a cultured person." His conclusion: "the agronomist must be in the vanguard of reshaping the entire ideology of the peasantry."

Some land personnel referred with condescension to the "ignorance, stagnation, and lack of culture" among the land-working population. Yet they frequently found that political officials serving in the local soviet were just as stubborn and ill informed. Specialists often cited their unsatisfactory relationship with local power as a cause of increasing work-related frustration. They asserted that the local soviet executive committees did not take them seriously as professionals, and, in fact, put enormous obstacles in their way. The volost' soviet assigned them incessant office responsibilities, which they called the "scourge of office work." Specialists complained bitterly that this flood of unnecessary paperwork kept them from devoting sufficient attention to their scientific and technical responsibilities, and it "paralyzed their creative work among the peasantry."[33] An agronomist in Gomel' province described "drowning in a sea of paper."[34]

A 1927 report highlighted extraordinary bureaucratization in the land agencies that hindered specialists' ability to serve the rural population.[35] An undercover investigator visited the offices of an unnamed provincial land section and made a simple inquiry in writing: "Where in the province can one purchase purebred sheep?" The investigator waited patiently for an answer, expecting to linger for several hours at the most. This request, however, had to move through a veritable maze within the provincial office. Clerks registered the letter six to eight times in various sections and subsections. On four occasions during its journey, the letter came to the attention of a different section head. Three times along the way, officials delayed the progress of the letter when deciding to whom it should be sent, as if it were not obvious that a question about sheep should go to the sheep specialist. The individual who actually possessed the authority and knowledge to answer the question was the twelfth person to receive the request. In all, the letter about sheep changed hands twenty-two times. On the third day, the expert in sheep matters actually received the request. On the fourth day, the patient Rabkrin investigator, still waiting in the office, finally got his answer. "This is the case," the author concluded, "for every simple question. This sheep specialist or any other responsible person could provide an answer in one minute, either orally or in writing, if only he were liberated from this bureaucratic road."[36] Another investigation revealed that land offices took an average of eight to ten months to answer letters from farmers. Experts clearly displayed a sense of wounded professional honor in their insistence that they be allowed to do their jobs without being burdened by mundane and irrelevant tasks unrelated to their scientific training and official duties.[37]

Another example illustrates the frustration and low status of the local agronomist. In the mid-1920s, the Commissariat of Agriculture, facing a tremendous shortfall of resources to support local agronomic work and a drastic shortage of specialists, discovered a new means of reaching the villages. The Commissariat requested and received a train, which they called the "V. I. Lenin Agro-train," and used it as a platform for traveling exhibitions.[38] This train traveled by rail all over the Russian Republic, carrying in its cars exhibits of the latest farm implements, seeds, and machinery. It was staffed by the provincial or county agronomist, who would board the train in his or her respective locale and demonstrate the equipment to any curious farmers who made their way to the station. Indeed, thousands of peasants did board the train at one of the many stops, curious about the tools, lectures, and especially the films. Many villagers saw a moving picture for the first time, and they were shown outdoors to audiences of more than a thousand people. Films were shown on themes having to do with everyday life in the village, including short pieces on the advantages of tractors, the benefits of electrification, and "the struggle against syphilis."

The report of the train's sixth trip in 1926, however, shows that programs could be less successful in practice.[39] At several stops in the five Black Earth provinces, the chairmen of the local soviet conscripted the agronomists, pulling them off the train and enlisting them in various projects around the county, including gathering firewood, repairing school houses, inspecting buildings, and collecting taxes. As one specialist put it, splendidly displaying his professional pride, local officials must not "turn the agronomist on a mass scale into a footman, a secretary, a stable boy, a furnace stoker, a janitor."[40] In most places, he went on, soviet employees "had no understanding of the essence of agronomic work." They simply treated specialists like yet another functionary. "They most often look upon the agronomist as a specialist invited not to serve the [peasant] population, but to serve the executive committee of the volost' soviet."[41]

Local executive committee chairmen were favorite targets of specialists' fusillades at the end of the 1920s. One agronomist from the Urals oblast' complained that he was ordered to play the accordion at the chairman's late-night drinking parties. When he refused, the agronomist was arrested as an "antisocial element."[42] Accusations of specialist baiting were also common. Agricultural experts demanded to be treated with the respect they felt their profession commanded, and they believed that local soviets stood in the way.[43] Like peasants, the heads of land administrations were usually "agronomically illiterate." As one specialist put it in late 1929, "We have to work with people who do not know the difference between rye and wheat."[44] An agronomist from Tver stated that "we see that even the heads of land organs, leaders who carry out agricultural policy in the localities, are completely illiterate in the area of technical construction in agriculture, and that this illiteracy puts up large obstacles for unleashing every measure."[45] These statements are in some senses reminiscent of the antagonism between tsarist officials and agricultural specialists before 1917. To some local councilors, as Kimitaka Matsuzato has pointed out, the word *agronomist* was synonymous with "antichrist, rebel, and plotter."[46]

Specialists and the Ambiguous Appeal of Modernization

In this context, many nonparty specialists supported the promise of a rapid transformation, at least in the way Party leaders touted the process in 1928 and early 1929. That is, they supported the accelerated modernization of the Russian countryside and its subsequent integration into urban Soviet society, not its reenserfment.[47] One must be careful not to look back at the plans made in 1928–29 through the prism of the utter catastrophe of later months and years. There is evidence that the "socialist reconstruction of the countryside" appeared to many in the agricultural apparatus to be a major step forward toward realizing all the newest agronomic possibilities to which they had dedicated themselves. To agronomists, it appeared that change was only very slowly taking hold in isolated, inward-looking villages that were frequently reluctant to accept innovations preached by outsiders.

Accelerated modernization promised massive state investment, which was seriously lacking before early 1928, in the "agronomization" (*agronomizatsiia*) of the countryside. Agronomization—a word, not surprisingly, that was invented by agronomists—meant the reorganization of peasant farming along modern lines, including dismantling the three-field system, ending frequent land partitions, and eliminating strip farming, all of which agronomists considered to be embarrassing blights on Russian farming. The promise of advances in mechanization—the wide-scale supply of machines and new tools—was also extremely appealing to specialists.[48] At least as initially planned, large-scale, agricultural collectives empowered agrarian specialists by promising them a chance to practice their professions in much-improved circumstances. Peasants would finally rationalize and intensify their production under the direction of the scientific elite who would be given power to plan, organize, and direct production on these grand, modern farming enterprises. Enthusiasm over the promise of "industrializing" production is visible in statements of some specialists in 1928–29, especially before the violent and disorganizing nature of the drive to collectivize was fully realized.[49]

Kendall Bailes has convincingly argued that the "discussion of the First Five Year Plan and rapid, state-directed industrialization after 1926 promised to enhance the position and importance of technical experts in government."[50] At the same time, just as in Europe and America, state-directed modernization plans lifted experts' social status, about which engineers had an almost obsessive concern. It must have appeared to many in the lower levels of the agrarian bureaucracy that the mechanization and urbanization of the countryside would embellish the professional status, prestige, working conditions, and living standards of rural specialists. The Soviet industrialization of the countryside promised abundant dwellings and workspace on progressive farms that would be run by well-paid, highly valued specialists in the agricultural sciences.

In January 1929, the close connections among the agronomists' three major concerns—improved working conditions, enhanced professional status, and the vision of a modern countryside were expressed by a certain Suvarov, a noncommunist regional agronomist in Siberia: "It is necessary to carry out a struggle for living conditions. The agronomists' daily living standard is extremely poor. . . . Of course, without the improvement in living conditions it will be very difficult to work. But I think that we are all concerned with this question only thanks to our sincere goal of rebuilding the old, dark, cold, dirty, half-capitalist village which we inherited."[51]

Specialists hoped to use plans to develop the country for their own ends. A new countryside, they hoped, would put an end to the stigma of work in the village. Collective farms would be oases of science and culture. These farms were advertised as the only places where "many achievements of agronomy and science can be applied." In the words of one agronomist in 1929, "The land organs should structure their work so that the modern achievements of science do not remain inside the walls of scientific institutes or stuck in the heads of their employees sitting in the bureaucracy, but are adapted to practical work in agriculture in a mass way."[52]

It was during this period that agronomists started calling themselves "agronomic-engineers." They labeled their work "agroeconomic service," dressing their own profession in the language of the modern industrial-technological state.[53] They compared their role in the new countryside to the revered, prestigious, and powerful place that the industrial engineer had enjoyed for a decade. A leading official in Narkomzem asserted that the director of every sovkhoz must be an agronomist. Or as N. M. Antselovich made same the point, "It would never even enter anyone's mind to organize a factory without an engineer."[54]

Most specialists who supported the transformation of the countryside did so because they believed it would result in modernization. They did not envision their role in collectivization in terms of class war, as a way of arming the exploited poor peasantry against the rich, avaricious kulak. It is unlikely that most specialists would have supported such a rigid class line. Agronomists, in line with Commissariat of Agriculture's policies, only very rarely discussed kulaks. Incendiary class rhetoric by party officials would have fallen on deaf ears among the agronomists. Generally, the language of specialists was class neutral. Rather, they employed the idiom of "overcoming backwardness," as they remained concerned with modernization and rationalization, not social differentiation. As one of the Narkomzem leadership said at the January 1929 Congress of Agronomists, in a clear effort to enlist the support of a group that was less than excited about a class-war-based vision of the countryside as a means of reaching socialism,[55] "raising the harvest among the mass of the peasantry — this is the victory of socialism."[56] Before this audience, the leading party officials chose to equate socialism with an increase in the productivity of the rural economy, and the formula appears to have been widely accepted by specialists.[57] Indeed, the party leadership left room in their invitation to specialists to support rural transformation without undue concern for the class line. They advertised the "socialist reconstruction of the countryside" via collectivization (still discussed as a gradual process) as a movement in which specialists would serve in the vanguard of a struggle to improve harvests and raise the cultural level of the country.

To be sure, many specialists were skeptical about plans to collectivize the village, and this response also must be considered. Some were appalled by the prospect, as the opposition of leading specialists in Moscow to the First Five Year

Plan indicates (see next chapter). Furthermore, specialists bristled at the charges of anti-Soviet "sabotage" brought against many of them that surfaced with 1928–29 mass investigations of state employees.[58] One Narkomzem leader complained that an article in *Pravda* had absurdly called for the complete elimination of agronomic assistance organizations as a holdover from "the era of the zemstvo." He sarcastically wondered aloud whether railroads and Karl Marx's writings should not also be eradicated as relics of the same era.

A variety of specialists predicted disorganization, anticipated a major divergence between the Party's grandiose goals and the actual allocation of resources, or expressed skepticism about the Five Year Plan's ambitious tempos.[59] Conversely, in some corners of the party, suspicion of nearly all nonparty agricultural specialists was pervasive. Sustaining its spirit of antagonism toward Narkomzem's leadership and specialists, the Commissariat of Agriculture's party cell complained that too many agricultural experts expressed reservations about the accelerating pace of industrialization. Lower-level party cell representatives argued that open support for socialist goals by experts was trickery that disguised a negative attitude toward the general line of the party.[60] Party personnel hawks were clearly very worried about the dedication of (overwhelmingly noncommunist and nonproletarian) local specialists to the construction of socialism as they understood it.

Yet extant material in the Rabkrin archives also indicates that, despite the vehemence of many inspectors' class-based hostility to nonparty, bourgeois experts, investigations did not turn up evidence of significant anti-Soviet feeling or activity among local agrarian specialists.[61] One report asserted that specialists were "Russian chauvinists." Some Bolsheviks openly appealed to this patriotism, celebrating "the enormous significance [of agronomists' work] for our country."[62] Even in the political environment of 1928–29 in which "hostile and alien elements" were hunted in every corner, Rabkrin did not consider most nonparty specialists to be anti-Soviet. For example, by 1929 only 8 percent of those 406 people purged as "socially alien elements" in fourteen local land sections investigated were agronomists.[63] As late as mid-1929, a Rabkrin inspector recommended promoting "honest specialists, who do work of high quality, accurately, clearly and rapidly, purely observing the class line."[64] Only 20 percent or so of the local cadres removed in 1929 were fired as "anti-Soviet elements."[65] Archival material also indicates that the entire Narkomzem leadership, even those who were intent on uncovering class enemies in the apparatus, assumed that local specialists were generally loyal, regardless of social origin.

Thus, the Communist Party, between late 1928 and mid-1929, rather than exclusively scapegoating and then purging local specialists, overtly appealed to their professional and cultural interests. The Communist Party did not hope to attract specialists by urging them to wage war against kulaks. Instead, the Soviet government invited specialists into the Soviet reconstruction project at least in part on the basis of healing their wounded professional pride, promising a privileged position and better working conditions in a new Soviet countryside. In early 1929, several party leaders openly, even enthusiastically, offered specialists an important role in the transformation. The chairman of the Central Executive Committee, M. I. Kalinin, delivered a speech at the Fourth Conference of RSFSR Land Workers in January 1929 in which he extended an invitation to nonparty agricultural specialists on the basis of the concerns that he understood were at the top of their agenda.[66] Kalinin first spoke about the primacy of their role in the economy, comparing their mission directly with engineers. "The land worker should play no less of a role in our soviet system and in our local executive committees than a worker of Vesenkha," that is, an engineer working in the industrial trusts. He flattered agronomists' aspirations to lead and direct rural reconstruction, addressing them grandly as "engineers of agricultural production." Deputy Chair of Sovnarkom USSR Rudzutak made many of the same appeals at the Second Agronomic Congress later that month.[67] The agronomist should not only be a consultant on agronomic questions, he asserted, but a real leader who makes serious decisions connected with raising the level of agriculture. Rudzutak envisioned the creation of "cultural centers" revolving around new collective farms, with the agronomists as their nucleus, which would lead millions of peasants in the massive reorganization of agriculture.

Kalinin went further, highlighting his sympathy with the specialists' cultural concerns as urban people in the village, tiny islands in a sea of rural backwardness. "Our party considers collectivization the most important task. It is therefore necessary to attract [talented and educated people] for work in this project, so that they can really create and build." During their time working in the village among the peasantry, specialists should not *omuzhichivat'sia* ("to become peasantized," from the word *muzhik*) or swallowed up by peasant culture and the rural milieu. On the contrary, specialists must maintain their urban ways, so that their work on collective farms allows them "to grow culturally."[68] Lunacharsky and other party leaders flattered specialists with references to their "superior culture."

Thus, local specialists' reactions to the prospect of large-scale construction of collective farms and the mechanization and industrialization of the countryside was mixed. We cannot consider specialists a monolithic group wholly united in their interests and reactions. Historians have not allowed sufficiently for the possibility that many nonparty, rural specialists, frustrated and discouraged by what must have appeared to be an unbreakable cycle of irrational state price policies, marketing shortfalls, and scissors crises endemic to NEP by 1928, interpreted the *promise* of the state's collectivization of Soviet agriculture as rationalizing, modern, progressive, and simultaneously a way of regenerating their wounded professional identities. Considering the great demand for specialists to serve on collective farms in 1928–29 in light of their rapid expansion, specialists found themselves arguing from a position of strength. Agronomists understood that the moment was right to insist on the recognition that was lacking earlier in the decade. Plans promised agrarian professionals greater power and a special place as architects who would design and execute plans for a new, modern, industrialized countryside.

Leading specialists and their political patrons in Moscow, however, many of whom were openly critical of collectivization and industrialization plans in this period, were treated much more harshly. Their open dissent had repercussions for themselves and for the entire organization.

6

Better Red than Bread?

Purge, Collectivization, and the Defeat of the People's Commissariat of Agriculture, 1927-1929

Contradictory impulses competed inside the party-state in 1928–29 as battles over methods of rural modernization and socialization intensified. The Commissariat of Agriculture's gradualist approach increasingly came under attack, as did its specialists and political leadership. How did the Commissariat's leadership react to peasants' unwillingness to deliver grain to the state in early 1928? How did the regime's intensified interest in purging "alien and hostile elements" affect the Commissariat in 1928–29, and how did the Commissariat leadership respond? What was the fate of Smirnov and his associates, who had long frustrated the very organizations that would carry out the 1928–29 purge? Specialists and officials whom Smirnov had been protecting for years came under withering fire from Stalin's associates after the defeat of the Left Opposition and the attack on the Right. Records of investigations of Narkomzem on the eve of collectivization reveal continuing struggles over class categories and ideas of "alienness" that permeated the revolutionary regime at the end of the decade. By the end of 1929, these battles ended in the defeat of the Moscow Commissariat of Agriculture's gradualist approach to remaking rural Russia.

Going Down with the NEP

Turning Points

In 1926 and 1927 opinions inside the party began shifting more strongly against the conciliation of the peasantry that was the heart of NEP. International and domestic developments contributed to a growing sense at the top ranks of the party that the country must more quickly secure increased funds for investment in industrial projects while guaranteeing the food needs of a growing city population and the agricultural raw material needs of industry.[1]

One reason why the tide turned against the Right beginning in 1926 was the death of Feliks Dzerzhinskii, widely regarded as one of the most powerful (together with Rykov) and prestigious of the Right's advocates. International developments also had a major impact. In May of 1927, the Tory government in Great Britain broke off diplomatic relations with the Soviet Union, causing a major war scare. Peasants hoarded food in anticipation of what party leaders publicly called an "inevitable" war with England, Poland, or another Western nation. Trade ties between the USSR and Great Britain, its largest trading partner, were severed. At almost the same time, an attempted revolution in China failed. Suddenly, the USSR's international isolation was felt very keenly. In light of saber rattling by the British, concerns about quickly building an industrial base sufficient for defending the country's borders became paramount. Concern about internal enemies also grew. The GPU swept through cities and villages, arresting several thousand Nepmen and kulaks.

Two branches of the Right wing, one headed by Stalin and the other by Bukharin, began to divide over questions of the tempo and methods of industrialization. Stalin and his group began to show frustration with the snail's pace of progress in the ninth year of the revolution, lurching to the left. By early 1927, patience was wearing thin among many party members with the notion that the USSR could gradually "grow into" socialism. Sharp disagreements in the party about the future course of agricultural policy and the state's relationship with the peasantry came to the fore that year. The left wing of the party, including Trotsky, the economist Evgenii Preobrazhenskii, and their supporters insisted on substantially increased investment into heavy industry and the collective farming sector. Arguing that unpredictable yields made it difficult to plan investment into heavy industry, they advocated higher taxation and a price policy that would extract more grain from the peasantry at a lower cost to the state. Grain procurement targets had fallen short by two hundred million puds in 1925–26, for example, which led to a decrease in investment plans for capital construction in industry. They did believe, however, that changes in taxation and price policy must be undertaken within the framework of NEP; none of the Left advocated forced collectivization.

Smirnov and the moderate Rightists who supported Bukharin continued to argue that party leaders did not sufficiently appreciate the complexity of the agricultural problem or the full gravity of agriculture in the national economy. Recovery in this sector could not be rushed, they insisted. As they had all decade, moderate party leaders turned to the agriculture commissariat to provide empirical data for a gradualist approach to the modernization of agricultural production without coercion. Smirnov had shared many of the positions of Bukharin,

Rykov, Tomskii, and other Rightists, a coalition that sided—at least in the conditions then current—with the interests of agriculture against party leftists and industrial interests. Although their complaints were directed in part against Trotsky's Oppositions, Narkomzem aimed its accusations more specifically at Vesenkha and other institutional proponents of investment in heavy industry at the expense of agriculture. (The United Opposition of 1926–27 joined Zinov'ev and Kamenev's Leningrad Opposition and Trotsky's Left Opposition. I will continue to refer to the Opposition grouped around Trotsky as the "Left.") In Gosplan, Commissariat specialists argued vigorously for granting agriculture "the place it deserved" both in economic and in financial plans, although Narkomzem's standing in that organization was weakening quickly.[2]

The Left also increasingly charged that party policy toward the peasantry benefited the kulaks and Nepmen private traders. Among Stalin's supporters in the party majority, including the OGPU, one sees in 1926 and 1927 more frequent references to *kulak-zazhitochnyi* agriculture, a term that eradicated the distinction between the peasant-exploiter and the "strong, sober, well-to-do" upper stratum of the middle peasantry.[3] Further, beginning in 1924, the OGPU had been compiling records of hundreds of instances of "kulak terror," including numerous instances of murder, assault, and threats against soviet officials.[4] These investigations of alleged kulak counterrevolutionary activities picked up steam in 1926. Not surprisingly, in light of the new suspicion of the kulak, Narkomzem would come under increased scrutiny for its long-held, sophisticated defense of the well-off strata in the village.

The Commissariat's Approach

While many party members viewed the production capacity of the countryside with "dangerous complacency"[5] in 1927, the officials and specialists of the People's Commissariat of Agriculture rejected this benign view. Key parts of the agricultural sector, they feared, still had not fully recovered to pre-war levels in important regions, and did not begin to approach the productivity of the Soviet Union's western European neighbors. As had been the case for decades, the countryside remained one bad harvest away from disaster. Smirnov wrote in an article that appeared in April 1927, "The general level reached by our agriculture is still lower than before the war."[6]

In the summer of 1927, People's Commissar Smirnov summed up his view of the Soviet countryside.[7] The development of agriculture in the USSR, he wrote, must pass through two stages. The first stage is "to transform our *agrarian* country into an *industrial-agrarian* country, and the second stage is to transform it from an industrial-agrarian country to an *industrial* country." The Soviet Union was moving very slowly through these stages. In its current condition, Smirnov wrote, the country was still solidly agrarian. The pace for advancing to the next stage was deliberate and depended on a number of factors, including the massive influx of machines into the village and the coincident intensification of farming. "The length of these stages is now difficult to determine. It depends on how quickly we succeed in introducing agricultural machines, making agriculture more intensive, and converting agriculture to superior forms of farming, which in turn must introduce profound changes in agriculture."

Smirnov's statement summarizes the Commissariat's ethos on the eve of Stalin's "revolution from above." The USSR would remain a peasant country into the foreseeable future. In some areas agricultural production had made impressive strides and had caught up to—even surpassed— pre-war levels, but as a whole it still had not recovered sufficiently. Production lagged especially compared to Western countries and was not gaining ground relative to them. The necessary preconditions for a wide-scale, socialist transformation of peasant farming simply were not yet in place; strong but balanced government policy was needed to advance the country, albeit slowly, to the next stage.

At a meeting of the Zemplan Plenum in November 1927, one of the Commissariat's leading economists, N. P. Makarov, developed these points. He noted that in most of the major producing regions agricultural output still had not reached pre-war levels.[8] More importantly, although the rate of growth of Soviet agriculture was slightly higher than the pre-war level, it had actually slowed since 1925. Meanwhile, the splintering of farms into smaller and less productive units continued unabated, as did population pressures and poverty. Yields in Denmark and Germany were four times higher than those in Samara and Saratov provinces, two important grain-producing areas. By illustrating just how far the USSR lagged behind these Western economies after years of reconstruction, Makarov's comparisons were devastating to a Commissariat and Party leadership intent on catching up.[9] The country's progress in matching the output of less industrialized countries such as China gave officials little comfort.

Another Narkomzem economist, A. A. Manuilov, agreed with Makarov, arguing that with regard to production and sown area, gains were slowing and most likely would not accelerate soon. Annual increases in sown area had begun to taper off in the previous three years. In addition, although the total amount of land dedicated to growing industrial crops was much greater in the Soviet era (nearly 17 percent in 1926 versus around 9 percent before the war), the proportion had not grown since 1924. Indeed, the land dedicated to industrial crops had dropped slightly, and certain crops had shown almost no expansion in sown area since 1922. Further growth in these stagnant areas, Manuilov argued, was impossible without the "reconstruction of agriculture." In conjunction with these negative trends, the sown area devoted to grains had increased, growing by 18–20 percent in 1926. Despite the progress that had been made in the 1920s, still over 80 percent of all sown area was planted with grain, a discouraging reflection of the continuing reliance on extensive forms of agricultural production. The growth in livestock farming had nearly stopped, an ominous sign since the transition to multifield farming largely depended on the availability and quality of draft animals. Together, these factors represented a potentially calamitous "deintensification" of agriculture on the horizon. Agriculture, Manuilov summed up, is regressing toward extensive grain farming, threatening what might become a "depression in intensive and technical cultures."[10]

An Unfilled Prescription for Growth

As late as December 1927, Narkomzem's priority remained the "fundamental reconstruction of the commune along more efficient and productive lines," not the headlong advance toward the construction of collective farms. The Commissariat emphasized that in the present conditions the ideal type of farming organization in most regions for the foreseeable future would remain the commune, which continued to control about 97 percent of the country's farmland. Professor N. Rudin, the author of the 1922 Land Code, stressed that the scientifically organized, well-equipped, and productive commune remained a viable form of socioeconomic organization. Rudin, a senior official in the Commissariat's Land Reorganization and Improvement Administration, argued that sufficient "objective preconditions" still did not exist for the rapid and extensive development of collective farms. Instead, he advocated that communal production should be reorganized so that it would "use territory rationally." The rationalized commune should have "improved, multifield crop rotation, with strips that are few, wide, and well-suited for working the land, . . . correctly organized pasturing of cattle, and twenty to thirty years between repartitions of land."[11]

Commissariat representatives also vigorously protested the "incorrect" price policies of the finance commissariat and the Central Committee. The Commissariat leadership urged the Commissariat of Finance to keep prices of industrial goods low and purchase prices for raw materials and crops produced by peasants relatively high. A 1927 article by Manuilov summarized the Commissariat's position on the persistent output and marketing problems of Russian agriculture.[12] In short, he argued that the hasty development of industry slighted the interests of agriculture and would harm the national economy in the long run. Manuilov blamed neither farmers nor Narkomzem for agriculture's lagging production. Rather, he laid the blame squarely on factors outside farmers' control, including inflation in the price of manufactures, the government's failure to export sufficient surpluses (resulting in trade imbalances), and the consequent inability of peasants to accumulate capital in cash. The greatest problem, however, had been the drop in the state-set purchase price of intensive crops. Low prices naturally discouraged sowings by farmers. Peasants could not afford to risk experimenting with growing nonfood crops if they could not sell them for a reasonable price, and as a result they had fallen back to growing staple food crops. The complete absence of incentives to grow technical crops created a shortfall in production and left industry with insufficient quantities to satisfy demand. Manuilov and other agricultural specialists urged decreasing the amount of state investment in heavy industry while increasing spending on developing consumer industries.[13] Most importantly, the government needed to adjust prices in favor of the rural producer, as it had during the 1923 scissors crisis, by lowering prices for industrial goods and raising them for agricultural produce. The government, therefore, must spend more on light industry to step up the production of consumer goods (this was also the position of Rykov and the Right wing). Narkomzem officials continued to point attention to these price imbalances, blaming central policymakers rather than the peasantry or its own land agencies for shortfalls in marketed produce.[14]

Along with the rebalance of prices, Narkomzem demanded an acceleration of the supply of equipment to the countryside. In a mid-1927 article, deputy commissar of agriculture Sviderskii looked toward the future of rural Russia. He envisioned a modern countryside with mechanized communal production.[15] The new village would "be evident in the transition of agriculture to better methods of production; in the transition to multifield farming and to better forms of land use; in the development of fruitful animal husbandry and more lucrative crops; in the extensive distribution and use of machines, mineral fertilizers, and improved seeds; in measures to raise our inordinately feeble harvests. [These measures will] increase the output of all agriculture and increase the well-being and living standards of the peasant masses."[16] Sviderskii emphasized the need to distribute technology to raise harvests and improve living standards. Technical progress was a prerequisite for building socialism. He closely linked the building of socialism with raising the technical level of peasant farming and, in particular, small-scale, communal peasant farming. This position was consistent with the line that the Commissariat had taken for six years. Only with a massive dedication of resources to the countryside could agriculture recover and the foundation for the socialist reconstruction of agriculture be laid. The reconstruction of communal farming still served as the dominant metaphor for the Narkomzem leadership.

In this period, it was progressively clear that Narkomzem had essentially become a "Commissariat of *Communal* Agriculture." Strongly discouraging the creation of separated households, the Commissariat's leaders also argued that the time was not yet right for the creation of kolkhozy on a large scale. The new emphasis at the Fifteenth Party Congress in December 1927 on intensifying the creation of collective farms increasingly made the Commissariat look like a relic of a bygone era, the era of traditional communal farming. Smirnov and his specialists seemed to represent a fading epoch.

Planning and Collective Farms

The Commissariat's Moscow leadership anticipated that the First Five Year Plan would create a great imbalance in the national economy due to its "neglect" of the proper place of agriculture. Narkomzem's leadership had come under attack earlier when it issued its "perspective" five year plans in 1923–24. These earlier plans had been more akin to general recommendations and predictions than to the rigid plans of the later years. In 1927, Narkomzem's specialists remained wholly unrepentant about the quality of their modest earlier plans. Most of their predictions, they claimed, had been on target. Deputy Commissar Teodorovich boasted about the earlier plans: "A feeling of realism, an understanding of peasant life guaranteed the completely rational and completely correct organization of Narkomzem's planning work."[17] This leitmotif of urging "realism" about the pace of industrialization continued for the next year, even as the Central Committee Secretariat and Vesenkha created incredible planning targets.[18]

When the Fifteenth Party Congress called for the accelerated creation of a substantial collective farm sector, the leadership of the Moscow Commissariat expressed skepticism that the countryside was prepared. The lack of financial resources and machines for these proposed collective farms led to pessimism among Commissariat officials. In 1928, state and collective farms still occupied only 2.7 percent of the country's sown area. Narkomzem did not even possess an accurate count of collective farms as late as early 1927, an indication of how little attention the agency devoted to them.[19] In 1927–28, neither Smirnov nor anyone else believed that the state would or should force peasants onto collective farms, nor did he anticipate that communal farming would soon be nearly eradicated altogether.[20] As late as the end of 1927, Gosplan's five year plan anticipated that the number of noncollectivized, communal households would actually increase to 26.5 million by 1932, as larger households continued to fragment into smaller ones.

Still, Smirnov was hopeful that the gradual creation of limited numbers of collectives would curtail this splintering, which he despised as a root of so many of Russian agriculture's problems.[21] He apparently had in mind the TOZ (association for the joint cultivation of land), the simplest type of production collective. In these voluntary associations, members did some of the farming jointly, but maintained family ownership of their equipment and most of their livestock and still controlled their land. Collective farms would raise the technical level of farming because they could more easily adapt to the introduction of technical crops, the presence of quality draft animals, better equipment and machines, and other innovations. Many farmers could have access to these animals and tools only on collective farms. At the same time, Narkomzem officials maintained that these newly established collectives could act as large model farms, demonstrating to neighboring villagers the benefits of scientifically organized and mechanized production.

The Attack Begins, 1927–1928

Over the course of 1927, both the Left Opposition (until its defeat in November) and, increasingly, Stalin's circle, launched ferocious attacks against the Commissariat's leading specialists. For their part, the Agrarian Marxists and their party supporters increasingly accused Narkomzem specialists of being "neopopulists," people who quietly harbored anti-Soviet sentiments. M. Ustinov derided the editorial board of the Narkomzem journal *Sel'sko-khoziaistvennaia zhizn'* for its "thoroughly Populist character" that represented "a throwback to Populist ideology."[22] In July, an article by the Oppositionist Zinov'ev in the Communist Party journal Bol'shevik accused Kondrat'ev of being the head of a "kulak party" that included Chaianov, Chelintsev, and Makarov.[23] Statements about the alleged political shortcomings of specialists and the party leaders who protected them appeared frequently, especially after the Fifteenth Party Congress in December 1927. Narkomzem's leaders found it increasingly difficult to shield their specialists from accusations that they favored the kulak. The Commissariat leadership continued to argue that a strong sector of "kulak agriculture," with its attendant exploitation of the poor and middle peasant, was not a serious likelihood or threat in the near term. Such positions left Narkomzem open to charges that its leadership, in league with Rykov and the Right wing, were "liberals" (later "wreckers") who continued to ignore a pernicious and expanding "kulak threat."

In the wake of the Central Committee's defeat of the Trotsky opposition in November 1927, a political offensive against Narkomzem lasted for more than a year, simultaneous with and parallel to the attack on the Right wing of the party. Stalin's followers took over the Left's critique of the NEP majority, subjecting the Right to precisely the same tactics that they had used against the Trotskyists. In the words of the historian Robert Daniels, "It would take uncanny dialectical subtlety to distinguish between the new Stalinist analysis and the warnings which the Left Opposition had been making for years."[24] In the political atmosphere of late 1927 and early 1928, the Commissariat's approach to rural reconstruction left it vulnerable to charges of "Right deviationism." At the Fifteenth Party Congress, Molotov, head of the party Committee on Work in the Village, outlined Narkomzem's "errors." Stressing that a vicious class struggle between capitalist and socialist elements was underway in the village, Molotov scolded Narkomzem for the persistent shortcomings of agricultural production and for the failure of agriculture to rebound to pre-war levels. More ominously, he attacked the "ideology of several professors from Narkomzem who completely support the line that calls for assisting the development of capitalist processes in the village." Molotov went on to accuse Kondrat'ev and other specialists of being both Trotskyists *and* Right deviationists (no easy feat): "The ideology of Trotsky accords with the ideology of these agrarian professors from Narkomzem and some other agencies. Although frequently they carry out very valuable specialized work, generally they aim to carry out an economic policy in the village that is . . . hostile to Soviet power. This is the line of the kulaks, the line of the bourgeoisie. Everyone should always remember this, especially the leaders of our land organs."[25]

Molotov issued a warning here to Narkomzem's leaders to remember that many of their specialists had designed policies favorable to capitalist "enemies" of the party. Such language, of course, borrowed wholesale the rhetoric of the Left Opposition that the Politburo majority had just succeeded in crushing. Indeed, Commissariat officials and specialists now found themselves under ferocious attack for having advocated policies that the party leadership had endorsed for years. In this sense, NEP itself had sown the seeds for the Commissariat's final destruction as the political paradigm under Stalin suddenly shifted from appeasement of the village to confrontation.

The Grain Procurement Crisis

By early 1928, Narkomzem RSFSR was viewed by the Stalinist group as a weed that had set its roots deep in the countryside. The organization was headed by a Central Committee member who had developed a gradualist strategy antithetical to the approach of the Stalin group. Smirnov had established a number of institutional bases, including the Orgburo and the Council of People's Commissars of the RSFSR, where he had served since 1925 as deputy chairman. Barraged with charges of vedomstvennost', he had stubbornly, with mixed success, fought battles over personnel, policies, and budgets. Employing the politics of expertise, he was fiercely protective of his experts, themselves under fire for their "neopopulist" or "capitalist" views. As head of the Commissariat for five years, he had made Narkomzem RSFSR an obstacle to groups who supported rapid industrialization at the expense of investment in agriculture. Identifying the interests of the countryside—and ultimately himself—with his organization, Smirnov continued to offer his vision of a modern, socialist countryside prospering within the confines of NEP as he understood it. Smirnov's position was increasingly at odds with the vision offered by Stalin.

The Stalin group understood that in order to rein in the Commissariat they would have to dislodge Smirnov. Only in his absence could Narkomzem be fundamentally reorganized. They strove to replace its political leadership and leading specialists with individuals more sympathetic to an accelerated collectivization of agriculture that would more quickly eradicate the vestiges of rural capitalism.

The grain procurement crisis of January 1928 created the conditions conducive to a full-scale assault on Narkomzem. By December 1927, state procurement organs had collected only about one-half to three-quarters of the grain that peasants had sold during the same period in 1926 as farmers delivered less to state collection points. In the face of low state purchase prices, peasants with surplus produce were, quite rationally, holding onto it to sell at higher prices in the winter and spring. Stalin used the crisis as a pretext for attacking the Right-dominated government and economic administrations, alleging they had ineptly managed agriculture, resulting in another year of very low peasant marketings.[26] Stalin immediately blamed kulaks for the crisis. He accused them of holding the country hostage, as they withheld grain at a time when the army and the cities lacked sufficient food. The regime reacted with emergency measures, invoking article 107 of the 1926 criminal code to arrest the "speculators" who "hoarded grain" by refusing to sell to procurement agencies. The government closed peasant markets and confiscated "surplus" grain stocks, copying the war communist methods of 1918–20. These confiscations later became known as the Urals-Siberian method (and they would be repeated the following spring). Stalin found fault with incompetent and alien local officials who allegedly appeased kulak and capitalist elements. Peasants reduced sowings and slaughtered animals, repeating farmers' reactions to requisitioning during the Civil War. The OGPU, whose powers were growing rapidly, was given extraordinary powers to arrest and imprison traders and "speculators," and the spring of 1928 saw a wave of violence in the countryside against villagers. Smirnov, Teodorovich, and the Commissariat's leading specialists vehemently opposed the grain requisitions that Stalin ordered during his foray into Western Siberia in January and February 1928. The Commissariat leadership anticipated the disastrous consequences of the drastic shifts in policy against the middle peasants and kulaks and, ultimately, against the great majority of the communal peasantry. Inside the Politburo, Bukharin and Rykov also denounced this "temporary" return to Civil War methods and the implicit destruction of the smychka partnership between peasant and proletarian. Ultimately, the grain crisis proved to many in the party that the policies of NEP could not supply the state with the resources necessary for industrialization, while highlighting the unreliability of much of the peasantry and the state apparatus.

Commissariat officials, meanwhile, dug in their heels, refusing to reproach farmers for the 1928 shortfalls. They did not frame the deficits as a consequence of rich peasants' criminal antagonism to the proletarian state (i.e., as kulak hoarding, unbridled speculation, or sabotage). A return to Civil War methods was not justified.[27] Instead, Narkomzem first blamed unfavorable weather in the grain regions in the spring and summer of 1927. The Commissariat's second explanation for the marketing shortfalls was the absence of manufactured goods available for purchase, especially the shortages of cotton, linen, and wool cloth whose production had either remained stable or declined in comparison with the previous year.[28] This shortfall greatly reduced farmers' incentive to sell their produce. The final, but most important reason for the marketing crisis, they argued, was irrational state-set prices for grain paid by government procurement agencies. Purchase prices had dropped sharply in the period between September and December to a level well below free-market prices. The Commissariat's leadership had been railing against these unbalanced prices for over a year. In effect, price policies forced farmers to direct their grain away from government purchasing agencies. As a logical response to the situation, farmers either used the grain to fatten their livestock, which they could still sell on the free market, or they sold grain for higher prices in peasant markets.

How did the Commissariat of Agriculture recommend that the party address the crisis? In general, specialists in the Commissariat of Agriculture (as well as in the Commisariat of Finance) called for the restoration of market equilibrium in the spirit of NEP. The state must provide the countryside with more manufactured goods. Collection agents in the localities must be allowed more flexibility to set higher purchase prices. Teodorovich argued that sown area must be increased by giving peasants in the grain regions better means of production, especially draft animals.[29] With the lessons of the Civil War in its institutional memory, Narkomzem correctly anticipated that requisitions would simply reduce peasant incentives to produce.

Stalin and much of the Communist Party, however, had tired of NEP's concessions to the "capitalist" peasantry. In the words of Lewis Siegelbaum, "In general one can say that the regime acted irrationally only in terms of the market principles it was increasingly anxious to overcome, and that especially for Stalin, political rationality [defeating the Right] had become paramount."[30]

Exit Smirnov

The Commissariat of Agriculture RSFSR, committed to the nonviolent stimulation of agricultural production through market and price mechanisms, could not long survive the abandonment of the New Economic Policy in its present form. In mid-February 1928, the Central Committee, dominated by Stalin, transferred Smirnov out of the Commissariat of Agriculture into a position in the Central Committee Secretariat. His deputies of the past five years, Teodorovich and Sviderskii, were dismissed within a month.[31] Along with the removal of these powerful communist patrons, nearly the entire political and specialist leadership of the Commissariat was ousted from the organization. They either were fired as political or social undesirables, resigned, or were transferred to other posts. On March 20, 1928, Kondrat'ev was officially dismissed from his positions in Zemplan and the finance commissariat, labeled untrustworthy because of his earlier sympathies with the Socialist Revolutionary Party.[32] The wholesale firings at Narkomzem boded ill for the Right wing of the Communist Party, serving as an early warning that trouble was on the horizon.

After Smirnov's transfer in February, forty-seven-year-old Nikolai Afanas'evich Kubiak became the new People's Commissar of Agriculture for the RSFSR. Born in 1881 into a worker's family, Kubiak worked in a variety of factories as an electrician in early adulthood. He spent several years in prison for revolutionary activity between 1908 and 1912, then spent many years in exile. From May to October 1917, he headed a zemstvo administration in Sestroretskaia. In October, local Bolsheviks transformed the zemstvo into a soviet, which he headed until March 1918. From May of 1919, Kubiak served as the Commissar of Agriculture for the Northern Oblast', and in 1920 he became chair of the Central Committee of the agriculture workers' trade union. A Central Committee member since the Twelfth Party Congress (1923), Kubiak was promoted to the Central Committee Secretariat in February 1927.[33] Ivan Evdokimovich Klimenko and Aleksandr Ivanovich Muralov were appointed Kubiak's deputies, replacing Sviderskii and Teodorovich.[34]

Narkomzem's new leaders immediately fired many provincial land officials for "inordinate delays and passivity in preparing the spring sowing campaigns."[35] The leadership announced new antikulak, anticommune, and procollectivization policies.[36] Kubiak's first speech in the Commissariat collegium introduced a much less tolerant class line as well as a new emphasis on collectivization. "In the interests of the socialist development of the village, and in the interests of the peasantry, we must carry out a defined class line in the village. We must lift up middle and poor peasant farms and direct them toward the only possible way that productive forces can develop—the path of cooperation and collectivization—while obstructing and paralyzing the growth of kulak elements in the village."[37] In correspondence of March 2, 1928, Kubiak (together with chief of the political police, Menzhinskii) noted that the Soviet economy was in an extremely serious economic crisis, blaming kulaks for economic sabotage, both intentional and unintentional, and noting that "the peasantry's mood is extremely bad and already is taking an outspoken, petty-bourgeois, counterrevolutionary form."[38]

Further, Narkomzem quickly issued an instruction that severely limited the ability of land agencies to create khutors, while calling for the creation of more kolkhozy within several months.[39] The Stalin circle had decided that the commune had resisted government food-collection efforts during the grain crisis. In its statements on the countryside, the party leadership now alleged that the commune had come under kulak domination. Collective farms were mostly composed of the poor and middle peasants. Specialists were even to undertake the reorganization of individual farms so that machines could help small- and medium-sized farms make the transition to the collective working of the land.[40] The plan still envisioned voluntary collectivization, and this was true until the fall of 1929. Nevertheless, agriculture had entered a new relationship with the heavily favored industrial sector. In the new environment, agriculture was a resource that existed primarily to sustain the frenetic pace of industrialization. At this critical moment in 1928–29, the Central Committee began to uproot Narkomzem RSFSR.

The Shakhty Affair and Its Repercussions

In March 1928, soon after Smirnov's removal from Narkomzem, Stalin instigated the show trial of the Shakhty engineers, most of whom were either German citizens or tsarist-era holdovers. During the trial, engineers were charged with attempting to undermine Soviet industry, even with beating and starving technical personnel working in their mines. The Shakhty trial swiftly brought to the surface lingering suspicions of "bourgeois specialists" in the state apparatus and increased pressure to expel them. Loudly discussed in the press between May and July, the trial sounded yet another alarm in Narkomzem (already shaken by the removal of Smirnov and its top specialists), an organization still crowded with holdovers in key positions. It was certainly no coincidence that Kondrat'ev and other top Commissariat specialists were dismissed just after the "unmasking" of the Shakhty "saboteurs" was announced.[41] In the spring and summer of 1928, some moderates in the party leadership—especially Rykov and Kuibyshev—tried to reassure engineers and other intimidated specialists that loyal experts would not be touched.[42] They cautioned zealous party members against an upsurge of specialist baiting. Nevertheless, the affair sent shock waves through the apparatus, including the Commissariat of Agriculture. Subsequent developments indicated that the balance of power on cadre issues had shifted permanently away from Rightist protectors of specialists and into the hands of Stalin and his allies in the Central Committee, Rabkrin, and the OGPU. The Shakhty Affair intensified pressure to replace bourgeois specialists and holdovers with recruits from the masses. The drive to remove alien elements progressed throughout 1928, when Stalinists tied them with the "Right deviationists" who were more likely to oppose rapid industrialization plans.

During the Shakhty investigations, the Central Committee established a commission headed by Lazar Kaganovich that supervised reviews of the bureaucracy for reliability in implementing party directives. The commission recommended that many specialists all over the state administration be removed and charged with various political transgressions. In the summer and fall of 1928, the OGPU undertook a massive review of nine thousand engineers and other specialists in the state apparatus, regularly announcing the unmasking and arrest of "wreckers" in the economic and governmental administrations.[43]

Similar to processes undertaken simultaneously in other economic administrations, investigations led by the OGPU and Rabkrin targeted the cadres of the Commissariat of Agriculture. As early as May 1928, the OGPU had already identified at least seventy-five people in the Commissariat's central offices as former nobles, people with prior affiliations with non-Bolshevik political parties, or as former White Army soldiers or officers.[44] Most were serving as senior specialists. Later in 1928, several former Commissariat officials and specialists were publicly disgraced in the press and were forced to confess errors of a "Right deviation." Teodorovich, Chaianov, and Chelintsev all admitted faults in their analysis and policy design.[45]

Assailing the Commissariat's cadres and policies, Rabkrin sought to undermine Narkomzem, a traditional institutional opponent whose planning and policymaking functions it was attempting to absorb.[46] In the fall of 1927, Rabkrin had called for a doubling of grain yields within ten years, an assault on the more moderate targets of Narkomzem. In July 1928, Rabkrin deputy Ia. A. Iakovlev publicly vilified the Commissariat specialists Oganovskii and Vainshtein as reactionaries. He decried the lack of specialists with "revolutionary enthusiasm" in senior positions. Even Kubiak, who had close ties to the OGPU and supported the crackdown on kulaks during the grain crisis, took a stand against Rabkrin's unrealistic targets. In November, he labeled goals for increasing yields and harvests by 30 to 35 percent in five years as utopian and irresponsible, arguing that they could undermine the entire economy. Rykov's Sovnarkom also harshly criticized Rabkrin's plan.[47] But in December 1928 the Right was forced to capitulate publicly in the planning debates, an action which anticipated Stalin's complete defeat of the moderates in February 1929.[48]

Cleansing the Commissariat of the Peasantry, 1928-1929

During this period, Stalin's circle pondered how to deal with an agency that was so closely identified with the increasingly discredited policies of NEP. Attention turned to removing suspect cadres. After the initial burst of firings in the wake of Smirnov's dismissal, two more rounds of "investigations" transpired in Narkomzem in late 1928 and 1929. Purges—still nonviolent—of nonparty personnel first heated up in late 1928. Rabkrin and the OGPU, both of which were headed by Stalin's allies, led the investigations of the people's commissariats.[49]

The Commissariat of Agriculture remained an agency filled with "suspect" personnel. In its Moscow offices, Narkomzem was one of the ministries with the smallest proportion of party members and employees from nonelite backgrounds. As late as 1929, in the midst of intensive efforts to "proletarianize" the state apparatus, fewer than one of ten employees at Narkomzem's headquarters met the ideal of a worker of peasant background, and they served almost exclusively as clerks and chauffeurs or in other auxiliary positions.[50]

While the social complexion of the Moscow offices was worrisome, the Commissariat's local cadres diverged so widely from the ideal that they were a prime target for Moscow watchdogs. The close proximity of the Commissariat's local personnel to the peasantry also concerned investigators, especially in light of the party's still negligible presence in the provinces. Although the state presence was nowhere strong in rural Russia before collectivization, the Commissariat's agronomic, veterinary, land reorganization, and other roving specialist personnel had a closer relationship to the peasantry than any other group of civil servants with the possible exception of schoolteachers. Thus, in the absence of respected party authority in the countryside, Moscow was clearly concerned that nonparty specialists could have an inordinate influence among a peasantry that was itself considered not wholly trustworthy.

The weak presence of communist party members was particularly striking among the ranks of local specialists. At the district level in 1929, fewer than one in thirty of the fourteen thousand agricultural specialists were party members.[51] The Commissariat's nonparty influence in the village was thus regarded as very pronounced, especially when combined with evidence that few party instructors paid visits to the countryside. By the eve of the collectivization offensive, central inspectors were expressing considerable concern that agricultural specialists in the village were something of a political time bomb. As one Central Statistical Administration report noted in 1929, the small percentage of party members and the large numbers of holdovers among local specialists "forces one to think carefully. The agencies of Narkomzem, which come into direct contact with the broad mass of peasants, are located in the politically most responsible sectors. They implement the most important directives of the party, but are nonetheless still very strongly choked with employees upon whom the legacy of the tsarist regime continues to weigh very heavily."[52] This anxiety was manifest despite evidence that many nonparty specialists in fact were open to appeals for more rapid rationalization and mechanization of the countryside.

Evidence also exists of disquiet about a pervasive SR presence. In 1929, people's commissar Kubiak wrote in a provocative secret report that as late as 1928, up to 60 percent of the leadership contingent of the krai and oblast' branches of Narkomzem had come from "other parties," primarily the SRs.[53] One must put Kubiak's accusation in the context of the heated political atmosphere of 1929, when ideologues were launching witch-hunts and spreading charges of disloyalty against *byvshie liudi* (so-called "former people" of the bourgeois or aristocratic classes tainted by association with the old regime). Although Kubiak's assertion may illustrate the exaggerated fears about SRs prevalent among some communists, it lends credence to the notion that the Commissariat of Agriculture had earned a reputation for sheltering persons with non-Bolshevik and even anti-Bolshevik inclinations.

The Purge Begins

Most historians have dated the opening of the purge of the state apparatus with a resolution of the April 1929 Sixteenth Party Conference.[54] In fact, archival materials from Rabkrin and Narkomzem demonstrate that a de facto purge began five months earlier, in November 1928. Although not officially termed a purge, but rather "research" or an "investigation" of the soviet apparatus in preparation for a later purge, the same patterns of stigmatization and unmasking personnel, defiance, and panic prevailed within the Moscow commissariats. These investigations created extraordinary disruptions in the work of the Commissariat of Agriculture and many other state agencies.

The united Rabkrin and Central Control Commission (NK RKI-TsKK USSR) conducted the purge of the central Narkomzem offices, under orders from the Central Committee and with the close cooperation of the OGPU. Kaganovich's Central Committee commission studying bureaucratism in the state apparatus formally instigated the process. In November 1928, a Central Committee Plenum declared that "government institutions are still full of elements of old officialdom and remnants of the former classes in whom hatred of the Soviet regime still resides." The Plenum's resolution called for a "radical purge" of the state and cooperative apparatuses. A November 27, 1928, directive of NKRKI-TsKK ordered an Inspectorate for Soviet Construction (ISS) within Rabkrin to devote itself to preliminary research for a "verification" of the qualifications and abilities of nonparty employees throughout the soviet apparatus.[55] The ensuing verification process proved to be formidable, encompassing all people's commissariats, cooperatives, trade unions, and soviets. In theory, at least, Rabkrin commissions were to investigate the class origins, qualifications, and competence of hundreds of thousands of people.

The investigation of the Commissariat of Agriculture began with an order from G. K. "Sergo" Ordzhonikidze in his capacity as People's Commissar of Rabkrin USSR. Ordzhonikidze instructed N. I. Il'in, the People's Commissar of Rabkrin RSFSR, to gather material on the personnel of Narkomzem RSFSR. In turn, Il'in ordered officials in local branches of Rabkrin to investigate and then provide pertinent information in a month's time regarding their "struggle with bureaucratism."[56] "For this purpose we request that you write up detailed, concrete examples of alien elements in the apparatus," in collaboration with local party organs. He also requested descriptions of the relationship of individual specialists with the village population. Rabkrin asked for specific examples of red tape, violations of the class line, ties with "alien elements," and other offenses.

Iakov Khristorovich Peters headed the Rabkrin group—the Commission for the Purge of the Soviet Apparatus—assigned to carry out preparatory work studying the personnel of the commissarial administration. Peters was a presidium member of both Rabkrin and the OGPU, and had a long association with the secret police going back to the Cheka. (Peters was not the only person to serve in this dual role, an indication of the close relationship between Rabkrin and the secret police during this period when Stalin was consolidating power.[57]) The group would present its conclusions to Ordzhonikidze, who would then base his report on "bureaucratism" at the upcoming Sixteenth Party Conference on this information.[58] Many commissariats were subjected to this "investigation" simultaneously.

According to Peters, this investigation of Narkomzem was not a full purge. Rather it would undertake only preliminary scrutiny of the personnel of the Commissariat's "most important" administrations, that is, those "responsible for implementing the party line in the countryside."[59] The investigation also intended to examine the "political face of the specialists." The process reflected two of the party leadership's primary sources of anxiety: first, that the state apparatus was not committed to implementing its orders, in part because it was full of noncommunists and social aliens not dedicated to the goals of Soviet power; and second, that its lower ranks were too corrupt or incompetent to fulfill the urgent new tasks of soviet construction. Ordzhonikidze emphasized that the struggle against bureaucratism would be even more challenging than implementing industrialization.[60]

Investigators focused on two types of nonparty officials. The first category included individuals who had either intentionally "violated the class line" in their work, or who, by virtue of their social or political background, were unlikely to be able to meet the new challenges of socialist construction. These included the "former people," a subgroup of which were the holdovers from the tsarist administration. Into a second group fell the incompetent, the corrupt, and the misplaced, including people who lacked initiative or enthusiasm.[61] Everyone involved in leading the investigations agreed that individuals who displayed overt hostility to Soviet power, engaged in criminal activities, or were conscious wreckers should be removed. All participants also agreed that the proletarianization of the apparatus was a worthy goal. Both of these objectives, presumably, would augment the dependability and effectiveness of the machinery of state. Beyond this common ground, however, disagreement arose. The imprecision of investigators' categories, a heavy dose of inflammatory class rhetoric, and the fact that some nonparty specialists supported the modernizing goals of Soviet power in the countryside, all contributed to confusion about which officials should be removed.

The category "former people" included the same groups that Rabkrin had targeted for purge in 1924–25.[62] Rabkrin concentrated on former priests, landlords, tsarist functionaries, White Army officers, zemstvo employees, and former SRs and Mensheviks. The children of these groups also merited a good deal of attention. Those considered politically suspect included employees who had openly expressed doubts about goals of the collectivization campaign. Another major target for purging was the so-called false specialists, employees who had exaggerated their qualifications and, despite a lack of proper education, obtained posts slotted for specialists. They had stolen jobs away from young, newly trained "red" specialists and from potential worker and peasant promotees.

In their research, Rabkrin inspectors used the same calculations that they had employed during the 1924–25 verifications. They found that the Moscow offices of Narkomzem employed more aliens than communists. On paper, Narkomzem seemed to be an apparatus likely teeming with anti-Soviet activities. As of January 1, 1929, for example, Rabkrin defined 43 of 139 employees in the Land Improvement and State Land Administration as aliens, while only 26 were communists; in the Agriculture Administration, 27 of 104 people were aliens and 21 were communists; in the Forest Administration, 26 of 86 employees were aliens, while 11 were party members.[63] These numbers disturbed Rabkrin watchdogs.

Nevertheless, disagreement persisted among the Rabkrin leadership regarding the objective of the purge, and these differences were reflected inside the broader party. Were all former people by definition hostile to Soviet power? And how should this hostility be determined? Should all suspect people be fired immediately? Should they be arrested? Or could some people from compromised social backgrounds still loyally serve Soviet power?

Rabkrin's policy during this period was inconsistent. For the most part, leaders acted cautiously, not wanting a campaign to fire all former people. Peters (with Ordzhonikidze's backing) insisted that inspectors and local party committees not purge officials solely on the basis of their social origins. Investigators must take into account ability and loyalty to Soviet power. Most of the Rabkrin leadership seemed to be concerned that specialist baiting might destroy the state apparatus's ability to carry out central party directives. The Rabkrin representative who oversaw the purge in Narkomzem agreed with the more wary approach of Ordzhonikidze and Peters.[64]

Despite this degree of caution, Rabkrin chief Ordzhonikidze undermined his own wary approach by repeating that at least some of the negative consequences of bureaucratism was rooted in the class origins of state personnel. For example, Ordzhonikidze agreed with more impatient investigators that the apparatus was full of alien elements and that the campaign to proletarianize the state was an integral part of the investigation. In other words, Rabkrin put forward an inherently contradictory policy, one that made for a potentially explosive combination. On one hand, Rabkrin's leaders cautioned against cleansing the apparatus solely on the basis of class origin. On the other hand, notions of irreconcilable class antagonism were at the heart of the purge. This basic idea was exploited by Rabkrin to expel undesirable employees, regardless of the possibly less zealous inclinations of Ordzhonikidze and others inside Rabkrin. In fact, when Peters kicked off the purge of the Commissariat of Agriculture in January

1929, he wasted no time reminding the Commissariat's party cell that many secret groupings of "aliens" who were "hostile to Soviet power" had been discovered in Vesenkha and other state agencies and that the Narkomzem party cell should keep its eyes open for similar groups.[65] The party cell took the hint as it looked for and, not surprisingly, located several similar groupings in Narkomzem.

"Disgraceful and Outrageous Mistakes": Purging Land Agencies in the Localities

In this period between November 1928 and April 1929, investigations of local officials moved forward much more quickly than purges of the Moscow headquarters. Local investigators often took the path of least resistance, taking action against all former people, regardless of current loyalty.[66] People's Commissar of Rabkrin RSFSR Il'in warned against local excesses in a circular letter to all krai, oblast', and provincial branches of Rabkrin on January 14, 1929.[67] He cautioned that in many localities purges had gone too far, too fast, and this had resulted in improper firings of former people. Il'in complained that local Rabkrin offices themselves were often left out of the purge process, which was presumably carried out exclusively by Party leaders in kangaroo courts. Because of this "campaign-shock" character of work, Il'in charged, many investigated agencies were left in a disorganized state for some time. Rabkrin tried to make sure that investigators dismissed only people who were actively anti-Soviet (that is, true wreckers) and those who were grossly incompetent. Rabkrin urged local officials to shift their attention to improving agencies' *implementation* of Moscow's instructions. One might say that in Il'in's view, the state administration was like a runaway train that should be brought under control, repaired, and steered by party leaders in the correct direction, but not destroyed.

Nevertheless, correspondence from local Rabkrin offices provides examples of improper investigative methods in many provinces in late 1928 and early 1929. It also sheds light on officials who were dedicated to purifying the apparatus and improving its quality but who balked at some of the extremes of the process that might undermine the party's goals. One person stands as a particularly interesting representative of the conflict found in the localities during the purge. The chief of a provincial Urals office of Rabkrin during the eviction of anti-Soviet elements from the land administration in 1928 and 1929 was a certain Studitov. He demanded that staffers who were hostile to Soviet power be tracked down and fired.[68] Studitov even chastised the OGPU for insufficient vigilance in their background checks, which had allowed hostile employees to have secretly penetrated the state apparatus.

At the same time that Studitov zealously hunted down "aliens," however, he was infuriated by a number of transgressions by party leaders and local Rabkrin officials in charge of cleansing the apparatus in his province. As he wrote to Peters, Studitov considered the process to have spun out of control, unjustly victimizing local employees. For example, a deaf man who worked twelve hours a day was denounced as politically unreliable because he did not take the time to read the newspaper regularly. In addition, Studitov pointed out the harm of purging solely on the basis of social origin. Loyal employees who had suffered the misfortune of being captured by the Whites during the Civil War were charged with actively working against the Reds during their captivity. Studitov also noticed that information about alleged aliens provided by the OGPU and local party cells was often incorrect. Many investigators involved in the purge were eager to unmask as many enemies as possible, and they perpetrated numerous excesses.

In such cases, Studitov was harshly critical of local purge commissions. Purges in the provinces have not been well organized, nor have they been undertaken carefully, he complained. In a wide array of okrugs, Rabkrin organs as well as party committees had ignored Moscow's instructions and given orders for indiscriminate, mass purges. "As a result, we have seen numerous disgraceful and outrageous mistakes by our regional Rabkrins." In Buyurslanskii okrug, for example, the party committee suggested that the local Rabkrin office carry out a purge, "but said nothing about how, or by whom, or which procedures to follow during the purge." Vague instructions led to excesses. In another case, the offices of Rabkrin carried out a massive purge of the local soviet apparatus under pressure from the local party committee. In one interrogation, an investigator asked a certain Novikov, an accountant in the okrug land administration, why he did not attempt to run from the White Army to Red partisans during the Civil War. Not satisfied with the answer, the commission dismissed the accountant for "working against the Reds." Studitov demanded that local inspectors avoid such fiascos.

Studitov's letter also belies the authorities' enormous difficulties in verifying any information about a person's past, especially denunciations received from anonymous informants. Accusations of sympathy with the White armies, for example, were almost impossible to prove or disprove. Judging the truth of the claims was left to the purge commissions. Studitov recommended that disparaging information should either be verified with particular care or thrown out. Since purge commissions are in such a rush, however, they do not take the time to corroborate data. Despite complaints of excesses, Rabkrin continued to solicit anonymous denunciations as hard evidence.[69] "Such methods terrorize the apparatus while discrediting our Rabkrin organs."

Defiance

As has been indicated, during the investigation of the central and local offices of the Commissariat of Agriculture, Rabkrin USSR regularly called on the OGPU to provide inspectors with essential data about all nonparty staff under scrutiny. The OGPU had been independently gathering information on Narkomzem's "bourgeois specialists" since the Shakhty Affair (and earlier), well before the Central Committee launched this latest investigation. Kondrat'ev, for one, had been under supervision by the OGPU since at least 1927.[70] The OGPU had accumulated "compromising material" about employees' service in White armies, social origins, and previous arrests that no other source could supply Rabkrin.[71] OGPU officers were very quick to provide valuable compromising evidence, and often responded to Rabkrin investigator's requests for information more quickly than Rabkrin's own local offices.

OGPU officials wrote confidently about the specific anti-Soviet activities of a number of Narkomzem employees. The head of one Commissariat section, for example, was a certain Panteleev, an agronomist who had attended Petrovskaia Agricultural Academy.[72] The OGPU uncovered information that "proved" that Panteleev had failed to reveal that his father had been a Cossack general who hated Soviet power. The OGPU report concluded that Panteleev "is nothing but a wrecker." He chased well-trained specialists out of his section, tried to discredit an honest party member, and greedily pursued a larger salary. This example is typical of investigators politicizing and labeling as sabotage the normal infighting and informal relationships and mechanisms of power present within all bureaucracies. Rabkrin and police inspectors translated the specialists' desire for improved material conditions into acts of political subversion. Such politicization became an incendiary factor in a ministerial system long wracked with inefficiency, petty corruption, bottlenecks, and red tape. These typical bureaucratic phenomena were considered by some zealots to be proof of wrecking by hostile elements.[73]

The OGPU "uncovered" more relationships that implicated the Commissariat's party leadership in efforts to mask its cadres' impure social origins. OGPU agents dug up information on employees who had resigned from the Moscow offices of the Commissariat "by their own request" in 1927 and 1928. At least twenty-seven people whom Narkomzem had expelled for concealing compromising information had been allowed to depart quietly, without publicity or penalty. (Several of them found jobs elsewhere in the state administration.) For instance, Narkomzem's Land Improvement and Reorganization Administration hired A. S. Filonenko as a senior geodesic engineer in October 1927. His boss— who was a party member—soon discovered that Filonenko had been a Menshevik between 1903 and 1917. Despite the unearthing of this dirty secret, Filonenko was allowed to resign quietly on October 31, 1928. The official reason for the departure noted on his record was that he left his position to enroll in an institute and prepare research for publication. Similarly, the Commissariat allowed a certain M. S. Kaftanovskii to quit because of poor health, although he had hidden from his employers that he had been born into a noble family.[74] Rabkrin's conclusion dripped with sarcasm: "So that the poor 'former people' did not have their feelings hurt, and so that they would not become unemployed, their boss called them to his office. The boss suggested that they submit a declaration stating that they were leaving their job. These people wrote resignation letters, even adding a statement about where they were going, with the help of Narkomzem. Or they wrote that Narkomzem had removed them under some type of pleasant pretext, [for example] as a consequence of 'staff reductions' or the 'reorganization of the apparatus.'"[75]

The ubiquity of such cases provides us with further evidence that, as late as 1927 and 1928, party chiefs in the state apparatus hired employees without conducting serious background checks or simply looked the other way when compromising background information came to their attention. Once Rabkrin began its investigation of the Commissariat, it found that Narkomzem's personnel department had recorded biographical information and then filed it away, unused. The accuracy of information supplied by applicants was not verified by documentation.[76] The Secret Section of the Narkomzem administration did not pass on information to the personnel department, and vice versa. Meanwhile, evaluations of the quality of employees' work or the reasons for dismissal were not recorded. As late as the end of 1928, Rabkrin complained that some land organs still did not even have complete lists of their employees. Because of these shortcomings in record keeping, Rabkrin chose to rely on informants willing to supply investigators with negative details, especially disgruntled members of the Commissariat's party cell. As had been the case earlier in the decade, the Commissariat's leaders remained more concerned with hiring people who possessed appropriate skills than with finding individuals with impeccable social or political credentials.

In another example that enraged investigators, Narkomzem officials permitted many social aliens to disguise their true social backgrounds in their labor books as sluzhashchie (white-collar worker) rather than the more damning "noble," "clergy," and so on. As one investigator complained, "According to rules on the compilation of labor lists . . . employees who do not belong to the category 'worker,' 'peasant,' or 'white-collar worker' should write down in their labor book the social position that they occupied before starting work in the soviet apparatus. This is not done. Instead these socially alien elements are counted as white-collar workers."[77] These tactics had their origin in the earlier efforts of Smirnov (and his assistants) to protect Narkomzem cadres.

The OGPU found another variety of "defiance" among the Narkomzem leadership in the phenomenon of "protectionism." With the help of information supplied by the OGPU and a Narkomzem Party cell eager to unmask "enemies," Rabkrin located informal patronage networks. Certain individuals with the power to hire specialists recruited their friends, noncommunist aliens who lacked the proper qualifications for a particular job, and then used their influence to protect these friends from investigators. According to investigators, N. P. Rudin, the former Socialist Revolutionary who wrote the 1922 Land Code, hired several such untouchables in his capacity as head of the Land Improvement and Reorganization Administration. The former assistant head of the same administration, B. F. Kopylov, who had himself served as a vice director of the tsarist Department of Agriculture, hired a certain Pushcharevskii, the son of a priest who lacked specialized training, as a senior engineer. Kopylov also brought in Sokolov, the son of a noble, as an engineer. Such a pattern repeated itself many times in Narkomzem. According to Rabkrin, one nonparty alien would hire two or three more people, both ill-suited for their posts and socially alien, creating a web of anti-Soviet treachery in investigators' minds. As the OGPU pointed out, Commissariat leaders had allowed many of them to resign quietly and find lucrative positions elsewhere in the apparatus.[78] Kopylov, for instance, managed to obtain work in the state Irrigation Committee and later ended up in Gosplan.[79] The particularly combustible factor here was that investigators labeled the state employees' rather banal bureaucratic pastimes, common to officialdom everywhere, to be hostile political actions, an indication of deliberate and organized anti-Soviet sabotage.

Rabkrin also pointed out that Narkomzem's leaders had continued to collaborate with certain employees to hide embarrassing or compromising facts in their backgrounds.[80] Managers and employees inside the government apparatus colluded with one another. Leaders desperate for qualified people allied themselves with the specialists they had hired to obscure the backgrounds of suspect staffers and to preserve the working integrity of their organizations. In May 1929, collegium member Gerasimovich wrote to Ordzhonikidze that Kopylov (the aforementioned former vice director of the tsarist Department of Agriculture) turned out to be an "unprincipled careerist who had cunningly been donning a Soviet mask" during his tenure at the Commissariat.[81] Klimenko, the hard-line deputy commissar whom Sovnarkom appointed to replace Teodorovich in 1928, fanned the flames of suspicion in an early 1929 letter to Rabkrin's Peters. He alleged that amid all the investigations, those old specialists who remained in Narkomzem had "moved to the left, so that no one would mistakenly think that they had not grasped the 'new course.'"[82] These accusations of feigned enthusiasm about rapidly changing economic plans among specialists—that they were "wearing a Soviet mask"—may have been true, of course, but many top communist officials were willing to play along as they struggled to protect these skilled skeptics.[83]

The Revenge of the Party Cell

Some communists inside the Commissariat—especially in its party cell—accused Narkomzem's party leadership of negligence. On January 29, 1929, the bureau of the cell reported that communist heads of administrations failed to supervise experts in their purview to ensure that they were observing the class line.[84] Rabkrin's deputy commissar Iakovlev denounced these rubber-stamping communists who shirked their responsibilities by allowing nonparty specialists and administrators to do the actual work of running the Commissariat. "Are communists administering the apparatus or is the apparatus administering the communists?"[85]

Not surprisingly, the Party cell reported to Rabkrin that Narkomzem's specialists were sluggish and greedy guardians of social aliens.[86] The Party cell launched a crusade against the Narkomzem party leadership that had frustrated them for so long. The cell alleged that opposition to Soviet policies inside the Commissariat came from "little clubs" that certain party members shielded. "It is disgusting that party members working in the apparatus do not try to learn about—indeed, do not even *glance at*—the people alongside whom they work." When the class line in their organization *was* violated, party leaders did not report these infractions to personnel agencies or to the party cell. This pattern of negligent supervision over noncommunist staff made it nearly impossible to conduct a purge either of incompetent people or of hostile elements. The party cell could not even mobilize Narkomzem's communists to offer information about nonparty specialists, an illustration of the passivity of the majority of Narkomzem's party members. The cell wondered how the communist leadership could have left so many aliens in specialized jobs. "How could the directives of the party and government be carried out by those 32 percent of leading cadres who were socially alien?"[87] According to their critics, these people psychologically were incapable of internalizing the new policies.[88]

The head of the Commissariat's agronomic aid section, the communist expert Lezhnev-Fin'kovskii, argued against the tactics of the Party cell. He insisted that Rabkrin's investigation of Narkomzem should concentrate only on the competence of the specialists, not purely on social origin. Concerned about the reliability of testimony against experts, he argued that investigators should focus on facts, not just hearsay, rumors, and ungrounded accusations. He worried aloud about depending on the "opinions of individual communists."[89] Lezhnev-Fin'kovskii feared that communists with a grudge against individual experts, or against specialists as a group, would try to humiliate them. Other leading party members feared disruption in the Commissariat's operations. The collegium member Gerasimovich urged Rabkrin investigators to undertake their research carefully, without distracting the specialists who were only just settling down after the 1927–28 reorganization of the Commissariat. The agency's crucial work must continue, with the participation of experts. We have to "avoid creating unhealthy moods among the specialists," Gerasimovich argued.

The party cell, however, was unmoved by requests for prudence. Party cell representatives believed that they had reversed the power relations of earlier years, which had kept them at a disadvantage relative to the Commissariat's political leadership, and they treasured this newfound position of strength. Cell members argued that most of the communists in the Commissariat of Agriculture had long been inert and passive. After all, the party cell had documented that Narkomzem's political leadership had helped to protect unsuitable elements in the past and were themselves guilty of malfeasance of duty. In perhaps its most outrageous move, the party cell assailed the communist M. I. Kozyrev in March 1929 for the sin of failing to reapply for his party card. Kozyrev was the head of the forestry administration and a Narkomzem collegium member of five years. The raion party committee expelled Kozyrev from the Communist Party.[90]

Panic Reigns

Investigators' aggressive actions created anger and opposition inside the Commissariat of Agriculture. A number of communists in the Commissariat were openly wary about the Party cell cooperating in secret with Rabkrin during the investigation. They called for *glasnost'*, or openness, in the investigations, meaning that every party member employed in Narkomzem should participate. The party bosses of each administration should evaluate the trustworthiness, the "political and social face," of the specialists who worked in their departments. Decisions of purge committees should be made public.[91]

A good deal more evidence exists of strong resistance inside the peoples' commissariats to Rabkrin's investigative methods. In late 1928 and early 1929, many people's commissars and other party leaders in the state apparatus feared that Rabkrin's investigations created an environment of fear in their organizations. Certainly, they recalled the Shakhty Affair, with its accusations of sabotage and espionage, its arrests and public trials. In December 1928, for example, R. E. Rudzutak, head of the Commissariat of Ways of Communications, wrote in a confidential letter that the special committees now investigating the personnel of the railroads would create hysteria among specialists. Five hundred individuals had already been fired.[92] All this was occurring, of course, *before* the official launch of the purge of the state apparatus in April 1929.

In February 1929, Deputy Chair of Sovnarkom RSFSR Lezhava wrote to Rabkrin's Iakovlev expressing concern.[93] Inquiring on behalf of the people's commissars of the Russian Republican commissariats, Lezhava asked whether Rabkrin had sanctioned the purge in the form of a "wide campaign." The people's commissars wanted Iakovlev to know that inside the apparatus "reign panic, confusion, and anxiety about the future. Work is suffering as a consequence." Everyone agreed that anti-Soviet elements should be removed. The question, however, was what form the process should take and what its methods should be. Lezhava pointed uneasily to an article by Peters in *Pravda* in which, like a commander going to war, he wrote of "mobilizing the light cavalry" for the operation. The campaign was producing a "colossal shock in every enterprise, one that would have a major influence on the work and ability of every agency and enterprise to fulfill its tasks." This was the wrong time to complete a disruptive cleansing, Lezhava concluded, just when there are such urgent missions in industry and agriculture. Lezhava's letter illustrates confusion in the state apparatus over the extent of Rabkrin's seemingly limitless powers, while demonstrating the people's commissariats' defensiveness toward Rabkrin. The OGPU had arrested many hundreds of specialists, especially in industry, and was issuing warnings about the likelihood that investigations would reveal massive amounts of sabotage among nonparty experts.[94] Employees of the state apparatus had reason to be concerned. Of course, the disruption engendered by this fear led to more charges of inefficiency and incompetence, which then led to growing charges of socially and politically based offenses. A vicious cycle was developing.

The Fate of the Promotees

In addition to bourgeois specialists and their party protectors, another group of employees who had reason to fear Rabkrin's investigations were the peasant promotees *(vydvizhentsy)* discussed in earlier chapters. In spite of programs to promote members of the laboring classes to the specialist and political elite, only a handful of peasants were ever appointed to the central offices of the people's commissariats during the NEP period. And in none of these organizations did more than a fraction of those promoted remain in responsible positions for long before they either quit or were removed by commissariat leaders.[95] In the Commissariat of Agriculture, an agency with over two thousand people in its Moscow offices, a total of only twenty-two people identified as "peasants" were recruited at the height of efforts between 1925 and 1928.[96] Not only did very few peasants occupy an important administrative or specialist position, only a handful of them remained in any posts in Moscow apart from the most menial. The original goal of mass peasant participation in the central organs of the revolutionary government was not being fulfilled. For their part, those few peasants who had been promoted complained that that communists and nonparty specialists alike resisted their assumption of important responsibilities, keeping them marginalized in the organization's culture.

And what was the fate of those promotees who remained in Narkomzem on the eve of collectivization? How did Rabkrin explain the poor results of the people's commissariats in promoting peasants into the government bureaucracy? One might imagine they would blame the noncommunist bourgeois specialists, and Rabkrin did sharply criticize "socially alien," nonparty specialists for ignoring rural promotees. But Rabkrin staff also found fault with the peasants themselves.

Rabkrin noted with indignation in 1929 that during the previous four years, the Commissariat had recruited far fewer promotees than the Central Committee had mandated.[97] Only nine continued to work in the Commissariat as of 1929. What happened to the rest? A typical Rabkrin report summed it up: "drunkenness, debauchery and discrediting Soviet power with their behavior." The report lists cases of promotees gone bad. For example: "Gagarin: Corrupted, became a drunk, currently hospitalized. Zimin [and Leskov]: Corrupted, became an alcoholic, sent to do local work."[98]

Why did these men become corrupted? The summary report gives us insight into official understanding of peasant character on the eve of collectivization. "Most peasant promotees are middle peasants [seredniaki] who need firm leadership. [The Commissariat of Agriculture] brought peasants to Moscow, paid them a salary . . . [but] did not give them work. There was nothing to do and they began to drink. They drank until they were sent back to the village."[99] In other words, these peasants, left unsupervised and unchallenged, reverted to their natural state as alcoholics. Whether the Rabkrin inspectors themselves—or the promotees' supervisors in the Commissariat of Agriculture—abused alcohol is addressed nowhere in this report.

The report demonstrated that peasants also could fall from grace in other ways: "In other instances, they accumulated money, sent it to their villages and became kulaks." This characterization points up a striking irony of the peasant-promotee experiment as it evolved on the eve of collectivization. The regime expends an enormous amount of time recruiting a select group of suitable villagers to the capital, pays them a salary that enables them to become relatively wealthy by rural standards, ultimately becomes dissatisfied with their work or their "outlook," returns them home, and proceeds to dekulakize them as class enemies.[100]

Once the course toward collectivization was set in 1929, peasants were among the first removed from local land administration. Purges occurred amid accusations that many farmer-officials were kulaks or middle peasants who, because of their loyalty to "reactionary" individual and communal farming, would try to sabotage progress toward socialist agriculture from within the government. Many in the party also came to believe that they brought lazy, undisciplined "peasant work habits" to the office, and were therefore unprepared for the attack "on the agrarian front."[101] By the end of the decade, the large numbers of specialists and administrative bosses from the peasantry were also labeled untrustworthy, since most were from middle peasant households. Party chiefs considered them incapable of managing the collectivization process, because they were overly wedded to traditional farming. Thus, peasants as well as specialists were presumed to have retained their "harmful" pre-Revolutionary mentalities.

Peasant promotees originally were brought to Moscow to legitimize the Bolshevik regime in the eyes of the peasantry, while simultaneously providing an avenue by which Moscow could learn about the situation in the countryside. They were to act in some sense as mediators within the state apparatus between the new regime and the local population. Yet once invited, the regime circumscribed their power and subjected them to mockery and stereotyping. Even those peasants whom party personnel chiefs considered to be the most likely to prosper in state administration—sober and hard-working poor and middle peasants who were veterans of the Red Army or soviet administration—proved themselves in the eyes of party inspectors to be unprepared for the task.

Crushing Narkomzem RSFSR

The attack on peasant promotees from the middle peasantry was part of the general, class-based cleansing of the state apparatus. Nevertheless, despite the mass firings in the wake of the Rabkrin-OGPU investigations of November 1928–April 1929, the party did not publicly refer to this as a purge, although the documents cited above show that nearly everyone involved considered it to be such. In early June, *Pravda* announced that a "full-blown purge" of Narkomzem would begin on July 10, 1929.[102]

The purge was delayed indefinitely, however, for reasons that went unstated at the time. The reasons for the delay were explained in a September 1929 decree of the Central Committee and the Central Control Commission, "On the purge of the Soviet apparatus," which declared that investigations to that date had been largely unsuccessful. Why? The Central Committee complained that Rabkrin could not undertake the purge without more enthusiastic support from the party, the unions, and the entire working class. Instead, the masses had participated only tangentially, and the Communist Youth League (Komsomol) had barely assisted. Many party leaders treated this crucial work passively. Heads of institutions continued to collaborate in a "conspiracy of silence," as *Izvestiia* put it. Party leaders of commissariats had frequently refused to cooperate with purge commissions, and in some cases they actively hindered the purge. They should be held responsible and even removed from their posts. *Izvestiia* complained that purge commissions often could not remove the high-level officials in an institution, and instead had to settle for dismissing petty clerks and low-level specialists.[103] This pattern repeated the phenomena seen in 1924–25, when Narkomzem successfully defended many leading specialists, while allowing lower-tier officials without specialized qualifications to be swept away.

The September decree highlighted Rabkrin's growing frustration at the enormous amount of foot dragging in this purge. The Central Committee now instructed Rabkrin to focus on a select group of organizations that were most responsible for carrying out the class line and that had the closest contact with the "wide masses." The Commissariats of Agriculture and Finance were at the top of the list.

The OGPU also concluded that the purge had gone poorly in the spring and summer of 1929 because party officials were not participating. In November of 1929, the OGPU leadership complained that the purge of the state apparatus again was not proceeding properly. Failures occured because the professional and party organizations had not participated adequately in the activities of the purge commissions.[104] It recommended that the purge should now refocus on the regional (okrug and oblast') apparatuses and "only after that [is completed] carry out an investigation and purge of the central apparatus."[105]

The Rabkrin investigations continued, but within two months Narkomzem RSFSR was essentially crushed with the establishment of a new agency in charge of organizing forced collectivization, Narkomzem USSR.[106] With the creation of Narkomzem USSR, a highly centralized organization that directed the mass, rapid collectivization of agriculture from above, Narkomzem RSFSR became a weak and withered agency of implementation.[107] This was a tried and true method of combating "bureaucratism"—the Commissariat was simply reorganized into impotency. The appointment of the Rabkrin deputy Ia. A. Iakovlev as People's Commissar of Agriculture USSR on December 8, 1929, was yet another indication that the interests of agriculture would permanently remain secondary to those of industry. Iakovlev had successfully argued for the unrealistic agricultural production targets that Narkomzem's political and specialist leadership, now in eclipse, had opposed so virulently.

The seeds of the Commissariat's destruction were planted well before 1928. In important ways, the state system was very fragile and tension-filled throughout the 1920s, as the party pursued two, often conflicting, goals—economic modernization and class politics. We must be cautious, of course, in generalizing about the state on the basis of one commissariat. Narkomzem, like many commissariats, had an agenda and interests that were in many ways incompatible with Stalinist plans. It is certainly clear, however, that the experience of the Commissariat of Agriculture can serve as an example during NEP of how the state apparatus served as a refuge for nonparty scientific intelligentsia as well as professionals and administrators of all backgrounds. Every commissariat contained people who, in the eyes of some party activists, were potentially disloyal by virtue of their social status or occupation before the revolution. Although the party could temporarily tolerate these skilled people until loyal "red specialists" could be trained, they would have to be removed eventually. Since each commissariat was packed with such alien officials, each was increasingly vulnerable to attack. Furthermore, in light of the party's weakness in the countryside, some Bolsheviks felt even more insecure with a local soviet system staffed by "untrustworthy" cadres. State officials who had extensive contact with the mass of peasants, themselves unpredictable and suspect, were of special concern. Consider the words of Iakovlev at the Sixteenth Party Conference in April 1929: "In the USSR there is a gap between, on the one hand, the political and economic foundation of this country, and, on the other, the apparatus that implements these tasks. . . . To a significant degree, we had to build our new apparatus using holdover people whom we inherited with the old foundation. Many parts of our apparatus were transferred already intact. Because of this, we as a Soviet country have no guarantee that the decisions of the governing organs of this apparatus (to a large degree alien to us in terms of personnel) will really be implemented."[108]

This study proposes that when the leaders of state agencies tried to deflect stigmatization away from their vulnerable personnel this stigma could pass from individuals to entire organizations. Rather than deflecting stigmatization with their strategies to defend vulnerable personnel, as their leaders hoped, organizations ultimately absorbed it. Beginning in 1927, Narkomzem as a whole was becoming branded in a way that implicated all, or nearly all, of its personnel. The March 1928 removal of Smirnov and the rest of the Commissariat leadership meant that they could not shoulder this burden any longer, exposing the staff to attack. This process was complete by 1929. One might call this phenomenon the institutionalization of stigma, reminiscent of—and intimately related to—the 1921–22 institutionalization of expertise. The phenomenon helps to explain why the party leadership tried simply to sweep aside much of the old state apparatus in 1929. Many organs of government (especially the people's commissariats), having sheltered aliens for so long in the name of modernization, productivity, and economic recovery, themselves became fully stigmatized as alien to the building of socialism in a new era.

The upheavals of 1928–29 thus took root a decade earlier in the labeling of most employees of the government as "alien and hostile elements" and in the subsequent instability of the immature administrative systems of the Soviet state. The social composition of the state administration fueled a growing suspicion among certain of the party elites that whole sections of the ministerial bureaucracy (and their local agencies) were unreliable and had to be circumvented before the Great Leap Forward could proceed. To carry out crash collectivization, Stalinists denounced Narkomzem RSFSR as untrustworthy and created new supercentralized union-wide agencies.[109] In 1929, the Red Army and other extra-administrative plenipotentiaries traveled to the village and stayed, ignoring the established state structures, with their cohort of suspect personnel. After its purge, Narkomzem was simply bypassed, rendered powerless in the creation and implementation of rural policy.

Epilogue

The fate of the individuals discussed in this book is almost uniformly grim. The leading specialists of Narkomzem and their patron Teodorovich were forced to publicly recant their positions in 1928–29, together with Rykov, Tomskii, and Bukharin. Although Smirnov was moved out of Narkomzem in the spring of 1928, he somehow avoided the public humiliation that the other Rightists endured in that year, keeping his distance from them politically. During the crucial 1928–29 plenums at which the various versions of the Five Year Plans were discussed, Smirnov said almost nothing.[110] It is unclear whether he remained silent as a result of his chronic illness, his sense that the Right could not defeat Stalin, his indecision about the course that agricultural policy should take during this moment of crisis, or a combination of these factors.

Smirnov apparently resisted direct pleas to sign on to the Right Opposition's platform when it was being drafted privately. As Tomskii recalled in 1933, leaders of the Right Opposition to Stalin, presumably including Bukharin and Rykov, were "at someone's dacha in 1928 or 1929," secretly composing their platform. "Foma [Smirnov] came in, completely by accident." Tomskii showed him a document outlining the Right platform. "I said, 'Here, Foma.' I then believed like many others that [since] Foma often uttered such Rightist things, that there was nowhere else to go—he would go with us. 'Here, Foma, listen to the document.' Foma listened, listened, and said—'No, this affair will not succeed; I won't go along with it.' He would not sign, he did not join us, and there were no [further] conversations about it."[111]

It is not entirely clear why Smirnov refused to join forces with Tomskii, Rykov, and Bukharin in 1928–29. It is hardly surprising that they believed that Smirnov would join them. On a number of issues he had agreed with the Right, including the tempo and methods of collectivization, downplaying the kulak danger, defending the nonparty specialists, and stimulating production by encouraging the well-off stratum in the village. Yet, unlike (and against) Rykov and Bukharin, he voted for the "optimal" variant of the First Five Year Plan in April 1929, which most nonparty specialists and all Right Oppositionists had severely criticized as impossibly unrealistic. Smirnov was not a target of the same savage condemnation by Stalinists in the press and at party gatherings that other leading Rightists were subjected to in late 1928 and 1929.

It may be that Smirnov was convinced that in a period of crisis, when war seemed to threaten, party unity had to be maintained at all costs, and this devotion to the strength of the party overrode his concerns about the effects of rapid industrialization. As Rykov came to believe, he may have feared that division in the party leadership at this critical moment would have provoked a civil war with the peasantry.[112] He may have felt, like some party members in 1928–29, that the relatively limited degree of collectivization called for in the First Five Year Plan was achievable, if very ambitious. Like some other party moderates who declined to support the Right platform at the decisive time, it is also possible that he had grave doubts about the ability of Bukharin, Rykov, and Tomskii to serve as effective leaders during the kind of crisis the USSR was facing.[113] A simple belief that Stalin seemed indomitable and would win the political struggle, at least for the near term, may have been a factor. Most likely his decisions were influenced by a combination of these factors.

Surely, however, Smirnov would have been disillusioned with the way collectivization actually proceeded—with mass dekulakization, extraordinary violence and social dislocation, the widespread killing of livestock, and famine in 1932–33. Smirnov apparently fell seriously ill and remained uninvolved in politics for perhaps two years or more after the collectivization drive began.[114]

Immediately following the launch of the forced collectivization drive, the OGPU fabricated at Stalin's prompting "the Case of the Laboring Peasant Party" (*Trudovaia Krest'ianskaia Partiia*, the TKP), in 1930. Leading agricultural specialists, including N. D. Kondrat'ev, A. V. Chaianov, N. P. Makarov, L. N Iurovskii, N. N. Sukhanov, and A. N. Chelintsev, were accused of leading this fictitious counterrevolutionary party. According to the police, the TKP included over two hundred thousand members. Focusing on Narkomzem's perspective plans formulated between 1924 and 1926, the OGPU accused the agrarian scholars of having attempted to sabotage the agricultural economy. These experts had endeavored to restore capitalism through their secret activities inside government agencies, including the agriculture and finance commissariats, Gosplan, and the Central Statistical Administration. The country's greatest experts on agriculture were arrested by the OGPU in the summer of 1930. Agents arrested Kondrat'ev and Chaianov on June 19, 1930; Sukhanov was picked up on July 20, Chelintsev on August 13. As had been the case in 1922, Soviet agricultural specialists tended to be arrested around harvest time.[115]

According to the OGPU, these counterrevolutionary agrarian scholars, in secret cooperation with wreckers in industry, attempted to reintroduce capitalism through the Nepmen, kulaks, and bourgeois intelligentsia, while deliberately destroying the Soviet economy and planning for the armed intervention of foreign imperialists. These wreckers had worked in Zemplan, which turned out to have been "completely in the hands of bourgeois restorationists," including the "kulak professors" mentioned above, plus Rudin and Teitel', who were also arrested. In the words of V. P. Miliutin, head of the Central Statistical Administration, "The agents of world capitalism inside our country, agents of the internal bourgeoisie, chose particular methods of struggle. They occupied important positions, and a number of them occupied very important positions in our central state institutions. . . . Kondrat'ev for a long while played a great role in Narkomzem and Narkomfin. Sukhanov did important work in the Commissariat of Trade and Narkomzem for a long time; Makarov had a responsible post in Narkomzem."[116] "Kondrat'ev, Groman and another couple of scoundrels most certainly ought to be shot," Stalin wrote to Molotov in August, a full six months before the trial of Groman (at which Kondrat'ev testified). The next month Stalin privately accused Teodorovich of acting as an intermediary between the kulak agent Kondrat'ev and the leaders of the Right Opposition.[117] Significantly, Stalin did not accuse Smirnov of acting as the intermediary. Rather, Smirnov's deputy Teodorovich was assigned the blame in attacks on the *Kondrat'evshchina*. Smirnov himself was still safe and kept his position (though he was apparently ill) in the Central Committee's Orgburo.

Although the Trial of the Laboring Peasant Party was never held, two other public trials served to air many of the ludicrous accusations against Narkomzem's specialists. The prosecution concocted links among these three "parties" and forced agricultural specialists indicted in the TKP affair to testify against experts in the other trials. The trial of the so-called Industrial Party (Prompartiia) was held in Moscow in November and December 1930.[118] According to the obviously coerced testimony of Leonid Ramzin, the Industrial Party decided in mid-1928 that Chaianov would become the Minister of Agriculture in a new anti-Soviet government.[119] Prosecutors scripted detailed and frequently absurd testimony for the defendants. Professor A. A. Rybnikov, for one, admitted to accepting money for his counterrevolutionary activities directly from the Pope. Soon after his court appearance, he suffered a nervous collapse and attempted to dig through the wall of his prison cell with his bare hands.[120]

The so-called Menshevik Trial in March 1931 also served as a public attack on the discredited remnants of the Right wing of the party. Kondrat'ev was forced to testify for the prosecution as a lead witness. Having spent nine months in prison, Kondrat'ev "confessed" that both the Laboring Peasant Party (of which he was the "ideological chief") and the "Menshevik Party" had supported the Right wing of the Bolsheviks.[121] Although the planned trial of the TKP was never held, the outlines of the case against the TKP are evident from Kondrat'ev's testimony at the Menshevik trial. In the docket, he incriminated many nonparty specialists in Gosplan, Narkomfin, Narkomzem and other agencies, in incredibly elaborate, often internally contradictory and ultimately nonsensical, counterrevolutionary conspiracies. According to Kondrat'ev's testimony, all his work in the 1920s had been on behalf of the restoration of capitalism and "kulak agriculture." He further stated that beginning in 1928, he decided to support the intervention of the British, French, and other foreign armies into the USSR.[122] Kondrat'ev declared all his positions of the 1920s to have been incorrect, and admitted that Stalin was right about all matters of policy, including the liquidation of the kulaks as a class.

In January 1932, Chaianov, Kondrat'ev, Makarov, and many other agrarian specialists were sentenced by a closed OGPU tribunal to terms in concentration camps ranging from five to eight years.[123] Most never left prison alive.

Famine struck the Soviet Union in 1932 for the second time in ten years.[124] A result of the brutal methods of forced collectivization, the famine affected Ukraine (where the government suspected peasants were holding back hidden stocks of hoarded grain) more than other areas, though the effects were also felt in the Volga, the North Caucasus, and Kazakhstan. Armed units went from village to village, and house to house, to violently seize grain stores, including seed for the coming planting season. When requisitions did not bring in enough food to satisfy Moscow, new waves of armed forces were sent back to take still more grain. Unlike the famine of 1921–22, when Lenin had solicited and accepted help from abroad, the 1932–33 events were never mentioned in the Soviet press and no help from abroad was accepted. Foreign diplomats, journalists, and aid workers were not allowed into the afflicted regions, though some learned of the famine and tried to bring attention to the suffering. The death toll reached its peak in the spring of 1933. Perhaps five million people died from starvation and disease. Archive documents demonstrate that the government chose to export grain abroad for hard currency even as reports of mass starvation came in from the localities. Although poor weather played a role in the small harvest, Moscow's brutal requisitioning policies and its failure to react to signs of catastrophe ultimately turned a partial crop failure into a massive famine.

In November 1932 former commissar of agriculture Smirnov was accused by an OGPU informant of serving as the leader of a small "Rightist antiparty group" that included N. B. Eismont, People's Commissar for Supply of the RSFSR, and V. N. Tolmachev, head of the road transportation administration of the RSFSR. (One must assume that it was no coincidence that charges were brought against Smirnov during the famine.) Upon his arrest in late November, Eismont asserted that Smirnov had exclaimed in early November, "Who will remove Stalin as General Secretary?" and "We can't go on living like this!" The OGPU claimed that, based on its interrogations, Smirnov "opposed the party line" on collectivization and was a longtime oppositionist. Providing evidence of Smirnov's alleged "fractional past," Karl Radek testified by letter that Smirnov had proposed a "right-left bloc" against Stalin in the spring of 1927. The details of this bloc cannot be verified, nor can its very existence. Smirnov was himself very ill, wracked by debilitating headaches, and could barely stand upright to testify. Speaking on January 12, 1933, before a joint Plenum of the Central Committee and the Central Control Commission, Smirnov categorically denied that he was involved in an anti-Stalin political grouping, though he conceded that he had complained about the effects of certain specific policies, especially those that had negative effects on livestock.

Nevertheless, some of the sentiments ascribed to Smirnov do seem consistent with what we know of Smirnov's beliefs in 1927. According to Radek's letter (handwritten on *Izvestiia* letterhead), Smirnov complained that "the party has no clear policy on the peasant question; it takes steps towards the peasants, and then negates them." According to Radek, Smirnov said that he "receives hundreds of letters from the village [writing that] 'we cannot live like this any more.'"[125] Further, Eismont alleged that Smirnov was particularly horrified by the methods of collectivization that caused a precipitous decline in the number of horses and cattle, and he predicted that the countryside would produce no meat before 1934. Many of these statements are consistent with Smirnov's positions in the 1920s, and may reflect his sentiments in 1932. In the final analysis, however, we cannot know to what degree Smirnov embraced any of the positions ascribed to him in this kangaroo court. On January 16, 1933, the Plenum unanimously voted to expel Smirnov from the Central Committee for his alleged failure to abandon "antiparty positions." Smirnov's group was found to have attempted to "restore capitalism, and in particular the kulaks."[126] In December of 1934, he was charged with continuing his oppositional activities and subsequently expunged from the ranks of the Communist Party.

Teodorovich, Kondrat'ev, Chaianov, Oganovskii, Sviderskii, Kubiak, Iakovlev, and the "peasant commissar" Iakovenko were killed in the Great Purges of 1937–38. In March 1937, while serving in an insignificant post in the Commissariat for Light Industry, Smirnov was arrested. On February 8, 1938, Aleksandr P. Smirnov was convicted under article fifty-eight of the Soviet Union's criminal code. He was shot two days later.[127]

Conclusion

In many ways the fate of the People's Commissariat of Agriculture RSFSR reflects the character, tensions, and fate of the New Economic Policy of 1921–28, while offering insight into the political victory of Stalin and his associates in 1928–29. This crucial Soviet state agency's internal culture, worldview, personnel, leadership, and political face offer a glimpse into the revolutionary regime in all its complexity. The Commissariat rested at the intersection of several fundamental, related currents during the 1920s. Aspiring to spread the revolution to the countryside as an element in the building of socialism, the government simultaneously needed to boost the output of peasant agriculture in an attempt to "catch and overtake" the Western industrial economies. Suspicion of the "petty bourgeois" peasantry simmered inside the Communist Party just as the party was forced to reach a modus vivendi with the noncommunist specialists who populated the economic and government administrations. The general, almost visceral, mistrust among many communists of bureaucracy in all its forms was pervasive, yet the ruling party was committed to using the machinery of state to reshape the Soviet countryside. The relationships among, and unexpected outcomes of, these trends are presented herein.

As one of many similar institutions the Bolsheviks designed to carry out the socialist transformation of the Soviet Union, the Commissariat of Agriculture provides a window into numerous dilemmas of early Soviet state construction. Narkomzem's political position and challenges in some ways mimicked those of other early Soviet organizations. Yet, in some senses the Commissariat of Agriculture reflected the regime's contradictions more intensely—and in unique ways—than other state agencies. This distinction was partly a consequence of its specific mission and partly a result of the regime's general distaste for the peasantry as an ignorant, stubbornly individualistic, and ultimately obsolete class. At the end of the 1920s, when the peasant problem seemed to many people to be more intractable than ever, enthusiasts grew impatient with the complaints and strategies of experts and bureaus. They solved the peasant "problem" once and for all by means of the immediate and violent collectivization of agriculture and the simultaneous liquidation of the kulaks.

During the chaotic first three years of the Revolution, the Commissariat of Agriculture, like the rest of the infant government, was pieced together spontaneously amid social upheaval and war. In 1917, the Bolsheviks had encouraged the breakdown of order in the countryside and the disintegration of the decrepit bureaucratized apparatuses of the Old Regime and the Provisional Government. Immediately after taking power, however, the Bolsheviks realized that they would need to protect or reconstitute much of the old administration. Narkomzem emerged as an amalgamation of three types of organization: first, wholly preserved structural legacies of the tsarist past; second, *ad hoc*, improvised organizations created to meet urgent problems as they arose; and third (but infrequently), planned, consciously created, new departments. The Bolsheviks did not create a new state from scratch in October; rather, they inherited one across the revolutionary divide. Structures and subdivisions mimicked the pre-October 1917 ministry. A glance at the Commissariat's organizational chart, with its sixty divisions and subdivisions, nearly all of which had precursors in the tsarist administration, would hardly have indicated that power had switched hands. Only the presence of a section devoted to "socialist" farms would have hinted at the change in government. The persistence of communal peasant farming, plus a continued commitment on the part of the regime to attack the deficiencies of "backward" peasant farming by means of state intervention, meant that government strategies for modernizing agriculture would fall back on certain patterns or models. Just as Tocqueville observed about the reemergence of centralized patterns of administration after the French Revolution, Soviet state building borrowed much from tsarist efforts. Crucial elements of the state apparatus—including structures, personnel, practices, and bureaucratic culture—made the transition.

In the months that followed the Bolshevik seizure of power, the leaders of the people's commissariats, from the party chiefs to the heads of the specialized divisions, had to find qualified labor to staff revolutionary agencies. Narkomzem thus absorbed a large number of employees from the tsarist administration and the Provisional Government. These holdovers from the Old Regime joined the Bolshevik Commissariat for various reasons. Some officials were desperate for sustenance. Others were dedicated to the realization of scientific land and agricultural reform. Some specialists had devoted themselves to service to the peasant population, in the tradition of Russian populism. Most noncommunist specialists and Bolsheviks could agree on the need for extensive state intervention to overcome what both groups considered the villages' profound underdevelopment. A great paradox—and this did not escape the Bolsheviks—is that the new regime inherited a huge (and growing) state administration populated by people whom many Bolsheviks considered to be social aliens and even class enemies. Yet, these were the very people whom they desperately needed to rebuild the economy and staff every agency of state.

During the Civil War, the Commissariat of Agriculture and its specialists remained in a precarious position in the government. The war destroyed networks of transportation and communications and greatly hindered the distribution of supplies and equipment not directly involved in the war effort. In this environment, extracting food to feed the armies and starving cities became the urgent mission to which the regime subordinated all other economic tasks. The party bypassed the Commissariat's system of land reform and agricultural assistance agencies, institutionalizing extralegal confiscation methods in the village. The contingencies of the emergency meant that the regime treated agricultural assistance as a low priority.

In wartime, noncommunist agrarian specialists had little real authority in the Commissariat. The leaders of the Commissariat, however, organized the agency into divisions and subunits that focused on particular branches of agriculture, most of which were headed by trained experts. These positions were relatively insignificant during the war when Narkomzem remained politically and economically on the margins. When NEP greatly accentuated the role of specialists in the economy, however, experts were in position to assume more authority both in Moscow and in the provinces. The recovery of agriculture constituted an essential precondition for the reconstruction of the economy in the 1920s and, ultimately, for the survival of the state and the Revolution. Optimism about the prospects for "rescuing" the countryside from its perennial backwardness accompanied the post-war emergence of a specialized institutional culture devoted to using the state to elevate production through the application of science and technology to agricultural organization. Indeed, the Commissariat should have been in a strong position when the party leadership introduced NEP policies aimed at conciliating the peasantry.

Nevertheless, the Commissariat remained weak for the first two years of NEP. Both internal and external factors abound to explain this continued frailty. Inside the Commissariat, ineffective leadership, a series of scandals, and insufficient contact with local branches kept Narkomzem less potent than it might have been. Moreover, agriculture's increased stature on the national agenda did not translate into substantially increased resources for the Commissariat in 1921 and 1922. Continuing biases against economic concessions to peasant capitalism in certain segments of the Communist Party also conspired against the allocation of large subsidies for agriculture and land work. The Commissariat's class-neutral outlook raised concerns that it favored better-off peasants. Uncertain loyalty to NEP among some party members worked against the Commissariat of Agriculture, which, more than any other, lobbied for, and then implemented, the "soft-line" policy of alliance between city and countryside that formed the heart of the new policies. During these two years, the Commissariat was unable to parlay the increased prominence of agriculture into more power for the organization.

Despite the Commissariat's unstable position, the government institutionalized the influence of specialists in the land administration in 1921–22. During this period, the role of trained experts throughout the government and economic agencies was elevated. Nonparty experts found protectors among the party leadership of the ministries. Inside Narkomzem, the planning commission Zemplan, directed by I. A. Teodorovich, became something of a haven for pre-revolutionary agrarian experts. The case of Narkomzem demonstrates how the state apparatus served as a type of refuge for nonparty scientific intelligentsia as well as middle-class professionals, administrators, and educated persons of all types. The list of eminent scholars of the rural economy whom the Narkomzem leadership recruited to the Commissariat reads like a veritable Who's Who of pre-war experts on the rural economy. All evidence points to the influence that these and other noncommunist specialists enjoyed inside the Commissariat. The fact that many of these specialists were believed to have had pre-October ties with the Socialist Revolutionary party (or were accused of having such ties), however, brought the frequent attention of hostile investigators.

In this context, Narkomzem remained a ministry closely associated with two nonproletarian social groupings: the noncommunist specialists (most of whom were white-collar workers and many of whom were holdovers from the tsarist administration) and the more productive sections of the peasantry. The regime desperately needed both groups to revive the economy and maintain the state: the specialists were essential for their indispensable expertise, and the peasantry was needed for the production of food and raw materials. There was an underlying tension and destabilizing factor during NEP, namely, the party's class-based approach to its own bureaucracy, an approach that tended to group personnel into "desirable" and "undesirable" social and political categories. In this case, A. P. Smirnov, while accepting the general premise that personnel from some social groups was better than others, employed numerous strategies to protect vulnerable personnel. With Smirnov's removal in the spring of 1928 in the wake of the grain crisis, those suspect staffers were much less likely to survive the scrutiny of the cadre hawks in party personnel agencies. Indeed, although many commissariats were subject to (still nonviolent) purges of their cadres in

1928–29, the Commissariat of Agriculture was one of the first targets, partly because of Smirnov's very success in protecting his agency's cadres in previous years.

A very useful analytical tool for examining the Commissariat under the leadership of A. P. Smirnov is the concept of *vedomstvennost'*—the notion that an institution has cultures, political interests, and constituencies that shape its actions, often in unexpected ways. Institutions in the Soviet period were both deeply political and deeply politicized. Struggles for cadres, influence, budgets, and policy were all shaped by politics and were couched in terms of the future of the Revolution. Competing, if often overlapping, worldviews lay at the heart of NEP life, and these battles over vision often took on inter-and intrainstitutional forms.

The Commissariat of Agriculture's leadership developed a specific, if sometimes contradictory, vision of the Soviet countryside in the transition period, one that embraced both the modernization and the socialization of farming. In their view, a productive rural sector was essential for the success of the Soviet economy and ultimately for the success of the revolution itself. The countryside had to be made prosperous through the introduction of new technology and forms of farming organization and the elimination of what they regarded as gross inefficiencies in traditional farming methods. In some senses, the leaders of the Commissariat of Agriculture were pragmatists. They understood that a large-scale transition to collective farming was nowhere on the horizon. Before 1928 collective farms were rare, unpopular with almost all farmers, expensive for the state to maintain, and relatively unproductive. All communists agreed that a socialized farming sector was the ultimate goal. Peasants' movement to collective farms should be voluntary, and everyone, including Narkomzem party chiefs, believed that it would occur eventually. The Commissariat's Moscow leadership, intent both on raising production and on overseeing the countryside's transition to socialism, demonstrated ambivalence toward collective farms, which showed little promise as vehicles for moving the countryside toward greater productivity or toward collectivism in agriculture. At the same time, Commissariat leaders understood that the other institutions they would have liked the peasantry to have accepted—the village soviet and the communist party—were also weak and largely rejected by rural inhabitants.

The Commissariat leadership understood that the repartitional commune had emerged from the Civil War stronger than before the Revolution and that, for the foreseeable future, the commune would remain the primary—and in most places the only—institution in the countryside through which peasants would make decisions about their lives as producers. For the near term, Narkomzem was intent on preserving the commune as the central institution in the state's relationship with the village. Indeed, it is one of the ironies of the situation that the institution most associated with peasant stagnation and backwardness before the Revolution became one that the Commissariat made every effort to protect and strengthen in the 1920s. Commissariat officials saw in the commune several positive features, maintaining that the regime could achieve many of its goals in a countryside still dominated by this traditional institution. Within the parameters of the commune, Commissariat specialists would locate, educate, and provide incentives to a progressive vanguard of farmers who were willing to adopt modern technologies and methods, and who would then serve as models for their neighbors.

In addition to counting on a more efficient commune to improve output and yields, Commissariat leaders believed that the commune would serve as a stepping-stone from which villagers could make the transition to the large, highly mechanized, collectivized production units that would eventually comprise the basis of the socialist countryside. The commune, in this view, was a preserver of "collectivism." With its emphasis on the redistribution of land and joint decision-making, the commune discouraged the individualism that might develop if peasants broke away from the commune onto separated homesteads. In addition, the commune was highly regarded as a foundation of the nationalization of land, serving as a bulwark against private property and the development of property consciousness. Narkomzem's emphasis on the commune also hints at a mistrust of certain spontaneous actions of villagers, even among those officials considered most supportive of the economic interests of the peasantry. The Commissariat leadership believed that using the commune as a means of controlling the negative actions of villagers was in the interest of the Soviet state.

Finally, Commissariat officials envisioned using the peasant commune in order to advance the organization's institutional interests. Commissariat officials wanted to play a role much greater than merely modernizing peasant farming; rather, they intended to oversee a gradual and controlled transition to productive socialism in the countryside. Like so many phenomena in the political life of NEP, these factors were inextricably linked. In the view of the Commissariat's leadership, this transition had to include a central and large institutional role for the Commissariat and its personnel. Smirnov tied the fate of the Revolution to the fate of "his" organization, just as he linked the fate of the organization to himself.

Another important pillar of the Commissariat vision during NEP was its minimization of social differentiation and class antagonisms; rural class struggle did not concern most Commissariat officials. Narkomzem's leading specialist and communist leadership argued that there was no real threat of the emergence of a dangerous kulak stratum. They argued that the state should aim its policies toward helping villagers who were hard working and productive but who did not take advantage of their neighbors. The Commissariat's Rightist policies—lobbying for easy credit for farmers and relatively high purchase prices for agricultural produce, while encouraging production by better-off (zazhitochnye) or strong (krepkie) farmers—left it open to charges that its specialists were influencing Narkomzem to make concessions to the peasantry at the expense of the proletariat. Narkomzem's persistent claim that social differentiation in the countryside was not a serious problem left it vulnerable to these accusations.

Meanwhile, local agricultural experts in the countryside found themselves in a very difficult situation during NEP. Despite NEP's emphasis on agricultural recovery, the wages and prestige of agricultural experts remained very low in comparison with their counterparts working in industry. Poor salaries combined with poor working and living conditions caused high turnover and fostered resentment among local workers toward a party and ministry leadership that seemed to ignore the plight of its civil servants. The implementation of land policy and programs to assist peasant agriculture had to be coordinated and carried out through an agency which was poorly funded and organized, suffered from massive turnover, and lacked sufficient numbers of educated and reliable officials.

There were several reasons why many within the professional strata of specialists, administrators, and planners in the state apparatus, especially at the local level, found it in their interest to support aspects of plans to accelerate agricultural modernization. Many members of these groups saw in plans to more rapidly reshape the village the means to achieve personal or collective goals. At least as initially planned, large-scale, collectivized agriculture promised agrarian specialists a chance to practice their trades in close to ideal circumstances. The state would compel the peasantry to rationalize production, eliminate three-field and strip farming, and obey the scientific elite that would manage production on these modern farms. Heightened professional satisfaction, combined with guarantees of higher pay, increased prestige, and more comfortable living and working conditions seems to have convinced many nonparty specialists to share in enthusiasm over industrializing and rationalizing agricultural production, especially before the violent and disorganizing nature of the drive to collectivize became clear.

Moreover, in the context of the tensions between the urban-based socialist regime and the traditional society it was trying both to govern and to transform, a yawning chasm opened between the goals of the Commissariat of Agriculture and its ability to accomplish those goals. Agriculture needed something akin to a technical revolution, which could be accomplished only through a massive influx of credit, equipment, and specialists. For a variety of financial and political reasons, these resources were not forthcoming. By the second half of the decade, a variety of other features out of the control of the Commissariat's leaders also contributed to undermining the agricultural administration's efforts, including the continuing reluctance of the party leadership to commit large resources to agriculture, in part a result of general ignorance in communist circles concerning the rural economy and the village in general and latent hostility toward the "petty bourgeois peasantry;" dilemmas involving the marketing of produce that the party never managed to resolve peacefully; red tape that tied the hands and wasted the time of specialists and officials alike; a severe shortage of qualified personnel, and many farmers' continuing mistrust of the regime, inflamed by price policies that provoked farmers to withhold surplus produce from government procurement agencies. Committed to the transformation of the Russian countryside, Commissariat leaders during NEP encountered staggering roadblocks to its achievement through peaceful methods.

Once the party line permanently turned against NEP in 1928, openly repudiating the policies Narkomzem had fought for since 1921, the Commissariat of Agriculture became the first government agency to be subjected to a large-scale, though still nonviolent, purge. When it became clear that the removal of Smirnov and his deputies in March 1928 had failed to ensure the reliability of the organization, the party's oversight agencies called for an investigation, then a purge, of noncommunist employees in late 1928 and 1929. Finally, with the full-scale collectivization drive, the party leadership under Stalin simply bypassed the entire organization in December 1929, creating new agencies to carry out the "socialist reorganization of agriculture." By the end of the decade, frustration with the traditional channels and methods of economic transformation led the Central Committee, under Stalin's direction, to utilize armed brigades, which circumvented established government agencies in collectivizing the villages by force. Narkomzem was rendered impotent. The Commissariat of Agriculture RSFSR—whose policies toward the peasantry had comprised the heart of the party's NEP-era policies toward the countryside, committed to gradualist change and a stable, if tenuous, peace with the village, and opposed to immediate, forced collectivization—was by no means the appropriate vehicle for overseeing the Stalinist revolution in the countryside.

Glossary and Abbreviations

batrak	a landless peasant laborer
bedniak	poor peasant
byvshie liudi	literally *former people*; individuals tainted by association with the old regime or with suspect political or social backgrounds
cherespolositsa	the division of communal lands into dispersed strips; strip farming
chernyi peredel	massive "black repartition" or redivision of land undertaken by peasantry during 1917–18
dal'nozemlia	strips located long distances from the village
Departament zemledeliia	The Department of Agriculture, a division found within the Imperial Ministry of Agriculture
desiatina	a unit of measurement that equals about 2.7 acres
droblenie	the splintering of households into smaller and smaller units
dvor	peasant household
GPU	the political police (Main Political Administration), 1922–23, formerly the Cheka (renamed OGPU in 1923)
khutor	homestead in which all of a household's arable land was concentrated in one place outside the village
kolkhoz	collective farm
kollegiia	the collegium—the advisory board of the people's commissar
krest'ianin	peasant
kulak	"wealthy" peasant
Ministerstvo zemledeliia	Imperial Ministry of Agriculture
mir	the peasant commune (a term used by peasants)
muzhik	colloquial term for a peasant man
na ziab	plowing fields in the fall for the spring sowing
narkom	narodnyi komissar, or people's commissar
Narkomfin	Narodnyi komissariat finansov, or People's Commissariat of Finance (NKF)
Narkomprod	Narodnyi komissariat prodovol'stviia, or People's Commissariat of Food Supply

Narkomzem	Narodnyi komissariat zemledeliia, or People's Commissariat of Agriculture (NKZ)
obshchina	the peasant commune (a term used mainly by intellectuals and officials)
OGPU	the political police, 1923–34 (Unified Main Political Administration)
otrub	homestead that concentrated only plowed land in one place outside the village, but the farm buildings, house, and garden plot remained in the village
pomeshchik	a noble estate owner before 1917
prodotriad	"food brigades" responsible for requisitioning food from villages during the Civil War
sel'sovet	the village soviet
seredniak	"middle peasant" or a peasant of "average" means
skhod	gathering of heads of village households
smychka	in official parlance, the link or alliance between the proletariat and peasantry during the New Economic Policy
sokha	the wooden peasant plow
sovkhoz	state farm in the Soviet period
Sovnarkom	Council of People's Commissars (SNK)
uchastkovye punkty	local agronomic stations
usad'ba	garden plot
vydvizhenets	a promotee; a person of peasant or working-class background promoted into an important position in a state or economic organization
zazhitochnyi	a well-off or better-off peasant; part of the upper stratum of the "middle" peasantry, but not a "rich" peasant (kulak)
zemleustroistvo	land reorganization
zemotdel	land section of a local soviet
Zemplan	the Commissariat of Agriculture's planning agency (Zemel'naia planovaia komissiia)
zemstvo	tsarist era units of local administration that employed many professionals, including doctors, statisticians, agronomists, teachers, and the like; known collectively as the third element

Notes

INTRODUCTION

1. This book focuses on the territory of the RSFSR, especially European Russia.

2. The best study of the contemporary problems facing the rural areas of the former Soviet Union is Stephen K. Wegren's *Agriculture and the State in Soviet and Post-Soviet Russia* (Pittsburgh, 1998).

3. R. W. Davies, ed., *From Tsarism to the New Economic Policy* (London, 1990), 154–57, 189–211.

4. I. Chernyshev, *Sel'skoe khoziaistvo dovoennoi Rossii i SSSR* (Moscow, 1926), 60–69. Agriculture comprised 49.4 percent of the national income; industry, 22.1 percent; trade, 20.5 percent; and transportation, 7.6 percent.

5. V. N. Meshcheriakov, *Organizatsiia Narkomzema* (Moscow, 1919), 8.

6. On changing social composition of the imperial bureaucracy and its impact on ministerial politics, see especially Alfred J. Rieber, "The Sedimentary Society," in Edith W. Clowes, Samuel D. Kassow, and James L. West, eds., *Between Tsar and People: Educated Society and the Quest for Public Identities in Late Imperial Russia* (Princeton, 1991). See also articles in D. K. Pintner and Walter Rowney eds., *Russian Officialdom: The Bureaucratization of Russian Society from the Seventeenth to Twentieth Century* (Chapel Hill, 1980); and Daniel T. Orlovsky, *The Limits of Reform: The Ministry of Internal Affairs in Imperial Russia, 1802–1881* (Cambridge, Mass., 1981); Richard Wortman, *The Development of a Russian Legal Consciousness* (Chicago, 1976).

7. Daniel Orlovsky pioneered the application of the concept of *vedomstvennost'* for the study of Russian bureaucracy. Important work on the Soviet civil service has been done by Orlovsky, who has identified the "white collar employees" *(sluzhashchie)* in the government apparatus as a serious subject for research. See, for example, his "Gimpelson and the Hegemony of the Working Class," *Slavic Review* 48: 1 (Spring 1989); "State Building in the Civil War Era: The Role of the Lower Middle Strata," in Diane Koenker et al., eds., *Party, State and Society in the Russian Civil War* (Bloomington, 1989), 180–209. See also his *Limits of Reform*; and Marc Raeff, "Bureaucratic Phenomena of Imperial Russia," *American Historical Review* 84, no. 2 (1979), 399–411.

8. S. Frederick Starr, *Decentralization and Self-Government in Russia, 1830–1870* (Princeton, 1972). Historians since E. H. Carr have noted the weakness of the Soviet state in the countryside. See, for example, his *Socialism in One Country*, vol. 2, (New York, 1970), 311 ff.

9. See, for example, P. A. Zaionchkovskii, *Pravitel'stvennyi apparat samoderzhavnoi Rossii v XIX v.* (Moscow, 1978); and *Rossiskoe samoderzhavie v kontse XIX stoletiia* (Moscow, 1970); Richard Robbins, *Famine in Russia, 1891–92: The Imperial Government Responds to a Crisis* (New York, 1975); George Yaney, *The Urge to Mobilize* (Urbana, 1982); Nancy Frieden, "The

Politics of Zemstvo Medicine," in Terence Emmons, ed., *The Zemstvo in Russia: An Experiment in Local Self-Government* (Cambridge, 1982).

10. On underfunding of local governments compared with Western Europe, see Michael F. Hamm, "The Breakdown of Urban Modernization: A Prelude to the Revolutions of 1917," in Michael F. Hamm, ed., *The City in Russian History* (Lexington, Ky., 1976), 182–200. On the third element, see Emmons, ed., *The Zemstvo in Russia*.

11. See especially Stephen F. Cohen, *Bukharin and the Bolshevik Revolution: A Political Biography, 1888–1938* (Princeton, 1971), and his "Bukharinism and Stalinism," and "Bukharin, NEP, and the Idea of an Alternative to Stalinism," in *Rethinking the Soviet Experience: Politics and History since 1917* (New York, 1985).

12. Stephen Cohen, *Bukharin and the Bolshevik Revolution*, 76.

13. Natalia P. Nosova's writing on the Commissariat of Agriculture represents an approach that similarly idealizes the NEP period. Natalia P. Nosova, *Upravliat' ili komandovat'? Gosudarstvo i krest'ianstvo sovetskoi Rossii, 1917–1929* (Moscow, 1993). The book appeared in 1993 but is based on her masters and doctoral dissertations, written between 1987 and 1991. Imbued with the Perestroika-era celebration of NEP as a peaceful, prosperous period before the sudden advent of Stalinist tyranny and collectivization, her study wholly accepts the Commissariat's own constructed public image. Nosova uncritically accepts the Commissariat's public proclamations of its own accomplishments. An effort to knock down the Stalinist straw men that dominated the field of historical study for decades in the USSR limits the analysis; her work tries to debunk oversimplified Stalinist and, later, Brezhnevite notions of a capitalist-restorationist commissariat without fully breaking out of the previous categories of analysis.

14. David R. Shearer has pointed out the limitations of this assumption. See his *Industry, State, and Society in Stalin's Russia, 1926–1934* (Ithaca, 1996), 14–17.

15. D. K. Rowney, *Transition to Technocracy: the Structural Origins of the Soviet Administrative State* (Ithaca, 1989); Kendall Bailes, *Technology and Society under Lenin and Stalin* (Princeton, 1978). Bailes's work was pathbreaking for its treatment of patronage and specialists in industry—what he calls the "technostructure"—especially for the 1928–1941 period.

16. Stephen Sternheimer, "Administration for Development: The Emerging Bureaucratic Elite, 1920–1930," in Pintner and Rowney, eds., *Russian Officialdom*, 335, 344. Kendall Bailes also emphasizes that during the 1920s, legislation "raised the social status of the technical intelligentsia." Bailes, *Technology and Society* (Princeton, 1978), 66.

17. See, for example, Merle Fainsod, *How Russia is Ruled* (Cambridge, 1953); Richard Pipes, *The Russian Revolution* (Cambridge, 1990); Orlando Figes, *A People's Tragedy* (New York, 1996).

18. Moshe Lewin, *The Making of the Soviet System* (New York, 1985); Roger Pethybridge, *The Social Prelude to Stalinism* (New York, 1974); and his *One Step Backwards, Two Steps Forward* (Oxford, 1990). Stephen Sternheimer, "Administration for Development: The Emerging Bureaucratic Elite, 1920–1930," in Pintner and Rowney, eds., *Russian Officialdom*, 317–54. The classic text on Communist Party officials is T. H. Rigby, *Communist Party Membership in the USSR 1917–1967* (Princeton, 1968).

19. Don K. Rowney, *Transition to Technocracy: The Structural Origins of the Soviet Administrative State* (Ithaca, 1989); Kendall Bailes, *Technology and Society under Lenin and Stalin*; David Shearer, *Industry, State and Society* and his "The Language and Politics of Socialist Rationalization: Productivity, Industrial Relations and the Social Origins of Stalinism at the end of NEP," *Cahiers du Monde Russe et Sovietique* 32(4): 581–608; Peter Holquist, *Making War, Forging Revolution: Russia's Continuum of Crisis, 1914–1921* (Cambridge, Mass., 2002). See also Stephen Kotkin, "The State: Is It Us? Memoirs, Archives, and Kremlinolo-

gists," *Russian Review* 61:1 (January 2002): 35–51. Susan Gross Solomon's work analyzes disagreements among agrarian scholars. See Susan Gross Solomon, *The Soviet Agrarian Debate: A Controversy in Social Science, 1923–29* (Boulder, 1977).

20. Several important recent monographs that treat the complex relations between state and society—and inside the state itself—in the early Soviet period are David Shearer, *Industry, State and Society*; Michael David-Fox, *Revolution of the Mind: Higher Learning among the Bolsheviks, 1918–1929* (Ithaca, 1997); Elizabeth Wood, *The Baba and the Comrade: Gender and Politics in Revolutionary Russia* (Bloomington, 1997); Daniel Peris, *Storming the Heavens* (Ithaca, 1998); and David Stone, *Hammer and Rifle: The Militarization of the Soviet Union* (Lawrence, 2000). John McCannon's *Red Arctic: Polar Exploration and the Myth of the North in the Soviet Union, 1932–39* (Oxford, 1998) is an example of an archive-based study of the 1930s that combines political, cultural, and institutional approaches.

21. For details on the relationships among leading institutional actors and the processes involved in the formation of policy toward the peasantry, see Markus Wehner, *Bauernpolitik im proletarischen Staat: Die Bauernfrage als zentrales Problem der Sowjetischen Innenpolitik 1921–1928* (Koeln, 1998). See also James W. Heinzen, "Politics, Administration, and Specialization in the Russian People's Commissariat of Agriculture" (Ph.D. dissertation, University of Pennsylvania, 1993).

22. See, for example, Donald Raleigh, *Experiencing Russia's Civil War: Politics, Society, and Revolutionary Culture in Saratov, 1917–1922* (Princeton, 2002); and his *Revolution on the Volga: 1917 in Saratov* (Ithaca, 1986); Orlando Figes, *Peasant Russia, Civil War: The Volga Countryside in Revolution (1917–1921)* (Oxford, 1989); Roger Pethybridge, *One Step Backwards, Two Steps Forward* (Oxford, 1990). On the peasant economy in the 1920s see the work of V.P. Danilov; and Stefan Merl, *Agrarmarkt und die neue okonomische Politik: die Anfange staatlicher Lenkung der Landwirtschaft in der Sowjetunion, 1925-1928* (Oldenbourg, 1981). On the prerevolutionary village, see David Moon, *The Russian Peasantry, 1600-1930: The World the Peasants Made* (London, 1999).

CHAPTER 1

1. Meshcheriakov, *Organizatsiia Narkomzema* (Moscow, 1919), 8.

2. Figures for 1909–10: agriculture, 9.1 billion rubles; industry, 4.5 billion rubles. I. Chernyshev, *Sel'skoe-khoziaistvo dovoennoi Rossii* (Moscow, 1926), 60–69. In 1913, agriculture comprised 50.7 percent of national income; industry, by contrast, provided only 21.4 percent. R. W. Davies, et al., eds., *The Economic Transformation of the Soviet Union, 1913–1945* (Cambridge, Eng., 1993), 272, table four. See also *Sel'sko-khoziaistvennaia zhizn'*, 1927, no. 16:1.

3. Stephen G. Wheatcroft et al., "Soviet Industrialization Reconsidered: Some Preliminary Conclusions about Soviet Economic Development between 1986 and 1941," *Economic History Review*, 39:2 (1986): 12. See also *Narodnoe khoziaistvo SSSR* (1932–1958), 70. Because the year 1913 produced an exceptionally good harvest, statisticians have instead relied on calculations based on an average of the five years between 1909 and 1913, as a benchmark for production on the eve of the war. Using this principle, for 1909–13, the average figure for millions of tons of harvested grain is approximately 68, while the unusually high total for 1913 alone equals 79 million tons. Davies et al., eds., *The Economic Transformation of the Soviet Union, 1913–1945* (Cambridge, Eng., 1994), table 19. A. M. Anfimov, "On the History of the Russian Peasantry at the Beginning of the Twentieth Century," *Russian Review* 51 (July 1992): 396–407. On the war, see also Alexis Antsiferov, et al., *Russian Agriculture during the War* (New Haven, 1930). For a provocative and exhaustive critique of the performance of Russian peasant agri-

culture in the late nineteenth and early twentieth centuries, focusing on the central grain producing region, see David Kerans, *Mind and Labor on the Farm in Black-Earth Russia* (Budapest, 2001). An excellent overview of the history of the Russian peasantry is David Moon, *The Russian Peasantry 1600–1930: The World the Peasants Made* (London, 1999).

4. R. W. Davies, ed., *From Tsarism to the New Economic Policy: Continuity and Change in the Economy of the USSR* (London, 1990), 18–19, citing Wheatcroft's unpublished works.

5. Alfred J. Rieber, "The Reforming Tradition in Russian History," in Alfred J. Rieber and Alvin Z. Rubinstein, eds., *Perestroika at the Crossroads* (Armonk, 1991), 4, 6–7.

6. For a discussion of agronomists employed in the tsarist credit cooperatives, who often regarded peasants as "backward," "primitive," and "dark," see Yanni Kotsonis, *Making Peasants Backward: Agricultural Cooperatives and the Agrarian Question in Russia, 1861–1914* (New York, 1999). For a similar interpretation of the discourse and worldview of economists, see Alessandro Stanziani, *L'economie en revolution: Las cas russe, 1870–1930* (Paris, 1998).

7. For vigorous critiques of this position, see Kotsonis, *Making Peasants Backward*, 1–12; and Judith Pallot, *Land Reform in Russia, 1906–1917* (Oxford, 1999), 16–19.

8 League of Nations, Economic and Financial Section, *International Statistical Yearbook 1926* (Geneva, 1927), 38–42, referring to average yields of wheat, rye, and barley for 1909–13.

9. See Theodore von Laue, *Sergei Witte and the Industrialization of Russia* (New York, 1969); and Alexander Gershenkron, *Economic Backwardness in Historical Perspective* (Cambridge, Mass., 1962); Alfred J. Rieber, "The Reforming Tradition in Russian History," 6–7. When discussing the net volume of agricultural production in Russia, both before and after the Revolution, there are many conflicting estimates. For an overview, see S. G. Wheatcroft and R. W. Davies, "The Crooked Mirror of Soviet Economic Statistics," in R. W. Davies, Mark Harrison, and S. G. Wheatcroft, eds., *The Economic Transformation of the Soviet Union, 1913–1945* (Cambridge, 1994), 24–37.

10. TsSU SSSR, *Narodnoe khoziaistvo SSSR v 1961 godu. Statisticheskii ezhegodnik* (Moscow, 1962), 7 (borders of USSR before 1939). The census listed the peasantry as comprising nearly 90 percent of the population, but since many peasants lived in cities most of the year or worked in forestry or other trades, a figure closer to 75 percent is more accurate. The 1897 census described 70 percent of Russians as "dependent" on agriculture. These figures can be compared with 10 percent in Great Britain and 39 percent in Germany in the same period. Three percent of the population accounted for landlords, their servants and household laborers, and temporary residents. V. P. Danilov, *Sovetskaia dokolkhoznaia derevnia: Naselenie, zemlepol'zovanie, khoziaistvo* (Moscow, 1977), 29. In 1905, one hundred thousand nobles possessed one third of the country's agricultural land, while twelve million peasant households occupied the remaining two thirds. Tsentral'nyi statisticheskii komitet M.V.D., *Statistika zemlevladeniia 1905 g.* (St. Petersburg, 1907), 164–67, appendices on pp. v, xx, xxii.

11. N. D. Kondrat'ev, "Foundations of the Perspective Plan," *Osoboe mnenie*, kn. 1: 344. Report at the Plenary Session of USSR Gosplan presidium, July 4, 1925. Figures based on 1916 census.

12. *Osnovnye elementy sel'skokhoziaistvennogo proizvodstva SSSR 1916 i 1923–27 gg.* (Moscow, 1930), 2–5.

13. The commune also had the right to lease land to other communes or to individuals.

14. Kerans, *Mind and Labor in Black-Earth Russia*, 248–49.

15. Viktor Danilov, using Commissariat of Agriculture figures, in *Sovetskaia dokolkhoznaia derevnia*, 278.

16. In Vologda province the average number of strips was thirteen, in Novgorod ten. In

Tambov the average family worked thirty-six strips; in Orel the average exceeded sixty strips. Many of these parcels were simply abandoned. See Danilov, *Sovetskaia dokolkhoznaia derevnia*, 133. The phenomenon of distant plots, or *dal'nozemlia*, was most pronounced in areas such as the Northern, Western, and Southeastern regions, where fertile land was scarce and scattered piecemeal among lakes, rivers, and forests. In some cases, individuals had to travel up to twenty-five kilometers to reach the farthest strips, occasionally on horseback, but usually by foot.

17. *Narodnoe khoziaistvo za 1958*, 348. Statistics drawn from 1910 census.

18. Zeml'no Planovaia Komissiia, *Materialy po perspektivnomu planu razvitiia sel'skogo Khoziaistva*, (Moscow, 1928), ch. 2, 63. A pood was equal to 16.38 kilograms or about 36 pounds.

19. *Agronomicheskaia pomoshch'*, 34. For the sake of clarity, GUZiZ will be referred to as the Ministry of Agriculture, though it did not receive that appellation until 1915.

20. Wayne D. Rasmussen and Gladys L. Baker, *The Department of Agriculture* (New York: 1972). Before 1905, zemstvos did not participate in agricultural aid programs.

21. *Agronomicheskaia pomoshch'*, 118–19. Between 1905 and 1914, the total amount in zemstvo budgets doubled. K. Matsuzato, "The Fate of Agronomists," *The Russian Review*: 55 (April 1996): 172–73.

22. *Agronomicheskaia pomoshch'*, 116.

23. Ibid., 164–65.

24. Ibid., 143–44.

25. Ibid., 163–72. An excellent survey of the work and outlook of agronomists in this period is Kimitaka Matsuzato, "The Fate of Agronomists in Russia: Their Quantitative Dynamics from 1911 to 1916," *The Russian Review*: 55 (April 1996): 172–200.

26. Matsuzato, "The Fate of Agronomists," 174. See also his "Stolypinskaia reforma i Rossiiskaia agrotekhnologicheskaia revoliutsiia," *Otechestvennaia istoriia*, no. 6: 194–200.

27. Matsuzato, "The Fate of Agronomists," 173.

28. On Tambov province, see Kerans, *Mind and Labor on the Farm*, 416–19.

29. On continuities in food supply and other practices across the 1917 divide, see Peter Holquist's exceptional and original work, including his *Making War, Forging Revolution: Russia's Continuum of Crisis, 1914–1921* (Cambridge, 2002), which appeared too late to receive full treatment in the present study. See also his "Information is the Alpha and Omega of Our Work: Bolshevik Surveillance in Its Pan-European Perspective," *Journal of Modern History* 69:3 (1997): 415–50.

30. In 1915, the regime created a separate "Ministry of Agriculture," which assumed the duties of GUZiZ and was headed by Aleksandr Krivoshein.

31. This policy actually led to higher prices, as peasants refused to sell to the government procurement agencies at state-fixed prices and instead sold on the black market, which flourished. Dorothy Atkinson, *The End of the Russian Land Commune*, 118.

32. Peter Gatrell, "The First World War and War Communism, 1914–1920," in *The Economic Transformation of the Soviet Union, 1913–1945* (Cambridge, England, 1994), 229.

33. Kerans, *Mind and Labor on the Farm*, 414; Matsuzato, "The Fate of Agronomists," 185–89.

34. K. Matsuzato cites several examples in "The Fate of Agronomists," 185–86.

35. A detailed discussion of the problems of the Provisional Government lies outside the parameters of this study.

36. V. M. Chernov, *The Great Russian Revolution* (New Haven, 1936), 236.

37. *Dekrety sovetskoi vlasti*, vol. 1, (Moscow, 1957) 57. All dates are old style.

38. L. Trotsky, *My Life* (New York, 1970), 337–38.

39. N. K. Krupskaia, *Vospominaniia o Lenine* (Moscow, 1968), 337.

40. Such commissariats were later called "union republican" commissariats. Other nonunited commissariats included international affairs, justice, health, enlightenment, and social welfare.

41. Rowney, *Transition to Technocracy*, 20.

42. Zaionchkovskii, *Rossiiskoe samoderzhavie v kontse XIX stoletiia* (Moscow, 1970); Rowney, *Transition*, 20.

43. In September 1918, 1,157 people worked in Narkomzem's Moscow offices. Only two government organizations had more: the Commissariat of Food Supply and the Commissariat of Ways and Communications, manager of the railroad network. The best basis for determining who comprised the staff of the Bolshevik Commissariat in the first year comes from a survey of the all the commissariats' central Moscow employees taken between August and September 1918. M. P. Iroshnikov, *Sozdanie sovetskogo tsentral'nogo gosudarstvennogo apparata. Sovet Narodnykh Komissarov i narodnye komissariaty (oktiabr' 1917 g.-Ianvar' 1918)* (Moscow, 1966), 184–85.

44. T. H. Rigby's work on the Council of People's Commissars is still the best account. Rigby, *Lenin's Government* (Cambridge, 1979).

45. *Sobranie uzakonenii* (hereafter 'SU'), 1917, no. 1, art. 3. For a collection of legislation affecting Narkomzem in this period, see *Sbornik dekretov i postanovlenii po Narodnomu komissariatu zemledeliia, 1917–1920* (Moscow, 1921).

46. SU 1917–18, no. 25, art. 346.

47. As of late 1919/early 1920, approximately twenty-three million desiatinas (about ten million acres) had been transferred to the peasantry in European Russia. V. P. Danilov, "Pereraspredelenie zemel'nogo fonda Rossii v rezul'tate velikoi oktiabrskoi revoliutsii," in I. I. Mints, ed., *Leninskii dekret o zemle* (Moscow, 1979) 261–310.

48. *Otchet Narodnogo komissariata zemledeliia RSFSR (IX Vserossiiskomu s"ezdu sovetov) za 1921* (hereafter *Otchet NKZ za 1921*) (Moscow, 1922), 5. See *Istoricheskii atlas revoliutsii*, 128. One desiatina equaled 2.7 acres.

49. B. N. Knipovich, in *O zemle*, 24.

50. On these processes, see also Teodor Shanin, *The Awkward Class* (Oxford, 1972), 145–61.

51. B. N. Knipovich, in *O zemle*, 29.

52. Ibid., 42; see the *Instruktsiia k sostavleniiu sel'sko-khoziaistvennykh kommun i dekret ob organizatsii i snabzhenii derevenskoi bednoty* (Petrograd, 1918).

53. For the laws and regulations that governed collectives see V. P. Danilov, ed., *Kooperativno-kolkhoznoe stroitel'stvo v SSSR, 1917–22: Dokumenty i materialy*, (Moscow, 1990), 52ff.

54. V. V. Kabanov, *Krest'ianskoe khoziaistvo v usloviakh voennogo kommunizma* (Moscow, 1988), 240–73.

55. Krupskaia, *Vospominaniia o Lenine* (Moscow, 1968), 38.

56. The initial period witnessed little stability in the Petrograd offices of the Commissariat. During the first six months, four different men held the post of Commissar of Agriculture. People's Commissars of Agriculture RSFSR between 1917 and 1921 included V.P. Miliutin (October 26–November 13, 1917); A. G. Shlikhter (November 13–November 24, 1917); L. Kolegaev (November 25, 1917–March 16, 1918); and A.P. Sereda (April 3, 1918–February 10, 1921).

57. *Sel'sko-khoziaistvennaia zhizn'*, 1922, no. 7. On the first months of Sovnarkom, see

Rigby, *Lenin's Government* (Cambridge, 1979), 1–40. See also M. P. Iroshnikov, *Sozdanie sovetskogo tsentral'nogo gosudarstvennogo apparata* (Moscow, 1966), 174.

58. See, for example, Iroshnikov, *Sozdanie*, 232; and T. H. Rigby, *Lenin's Government*, 47.

59. The Bolsheviks and SRs disagreed over the distribution of large, intensively cultivated estates and breeding farms. They also parted ways on the issue of whether or not land committees should distribute all agricultural land (the Bolshevik position), or whether individual peasant holdings should be off limits (the SR position).

60. Kabanov, in *O zemle* (Moscow, 1977), 82; and Ozimyi in *Sel'sko-khoziaistvennaia zhizn'*, 1922, no. 7: 35. Kolegaev was considered the Left SR expert on agrarian matters. By July 1918, he had renounced his association with the Left SRs, joining the Bolsheviks in November. Oliver Radkey, *The Sickle under the Hammer* (New York, 1963); Carr, *The Bolshevik Revolution 1917–1923* (New York, 1952), vol. 2: 41; *The Trotsky Papers*, 1917–22, vol. II, Jan M. Meijer, ed., 469, 473.

61. *Delo naroda*, December 20, 1917.

62. Carr, *Bolshevik Revolution*, vol. 2: 147; A. Andreev, in *O zemle*, 46.

63. Gosudarstvennyi Arkhiv Rossiiskoi Federatsii (GARF), f. 130, op. 2, d. 1, ll. 172, 185.

64. Meshcheriakov, *Organizatsiia*, 5; *Sel'sko-khoziaistvennaia zhizn'*, 1922, no. 7: 31.

65. Meshcheriakov, *Organizatsiia*, 5; *Vladimir Il'ich Lenin: Biograficheskaia khronika* (Moscow: 1970–82), vol. 5: 356.

66. The Commissariat of Agriculture, like the new commissariats of health and education, combined several organizational structures from pre-revolutionary ministries. D. K. Rowney, "The Scope, Authority, and Personnel of the New Industrial Commissariats in Historical Context," in William G. Rosenberg and Lewis H. Siegelbaum, eds., *Social Dimensions of Soviet Industrialization* (Bloomington, 1993), 126.

67. For Bolshevik denunciations of SR "untruths, misunderstandings [and] conscious lies," see V. Meshcheriakov, *Zemel'naia politika kommunistov* (Petrograd, 1919), 6 ff.

68. Meshcheriakov, *Organizatsiia*, 5. A year after the Bolshevik seizure of power, Commissariat leaders still considered their problems overwhelming and felt the need to bring them to Lenin's attention. On November 9, 1918, Meshcheriakov sent Lenin a blistering memo entitled "What still has not been done in the Commissariat of Agriculture." Rossiiskii Gosudarstvennyi Arkhiv Sotsial'noi i Politicheskoi Istorii (hereafter RGASPI), f. 5, op. 1, d. 1200, ll. 2–4. Meshcheriakov had taken upon himself responsibility for transforming the agency into a vehicle for rapid change in the countryside. In the memo, he expressed great frustration with the snail's pace of progress, focusing on poor organization and coordination between Moscow and the local land sections. Moscow rarely received accurate information about the rural situation. Meshcheriakov's conclusion: "The Commissariat has no organization. The Commissariat has no program." On the lack of coordination, see November 1920 letter to Sereda from Grigor'ev, in Rossiiskii Gosudarstvennyi Arkhiv Ekonomiki (RGAE), f. 478, op. 1, d. 366, ll. 23–24a.

69. Meshcheriakov, *Organizatsiia*, 8. In its first years, personnel matters took precedence over organizational issues for the Commissariat's leaders. They considered the expulsion of Right SRs and the Kadets from prominent administrative posts to be the most urgent task. Over the course of 1918, local land committees were gradually abolished, merged into land sections, or simply renamed soviet land sections.

70. N. Turchaninov, in *Sel'sko-khoziaistvennaia zhizn'*, 1922, no. 7: 34–35.

71. Gareth Morgan, *Images of Organization* (Beverly Hills, 1986), 56–58, 60–61.

72. *Sel'sko-khoziaistvennaia zhizn'*, 1922, no. 7. The Forest Department was slightly restructured and renamed the Central Forest Administration of the Republic. Meshcheriakov,

Organizatsiia, 7. RGAE, f. 478, op. 1, d. 216, l. 44.

73. V. I. Lenin, *Pol'noe sobranie sochinenii*, fifth edition (hereafter PSS), vol. 34: 307.

74. On the organization and structures of the Imperial Ministry of Agriculture, see N. P. Eroshkin, *Istoriia gosudarstvennykh uchrezhdenii dorevoliutsionnoi Rossii* (Moscow, 1983).

75. On this phenomenon in the League of the Godless, see Daniel Peris, *Storming the Heavens*.

76. Meshcheriakov, *Organizatsiia*, 6.

77. Iroshnikov calculates that 58.8 percent of all Narkomzem employees were holdovers. *Sozdanie*, 424–31. RGAE, f. 478, op. 1, d. 19, ll. 1–9 (Narkomzem Collegium protocols); RGAE, f. 478, op. 1, d. 1534, ll. 8–13.

78. For an overview of the phenomenon of bourgeois specialists in the state apparatus, "indispensable for the success of the regime," see Lewin, "Society, State and Ideology during the First Five Year Plan," and Lewin, "Leninism and Bolshevism" in *The Making of the Soviet System*. See also E. H. Carr, *The Bolshevik Revolution, 1917–1923* (New York, 1952), 2: 182–87; *Socialism in One Country* (New York, 1958), 1:115–22, 379–81; and Carr and R. W. Davies, *Foundations of a Planned Economy, 1926–1929* (London, 1969), vol. 1: 574–604. Siegelbaum, *Soviet State and Society*, 54–61; Sheila Fitzpatrick, "Stalin and the Making of a New Elite, 1928–1939," in *The Cultural Front: Power and Culture in Revolutionary Russia* (Ithaca, 1992), 149–70. For interesting conclusions based on a quantitative and structural analysis of several people's commissariats, see Rowney, *Transition to Technocracy*.

79. RGAE, f. 478, op. 12, d. 285, l. 12 ob.

80. Iroshnikov, *Sozdanie*, 431.

81. Daniel Orlovsky has shown that the sluzhashchie played a crucial role in Soviet institution building in the early Soviet period. See, for example, his "Gimpelson and the Hegemony of the Working Class," *Slavic Review* 48:1 (Spring 1989): 104–6. See also his "State Building in the Civil War Era: The Role of the Lower Middle Strata," in Diane Koenker, et al., eds., *Party, State and Society in the Russian Civil War* (Bloomington, 1989), 180–209.

82. In 1924, 97 percent of the leading officials and specialists who worked in the central offices of Narkomzem were sluzhashchie. Bineman and Kheinman, *Kadry gosudarstvennogo apparata*, 24. For a 1920 census of sluzhashchie in Moscow, see RGAE, f. 478, op. 1, d. 286, l. 197.

83. Fewer than 2 percent of Narkomzem officials identified themselves as having been members of the industrial working class before the revolution. This total was among the smallest of all the surveyed organizations. See Rigby, *Lenin's Government*, chs. 4 and 10.

84. One of the most balanced accounts of war communism is Lewis Siegelbaum, *Soviet State and Society between Revolutions, 1918–1929* (Cambridge, Eng.: 1992).

85. Iroshnikov, *Predsedatel'*, 390–91.

86. On interinstitutional strife between Narkomprod and Vesenkha during the Civil War, see Siegelbaum, *Soviet State and Society*, 18–20; and Patenaude, "Bolshevism in Retreat," 51–52.

87. Meshcheriakov, in *Sel'sko-khoziaistvennaia zhizn'*, 1922, no. 7: 32.

88. Meshcheriakov, in *Organizatsiia*, 9.

89. RGASPI, f. 5, op. 1, d. 1200, 1.2 (November 1918).

90. L. N. Litoshenko, *Sotsializatsiia zemli v Rossii* [1922], unpublished manuscript, cited in Bertrand M. Patenaude, "Peasants into Russians: The Utopian Essence of War Communism." *Russian Review*: 54 (October 1995): 558.

91. For a detailed breakdown of the commissariat's budget from 1918 to 1921, see *Otchet Narkomzema za 1921*, 26–27.

92. RGASPI f. 5, op. 1, d. 1200, l. 2.

93. Ibid.

94. *Pravda*, December 12, 1920. As cited in Lars Lih, *The Bolshevik Sowing Committees*, 27. See also Bogdanov's article in *Ekonomicheskaia zhizn'*, October 16, 1920.

95. Patenaude, "Bolshevism in Retreat," 35.

96. *Agronomicheskaia pomoshch' v Rossii*. In 1890, the Russian empire contained forty-three agricultural schools for peasants, with a total of 2,715 students, and three agricultural colleges. In 1893, only six uezd zemstvos employed agronomists; by 1897 nine provincial (*guberniia*) and thirty-eight district zemstvos had hired them.

97. N. P. Nosova, "Formirovanie kadrov spetsialistov sel'skogo khoziastva v sovetskoi dokolkhoznoi derevne (1917–29)" in R. P. Tolmacheva, ed., *Naselenie i trudovye resursy Ural'skoi sovetskoi derevni* (Sverdlovsk, 1987), 6. Many of those agronomists worked not for the state in agronomic aid organizations but as private agronomists on large estates. Kimitaka Matsuzato, "The Fate of Agronomists." See also *Agronomicheskaia pomoshch'*, 135–38, for statistics broken down by specialty, as well as a complaint that the number began growing only "most recently."

98. For example, RGAE, f. 478, op. 1, d. 457, ll. 1–22; RGAE, f. 478, op. 1, d. 458, ll. 1–6; and RGAE, f. 478, op. 12, d. 285, l. 107.

99. Turchaninov, in *Sel'sko-khoziaistvennaia zhizn'*, 1922, no. 7: 36; see also RGAE, f. 478, op. 1, d. 428, ll. 13–14, 35, 39.

100. RGAE, f. 478, op. 12, d. 285, ll. 11–12, letter of March 20, 1920.

101. RGAE, f. 478, op. 12, d. 285, l. 12.

102. On the hazards of local land work, see the police report in RGAE, f. 478, op. 1, d. 363, l. 40.

103. Berzin, in *O zemle*, 169–70. Emphasis in original.

104. Ibid., 169–70.

105. On competition for specialists, see RGAE, f. 478, op. 12, d. 285, l. 12 ob.

106. RGAE, f. 478, op. 1, d. 366, l. 9. Iroshnikov, *Sozdanie*, 184–85.

107. Lenin, *PSS*, vol. 50: 105, June 22, 1918.

108. For more on this process, see James Heinzen, "Politics, Administration, and Specialization in the Russian People's Commissariat of Agriculture." (Ph.D. dissertation, University of Pennsylvania, 1993). Protocols of the First Congress of Land Departments, Committees of the Poor and Kommuny, and many of the speeches given there, are contained in V. P. Danilov, ed., *Kooperativno-kolkhoznoe stroitel'stvo*, vol. 1: 65–110. For a stimulating interpretive study stressing continuity between Bolshevik policies toward the countryside during the Civil War and the Stalinist collectivization of agriculture, see Andrea Graziosi, *The Great Soviet Peasant War: Bolsheviks and Peasants, 1917–1933* (Cambridge, Mass., 1996).

109. *Dekrety sovetskoe vlasti*, vol 4: 362–89.

110. I. A. Teodorovich, *O gosudarstvennoi regulirovanii krest'ianskogo khoziaistva* (Moscow, 1920).

111. A series of articles on state regulation that appeared in *Pravda* can be found in V. V. Osinskii, *Gousudarstvennoe regulirovanie krest'ianskogo khoziastva. Sbornik statei* (Moscow, 1920).

112. N. Osinksii, *Gousudarstvennoe regulirovanie*, 10, 17.

113. *Ekonomicheskaia zhizn'*, September 16 and December 2, 1920.

114. See *Sel'sko-khoziaistvennoe vedomstvo za 75 let ego deiatel'nosti (1837–1912 gg.)*, (Petrograd, 1914), appendix V, 57–59.

115. A December 23, 1919 decree granted special benefits to specialists in fields vital to government interest, including higher pay, exemption from military service, and better housing.

116. See Rowney in *Transition to Technocracy*, 85. Rowney discusses the People's Commissariat of Health as an example of this phenomenon.

117. *Narodnyi komissariat zemledeliia, Sel'sko-khoziaistvennyi uchenyi komitet. Kratkii ocherk ego deiatel'nosti i zadach* (Moscow, 1919), 4. The passages in the following section are all drawn from this book, pages 2–19.

118. *Agronomicheskaia pomoshch' v Rossii*, 84–85 on allotments for GUZiZ.

119. Alexis de Tocqueville, *The Old Regime and the French Revolution*, trans. Stuart Gilbert (New York, 1955), 61–63.

120. Ibid, p. 68.

121. See especially Peter Holquist, *Making War, Forging Revolution*. See also Lars Lih, *Bread and Authority in Russia, 1914–1921* (Berkeley, 1990); George Yaney, *The Urge to Mobilize: Agrarian Reform in Russia, 1861–1930* (Urbana, 1982); Donald Raleigh, *Experiencing Russia's Civil War: Politics, Society, and Revolutionary Culture in Saratov, 1917-1922* (Princeton, 2002).

122. See Holquist's discussion of Alexander Krivoshein in *Making War, Forging Revolution* (Cambridge, 2002), 17–20.

123. Bitsenko, in *Sel'sko-khoziaistvennaia zhizn'*, 1922, no. 7: 44.

124. TsSU SSSR, *Sbornik statisticheskikh svedenii po Soiuzu SSSR, 1918–1923* (Moscow, 1924), 28. Up to 99 percent of land in agricultural regions of the RSFSR was farmed in repartitional communes.

125. B. N. Knipovich, *O zemle*, 42.

126. For the circular, see Danilov, ed., *Kooperativno-kolkhoznoe stroitel'stvo v SSSR 1917–1922: Dokumenty i materialy*, vol. 1 (Moscow, 1990), 230.

127. B. N. Knipovich, *O zemle*, 42.

CHAPTER 2

1. *Tsentral'oe upravlenie zemledeliia i sovkhozov v svete Novoi Ekonomicheskoi Politiki* (Moscow, 1921). Henceforth cited as *TsUZem v svete Novoi Ekonomicheskaia Politika*. The nickname "the brains of the country" was coined in a report summarizing a 1922 investigation of the Commissariat of Agriculture undertaken by the People's Commissariat of Workers' and Peasants' Inspectorate (Rabkrin). RGAE, f. 478, op. 3, d. 1403, ll. 36–53.

2. A textile engineer named Fedotov noted that, for him and his specialist colleagues, NEP was akin to "emerging from an airless crypt, starting to breathe, rolling up one's sleeves, and getting down to real work." N. V. Valentinov, *Novaia Ekonomicheskaia Politika i krisis partii posle smerti Lenina* (Palo Alto, 1971), 25.

3. On the civilizing mission of agronomists, see Kerans, *Mind and Labor on the Farm*, part 5. On pre-war and wartime professionals, see Holquist, *Making War*, chap. 1.

4. *Sotsial'isticheskoe stroitel'stvo SSSR* (Moscow, 1934), 2–3; I. A. Gladkov, *Sovetskoe narodnoe khoziaistvo (1921–25)* (Moscow, 1960), 151, 316, 357; *Statisticheskii spravochnik po narodnomu khoziaistvu, vyp. 2, Promyshlennost'* (Moscow, 1923), table no. 8, p. 26; *Promyshlennost' SSSR: statisticheskii sbornik* (Moscow, 1964); Wheatcroft, "Agriculture," in Davies, ed., *From Tsarism to the New Economic Policy* (Houndmills, 1990), 94.

5. The decline in grain production was the result of a 24 percent drop in sown area and a 29 percent fall in yields. Wheatcroft in Davies, ed., *From Tsarism to the New Economic Policy*, 94. See also the report of Chaianov at session of the Presidium of Gosplan, the agricultural section, and representatives of Narkomzem, 23 November 1921. V. P. Danilov, ed., *Kooperativno-kolkhoznoe stroitel'stvo v SSSR, 1917–1922*, (Moscow, 1990), 322, and excerpted in *Ekonomicheskaia zhizn'*, 29 November 1921. For the decline in the southeastern area of European Russia,

see A. P. Smirnov, *Pomoshch' krest'ianskomu khoziaistvu*, 11; and *Otchet NKZ za 1921*, 80.

6. Numbers on livestock according to a Narkomzem estimate. *Kontrol'nye tsifry 1926–27* (Moscow, 1926), 338; see also data in Narkomzem report from March 1923 in RGAE, f. 478, op. 15, d. 5, ll. 99–108. On pig and sheep farming, see *Trudy TsSU*, xviii (Moscow, 1925), 136–39; *Kontrol'nye tsifry narodnogo khoziaistva SSSR na 1925–26 god* (Moscow, 1925). For numbers on draft animals, see Wheatcroft in Davies, ed., *From Tsarism to the New Economic Policy*, 98.

7. Sugar beet production dropped by two thirds. I. A. Teodorovich, *K voprosu o sel'skokhoziaistvennoi politike RSFSR* ([n.p.], 1923). V. P. Danilov, *Sovetskaia dokolkhoznaia derevnia: naselenie, zemlepol'zovanie, khoziaistvo* (Moscow, 1977), 293.

8. TsSU, *Trudy*. Vol. 6, ch. 3, *Ekonomicheskoe rassloenie krest'ianstva v 1917 i 1919 g.* (Moscow, 1922), 21; TsUKhU Gosplan SSSR, *Zhivotnovodstvo SSSR za 1916–1938 gg.*, *Statisticheskii sbornik* (Moscow-Leningrad, 1940), 4.

9. *Itogi desiatiletiia sovetskoi vlasti v tsifrakh, 1917–1927* (n.p. [1927]).

10. PSS, vol. 41:359.

11. On the crises surrounding the Tenth Party Congress, see Paul Avrich, *Kronstadt 1921* (Princeton, 1971). On the opposition in the party to the introduction of NEP, and Lenin's vigorous efforts to push it forward, see N. V. Valentinov, *Novaia Ekonomicheskaia Politika i krizis partii*, 28–36.

12. Lenin, PSS, vol. 43: 18. March 15, 1921 (emphasis mine).

13. Lenin, PSS, vol. 43: 57.

14. For a moving and graphic eyewitness description of conditions on the Volga in the summer of 1921, see C. E. Bechhofer, *Through Starving Russia* (Westport, 1977). This is a reprint of the 1921 edition.

15. The 1921–22 famine was a seminal, but understudied event in the history of the USSR. Roger Pethybridge's thorough treatment is an exception to this rule. See his *One Step Backwards, Two Steps Forward* (Oxford, 1990), 91–119. See also Markus Wehner, "Golod 1921–22 v Samarskoi Gubernii i reaktsiia Sovetskogo pravitel'stva," *Cahiers du Monde Russe* 38:1–2 (January–June 1997): 223–42, for a study in relations between Moscow and one important provincial capital at the center of the famine. Edmundson's unpublished dissertation is still the most useful single work devoted to a study of the famine from the Soviet side. Charles M. Edmundson, "Soviet Famine Relief Measures, 1921–23" (Ph.D. dissertation Florida State University, 1970). On the basis of Soviet archival sources, Wehner reaches many of the same conclusions about Moscow's slow and ineffective response as Edmundson, who relied on published sources. See also Christopher Williams, "The 1921 Russian Famine: Centre and Periphery Responses," *Revolutionary Russia* 6:1 (December 1993): 277–314; and S. Wheatcroft, "Famine and Epidemic Crises in Russia, 1918–1922: The Case of Saratov," *Annales de Demographie Historique*, (1983): 329–52. An excellent recent addition to the literature on the famine, focusing on the American relief effort and including detailed descriptions of conditions among the peasantry, is Bertrand Patenaude, *The Big Show in Bololand: The American Relief Expedition to Soviet Russia in the Famine of 1921* (Stanford, 2002). See also Benjamin M. Weissman, *Herbert Hoover and Famine Relief to Soviet Russia, 1921–23* (Stanford, 1974); and H. H. Fisher, *The Famine in Soviet Russia, 1913–1923: The Operations of the American Relief Administration* (New York, 1927). When Soviet historians wrote about the famine, they provided little detail and tended to glorify Soviet relief efforts. See, for example, Iurii Poliakov, *1921-i— Pobeda nad golodom* (Moscow, 1975).

16. Charles M. Edmundson, "The Politics of Hunger: The Soviet Response to the Famine of 1921," *Soviet Studies*, vol. 29, no. 4 (October 1977), 506–18. The invaluable document collection, *Sovetskaia derevnia glazami VChK-OGPU-NKVD: Dokumenty i materialy. Tom 1.*

1918–1922 (Moscow, 1998) and *Tom 2. 1923–1929* (Moscow, 2000) contains excerpts from hundreds of documents produced by the police detailing their observations of local conditions during the famine. See also the so-called land reports of the GPU located in the Narkomzem archive: RGAE, f. 478, op. 15, dd. 8–10.

17. GARF, f. 4085, op. 9a, d. 870, l. 242.

18. Markus Wehner, "Golod 1921–22 gg. v Samarskoi guberniia," 223; Alan Ball, "State Children: Soviet Russia's *Besprizornye* and the New Socialist Generation," *Russian Review* 52 (April 1993): 228–47.

19. TsK Pomgol, *Chto govoriat tsifry o golode?* [n.p., n.d.], 4.

20. I. A. Teodorovich, *K voprosu*, 7.

21. See the report by A. V. Chaianov located in the protocol materials of June 23, 1921. RGAE, f. 478, op. 1, d. 473, l. 161. For more on Chaianov's report, see Heinzen, "Politics, Administration, and Specialization", 257.

22. *Snabzhenie krestianskogo naseleniia sel'skokhoziaistvennymi mashinami i orudiiami* (Moscow, 1925), 32.

23. Orlando Figes, *Peasant Russia, Civil War*, 268–275.

24. See Radek's comments from October 1921 in Charles M. Edmundson, "Soviet Famine Relief Measures," 55. Chicherin made a similar comment to Carl Bechhover, noting that the famine was in part a result of Bolshevik policies during war, but that requisitioning was the only way to defeat the Whites. *Through Starving Russia*, 157.

25. Turchaninov, *Sel'sko-khoziaistvennaia zhizn'*, 1922, no. 7: 36.

26. On the debates surrounding the introduction of NEP, see Bertrand M. Patenaude, "Bolshevism in Retreat: the Transition to the New Economic Policy, 1920–22" (Ph.D. dissertation Stanford University, 1987); and Lewis Siegelbaum, *Soviet State and Society between Revolutions, 1918–1929* (Cambridge, 1992), 67–126. Siegelbaum's book still stands as the best one-volume treatment of the period.

27. Patenaude, "Bolshevism in Retreat," 241–42.

28. On the anger at food brigades expressed by nonparty metal workers in February 1921, see Patenaude, "Bolshevism in Retreat," 133. On taxes, see Carr, *The Bolshevik Revolution*, vol. 2, 286. For food brigades, see *Otchet Narodnogo komissariata zemledeliia za 1922 g.* (Moscow, 1923), 6 (henceforth *Otchet NKZ za 1922*).

29. For example, on 4 April 1921 the collegium resolved to "form a coalition" in STO against Narkomprod over the tax on meat. RGAE, f. 478, op. 1, d. 473, l. 52. Narkomzem's position on the tax in kind in meat was laid out in Gosplan's agricultural section in November 1921. See Danilov, ed., *Kooperativno-kolkhoznoe stroitel'stvo v SSSR*, 322–34, especially 332.

30. *Desiatyi Vserossiskii s"ezd sovetov RSFSR* (Moscow, 1923), 171. Comment by Budyennyi.

31. See commissar of food supply Briukhanov's comments in *Pravda*, July 21, 1922, p. 3; and see the veiled attack on Briukhanov by Osinskii in *Pravda*, August 11, 1922, p. 1.

32. Edmundson, "Soviet Famine Relief Efforts," 214–19.

33. *Izvestiia*, August 10, 1922; *Pravda*, August 11 and 12, 1922, p. 1. *Izvestiia*, September 20, 1922, p. 1; October 5, 1922, p. 3; October 14, 1922, p. 2.

34. *Sovetskaia derevnia glazami VChK-OGPU-NKVD*, tom 1, 667, 680–717 ff.; ibid., tom 2, 57–139 ff.

35. Edmundson, "Soviet Famine Relief Efforts," 335, citing U.S. State Department, Internal Affairs of Russia and the Soviet Union, Roll 133, frame no. 0337.

36. Briukhanov forced the issue at a joint meeting of the Central Committee and the Politburo, although neither body apparently took any steps to limit Narkomzem. *Vladimir*

Il'ich Lenin: Biograficheskaia khronika (Moscow, 1970–82), vol. 12, 322.

37. See Briukhanov's letters to the Central Committee in the fall of 1922 complaining of the Narkomzem "campaign" in RGASPI, f. 17, op. 84, d. 428, ll. 51–53, 122, 161.

38. See undated 1923 circular to provincial land sections. RGAE, f. 478, op. 15, d. 5, l. 1. For more on Narkomprod's disappearing powers, see Carr, *The Interregnum*, 141.

39. Speakers at the First Conference of Land Organs, which began on 29 November 1922, took up this theme. See reports of Mesiatsev's speech in *Sel'sko-khoziaistvennaia zhizn'*, 1922, no. 11: 12–16.

40. V. P. Danilov, ed., *Kooperativno-Kolkhoznoe stroitel'stvo v SSSR, 1917–1922*, (Moscow, 1990), 333.

41. *Otchet Narodnogo komissariata zemledeliia RSFSR (IX Vserossiiskomu s"ezdu sovetov) za 1921* (Moscow, 1922), 21. Statement at First Congress of Land sections, December 1921.

42. Stenographic report of First Conference of Narkomzem Instructors, RGAE, f. 478, op. 3, d. 1266, l. 3 ob.

43. One Narkomzem publication illustrates the Commissariat's ambitious goals. For specialists in the field, "The goal of agricultural work is not only to raise grain harvests, but also to get two buckets of milk instead of one, two pounds of meat instead of one, to increase the quantity of hay, wool, eggs, cabbage, etc. Results like this should be achieved everywhere. Productivity should be raised in the garden, and in the orchard, and in the cattle yard, and in the meadows, and in the pasture, and in the forest, as well as in the field." *TsUZem v svete Novoi Ekonomicheskaia Politika*, 27. In January 1922 Sovnarkom concentrated all agricultural education in the Commissariat. The Commissariat began distributing simple agronomic literature, and its instructors taught introductory courses to farmers, though they were sparsely attended. The section in charge of task this remained poorly funded and short of staff and materials, however.

44. Yanni Kotsonis, in his book *Making Peasants Backward*, argues that pre-revolutionary agronomists believed that peasants were profoundly and permanently "irrational." The present study indicates that many agronomists in the Soviet period did not hold these views. The question also arises whether Kotsonis's generalization applies to all agronomists, or only to those in the pre-revolutionary cooperative movement, the subject of his study.

45. *Sel'sko-khoziaistvennaia zhizn'*, 1922, no. 1: 18.

46. *Sel'sko-khoziaistvennaia zhizn'*, 1922, no. 2: 1.

47. Quoted in a report of the Workers' and Peasants' Inspectorate (Rabkrin), RGAE, f. 478, op. 3, d. 1403, l. 37.

48. GARF, f. 4085, op. 9a, d. 870, l. 242. A. Kh. Mitrofanov, *Samodeiatel'nost krest'ianstva v velikuiu kampaniiu* (Moscow, 1921), 9–10. *TsUZem v svete Novoi Ekonomicheskaia Politika* (Moscow, 1921), 34.

49. On cutbacks in education, see Siegelbaum, *Soviet State and Society*, 93–94.

50. Shefler in *Ekonomicheskaia zhizn'*, October 1, 1921. M. E. Shefler (b. 1889), had been a Party member since 1917, was the son of an agronomist and was university educated, then worked on the southern front doing food work during Civil War. Shefler became a collegium member of Narkomzem in March 1920. His personnel file is RGAE, f. 478, op. 12, d. 10933.

51. Mitrofanov, *Samodeiatel'nost krest'ianstva*, 9–10.

52. For another call to "liquidate agricultural illiteracy," see *TsUZem v svete Novoi Ekonomicheskaia Politika*, 9; Mitrofanov, *Samodeiatel'nost krest'ianstva*, 13.

53. Valentinov, among others, makes this observation in *Novaia ekonomicheskaia politika*, 30–32.

54. Sapronov went further: "This is a kind of game—in some sense it is like playing with

fire, perhaps. The little peasant will have tasted the sweet and will not want the sour, having tasted a little power he will want to climb higher." RGASPI, f. 45, op. 1, d. 35, l. 61.

55. Lenin, PSS, vol. 38, 166–67.

56. Political Report of the Central Committee of the RKP(b), given to the 11th Party Congress, March 27, 1922. *Odinadtsatyi s"ezd RKP(b), mart-aprel' 1922 goda. Stenograficheskii otchet* (Moscow, 1961).

57. See *TsUZem v svete Novoi Ekonomicheskaia Politika*, 6–8.

58. For the work of organizational theorists (especially Henry Mintzburg, Danny Miller and Peter Friesen) on this species of "machine bureaucracy" and "divisionalized form," see Gareth Morgan, *Images of Organization* (Beverly Hills, 1986), 56. See also records of investigations located in GARF, f. 4085, op. 9a, d. 870, l. 162–186 ob.; GARF, f. 5446, op. 26, d. 8, ll. 1–23; and RGAE, f. 478, op. 3, d. 1403, ll. 36–53.

59. Among others, the "enthusiasts" whom Narkomzem had recruited to staff sowing committees at the end of 1920 and the first two months of 1921 were slow to accept NEP.

60. A. V. Kvashonkin et al. eds., *Bol'shevistskoe rukovodstvo. Perepiska. 1912–1927* (Moscow, 1996), 204–5.

61. Danilov, ed., *Kooperativno-kolkhoznoe stroitel'stvo*, 349–50. Lead editorial in *Pravda* of August 6, 1922.

62. See Crozier on this tendency in bureaucracies: *The Bureaucratic Phenomenon* (Chicago, 1964).

63. *Sel'sko-khoziaistvennaia zhizn'*, 1922, no. 11: 12–16.

64. *TsUZem v svete Novoi Ekonomicheskaia Politika*, 13–15.

65. Ibid., 4.

66. Ibid., 15, 16–17. See Jerome Blum, *The End of the Old Order in Rural Europe*, for his argument that yields were improved in Europe largely as a consequence of state intervention.

67. *TsUZem v svete Novoi Ekonomicheskaia Politika*, 17.

68. Morgan, *Images of Organization* (Beverly Hills, 1986), 56.

69. On Glukhov, see *Sel'sko-khoziaistvennaia zhizn'*, 1928, no. 4: 10. For a biographical sketch on the occasion of Teitel's thirtieth year in land work, see *Sel'sko-khoziaistvennaia zhizn'*, 1928, no. 46: 11.

70. RGASPI, f. 17, op. 2, d. 53, l. 1.

71. *Vladimir Il'ich Lenin: Biograficheskaia khronika* (Moscow, 1970–82), vol. 9: 624, 628. The introduction of NEP greatly accelerated this process.

72. RGASPI, f. 2, op. 1, d. 22430; RGAE, f. 478, op. 1, d. 473, l. 86. *Sel'sko-khoziaistvennaia zhizn'* 1922, no. 9: 7.

73. For details on the creation, organization, and staffing of the Commissariat's planning agencies, see Heinzen, "Politics, Administration, and Specialization," 165–69.

74. Zemplan was established at the same time as Gosplan, the State Planning Commission. Gosplan worked within STO. Affiliated planning agencies were established in all economic commissariats. SU RSFSR, 1921, no. 17, st. 106. For Zemplan see RGAE, 478, op. 1, d. 473, l. 72.

75. *Otchet NKZ za 1921*, 222. In fact, Zemplan was modeled after Gosplan. For more on Gosplan, see Bailes, *Technology and Society under Lenin and Stalin* (Princeton, 1978), 62–63.

76. The *Ekonomicheskoe soveshchane* was created as an agency "which unites scientific and practical forces and is to help Narkomzem design measures for the recovery of the country's agriculture." Initially, EKOSO used the technical apparatus of the section of agricultural economy and statistics, which in August 1921 became the Secretariat of Zemplan and EKOSO. Teodorovich had earlier appointed Chaianov as chair of the Section of Agricultural

Economics and Statistics. Chaianov served as the Director of the Institute on Agricultural Economics of Timiriazev Academy between 1922 and 1930.

77. At times Teodorovich publicly distanced himself from Chaianov, who was strongly criticized by some Bolsheviks. See, for example, *Sel'sko-khoziaistvennaia zhizn'*, 1922, no. 14: 21–23. The collegium appointed Zemplan's members and its Presidium, and in turn, Zemplan reported to the collegium.

78. For more on the relationships among institutions involved in agrarian policy making, see Markus Wehner, *Bauernpolitik im proletarischen Staat: Die Bauernfrage als zentrales Problem der sowjetischen Innenpolitik 1921–1928* (Koeln, 1998). See also Heinzen, "Politics, Administration, and Specialization."

79. N. D. Kondrat'ev and D. I. Oparin, *Bol'shie tsikly kon'iunktury* (Moscow, 1928). See the study of Kondrat'ev's economic thinking by Vincent Barnett, *Kondrat'ev and the Dynamics of Economic Development* (Houndmills, Eng., 1998).

80. N. D. Kondrat'ev, *Rynok khlebov i ego regulirovanie vo vremia voiny i revoliutsii* (Moscow, 1922).

81. A. P. Efimkin, *Dvazhdy reabilitirovannye* (Moscow, 1991), 62.

82. *The Works of Nikolai D. Kondrat'ev*, vol. 4, 284. Beginning in 1922, Kondrat'ev also edited the publication of the Conjuncture Institute (Kon'iunkturnyi Institut), the *Economic Bulletin*. Kondrat'ev enjoyed influence with People's Commissar of Finance G. Ia. Sokol'nikov (July 1923–January 1926) and leading economist L.N. Iurovskii, who often attended Zemplan meetings. The Conjuncture institute was under Narkomfin's jurisdiction.

83. In late 1921, the Tenth Congress of Soviets ordered Narkomzem to rewrite the Land Code. The 1922 Land Code's 340 articles superseded all previous Russian Republican and Imperial land legislation.

84. The law was passed by the IV session of the All-Russian Central Executive Committee (VTsIK) on October 30, 1922, as the "Land Code of the RSFSR" and became law on December 1, 1922.

85. *Sel'sko-khoziaistvennaia zhizn'*, 1922, no. 7:16. Pavel A. Mesiatsev had joined the Bolsheviks in 1906, and was a graduate of the Petrovskaia-Razumovskaia agricultural academy.

86. Households could separate without consent only if a group of separating households was equal to more than one fifth of the membership of the commune or fifty dvors. Structures and all other property and crops were considered the personal property of the peasant household.

87. *Deviatyi s"ezd sovetov RSFSR, Stenograficheskii otchet* (Moscow, 1922), 146.

88. *TsUZem v svete Novoi Ekonomicheskaia Politika*, 5. See also the article by P. Pershin in *O zemle. Sbornik statei o proshlom i budushchem zemel'no-khoziaistvennogo stroitel'stva* (Moscow, 1922), 1, 50–78, which also argued that homesteads were often a rational choice for peasants.

89. *O zemle*, 1: 7. The book's Introduction is dated December 18, 1921. In this collection, the former SR and future author of the RSFSR Land Code, N. P. Rudin, argues that the leasing of land and the hiring of labor should be legalized (44–49). See also the article by collegium member V. Kuraev in *Ekonomicheskaia zhizn'*, September 9, 1921; and his letter to Lenin of August 1921 in RGASPI, f. 5, op. 1, d. 1122, ll. 1–7. According to A. P. Smirnov (who in 1923 became the People's Commissar of Agriculture), the first draft of the code written by Narkomzem permitted private property in land. Lenin strongly opposed this idea, and the Commissariat dropped it. See A. P. Smirnov's letter to Rykov, RGASPI, f. 17, op. 85, d.135, ll. 127–29; and *TsUZem v svete Novoi Ekonomicheskaia Politika.*, 6. On the Land Code, see P. Mesiatsev, "The Direction and Character of Current Land Policy," in *Sel'sko-khoziaistvennaia*

zhizn' 1922, no. 5: 1–3.

90. N. P. Oganovskii, "Obshchina i zemel'noe tovarishchestvo," in *O zemle*, vyp. 1, 89. David Kerans calls this peasant elite the "pioneers." Kerans, *Mind and Labor on the Farm*, 190.

91. *Pravda*, December 21, 1921.

92. *Sel'sko-khoziaistvennaia zhizn'*, 1922, no. 5: 1–3. (Emphasis mine)

93. See Moshe Lewin in *Russian Peasants and Soviet Power: A Study of Collectivization* (New York, 1968), and his essay "Who Was the Soviet Kulak?" in *The Making of the Soviet System*; and Teodor Shanin, *The Awkward Class* (Oxford, 1972). On the category "worker," see for example, David Hoffman, *Peasant Metropolis: Social Identities in Moscow, 1929–1941* (Ithaca, 1994); and Carr, *Socialism in One Country*, vol. 1: 89–94. Although there is not space to treat this issue in detail here, I wish to emphasize the regime's persistent concern that "workers," and especially "workers from the bench," be employed throughout the state apparatus.

94. Sheila Fitzpatrick, "Ascribing Class: The Construction of Social Identity in Soviet Russia," *Journal of Modern History* 65:4 (December 1993): 745–70. On the "declassing" phenomenon, see also Lewin, "Leninism and Bolshevism: The Test of History and Power," in *Making of the Soviet System* (New York, 1985), 191–208.

95. Statisticians generally considered landless rural laborers *(batraki)* to be proletarians.

96. When determining a person's social class in consideration for employment in the state apparatus, the Bolsheviks were generally most concerned with one's *proiskhozhdenie*, or social origin, which meant parents' background as of 1917. Sometimes statisticians also used the category "social situation" *(polozhenie)*, defining a person's social position or occupation in 1917 or if a party member, when one joined the party. In any case, the imprecision of these categories cautions one to take these figures as approximations, rather than as precise numbers. In late 1918, fewer than 2 percent of Narkomzem's personnel had been workers in 1917. Most other commissariats employed more workers, though only slightly more.

97. The worker contingent reached only 4 percent by 1927. RGASPI, f. 17, op. 74, d. 18, l. 9 (1930 report on agricultural cadres by allocation department of Central Committee). See also RGASPI, f. 17, op. 74, d. 18. In October 1929, 11.9 percent of all employees in the people's commissariats were former workers and 4.5 percent were children of workers.

98. RGASPI, f. 17, op. 74, d. 18, l. 14.

99. RGASPI; f. 17, op. 84, d. 252, l. 4.

100. "Svodka svedenii za Mart-Aprel' o nastroenii i zaprosakh krest'ian." RGASPI, f. 17, op. 85, d. 135, l. 83.

101. See Lenin, PSS, 54: 563. On November 18, 1921, the Politburo again resolved that "the people's commissar should be a peasant, one practicing agriculture."

102. RGAE, f. 478, op. 1, d. 610, ll. 4–5, letter to Sovnarkom from Osinskii and excerpt from Sovnarkom session of May 18, 1922. The Politburo discussed the situation of the Narkomzem collegium on April 27, and May 4, and the Orgburo did so on 2 May. *Vladimir Il'ich Lenin: Biograficheskaia khronika* (Moscow, 1970–82), vol. 12, 302, 309, 310, 322.

103. *Otchet Narodnogo komissariata zemledeliia RSFSR XII-omu Vserossiiskomu s"ezdu sovetov za 1923–24 g.* (hereafter *Otchet NKZ za 1923–24*)(Moscow, 1925), 585.

104. RGASPI, f. 17, op. 84, d. 252, l. 4.

105. Lenin, PSS, 52: 85–86. See also the Central Committee telegram to provincial party committees in RGASPI, f. 17, op. 84, d. 252, ll. 3–4.

106. See Cathy Frierson, *Peasant Icons: Representations of Rural People in Late Nineteenth-Century Russia* (New York, 1993), especially chapter six, for discussions of the peasant "types" created in the art of V. G. Perov and I. N. Kramskoi.

107. Robert Darnton, in *Kiss of Larmourette* (New York, 1990), 9.

108. The worker, meanwhile, wore boots, a blacksmith's apron, and was clean-shaven. See Victoria E. Bonnell, "The Representation of Women in Early Soviet Political Art," *Russian Review*, 50:3 (1991): no. 3 277–87; and her *Iconography of Power: Soviet Political Posters under Lenin and Stalin* (Berkeley, 1997).

109. On the quick dismissal of the first three promotees, see the letter to the Orgbiuro from Teodorovich and Iakovenko of April 22, 1922. RGASPI, f. 17, op. 84, d. 417, ll. 44.

110. See, for example, Lenin, PSS, vol. 52, 83–86; vol. 54, 563.

111. RGASPI, f. 2, op. 1, ed. khr. 22443, ll. 2–4. His Politbiuro confirmation is in RGASPI, f. 17, op. 3, d. 248, l.2. The troika was confirmed on January 17, 1922. RGASPI, f. 17, op. 3, d. 253, l. 2.

112. See Lenin's letter to Iaroslavskii of December 24, 1921, in Lenin, PSS, 54, 92–93; and to Molotov for the Politburo of December 25, 1921. Lenin, PSS, 54: 93–94.

113. On the social composition of the Council of People's Commissars between 1917 and 1922, see T. H. Rigby, *Lenin's Government*, ch. 11.

114. RGASPI, f. 2, op.1 ed. khr. 22443, ll. 2–4.

115. Mikhail I. Kalinin, a man of peasant origin, was appointed Chairman of VTsIK in 1919 after the death of Sverdlov. He was subsequently known as the *vserossisskii starosta*, or the all-Russian village elder (see A. I. Mikoian, *V nachale dvadtsatykh*, (Moscow, 1975) 311ff). When Lenin appointed Kalinin, he stated that Kalinin was to "organize a series of direct relations between Soviet power and the middle peasant." Unlike Iakovenko, Kalinin had been a party member for twenty years. Kalinin was the only leading Bolshevik to visit the affected areas during the famine.

116. On the public controversy over the essence of the "peasant soul" in the second half of the 19th century, see Frierson, *Peasant Icons*.

117. RGASPI, f. 2, op. 1, ed. khr. 22443, ll. 2–4.

118. *Izvestiia*, February 16, 1922.

119. *Sel'sko-khoziaistvennaia zhizn'*, 1927, no. 44–45: 43. The conversation occurred early in 1922.

120. *Izvestiia*, February 16, 1922.

121. At the Eleventh Party Congress in March 1922, for example, Lenin referred to deputy commissar Osinskii as the leader of Narkomzem, apparently forgetting that he had appointed Iakovenko a few months earlier. *Odinatsatyi s"ezd RKP(b), mart-aprel' 1922 goda. Stenograficheskii otchet* (Moscow, 1961), 144.

122. The interview with Iakovenko that appeared in *Izvestiia* seemed to be trying to dispel misconceptions that Iakovenko was not literate. He is "a man of few words," the iconic village elder. There is a *type*, a stereotyped image of the peasant patriarch: mysterious, quiet, wise, yet difficult for the outsider to understand.

123. Iakovenko's comment appeared in *Sel'sko-khoziaistvennaia zhizn'*, 1922, no. 12–13: 1–2.

124. See Sapronov's letter to Lenin (December 2, 1921) in which he asks Lenin to seat up to "thirty bearded *muzhiki*" in VTsIK. The peasant section of VTsIK "would be the representation of the petty bourgeoisie in VTsIK." RGASPI, f. 45, op. 1, d. 35, l. 61.

125. See Don K. Rowney's analysis in *Transition to Technocracy: The Structural Origins of the Soviet Administrative State* (Ithaca, 1989).

126. Orlovsky, "Professionalism in the Ministerial Bureaucracy on the Eve of the February Revolution of 1917," in Harley Balzer, ed., *Russia's Middle Class: The Professionals in Russian History* (New York, 1996), 270–71.

127. Orlovsky, "Professionalism in the Ministerial Bureaucracy," 288. For a survey of the

literature on professionalization, see Harley Balzer, "Introduction," in Balzer, ed., *Russia's Missing Middle Class*, 3–38.

128. Indeed, they employed some of the same rhetoric in these arguments that the Ministry of Agriculture had used between 1905 and 1914. Using phrases that echoed the language of their Tsarist predecessors, Commissariat leaders argued that the government of an agrarian nation must diligently defend the interests of agriculture. For a description of the Commissariat's mission as "defending the interests of agriculture," see A. V. Chaianov's report on the Commissariat's general plan to the Presidium of Gosplan and the Gosplan agricultural section, in *Ekonomicheskaia zhizn'*, November 29, 1921. For a later example, see the article by A. Andreev in *Sel'sko-khoziaistvennaia zhizn'*, 1925, no. 21:13, in which he writes: "The land organs are called upon to defend the interests of agriculture."

129. *Ekonomicheskaia zhizn'*, December 6, 1921. For more on the "battle for the budget," see Heinzen, "Politics, Administration, and Specialization," 259–64.

130. *Otchet NKZ za 1921*, 28.

131. A 1922 Rabkrin report confirmed that the sections of Narkomzem that were well funded "came alive." RGAE, f. 478, op. 3, d. 1403, l. 50. For Rabkrin's investigations of Narkomzem in 1921, 1922, and 1923, see, for example, GARF, f. 4085, op. 9a, d. 870, ll. 162–86 ob.; GARF, f. 5446, op. 26, d. 8, ll. 1–23; and RGAE, f. 478, op. 3, d. 1403, ll. 36–53.

132. *Otchet NKZ za 1921*, 21. In 1922, Narkomzem did somewhat better, though Narkomfin supplied only a quarter of its request. Closed letter to Central Committee in RGASPI, f. 17, op. 84, d. 295, ll. 66, 71; *Otchet NKZ za 1922*, 57.

133. *Otchet NKZ za 1921*, 21. See also the letter from Kondrat'ev to Chaianov of December 5, 1921, in which he complains that specialists were not being paid and were trying to find work in other agencies. N. D. Kondrat'ev, *Osoboe mnenie*, kn.1, 134–5 (Moscow, 1993).

134. *Deviatyi s'vezd sovetov RSFSR, Stenograficheskii otchet*, 100.

135. Speech of Latsis, *Deviayi s"ezd sovetov RSFSR*, 62–64.

136. RGASPI, f. 17, op. 87, d. 209, ll. 90–91.

137. N. V. Turchaninov, head of the statistical section of the Agriculture Administration, wrote the article. Turchaninov had worked in the Ministry of Agriculture since 1906. *Sel'sko-khoziaistvennaia zhizn'*, 1922, no. 11: 2–4.

138. *Deviatyi s"ezd sovetov RSFSR*. In 1925, a graduate of the Timiriazev Agricultural Academy wrote that the horror of the famine had inspired him to study agronomy and ultimately to join the Commissariat of Agriculture. One can assume that many more such idealists entered the civil service. RGASPI, f. 17, op. 69, d. 20, l. 52.

139. For details on commercial accounting, see Heinzen, "Politics, Administration, and Specialization," 192–94.

140. *Ekonomicheskaia zhizn'*, November 16, 1921. *Sel'sko-khoziaistvennaia zhizn'*, 1922, no. 1:20.

141. SU 1923, no. 9, st. 904–05; *K soveshchaniiu gubernskikh zemelnykh upravlenii (tezisy dokladov upravlenii i khozorganov NKZ)* (Moscow, 1924).

142. *Otchet NKZ za 1922 g.* (Moscow, 1923), 21; *Otchet Narodnogo komissariata zemledelia za 1924/25 g.* (Moscow, 1926), 162. (Henceforth *Otchet NKZ za 1924/25*.)

143. Letters to Central Committee Secretariat. RGASPI, f. 17, op. 84, d. 295, l. 68; RGASPI, f. 17, op. 84, d. 295, ll. 71–2.

144. When making its arguments about inadequate allotments, Narkomzem compared its budgets with those that the Tsarist state supplied to agricultural agencies. The Commissariat leadership claimed that the proportion of the national budget devoted to agriculture was only one half or less of allotments before the Revolution, when the tsarist state slighted agriculture

with horrible results. Chaianov complained that, as in tsarist times, "the agriculture agency stands in twentieth place for funding. Russia lives off agriculture, and we cannot keep it on a 'subsistence diet.' It must be given the kind of food from which it can not only survive, but work." See RGAE f. 478, op. 3, d. 1403, ll. 36–53.

145. See Naum Jasny, *Soviet Economists of the Twenties: Names to be Remembered* (Cambridge, England, 1972). See also E. H. Carr, *Socialism in One Country*, vol. 1, 102–50.

146. One can compare Narkomzem, where the experts were frequently former SRs, with Vesenkha and Narkomfin, where former Mensheviks dominated. See especially N. V. Valentinov, *Nasledniki Lenina* (Moscow, 1991), 132–38. See also Jasny, *Soviet Economists of the Twenties*.

147. For a 1922–23 characterization by an unknown Narkomzem superior (probably I. A. Teodorovich) of N. D. Kondrat'ev as "formerly an active and political worker of SR inclination who has moved away from this inclination and is politically completely reliable" that is located in the files of the Commissariat's personnel department, see RGAE, f. 478, op. 12, d. 957, l. 34. In the same report, N. P. Oganovskii is characterized as politically completely loyal but as having earlier possessed a "purely *narodnik* ideology."

148. A 1926 GPU report at a closed session of the Penza provincial party cell warned of the possibility of terror by SRs and members of other parties. Partiinyi arkhiv Penzenskoi oblasti (PAPO), f. 36, op. 1, d. 1138, l. 37 (Protocols of Secret session of the biuro and secretariat of Penza provincial committee of VKP(b), 1922). See also the reports from the FSB archive, selections of which are reproduced in *Sovetskaia derevnia glazami VChK-OGPU-NKVD. Dokumenty i materialy*, Tom. 1: 1918–1922 (Moscow, 1998); and Tom 2: 1923–1929 (Moscow, 2000). The Smolensk archive also records police concern about purported SR activities in the 1920s. Fainsod, *Smolensk under Soviet Rule* (New York, 1963), 44.

149. Valentinov, *Novaia Ekonomicheskaia Politika*, 4.

150. In some senses, their outlook mirrors that of the émigrés in the Changing Signposts movement. On this group, see Hilde Hardemann, *Coming to Terms with the Soviet Regime: The Changing Signposts Movement among Russian Émigrés in the Early 1920s* (DeKalb, 1994).

151. Valentinov, *Novaia Ekonomicheskaia Politika*, 22–23.

152. E. Ostovskii, "Pereproizvodstvo agrospetsialistov ili neratsional'noe ikh ispol'zovanie" in *Sel'sko-khoziaistvennaia zhizn'*, 1927, no. 46:26–27. In addition, because 1917 had seen the dominance of land committees by SRs and because the Provisional Government's Ministry of Agriculture had been controlled by the SRs, the revival of the local agronomic aid network at the beginning of NEP naturally attracted many administrators and experts who sympathized with the party that had been prominent in land affairs between the dual revolutions of 1917.

153. See Lenin's letter to Stalin of July 17, 1922, discussing the deportation of Mensheviks, Popular Socialists, and Kadets. Koenker and Bachman eds., *Revelations*, 232.

154. *Sel'sko-khoziaistvennaia zhizn'*, 1922 no. 34. See *Vladimir Il'ich Lenin: Biograficheskaia khronika*, vol. 12, 316, 332, 338.

155. Lenin, PSS, vol. 54:262.

156. The agricultural economist B. D. Brutskus was exiled from the Soviet Union in the summer of 1922, apparently for advocating similar measures. See Lenin's letter of September 18, 1922 to Unshlikht of the GPU, and Unshlikht's reply, with a list of names for exile including Brutskus, in Diane Koenker and Ronald D. Bachman, eds., *Revelations from the Russian Archives*, 233. See also Poliakov, *Perekhod*, 346–7.

157. Letter of June 19, 1922. Teodorovich sent a handwritten reply to Stalin the next day: "At the head of the editorial committee stood the agronomist-communist Morosanov, responsible for all publications of Narkomzem. Specifically, the collection *O zemle* was prepared for

press by the Land Improvement and Reorganization Administration, the head of which is the collegium member Mesiatsev." RGASPI, f. 17, op. 84, d. 417, l. 69; RGASPI f. 17, op. 84, d. 428, l. 81.

158. Marc Jansen, *A Show Trial under Lenin: The Trial of the Socialist Revolutionaries, Moscow 1922* (The Hague, 1982), 18, 101.

159. On the arrest of the Zemplan specialists, see RGAE, f. 478, op. 2, d. 168, ll. 55 and 116 (Zemplan materials). See also, Kondrat'ev, *Osoboe mnenie*, kn. 2 (Moscow, 1993), 449–50. The former Menshevik Valentinov notes that many nonparty specialists and administrators feared "undesired attention" from the GPU in this period. *Novaia Ekonomicheskaia Politika*, 4.

160. This oversight went beyond Tsiurupa's regular duties as the deputy chair of Sovnarkom with responsibility for a number of commissariats (including agriculture). A memo from deputy Sovnarkom chairman Kamenev to Stalin noted: "I believe that the only way to improve it is to assign one of the deputy commissars of STO (Tsiurupa) specially to supervise Narkomzem." RGASPI, f. 17, op. 84, d. 417, l. 121. Narkomzem made special reports of its activities to Tsiurupa. See, for example, RGASPI, f. 17, op. 84, d. 127, l. 127, RGAE, f. 478, op. 1, d. 851, ll. 1–11, 12–17; and RGASPI, f. 17, op. 84, d. 385, ll. 102–03.

161. GARF, f. 4085, op. 9a, d. 1133, l. 60.

162. RGASPI, f. 17, op. 84, d. 417, l. 40. The letter was addressed to Lenin, who forwarded it to Stalin. Lenin undertook some old-fashioned pork barrel politics, sending extra aid "to the peasants in Northern Kansk uezd, Eniseisk guberniia," Iakovenko's home district. This aid was probably considered crucial for preserving Iakovenko's reputation among the population of his home area. *Vladimir Il'ich Lenin: Biograficheskaia khronika*, vol. 12: 299.

163. GARF, f. 5446, op. 26, d. 8, l. 27.

164. Rowney, *Transition to Technocracy*, 5–9.

165. *Sel'sko-khoziaistvennaia zhizn'*, 1923, no.1–2:1.

CHAPTER 3

1. Three major published sources are central to any social analysis of the Soviet state in the 1920s. The first is a 1922 survey of government employees, the results of which have been compiled by V. I. Vasiaev, et al., *Dannye perepisi sluzhashchikh 1922 goda o sostave kadrov narkomatov RSFSR* (Moscow, 1972). The second and third are the Central Statistical Administration (TsSU) and Gosplan surveys of the state and cooperative apparatuses: Tsentral'noe Statisticheskoe Upravlenie SSSR, *Gosudarstvennyi apparat SSSR, 1924–1928 gg.* (Moscow, 1929); and Ia. M. Bineman and S. Kheinman, *Kadry gosudarstvennogo i kooperativnogo apparata SSSR* (Moscow, 1930).

2. TsSU SSSR, *Gosudarstvennyi apparat SSSR*, 28. Vesenkha and the Central Statistical Administration also had the status of ministries; each was about a quarter the size of Narkomzem. The finance commissariat was slightly smaller than Narkomzem, having suffered severe cutbacks after 1926.

3. TsSU SSSR, *Gosudarstvennyi apparat SSSR*, table 3: 12, and GARF, f. 406, op. 25, d. 41, l. 78 ob.

4. See TsSU SSSR, *Gosudarstvennyi apparat SSSR*, 16, for an accounting of the staffs of each commissariat in these years.

5. See, for example, Smirnov's letters to the Central Committee, RGASPI, f. 17, op. 68, d. 239, ll. 146–48, February 23, 1925.

6. GARF, f. 5446, op. 26, d. 8, l. 34.

7. See, for example, the excerpt from Smirnov's speech in Sovnarkom, dated "no earlier than October 10, 1918," in which he extols the virtues of the provincial branches of Narkom-

prod as "strictly centralized" and "disciplined." *Sovetskaia derevnia glazami VChK-OGPU-NKVD: Dokumenty i materialy, Tom 1. 1918–1922* (Moscow, 1998), 88–89.

8. Similarly, Dzerzhinskii, who was head of Vesenkha between February 1924 and June 1926, brought many associates to Vesenkha from the political police (GPU).

9. Patenaude, "Bolshevism in Retreat: The Transition to the New Economic Policy, 1920–22" (Ph.D. dissertation Stanford University, 1987): 12. Tsiurupa's deputy, Briukhanov, was also from Ufa.

10. For documents produced by the commission that set salaries for these specialists, and that include evaluations of their reliability, see the materials for the administrative-financial administration's *obshchii otdel*. RGAE, f. 478, op. 12, d. 957, ll. 1–17. The documents argue that these specialists should get higher salaries than they were assigned "in view of the especially high qualifications of the employees necessary for such work" (l. 29).

11. RGAE, f. 478, op. 15, d. 5, ll. 10–12.

12. Again, there were parallels with Dzerzhinskii's leadership of the commissariat of transport and later at Vesenkha. Valentinov describes the fear of arrests and shootings (which did not come about) among Vesenkha staff upon Dzerzhinskii's appointment in February 1924. In November 1924, in a speech to the all-union conference of metalworkers, he promised to rule "with an iron hand." "To many people, it is well known that I have a heavy hand that can inflict heavy blows. I will not allow work to continue as it did earlier, anarchically" Valentinov, *Novaia ekonomicheskaia politika*, 101–2.

13. *Sel'sko-khoziaistvennaia zhizn'*, 20 May 1923: 1.

14. Lenin, PSS, vol. 43:266–91; vol. 36:137; vol. 40:213; and vol. 42:156–7, 339.

15. Merle Fainsod noted "the extreme weakness of the party" in the Smolensk countryside. Fainsod, *Smolensk under Soviet Rule* (New York, 1963), 44. As he pointed out, "To read the Party records of 1925–26 is to catch something of the flavor of an army of occupation in hostile territory." *Smolensk under Soviet Rule*, 123. See also Roger Pethybridge, *One Step Backwards, Two Steps Forward*, on the failure of Bolshevik policy in the 1920s to take into account local conditions.

16. *Spravochnik o spetsialistakh sel'skogo khoziastva SSSR* (Moscow-Leningrad, 1924), 73. At the beginning of 1923, the Main Bureau of Technical Forces in the Commissariat of Labor undertook the re-registration of all agricultural specialists. As a result, for the first time the executive organs of the party and state as well as Narkomzem had at least a general picture of who worked in the land administration. A small number of these holdovers were peasants who had moved into the civil administration between 1905 and 1917.

17. *Otchet Narodnogo komissariata zemledeliia RSFSR za 1924–25* (Moscow, 1926), 577.

18. RGAE, f. 478, op. 3, d. 2979, l. 48 (quarterly and monthly reports of provincial land sections).

19. RGAE, f. 478, op. 1, d. 1433, l. 37. Report from 1925.

20. RGASPI, f. 17, op. 3, d. 469, pt. 22; and d. 480, pt. 26 and supplement. A decree of the Orgburo of November 30, 1923, made many of the same points.

21. It was not uncommon for local party agencies to conscript all employees of the soviets for the pressing task of the day, such as food requisition or tax collection. This involuntary recruitment disrupted the work of the soviets' many specialized departments. The Moscow Party Committee also mobilized leading Narkomzem employees without coordinating its plans with the Commissariat ahead of time. This drew an angry protest from Smirnov in February 1924. RGAE f. 478, op. 1, d. 1429, l. 10.

22. RGASPI, f. 17, op. 34, l. 368, l. 15. Letters followed in May 1923, September 1923, January 1924, July 1924, February 1925, April 1925, and June 1925. See RGASPI, f. 17, op. 34, d. 368,

l. 3; f. 17, op. 68, d. 239, ll. 60 and 146–54; f. 17, op. 34, d. 365; f. 17, op. 84, d. 1007, l. 67. The Central Committee sent a circular letter to all provincial and oblast' party committees on May 25, 1923 incorporating many of Smirnov's complaints. Based on a letter drafted by Smirnov, the circular lamented the lack of sufficient attention to the Commissariat's work. The letter went on to state that "the removal of chiefs of provincial land administrations and their deputies should be done with great caution and in every instance with the agreement of the Central Committee. . . . [Removal of] chiefs of the uezd land administration should be done with the agreement of the provincial party committee."

23. RGAE f. 478, op. 15, d. 44, l. 50. The circular was approved by the Orgburo.

24. Ibid., ll. 46–47. The letter went out above the signature of Smirnov and the Central Committee Secretariat.

25. See the triumphant article by Iun'ev, the chief of the administrative-financial section, in *Sel'sko-khoziaistvennaia zhizn'*, 1927, no. 27: 23.

26. On the background to the Face to the Village campaign and its many internal contradictions, see Markus Wehner, "Litsom k derevne: Sovetskaia vlast' i krest'ianskii vopros," *Otechestvennaia Istoriia* 5 (1993): 86–107. See also his *Bauernpolitik im proletarischen Staat: Die Bauernfrage als zentrales Problem der sowjetischen Innenpolitik 1921–1928* (Koeln, 1998). See also E. H. Carr, *Socialism in One Country*, vol. 1: 195ff.

27. On the scissors crisis, see Carr, *The Interregnum*, 86–147; and *Otchet Narodnogo komissariata zemledeliia RSFSR XII-omu Vserossiiskomu s"ezdu sovetov za 1923–24 g.* (Moscow, 1925).

28. Letter from Smirnov to Molotov dated October 17, 1924. RGAE, f. 478, op. 1, d. 1428, l. 12.

29. Carr, *Socialism in One Country*, vol. 1: 214–216.

30. *Pravda*, January 1, 1924.

31. For a policy statement in 1925, see RGASPI f. 17, op. 84, d. 1007, l. 109–12, June (or July) 19, 1925.

32. *Pravda*, January 1, 1924.

33. *XI Vserossiiskii s'ezd Sovetov RSFSR, Stenograficheskii otchet*, January 20, 1924, 17–36.

34. *Sel'sko-khoziaistvennaia zhizn'*, 1925, no. 16:1–2, 25–26.

35. RGAE, f. 478, op. 3, d. 3222, ll. 3–4. As early as November 1923, Smirnov called the budgetary position of the land organs "completely abnormal." See his *Na pomoshch' krest'ianskomu khoziaistvu*, 10.

36. RGAE, f. 478, op. 1, d. 1428, ll. 1–4.

37. See also RGAE, f. 478, op. 1, d. 1080, ll. 60–61, on the "extremely insignificant allotments" to local budgets.

38. RGAE, f. 478, op. 1, d. 1810, l. 95.

39. The "Face to the Countryside" campaign could not save the Narkomzem journal *Sel'skoe i lesnoe khoziaistvo*, which ceased publication in the spring of 1925 because of its "miserly financial situation." It was merged with *Uspekhi agronomii*, which, under the auspices of the Timiriazev Agricultural Academy, had also gone broke, to form *Puti sel'skogo khoziaistva*. *Puti sel'skogo khoziaistva*, 1925, no. 1–2: 3.

40. R. W. Davies, *The Development of the Soviet Budgetary System* (Cambridge, 1958), 4–5, 83–84.

41. Report of Narkomzem to the 11th Congress of Soviets, January 1924, as reported in *Sel'sko-khoziaistvennaia zhizn'*, 1924.

42. Protocols of session of the Zemplan Plenum from November 1, 1927. RGAE, f. 478, op. 2, d. 371a, ll. 3–4.

43. Letter to the Politburo of 1926 in RGAE, f. 478, op. 1, d. 1438, ll. 28–29.

44. See RGAE, f. 478, op. 1, d. 1139, ll. 5–6 and d. 1801, l. 27; also Stephen Sternheimer, "Administration" in Pintner and Rowney, *Russian Officialdom*, 336.

45. *Otchet Narkomzema za 1923/24*, 168.

46. RGASPI, f. 17, op. 68, d. 508, l. 7.

47. A. A. Alymov and S. Studenikin, "Rekonstruktsiia gosapparata," in E. B. Pashukanis, ed., *Piatnadtsat' let sovetskogo stroitel'stva* (Moscow, 1931), 253.

48. RGAE, f. 478, op. 15, d. 1, ll. 10–12.

49. RGASPI, f. 17, op. 2, d. 154, str. 48–54.

50. RGAE f. 478, op. 1, d. 1810, ll. 84–85. For a blistering attack by a Narkomzem collegium member on the finance commissariat's stinginess, see Latsis's comments at the 12th All-Russian Congress of Soviets, reported in *Sel'sko-khoziaistvennaia zhizn'*, 1925, no. 18: 1.

51. See, for example, D. R. Shearer, "The Language and Politics of Socialist Rationalization: Productivity, Industrial Relations and the Social Origins of Stalinism at the End of NEP," *Cahiers du Monde Russe et Sovietique*, 32(4), 581, 608; and Shearer, *Industry, State, and Society in Stalin's Russia*. On Dzerzhinskii, see N. V. Valentinov, *Nasledniki Lenina* (especially the article "Doktrina pravogo kommunizma"), and *Novaia Ekonomicheskaia Politika*. See also Sheila Fitzpatrick, "Ordzhonikidze's Takeover of Vesenkha: A Case Study in Soviet Bureaucratic Politics," *Soviet Studies* 37:2 (April, 1985): 153–72; Carr and Davies, *Foundations of a Planned Economy*, vol. 1: 574–604; Oleg Khlevniuk, *In Stalin's Shadow: The Career of 'Sergo' Ordzhonikidze* (Armonk, 1995). In *Technology and Society under Lenin and Stalin* (Princeton, 1978), Kendall Bailes very briefly discusses the twenties (before the Shakhty trial) (63–66); V. N. Ipatieff, *Life of a Chemist* (Stanford, 1946); Naum Jasny, *Soviet Economists of the Twenties: Names to Be Remembered* (Cambridge, 1972).

52. *Novaia ekonomicheskaia politika*, 127. See also, for example, Dzerzhinskii's letter to Kuibeshev of February 1, 1926, concerning a clash with Miliutin in the Sovnarkom cafeteria. Kvashonkin, et al., *Bol'shevistskoe rukovodstvo*, 318–19 (doc. 199).

53. In a manner similar to Smirnov, Feliks Dzerzhinskii had also undergone something of a transformation in his leadership style when he took charge of Vesenkha in 1924. "Going into Vesenkha, into this complicated agency with the complex problems standing before it, Dzerzhinskii felt he could not direct this organization by means of methods that relied on Chekist fear." Valentinov makes the (almost) touching observation that, when Dzerzhinskii began his tenure at Vesenkha, he actually was dismayed that the employees of Vesenkha were deathly afraid of him (*Novaia ekonomicheskaia politika*, 102–3). Smirnov betrayed no such sentiments.

54. Between 1919 and 1922, the organization had been called the People's Commissariat of State Control. Two useful treatments of Rabkrin's activities in the 1920s are Mark Beissinger, *Scientific Management, Socialist Discipline, and Soviet Power* (Cambridge, Mass., 1988); and E. A. Rees, *State Control in Soviet Russia: The Rise and Fall of the Workers' and Peasants' Inspectorate, 1920–34* (Houndmills, 1987).

55. L. Schapiro, *The Communist Party of the Soviet Union* (New York, 1960), 242. Initially intended to moderate disputes between party members, the Central Control Commission ended up as an agency that disciplined members for various infractions. It also kept thick files on party members, and those files were housed, not coincidentally, behind locked steel doors together with Stalin's secretariat on the sixth floor of the Central Committee building.

56. Just before his final stroke, Lenin criticized Rabkrin, and implicitly Stalin's leadership, in two articles published in *Pravda* in January and March 1923: "Kak nam reorganizovat' Rabkrin" ("How we should reorganize Rabkrin") and "Luchshe men'she da luchshe" ("Better fewer but better"). See also L. Krasin's critique of Rabkrin at the Twelfth Party Congress in

Dvenadtsatyi s"ezd rossiiskoi kommunisticheskoi partii (bol'shevikov): Stenograficheskii Otchet (Moscow, 1923), 42, 45, 113–22, 174.

57. This phrase is from Orlovsky, "The Anti-Bureaucratic Campaigns of the 1920s" in Theodore Taranovski, ed., *Reform in Modern Russian History: Progress or Cycle?* (New York, 1995), 295.

58. RGAE, f. 478, op. 1, d. 1534, l. 6 ob.

59. By 1921, the communist contingent was just 3 percent, approximately the same figure as in 1918. RGASPI, f. 17, op. 65, d. 175, l. 48 (correspondence between the Commissariat of Agriculture and the Communist party fraction). One party inspector complained that when the Commissariat was reorganized in 1923 into five large divisions, each of which oversaw ten or more subsections that concentrated on technical issues, most subsections were completely devoid of communists. T. H. Rigby, *Communist Party Membership in the USSR, 1917–1967* (Princeton, 1968), 420. On 1928–29, see Bineman and Kheinman, *Kadry gosudarstvennogo apparata*, 24.

60. RGAE, f. 478, op. 1, d. 1810, ll. 75–76 (correspondence between Narkomzem and Central Committee, 1925).

61. *Piatnadtsatyi s"ezd VKP (b), dekabr' 1927 goda, stenograficheskii otchet* (Moscow, 1961), 1: 446–47. The commissariat with the highest proportion of communists, Narkomtrud, had 28 percent. Narkomtorg was close behind with 27.6 percent. At the Sixteenth Party Conference in April 1929, it was reported that 11.7 percent of all employees were communists. This figure jumped to 25 percent for those in administration. *Shestnadtsataia konferentsiia VKP (b), aprel' 1929 goda: Stenograficheskii otchet* (Moscow, 1962), 458–59.

62. The verification may have been connected to expulsions of Trotsky's followers from the party and the state apparatus carried out in 1923–24, although there were very few, if any, Trotskyists in Narkomzem.

63. RGASPI, f. 17, op. 68, d. 508, l. 10.

64. RGASPI, f. 17, op. 68, d. 510, l. 5a. The commission recommended that other leading party members be removed, including P. I. Lezhnev-Fin'kovskii, A. A. Andreev, Ivan A. Mirtov, and M. A. Sakharov.

65. Protocols of investigation, RGASPI, f. 17, op. 68, d. 510, l. 5a. Telegram to Stalin from Smirnov, dated April 24, 1924. RGASPI, f. 17, op. 68, d. 508, l. 10.

66. RGAE, f. 478, op. 12, d. 1061, ll. 1–18 ob. contains the protocols of the Central Commission for Reducing the Staff of Narkomzem. In attendance were representatives of the divisions being reviewed, members of the party cell, and a representative of the Commissariat's Uchraspred section. Only those candidates about whom there was opposition to removing (or transferring) were mentioned in the protocols. Two hundred ninety-three people were listed in the protocols. The protocols do not cite the grounds for the Commissariat's objections, nor do they always note the reason why the Commission wanted them removed. See a Central Committee and Central Control Commission circular explaining the need for a verification of the whole apparatus, one that would not indiscriminately target nonparty specialists, intelligentsia, and *sluzhashchie*, in the Politburo fond, RGASPI, f. 17, op. 3, d. 480, ll. 13–14.

67. Each people's commissariat contained a branch of Uchraspred, which was, in the words of an Orgburo report, "a record keeping bureau that is small, but comprised of cadres selected for their good quality. Uchraspred focuses on nonparty individuals." The Central Committee, then, could count on its branch offices of Uchraspred for regular research on the state apparatus. RGASPI, f. 17, op. 34, d. 124, l. 38; RGASPI, f. 17, op. 34, d. 125, ll. 53–56. For more on Uchraspred, see Jeremy Azrael, *Managerial Power and Soviet Politics* (Cambridge, Mass., 1966), 71–82.

68. As late as 1924, 35 percent of the sixty-six people who comprised the top leadership group of Narkomzem were "from the nobility" *(iz dvorian)*. Of these, seven had been landowners *(pomeshchiki)*. RGAE, f. 478, op. 1, d. 1534, l. 2 ob.

69. The Orgotdel (the Organization and Instruction Department) and Uchraspred (the Records and Assignments Department) merged in 1924 into Orgraspred, which was charged with the allocation of party personnel. See *Bol'shevik*, April 30, 1928, no. 8: 66–71. On Orgraspred, see Carr, *Socialism in One Country*, 2:203–5, and Carr and Davies, *Foundations of a Planned Economy* (New York, 1959), 2:123–126.

70. See the instruction from the Central Committee's Uchraspred to pay special attention to the Agriculture Administration, in RGASPI, f. 17, op. 34, d. 126, l. 16. The agricultural and financial commissariats were singled out more than other ministries for this kind of investigation into the background of their cadres.

71. RGAE, f. 478, op.1, d. 1534, ll. 8–13. Smirnov's response is in the same delo, ll. 2–7, dated October 10, 1924.

72. In 1929, 24 percent of higher and midlevel officials at the okrug level and 27 percent at the oblast' level were holdovers. Bineman and Kheinman, *Kadry gosudarstvennogo apparata*, 28.

73. RGAE, f. 478, op. 1, d. 1534, l. 4.

74. Ibid., l. 7.

75. On Uchraspred, see T. H. Rigby, "Staffing USSR Incorporated: The Origins of the Nomenklatura System," *Soviet Studies*, 40 (1988); and Leonard Shapiro, *The Communist Party of the Soviet Union* (New York, 1971), 250, 253–54, 319–21.

76. In 1923 and 1924, Uchraspred complained that Narkomzem was very slow to establish a functioning branch of Uchraspred, noting that Smirnov simply chose staff based on personal acquaintance. See, e.g., RGASPI, f. 17, op. 34, d. 125, l. 89 and l. 125; op. 34, d. 126, l. 52.

77. "Lushche men'she da lushche" first appeared in *Pravda* on March 4, 1923. Smirnov often used Lenin's last writings as a springboard for defending his commissariat and for launching attacks on political enemies

78. RGAE, f. 478, op. 1, d. 1604.

79. TSGA RSFSR, f. 406, op. 1, d. 524, l. 5.

80. Report of Rabkrin, RGAE f. 478, op. 1, d. 1742, l. 5.

81. GARF, f. 406, op. 25, d. 41, ll. 1–2 ob.

82. A detailed analysis of the scholarly debate between the Agrarian Marxists and the Organization-Production School is contained in Susan Gross Solomon, *The Soviet Agrarian Debate: A Controversy in Social Science, 1923–29* (Boulder, 1977). Larin also frequently attacked Vesenkha's former Menshevik experts in print.

83. RGASPI, f. 17, op. 3, d. 370, ll. 12–13 (Politburo protocols, August 9, 1923).

84. Quoting Valentinov, *Nasledniki Lenina*, 135. See also his *Novaia ekonomicheskaia politika*, 22–23.

85. In 1921, the two scholars had tried to return to Soviet Russia: Makarov from the USA and Chelintsev from Serbia. They had been delayed, in part because of a lack of hard currency. RGAE, f. 478, op. 1, d. 473, l. 245, collegium protocols from September 21, 1921. N. P. Makarov (1886–1980) had been a member of the League for Agrarian Reform. He apparently was offered a job at Cornell University in 1923. He worked in Timiriazev Academy in 1927–28 and in Gosplan during the 1920s. A. N. Chelintsev (1874–1938?) was trained as an economist. He held posts in Gosplan and the Timiriazev Academy between 1923 and 1928.

86. RGAE, f. 478, op. 1, d. 1810, ll. 75–76, letter to Presidium of TsKK, tov. Iaroslavskii. Copies to members of Politburo.

87. Smirnov's objections are reminiscent of Dzerzhinskii's reply to Larin's accusation that "in Vesenkha Mensheviks dominate." As Dzerzhinskii put it, "I wish that in other commissariats there was such domination. Former Mensheviks occupying important posts are superb workers. We need to value them. We would lose very much if they were not there." Valentinov, *Nasledniki Lenina*, 135. See his comments to the Fourteenth Party Conference (1925), 173–74: "Without them we will not be able to conquer bourgeois Europe economically." Dzerzhinskii nearly always took the side of noncommunist technical personnel against their "arrogant" communist superiors. Valentinov, *Novaia ekonomicheskaia politika*, 132.

88. RGAE, f. 478, op. 1, d. 1810, l. 76.

89. Also in April 1925, an editorial in *Na agrarnom fronte* alleged that the writings of Kondrat'ev and N. P. Oganovskii "showed extraordinary contempt" for Soviet power. Apparently the fuss came because the article was found to contain several errors of arithmetic. The editors pointed out that the scholars were not Marxists or Leninists and accused them of deliberate sabotage: "Specialists like Kondrat'ev must be mercilessly exposed." According to the editors, their writings were sufficiently counterrevolutionary to commend their cases to a court for review. Smirnov responded in *Pravda* by recommending that the authors of this editorial (apparently Kritsman and Larin, in the main) were more deserving of an appearance before the court. To reject these specialists' work because they are not Leninists would be "a sin" and "foolish baiting," Smirnov wrote, "the most harmful arrogance against which we must always wage a decisive struggle." Smirnov wrote glowingly of Kondrat'ev's qualities. "For the two years that I have led Narkomzem, I have had every opportunity to be confident that in the person of Professor Kondrat'ev we have in the highest degree a conscientious, energetic, and knowledgeable colleague who works untiringly." *Na agrarnom fronte*, 1925, no. 4: 190–91; *Pravda*, May 9, 1925; GARF, f. 4359, op. 1, d. 40, ll. 42–44.

90. Valentinov notes that in 1924–25, the GPU made arrests all over the country, though he does not specify whom, exactly, was arrested. There were none, however, in Vesenkha, thanks to Dzerzhinskii's intervention, and specialists in Vesenkha were grateful for his leadership. Valentinov quotes one as saying, "He valued and protected us specialists. [Under his leadership] you could sleep peacefully at night. You weren't afraid of the GPU." Valentinov, *Novaia ekonomicheskaia politika*, 101. One would guess that Narkomzem's specialists were equally grateful to Smirnov. In any case, the observation reveals that employees in the state administration understood that the GPU was active in harassing specialists and that the people's commissar had to defend them. But Smirnov was not Dzerzhinskii, who, with his close personal ties to Stalin, could be more direct. Smirnov had no such relationship. Thus, he had to be more creative in devising strategies for defending his staff.

91. The letter was marked "top secret, for your hands only," although a copy was sent to Uglanov, the Moscow party chief. RGASPI, f. 17, op. 85, d. 134, ll. 55–64.

92. The material is located in GARF, f. 374, op. 27, d. 702.

93. Undated report on VSNKh, probably late 1923, from Uchraspred. RGASPI, f. 17, op. 34, d. 125, l. 102.

94. As Valentinov noted, "[Dzerzhinskii] was a very 'vedomstvennyi' person, and he wanted his *vedomstvo* [agency]—Vesenkha—to be better than all others, to sparkle like glass in the sunlight. He wanted the best specialists in the USSR to work in his agency and to this end he was prepared to poach them from other commissariats." Valentinov, *Novaia ekonomicheskaia politika*, 127. See Lunacharsky's denial to Lenin that he was guilty of *vedomstvennost'* in a dispute with the Commissariat of Agriculture. Letter of January 12, 1922, in RGASPI, f. 17, op. 84, d. 420, l. 9. For a pioneering treatment of Bolshevik institutional and political culture, see Mark von Hagen, *Soldiers in the Proletarian Dictatorship: The Red Army and the Soviet State*

(Ithaca, 1990). See also Sheila Fitzpatrick, "Ordzhonikidze's Takeover of Vesenkha: A Case Study in Soviet Bureaucratic Politics," *Soviet Studies* 37:2 (April 1985): 165–67.

95. For an excellent study of the complex relationship among rank-and-file communists, specialists, and political leaders in an economic administration, see Robert Argenbright, "Marking NEP's Slippery Path: The Krasnoshchekov Show Trial," *Russian Review* 61 (April 2002): 249–75; see also Alan Ball, *Russia's Last Capitalists: The Nepmen, 1921–1929.* (Berkeley, 1987).

96. GARF, f. 374, op. 27, d. 702, l. 148. This file contains materials on the "Affair of the Narkomzem Party Cell," as investigated by the Central Control Commission and Central Committee in 1926–27.

97. Narkomzem's aggressive actions on behalf of its cadres can be contrasted with Fitzpatrick's characterization of Vesenkha's "embarrassed and intimidated silence" amid harassment from Rabkrin in 1929–30. The Commissariat of Agriculture was anything but silent, and such aggressiveness in defending institutional interests was likely the norm, not the exception, at least during the NEP period. Sheila Fitzpatrick, "Ordzhonikidze's Takeover of Vesenkha."

98. See Rabkrin's suspicious comment about categories in a letter from Shvernik to Smirnov in RGAE, f. 478, op. 1, d. 1534, ll. 9.

99. The protocols of these verifications are located in RGAE, f. 478, op. 12, d. 1061.

100. RGAE, f. 478, op. 12, d. 1061, l. 9 ob.

101. See RGAE, f. 478, op. 1, d. 1534, l. 2–7 ob.

102. RGAE, f. 478, op. 12, d. 1061, l. 9 for the case of N. M. Kormilitsyn, a specialist on financial matters in the forest administration who had been fired from Narkomzem once before.

103. A brief account is contained in *Otchet NKZ za 1923–24 g.*, 583–84.

104. *Pravda*, 1924, no. 290 and Narkomzem's undated response in a letter to the TsKK, RGAE, f. 478, op. 3, d. 1141, l. 9. Also of interest is Smirnov's 1924 letter to Rabkrin (RGAE, f. 478, op. 1, d. 1534, ll. 2–7) and 1926 Rabkrin letter to the Central Control Commission (GARF, f. 374, op. 27, d. 372, l. 5 ob.). See also materials directing the heads of local land sections to seek out former estate owners and report them to Moscow. RGAE, f. 478, op. 15, d. 41, ll. 11, 47. All this occurred at the same time as efforts to evict from their estates those few estate owners who somehow had held onto their lands. See RGAE, f. 478, op. 15, d. 17, ll. 27–28, 34, 48–51.

105. RGAE, f. 478, op. 12, d. 1061, l. 4 and ll. 5 ob.– 6.

106. GARF. f. 374, op. 27, d. 372, l. 5 ob. Former landlords had been less than one-fifth of 1 percent of employees in the entire land administration, and in twenty-three provinces there had been none at all. *Otchet NKZ za 1923–24 g.*, 584.

107. Former White Army officers were to be used "only in the center" and were "by no means to be sent to the localities." RGAE, f. 478, op. 12, d. 487, l. 11.

108. RGAE, f. 478, op. 12, d. 1061, l. 5. Bailes notes the "division of labor" and "uneasy truce" that developed between specialists in industry and their communist superiors in the 1920s. Bailes, *Technology and Society under Lenin and Stalin*, 64.

109. This phenomenon of defending cadres was not limited to Narkomzem of course. Narkomfin and Vesenkha faced the same problems, though their strategies have not been documented.

110. Sheila Fitzpatrick, "Ascribing Class: The Construction of Social Identity in Soviet Russia," *Journal of Modern History* 65 (December 1993): 749.

111. It is also important to note that despite some resistance, provincial and county apparatuses absorbed peasants into the soviets and their various sections in very large numbers, although a detailed treatment of the rapidly growing cohort of peasants by social origin in *local*

soviet administration lies outside the parameters of this book. Villagers were to be given practical experience in management and administration in local soviets. One half of the approximately three hundred county land section chiefs were of peasant origin by 1925, as were one half of their deputies. Few had more than a primary education. Outside Moscow, then, promotion was fairly widespread—indeed local soviets were an excellent source of social mobility for peasants—and serves as an example to which we can compare the central efforts.

112. For Voroshilov's letter, see *Voennye arkhivy Rossii*, vypusk I (Moscow, 1993), 408–10.

113. For more on the phenomenon of peasant promotion, see Heinzen, "'Peasants from the Plow' to 'Professors from the Plow': The Culture of the Soviet People's Commissariat of Agriculture, 1921–1929," *Journal of Peasant Studies* 25:2.

114. The quote is from Orlovsky, "The Hidden Class: White Collar Workers in the Soviet 1920s," in Lewis Siegelbaum and Ronald G. Suny, eds., *Making Workers Soviet: Power, Class, and Identity* (Ithaca, 1994), 225. Orlovsky goes on: "Neither social nor even political reality corresponded to the requirements of ideology."

115. Smirnov's self-identification as a "peasant" was taken at face value by Soviet-era historians. See, for example, Nosova, "Formirovanie kadrov spetsialistov sel'skogo khoziaistva v sovetskoi dokolkhoznoi derevne," in R. R. Tolmacheva, ed., *Naselenie i trudovye resursy ural'skoi sovetskoi derevni* (Sverdlovsk, 1987), 10–11.

116. See, for example, stenograms of collegium meetings located in RGAE, f. 478, op. 1, d. 1544.

117. See the introductory biographical sketch in A. P. Smirnov, *Zadachi nizovoi vlasti v oblasti sel'skogo khoziaistva* (Moscow, 1926), 5–8.

118. *Biulleten' soveshchaniia krest'ian-chlenov VTsIK pri Narkomzeme RSFSR*, no. 3 (Moscow, 1924), 15.

119. This posturing anticipated the fact that beginning in 1930, the names of some top Bolsheviks (such as Ordzhonikidze and Kaganovich) appeared in print with the letter "r" for *rabochii* (worker) in parentheses following their names. Merridale, *Moscow and the Rise of Stalin*, 120.

120. RGAE, f. 478, op. 3, d. 3178, l.1.

121. A. P. Smirnov, *Zadachi nizovoi vlasti*, 7. Smirnov explicitly notes that he "broke ties with the village in 1895–97."

122. See RGAE, f. 478, op. 1, d. 1553, l. 19.

123. See, for example, Smirnov's letters to Rabkrin in RGAE, f. 478, op. 1, d. 1534, ll. 8–13; RGAE, f. 478, op. 1, d. 1604; RGAE, f. 478, op.1, d. 1810, ll. 75–76.

124. Interestingly, his patron, Smirnov, who was approximately the same age, joined the party at approximately the same time, and also identified himself as a worker when asked to list his social origin on the application in his Narkomzem personnel file.

125. Sheila Fitzpatrick, "The Problem of Class Identity in NEP Society," in Sheila Fitzpatrick, Alexander Rabinowitch, and Richard Stites, eds., *Russia in the Era of NEP: Explorationss in Soviet Society and Culture* (Bloomington, 1991) 26.

126. RGASPI, f. 17, op. 68, d. 239, l. 28.

127. RGAE, f. 478, op. 15, d. 41, ll. 37–37 ob.

128. GARF, f. 374, op. 28, d. 3061, ll. 16–17.

129. TsGA RSFSR, f. 406, op. 25, d. 362, ll. 22–24. "Results of purge of apparatus in land organs sent to comrade Ordzhonikidze."

130. This tension is revealed in the protocols of a 1925 meeting between the commissariat's *krest'iane-vydvizhentsy* and their supervisors RGAE, f. 478, op. 3, d. 3188, ll. 1–5. See also TsGA RSFSR, f. 406, op. 25, d. 1165, ll. 193–94. Unfortunately, we do not have information about

whether promotees brought their families with them to Moscow.

131. TsGA RSFSR, f. 406, op. 25, d. 1165, l. 194–3: "O vydvizhencheskoi rabote v Narkomzeme."

132. RGAE, f. 478, op. 3, d. 3188, ll. 10–11.

133. "Otchetnyi doklad Penzenskogo gubzemupravleniia za II-y kvartal 1924/5 goda." RGAE, f. 478, op. 3, d. 2979, 74 ob. For excerpts from hundreds of secret police reports on conditions during the 1924 crop failures, see *Sovetskaia derevnia glazami VChK-OGPU-NKVD, Tom 2. 1923–1929* (Moscow, 2000), 170–235

134. GARF, f. 374, op. 27c, d. 3061, ll. 12–25.

135. RGAE, f. 478, op. 1, d. 1810, ll. 75–76.

136. N. D. Kondrat'ev. *Osoboe mnenie.* Kn. 1 (Moscow, 1993), 253. The stenograms of this meeting are located in RGAE, op. 1, d. 1209, ll. 147–50.

137. Merridale, 195.

138. RGAE, f. 478, op. 1, d. 1427, l. 11.

CHAPTER 4

1. Stenographic report of collegium meeting, June 6, 1925. RGAE, f. 478, op. 1, d. 1549, l. 2.

2. RGAE, f. 478, op. 1, d. 1549, l. 3.

3. *Sel'sko-khoziaistvennaia zhizn'*, 1926, no. 10:2–3.

4. RGAE, f. 478, op. 1, d. 1544, l. 13 ob.

5. "Theses on organizational tasks in the further regulation of the work of Narkomzem," GARF, f. 406, op. 25, d. 41, l. 70.

6. Aspects of the debates over the agricultural economy in the 1920s have been covered in detail in several valuable works. See Alexander Erlich, *The Soviet Industrialization Debate, 1924–1928* (Cambridge, 1960); E. H. Carr, *The Interregnum* and *Socialism in One Country*; Carr and R. W. Davies, *Foundations of a Planned Economy*; Dorothy Atkinson, *The End of the Russian Land Commune* (Stanford, 1983); Isaac Deutscher, *The Prophet Unarmed: Trotsky, 1921–1929* (London, 1959); and Moshe Lewin, *Russian Peasants and Soviet Power* and *The Making of the Soviet System*.

7. From Lenin's "Political Report of the Central Committee of the RKP(b) to the Eleventh Party Congress," March 27, 1922. In *Lenin*, PSS, vol. 45:69–116.

8. Regarding the net volume of agricultural production in Russia, both before and after the Revolution, there are a large number of conflicting estimates. Stephen Wheatcroft's revised estimates must be considered definitive. See Wheatcroft in R. W. Davies, ed., *From Tsarism to the New Economic Policy* (London, 1990), 79; and Wheatcroft and Davies, "Agriculture," in Davies et al., eds., *The Economic Transformation of the Soviet Union, 1913–1945*.

9. *Sotsialisticheskoe stroitel'stvo* (1934), 4–5.

10. Wheatcroft and Davies, "Agriculture," in Davies et al, eds., *The Economic Transformation of the Soviet Union, 1913–1945*, 111. A. P. Smirnov, "Ocherednye zadachi razvitiia sel'skogo khoziaistva," in *Sel'sko-khoziaistvennaia zhizn'*, 1927, no. 16:2.

11. Figures declined from an average of almost eight million tons between 1909 and 1913 to fewer than two million tons in 1925–26. Barely two and a half million tons were exported the following year. Girkovich and Ozerov in *Ekonomicheskii biulleten' koniunkturnogo instituta*, 1927, no. 11–12: 60. See also A. P. Smirnov, "Ocherednye zadachi razvitiia sel'skogo khoziaistva," in *Sel'sko-khoziaistvennaia zhizn'*, 1927, no. 16:2.

12. The quantity of potatoes produced for market dropped by nearly half, from 5.6 to 2.9 million tons. *Narodnoe khoziaistvo za 1958*, 351. Danilov emphasizes large increases in sown area devoted to land sown with potatoes, without discussing marketings. *Sovetskaia dokolkhoz-*

naia derevnia, 288.

13. Davies, *The Soviet Economy in Turmoil* (Houndmills, 1989), 21.

14. If we take the 1924–28 average for the USSR, the picture improves slightly since the famine years are excluded. The average yield would then be 7.6 centners per hectare rather than 6.4. The 1925–29 average, which excludes the poor 1924 harvest, jumps slightly to 7.9 centners per hectare. V. P. Danilov, *Sovetskaia dokolkhoznaia derevnia*, 284–85. A centner is equivalent to 50 kilograms.

15. *Otchet Narodnogo komissariata zemledeliia za 1923* (Moscow, 1924), 18.

16. See Kerans, *Mind and Labor on the Farm*, 385–429, on pre-war agronomic aid programs.

17. *Itogi desiatiletiia sovetskoi vlasti v tsifrakh, 1917–1927*, (n.p., [1927]), 100–101. Smirnov set the figure at 99 percent, though this is a higher number than one generally finds. Smirnov, *Na agrarnom fronte*, 1926, no. 11–12:131.

18. On the commune in pre-war Russia, see David Moon, *The Russian Peasantry, 1600–1930: The World the Peasants Made* (London: 1999). The terms *mir*, *commune*, and *land society* were generally used interchangeably.

19. On this theme, see D. J. Male's valuable study of the commune during the mid to late 1920s, *Russian Peasant Organisation before Collectivisation: A Study of Commune and Gathering, 1925–1930* (Cambridge, Eng., 1971), 15–83. A weakness of Male's study is his tendency to see "the Soviet government" as an undifferentiated whole (pp. 4, 87, and 99, for example).

20. A. P. Smirnov, *Na pomoshch' krest'ianskomu khoziaistvu. Sbornik statei*. 2-e izdanie (Moscow, 1926), 19.

21. See, for example, Kondrat'ev discussing "irrationality in the organization of farms," in "Foundations of the Perspective Plan." Kondrat'ev, *Osoboe mnenie*, kn. 1:346.

22. Narodnyi komissariat zemledeliia, *Materialy po perspektivnomu planu razvitiia sel'skogo khoziastva RSFSR* (Moscow, 1928), 157; Gurov, "Predvaritel'nye itogi zemleustroistva," in *Na agrarnom fronte*, 1925, no. 10:77. See also Pershin, *Zemel'noe ustroistvo dorevoliutsionnoi derevni* (Moscow, 1928).

23. Peasants often had good reason not to till the fallow field in April, including the fact that cattle grazed on that field so their food would be lost if it were plowed under. There often were no other sources of fodder that early in the season. Surveyors also charged a hefty sum to widen narrow strips. On early plowing of fallow, see Kerans, *Mind and Labor on the Farm*, 37–41.

24. For pre-war agronomic strategies for attacking the three-field system, see Kerans, *Mind and Labor on the Farm*, 248–87.

25. Danilov, *Sovetskaia dokolkhoznaia derevnia*, 278.

26. Ibid., 143.

27. For a discussion of the challenges to peasants that were inherent in switching from three-field to multifield farming, see Kerans, *Mind and Labor on the Farm*, 272–77.

28. "Summary report about work on peasant letters for the period from November 1, 1924 to January 1, 1926." RGAE, f. 478, op. 3, d. 2813, l. 153. See also *Otchet Narodnogo komissariata zemledeliia za 1924–25* (Hereafter Otchet NKZ za 1924–25.) (Moscow, 1926), 207–9.

29. RGAE, f. 478. op. 3, d. 2813, l. 153. Of 10,992 letters surveyed, 72 complained about bribery among local land section personnel, 433 about drunkenness, and 419 about bureaucratism.

30. *Osnovnye elementy sel'sko-khoziaistvennogo proizvodstva SSSR 1916 i 1923–27 gg.* (Moscow, 1930), 2–5; Danilov, *Sovetskaia dokolkhoznaia derevnia*, 212. The equivalent figures for the RSFSR were 14.4 million and 17.1 million households, an 18.6 percent increase.

31. *Statisticheskii spravochnik za 1927 g.* (Moscow, 1927), 64–65; A. Bol'shakov, *Sovremen-*

naia derevnia v tsifrakh (Moscow, 1925). See also A. P. Smirnov, *Na pomoshch' krest'ianskomu khoziaistvu*, 18.

32. By 1927, the average household allotment in the RSFSR was 13.23 hectares, increasing from 10.08 in 1913. This indicated that the growth in the amount of land used by peasants after the 1917–18 mass repartitions, together with the large (approximating 6 percent a year) growth in sown area after 1922, more than countered the growth in households. Danilov, *Sovetskaia dokolkhoznaia derevnia*, 218, 219. Figure exclusive of autonomous republics.

33. Danilov, *Sovetskaia dokolkhoznaia derevnia*, 278–79.

34. 17,740,000 hectares.

35. A. P. Smirnov, *Na pomoshch' krest'ianskomu khoziaistvu*, 91.

36. Narodnyi Komissariat Zemledeliia *Osnovy perspektivnogo plana razvitiia sel'skogo i lesnogo khoziaistva* (Moscow, 1924).

37. A. P. Smirnov, *Na pomoshch' krest'ianskomu khoziaistvu*, 20.

38. From 35.8 to 24.1 million head. TsUNKhU Gosplana SSSR, *Zhivotnovodstvo SSSR za 1916–1938 gg., Statisticheskii sbornik* (Moscow-Leningrad, 1940), 4.

39. *Sel'sko-khoziaistvennaia zhizn'*, 1925. See also Smirnov, *Na pomoshch' krest'ianskomu khoziaistvu*, 39.

40. R. W. Davies et al., eds., *The Economic Transformation of the Soviet Union*, table 20, 289.

41. The figure grew from 7.5 million hectares to 14.2 million. *Sotsialisticheskoe stroitel'stvo SSSR* (Moscow, 1934), 176–77.

42. Flax reached its pre-war level by the late 1920s and sugar beets recovered by 1927, as did cotton. Although the yields for flax and sugar beets declined, this was compensated for by an increase in sown area. By 1928, the production of potatoes, fruits, and other vegetables was up to 42 percent higher than before the revolution. Wheatcroft, in *The Economic Transformation of the Soviet Union*, 111–12.

43. A. P. Smirnov, *Na pomoshch' krest'ianskomu khoziaistvu*, 82–83. Narkomzem's leadership argued that the poorer peasants should be given long-term credit to buy desperately needed inventory, while the better off could buy it out of pocket. See also *Snabzhenie krest'ianskogo naseleniia sel'skokhoziaistvennymi mashinami i orudiiami* (Moscow, 1925), 32.

44. Comments of the peasants Kireev, of Tambov guberniia and Ryndin of Saratov. RGASPI, f. 17, op. 85, d. 135, l. 78 and l. 79 ob-80.

45. Kerans, *Mind and Labor on the Farm*; R. W. Davies, *The Industrialisation of Soviet Russia. Vol. 1. The Socialist Offensive* (Cambridge, Mass., 1980), 9.

46. Danilov, *Sovetskaia dokolkhoznaia derevnia*, 275–76. *Narodnoe khoziaistvo za 1958*, 224, 444.

47. R. W. Davies, *The Industrialisation of Soviet Russia. Vol. 1. The Socialist Offensive*, 9.

48. This discussion is based on Danilov, *Sovetskaia dokolkhoznaia derevnia: Sotsial'naia struktura, sotsialnye otnosheniia* (Moscow, 1979), 208–16. On party policy toward cooperatives, see also Moshe Lewin, *Russian Peasants and Soviet Power: A Study of Collectivization* (New York, 1975), 93–102; and Markus Wehner, "Litsom k derevne."

49. RGAE, f. 478, op. 1, d. 1549, l. 3. Stenographic report of collegium session, June 6, 1925.

50. *Sovetskaia derevnia glazami VChK-OGPU-NKVD: Dokumenty i materialy*, Tom 2. 1923–1929 (Moscow, 2000), 199.

51. RGASPI, f. 17, op. 85, d. 135, l. 85. See also the 1926 comments of the peasant Khromushin of Vladimir province, who demanded that the sovkhoz land be given to the peasants. RGASPI, f. 17, op. 85, d. 135, l. 75 ob.

52. *Itogie desiatiletiia sovetskoi vlasti v tsifrakh, 1917–1927* ([n.p.] [1927]), 100–1. In 1928, the figures climbed to 1.2 percent for kolkhozy and 1.5 percent for sovkhozy.

53. The figure is given in TsSU SSSR, *Narodnoe khoziaistvo SSSR* (Moscow, 1933), 130.

54. "Protokol ob'edinennogo zasedaniia Prezidiuma Gosplana, Sel'sko-khoziaistvennoi sektsii i prestavitelei Narkomzema," 23 November 1921, in Danilov, ed., *Kooperativno-kolkhoznoe stroitel'stvo v SSSR, 1917–1922*, 329. For reports, see, for example, the late 1922 reports on state farms in Kashirsk uezd. RGASPI, f. 17, op. 84, d. 417, ll. 130–1; RGAE, f. 478, op. 1, d. 1372, l. 134. See also RGAE, f. 478, op. 1, d. 1810, ll. 71 and 84–85; and Smirnov's letter to the Politburo of 14 March 1924. RGAE, f. 478, op. 1, d. 1429.

55. A. P. Smirnov, *Na pomoshch' krest'ianskomu khoziaistvu*, 8. Provincial sovkhozy were grouped together in *gubseltresty*, or "trusts." These in turn answered to the state farm syndicate, Gossel'sindikat, which was attached to the Commissariat of Agriculture.

56. *Osnovy perspektivnogo plana razvitiia sel'skogo i lesnogo khoziastva* (Moscow, 1924).

57. RGAE, f. 478, op. 1, d. 1553, ll. 20–20 ob.

58. For more on the party debates on the definition of the "kulak," see Lewin, "Who Was the Soviet Kulak?" in *The Making of the Soviet System* (New York, 1985), 121–41; and Atkinson, *End of the Russian Land Commune, 1905–1930*, 278–88.

59. E. H. Carr was disdainful of the party's Right wing (including those in the Commissariat of Agriculture), which urged a go-slow approach in encouraging rural recovery. Carr framed nearly all debates over agrarian policy between 1922 and 1929 as struggles between "pro-kulak" and "anti-kulak" forces, with the pro-kulak group triumphant between 1923 and 1927. Appropriating the language and vocabulary of politicians and scholars hostile to the party's Rightists, Carr overestimates the power of "the kulak." In his discussion of rural social classes, for example, Carr relies on the evidence of the Agrarian Marxists, indicated by his sympathetic citations of people like L. N. Kritsman. He frequently relies on their journal, *Na agrarnom fronte*, for information about the countryside. Phrases such as the following about the spring of 1925 pervade Carr's work: "The kulak had proved victorious. The cities were once more being held to ransom." *Socialism in One Country*, vol. 1, 193. Or, concerning state grain purchases in autumn 1925: "The kulak had shown himself master of the situation." *Socialism in One Country*, vol. 2, 295. Furthermore, while he mentions the Commissariat of Agriculture only rarely, he ties the Commissariat to these "kulaks" and implicates its leadership (together with other party moderates) in serving as toadies for their interests. For example, on the winter of 1924–25: "High prices were thus readily tolerated in those official circles which supported the development of kulak agriculture, and looked without disfavor on the growing social and economic differentiation in the countryside." *Socialism in One Country*, vol. 1, 195. He believes that the Commissariat of Agriculture's leadership advanced the interests of the capitalist "kulaks" and served as some of their "powerful protectors in the Party." Carr's understanding of the Commissariat of Agriculture is a byproduct of his ambivalent view of NEP as a temporary period of reaction en route to the establishment of a planned economy. He expresses impatience with the "conciliation of the peasant" that lay at the heart of the Rightists' understanding of the transition period. Carr, *Interregnum*, 86–87. In private correspondence, Carr wrote that "the peasants were a primitive, cunning, ignorant, and brutish lot." Haslam, *The Vices of Integrity*, 247. Thus, Carr regarded the Commissariat of Agriculture as something of a reactionary force that served the narrow interests of small-scale rural capitalists. Until the late 1980s, historians working in the Soviet Union went further along these lines, condemning the Commissariat's political and specialist leadership for their alleged dedication to the "restoration of capitalism in the countryside." They mimicked the Central Committee's vicious condemnation of the Right and leading agrarian specialists in 1928–31 after their political defeat,

accusing noncommunist specialists of surreptitiously attempting to establish property in land and encourage "kulak" exploitation.

60. Valentinov, *Naslredniki*, 117.

61. F. Sulikovskii, "Ne terminologicheskaia, prosto putanitsa," in *Bol'shevik*, 1925, no. 17–18:51–59. The best study of the Agrarian Marxists is Susan G. Solomon, *The Soviet Agrarian Debate: A Controversy in Social Science, 1923–29* (Boulder, 1977). The present study disagrees with Solomon's conclusion that the Agrarian Marxists tried to stay out of questions of policy and politics before 1928 and that "the politicization of rural inquiry did not begin until late 1928" (Solomon, 17–18, 178). Statements such as Gaister's alleging that Smirnov was denying the existence of the kulak were deeply political and incendiary, and they infuriated Smirnov and his supporters. This is not to say that the research undertaken by Agrarian Marxists and the members of the Organization-Production group was politically motivated, or that the field of rural social studies was merely a servant of politicians. Rather, I would argue that the many participants understood the larger political debate and took sides, using the conclusions they drew from their research as ammunition in policy disputes.

62. RGAE, f. 478, op. 1, d. 1810, l. 47. Emphasis in original.

63. *Sel'sko-khoziaistvennaia zhizn'*, 1922, no.3:2–3. Soviet historians exaggerated the level of peasant support for collective farms and for the expropriation of kulaks, in order to demonstrate that the preconditions for mass collectivization had been laid by 1929. See, for example, M. P. Iroshnikov, *Sozdanie Sovetskogo tsentral'nogo gosudarstvennogo apparata: Sovet Narodnykh Komissarov* (Moscow, 1980); E. B. Genkina, *Lenin: Predsedatel' Sovnarkoma i STO* (Moscow, 1984); E. N. Gorodetskii, *Rozhdenie sovetskogo gosudarstva* (Moscow, 1986). Iurii Poliakov, *Perekhod k NEPu* (Moscow, 1967); I. E. Zelenin, *Sovkhozy SSSR v gody dovoennykh piatiletok, 1928–1941* (Moscow, 1982); and his *Sovkhozy v pervoe desiatiletie sovetskoi vlast', 1917–1927* (Moscow, 1972). On Kritsman, see Solomon, *The Soviet Agrarian Debate*, 25ff, 189.

64. See Smirnov discussing this strategy in RGASPI, f. 17, op. 85, d. 135, l. 266.

65. *Sel'sko-khoziaistvennaia zhizn'*, 1922, no.3:2–3.

66. A. P. Smirnov, *Na pomoshch' krest'ianskomu khoziaistvu*, 37–45.

67. See the articles by Smirnov in *Pravda*, April 7, 1925, and Bogushevskii in *Bol'shevik*, June 1, 1925, no. 9–10:59–64. Bukharin echoed these distinctions between the kulak and zazhitochnyi. See, for example, *K itogam XIV s"ezda VKP(b)* (Moscow, 1926).

68. See, for example, A. I. Khriashcheva, *Gruppy i klassy v krest'ianstve*, 2nd ed. (Moscow, 1926); S. M. Dubrovskii, "Rassloenie krest'ianstva i zadachi partii v derevne," in *Na agrarnom fronte*, 1927, no. 11–12.

69. Smirnov, *Nashi osnovnye zadachi po podniatiiu i organizatsii krest'ianskogo khoziastva* (Moscow, 1925), 21–22. Much of this pamphlet is based on his speech at the October 1924 Central Committee Plenum. RGASPI, f. 17, op. 2, d. 154, str. 48–53.

70. RGAE, f. 478, op. 1, d. 1544, l. 13.

71. See, for example, Smirnov's comments at the collegium session of May 29, 1926. RGAE, f. 17, op. 85, d. 135, l. 109. Carr used a less nuanced breakdown to describe the differences between kulaks and the well-off farmers: "kulaks and would-be kulaks." Carr, *Socialism in One Country*, vol. 1, 297–98.

72. For the thinking of N. D. Kondrat'ev on this theme see, for example, his "Sovremennoe sostoianie narodnokhoziaistvennoi kon'iunktury v svete vzaimootnosheniia industrii i sel'skogo khoziaistva." *Sotsialisticheskoe khoziaistvo*, 1925, no. 6.

73. A recent addition to the historical literature treating the interaction among specialists, the state, and the peasantry is the work of Yanni Kotsonis, who has examined the rural cooperative movement between 1861 and World War I. *Making Peasants Backward: Agricultural*

Cooperatives and the Agrarian Question in Russia, 1861–1914 (London, 1999). The work adds texture and depth to our understanding of the worldview of some prerevolutionary professional groups and their struggles for professional autonomy. Kotsonis's provocative book argues that agronomists in the pre-World War I cooperative movement were taken with painting groups of peasants with negative labels—especially kulak—and ascribing to this group as a collectivity (and the communities that supported them) certain negative features that needed to be wiped out, using coercion, if necessary, for the good of the state and peasant society. Whereas he acknowledges that cooperators could have never anticipated the Stalinist attack on the kulaks "as a class," and his detailed study ends in 1914, he does argue in his epilogue that the "intellectual construct and social dynamic" of the agronomists he studied exhibit continuity with those who implemented dekulakization in 1929–30. Drawing connections between pre-war cooperative agronomists and Stalinist dekulakization policies does raise certain questions. Was it a matter of Soviet policy in the twenties to stigmatize and persecute kulaks, and did professional agricultural specialists support this persecution? He writes that cooperative agronomists were mostly interested in mobilizing peasants as part of a social engineering project. One might ask, however, whether the cooperative agronomists were typical of all agronomists in the country. One might also inquire about the activities of agronomists who did not work in the cooperative movement, and who made up the great majority of the country's agronomists after 1905. Did the noncooperative agronomists have a different agenda? Can one generalize about the activities, worldview, and attitudes of agricultural specialists in the Soviet period on the basis of the agronomists in the pre-war financial cooperatives?

74. For similar fears, see the report from the Gomel' gubkom, RGAE, f. 478, op. 1, d. 1433, l. 37. Narkomzem officials approvingly cited Lenin's 1919 speech at the Eighth Party Congress in which he warned his audience that although a civil war must be waged against the kulaks, officials must not confuse the kulak-exploiter with the "strong middle peasant." It would be a gross error for local party members to make snap judgments without understanding the entire economic context. See, for example, A. P. Smirnov, *Na pomoshch' krest'ianskomu khoziaistvu*, 38.

75. A. P. Smirnov, *Na pomoshch' krest'ianskomu khoziaisvu*, 37.

76. *Deviatyi s'ezd sovetov RSFSR, Stenograficheskii otchet*, 215–16. Narkomzem used every opportunity to argue for the need to encourage the "vanguard" stratum of producers. The materials they supplied the Central Committee (including selections of peasant letters to Narkomzem and to rural newspapers) always backed this claim. In 1924, *Novaia derevnia*, Narkomzem's publishing house, issued a book in 20,000 copies, introduced and edited by A. Sosnovskii, entitled *Derevnia pri NEP'e: Kogo schitat' kulakom, kogo—truzhenikom. Chto ob etom govoriat krest'iane?* A collection of letters to the peasant newspaper *Bednota*, the book uses letters to support the idea that villagers themselves understand the difference between the kulak and the "strong" middle peasant. See also RGAE, f. 478, op. 1, d. 1080, l. 3. Narkomzem's top officials were united in their view of the absence of a current serious kulak threat. See Latsis's comments on the *krepkii trudovoi krest'ianin*, in *Sel'sko-khoziaistvennaia zhizn'*, 1925, 16:1–2.

77. Smirnov, *Na pomoshch' krest'ianskomu khoziaistvu*, 43.

78. RGASPI, f. 17, op. 2, d. 154, str. 48–50. The same sentiments are expressed in A. P. Smirnov, *Nashi osnovnye zadachi*, 21.

79. RGAE, f. 478, op. 3, d. 2813, l. 151 ob-152.

80. See, for example, the report of a traveling control commission, authored by Dyshin, October 27, 1925, in RGASPI, f. 17, op. 67, d. 138, l. 59.

81. *Osnovy perspektivnogo plana razvitiia sel'skogo i lesnogo khoziaistva* (Moscow, 1924).

Discussions of the plan which took place in meetings of the Gosplan Presidium in July–August 1925 are presented in *Puti sel'skogo khoziastva*, 1925, no. 4–5; and 1926, no. 1–3. The writings of the Agrarian Marxists are found in *Na agrarnom fronte*, the journal of the Agrarian Section of the Communist Academy. Criticisms of the *Fundamentals of the Perspective Plan* can be found in *Na agrarnom fronte* 1925, no. 1–3. See also Susan G. Solomon, *The Soviet Agrarian Debate: A Controversy in Social Science, 1923–29* (Boulder, 1977) for a closer examination of these disputes.

82. See Iurii Felshtinskii, compiler, *Arkhiv Trotskogo: Kommunisticheskaia oppozitsiia v SSSR 1923–27* (Benson, 1988), vol. 4: 150; see also vol. 1: 252 and vol. 2: 52, 91.

83. See the article by Larin in *Pravda*, December 16, 1925; and the reply by Smirnov in *Sel'sko-khoziaistvennaia zhizn'*, 1926, no. 1:1–5. Kondrat'ev agreed with Smirnov that the threat of differentiation was overblown by some in the party. "K voprosu o 'Proekte osnovnykh nachal zemlepol'zovaniia i zemleustroistva KZP," *Osoboe mnenie*, vol. 2, 99–102."

84. N. V. Valentinov, *Nasledniki Lenina* (Moscow, 1991), 88–89. Valentinov served as deputy editor of *Torgovo-promyshlennaia gazeta* from 1922 until 1930, at which time he emigrated to Paris.

85. Smirnov, *Nashi osnovnye zadachi*.

86. Valentinov, *Nasledniki Lenina*, 152.

87. On the "canon of differentiation," see Valentinov, *Nasledniki Lenina*, 150–52.

88. Valentinov, *Nasledniki Lenina*, 111.

89. See *Bol'shevistskoe rukovodstvo*, 329; letter from Dzerzhinskii to Iagoda (doc. 210). In November 1923–March 1924 the GPU began operations against "speculators and speculating elements" in Moscow and other major cities. See also *Bol'shevistskoe rukovodstvo*, 277–78, letter from Dzerzhinskii to Stalin of October 22, 1923.

90. Alan Ball, *Russia's Last Capitalists: The Nepmen, 1921–1929* (Berkeley, 1987), 33.

91. V. K. Vinogradov, citing report by Iagoda in FSB archives, "Introduction," in *Sovetskaia derevnia glazami VChK-OGPU-NKVD, Tom. 2* (Moscow, 2000), 36.

92. For an examination of the tension between economic productivity and party control that focuses on campaigns for "communist ethics," see Robert Argenbright, "Marking NEP's Slippery Path."

93. Each commune served significantly fewer people than the average village soviet, which buttressed its popularity as a forum for making decisions, while weakening the position of the soviet network. In 1927, a commune generally represented 150–500 people. The average number of persons served per village soviet ranged from 1500 in Kursk to 5500 in Tambov. *Entsiklopediia mestnogo upravleniia i khoziastva* (Moscow, 1927), 665.

94. See the stenographic report of the July 18, 1927 Orgburo session located in RGAE, f. 478, op. 1, d. 2044, ll. 4–49. At this session, Poluian complained that in Smolensk the village soviets play no role in local affairs. On Penza in 1925, see also RGASPI, f. 17, op. 67, d. 138, l. 4 ob. Pethybridge discusses the traveling TsKK comissions in *One Step Backwards, Two Steps Forward* (Oxford, 1990), 302–8.

95. Another speaker noted that the only thing the village soviets ever did was to investigate land disputes that arose on their territory. In the absence of such disputes, they did absolutely nothing. "Village soviets have insufficient rights, insufficient material base, unclear functions." RGAE, f. 478, op. 1, d. 2044, l. 5. In 1927, Smirnov argued in the Orgburo, "I do not believe that the village soviet will do what we want. Battles [among peasants] over how to divide the land and so on will turn the village soviet into a skhod." RGAE, f. 478, op. 1, d. 2044, ll. 4–49. See also GARF, f. 374, op. 27, d. 508, l. 25 (report of inspector Magidov).

96. For similar examples, focusing on Tver province, see Pethybridge, *One Step Back-*

wards, 293–301. Letter to TsKK member Iaroslavskii, "Seventh letter." GARF, f. 374, op. 27, d. 508, l. 57. On Penza, see also N. Rosnitskii, *Litso derevni* (Leningrad, 1926), 30–46.

97. "O polozhenii v Penzenskoi gubernii." Stenographic report of Orgburo TsK RKP session, December 8, 1924, in RGASPI, f. 17, op. 84, d. 656, ll. 320b–360b. Oral report of Secretary of the province Communist Party Committee Orlov.

98. On this theme, see Male, *Russian Peasant Organisation before Collectivisation*, 87–155. Atkinson's useful work overlooks the varying and conflicting agendas of the institutional actors. Dorothy Atkinson, *The End of The Peasant Land Commune*. See also Lewin, *Russian Peasants and Soviet Power* and Teodor Shanin, *The Awkward Class* (Oxford, 1972), 165–69.

99. SU RSFSR, 1922, no. 68.

100. See, for example, *Na agrarnom fronte*, 1926, no. 9:99. Male, *Russian Peasant Organisation*, 157–61. Once again, Rabkrin was the leading institutional opponent of the Commissariat over the issue of the desirability of maintaining the commune. See Kindeev, in *Na Agrarnom Fronte*, 1926, no. 10:77 ff.

101. Kondrat'ev, "Osnovy perspektivnogo plana razvitiia sel'skogo i lesnogo khoziaistva," report at the plenary session of Gosplan Presidium, July 4, 1925, in *Osoboe mnenie*, Tom. 1:365.

102. RGAE, f. 478, op. 1, d. 1141, l. 1.

103. See, for example, *Sobranie Uzakonenii*, 1927, no. 32, art. 213; RGASPI, f. 17, op. 85, d. 135, l. 263.

104. Smirnov called the Sovnarkom RSFSR version "the draft of Narkomzem," though it was officially referred to as the "Sovnarkom RSFSR draft." Narkomzem essentially drafted the law for the RSFSR government. *Na agrarnom fronte*, 1926, no. 11:131.

105. For the drafts of the laws, and discussions of them in the Communist Academy, see *Na agrarnom fronte*, 1926, nos. 5–6, 9, and 10 and 1927, no. 1. At the same time, the Commissariat's leaders argued against transferring any of the commune's legal rights to the village soviet.

106. This dimension of the commune has not been sufficiently recognized by historians. Alone among historians, Carr and Davies make this important point in *Foundations*, vol. 1: 122–24. They do not, however, link the preservation of the commune with Narkomzem's institutional interests. See also Carr, *Socialism in One Country*, vol. 1:210–6, 247–9, 267.

107. Sviderskii, *Na agrarnom fronte*, 1926, no. 9:117. (Emphasis in original)

108. Ibid. See also, "Ob obshchikh nachalakh Vsesoiuznogo zakonodatel'stva v oblasti zemleustroistva i zemlepol'zovaniia," in *Sel'sko-khoziaistvennaia zhizn'*, 1926, no. 49:4–5.

109. Letter of Smirnov to Rykov (copies to Stalin and Molotov), July 26, 1926, in RGASPI, f. 17, op. 85, d. 135, ll. 127–29.

110. The draft legislation would also have stretched the period during which a peasant had the right to unlimited land usage. Smirnov may have had in mind the Belorussian SSR, where the commune had effectively disintegrated since the war. *Na agrarnom fronte*, 1928, no. 8: 124.

111. A. P. Smirnov, *Nashi osnovnye zadachi*, 22.

112. See, for example, Kindeev, *Voprosy zemleustroistva*, (n.p., 1925); and his article in *Na agrarnom fronte*, 1926, no. 10: 77ff.

113. Pashukanis, *Na agrarnom fronte*, 1926, no. 9:81–83. See also Kubanin, "Obshchina pri diktatury proletariata (otvet N. N. Sukhanovu)," *Na agrarnom fronte*, 1926, no. 11–12.

114. Pashukanis, *Na agrarnom fronte*, 1926, no. 9:81.

115. Danilov, *Sovetskaia dokolkhoznaia derevnia*, 139–40. By 1923, ten percent of all land reorganized was being converted into homesteads. In the Western provinces, where the communal tradition was less dominant than in central Russia, the figure was 38 percent, and in the

Northwest it was 23 percent. In 1927, homesteads made up 16 percent of all sown land in the West, 11 percent in the Northwest and 5 percent in the central industrial region. In other regions, the total was very small, less than 2 percent. *Itogi desiatiletiia Sovetskoi vlasti v tsifrakh, 1917–27* (n.p., [1927]), 120–21.

116. See, for example, Mesiatsev, "Zemel'nyi vopros v sovremennoi postanovke," in Sel'sko-khoziaistvennaia zhizn', 1922, no. 7:15–22.

117. Teodorovich, *K voprosu*, 16.

118. *Sel'sko-khoziaistvennaia zhizn'*, 1924, no. 9:1.

119. *Stenograficheskii otchet III-go Vserossiiskogo soveshchaniia zemorganov 28 fevralia - 7 marta 1926 g.* (Moscow, 1926), 425.

120. *Sel'sko-khoziaistvennaia zhizn'*, 1922, no. 12–13:3–5. Carr and Davies, *Foundations of a Planned Economy*, vol. 1, 184–5.

121. "V Zemplane," in *Sel'sko-khoziaistvennaia zhizn'*, 1927, no. 12:28–30.

122. Smirnov's position on separation from the commune was controversial and, in fact, was mentioned in a Central Committee investigation of the "Affair of the Narkomzem Party Cell." See the letter among the materials of the TsKK-RKI investigation in GARF, f. 374, op. 27, d. 702, ll. 177–78 (January 27, 1926), in which Sviderskii writes to the Presidium of TsKK that comrade Smirnov "still considers that it would be extremely harmful for most regions of our Republic if even [only] a part of the peasantry went along the path of khutorization." In this debate about the commune's place, Smirnov agreed with the outspoken former Menshevik N. N. Sukhanov, who served on the Zemplan Presidium. See, for example, Sukhanov's speech at the Communist Academy, published in *Na agrarnom fronte* as "Obshchina v sovetskom agrarnom zakonodatel'stve," 1926, no. 11–12:98–109. Sukhanov agreed with Smirnov that, when judging the commune, economic development should not take precedence over the more important goal of the movement toward socialism.

123. A. P. Smirnov, *Na pomoshch' krest'ianskomu khoziaistvu*, 20. Narkomzem sent circulars to its local employees urging minimal allocation of land to khutors. An October 24, 1924, circular is cited in GARF, f. 374, op. 27, d. 702, l. 214. It is incorrectly dated as "1925" here. See also *Tretii S'ezd sovetov SSSR* (Moscow, 1925), 323–358.

124. Smirnov, *Na pomoshch' krest'ianskomu khoziaistvu*, 57.

125. Collegium protocols in RGAE, f. 478, op. 1, d. 1212, l. 187.

126. *Biulleten' soveshchaniia krest'ian—chlenov VTsIK pri Narkomzeme RSFSR*, July 4–7, 1924, no. 2:24–25.

127. A. P. Smirnov, *Na pomoshch' krest'ianskomu khoziaistvu*, 20. N. P. Rudin, the author of the 1922 Land Code and a former SR, argued that "our agricultural development for many years to come will consist of movement from the three-field, narrow strip system to the improved commune with wide plots." *Na agrarnom fronte*, 1926, no. 10:69ff. His words were echoed by Sviderskii in *Na agrarnom fronte*, 1926, no. 11–12:142ff.

128. It is difficult to know the degree to which specialists in the localities enforced these anti-khutor laws. On payment scale, see SU RSFSR, 1923, no. 60, st. 567. On credit problems, see A. P. Smirnov, *Na pomoshch' krest'ianskomu khoziaistvu*, 20. Beginning in 1925, land reorganization services for "poor peasants" were covered by the state budget. In 1927, the party resolved to pay for land reorganization for all but the *zazhitochnye* and kulaks. RGASPI, f. 17, op. 85, d. 276, l. 5.

129. That month, Smirnov wrote of the "ruinous dispersion into khutors." *Sel'sko-khoziaistvennaia zhizn'*, 1924, no. 46:1.

130. Smirnov, *Na pomoshch' krest'ianskomu khoziaistvu*, 57; Narkomzem RSFSR, *K voprosu ob ocherdnykh zadachakh raboty v derevne*, 112. Sobranie zakonov, 1928, no. 13: 21; *Dva*

goda raboty pravitel'stva, 59.

131. Copies to Molotov and Stalin. RGASPI, f. 17, op. 85, d. 135, ll. 127–29.

132. Smirnov was referring to the third paragraph of the 1922 Land Code, which states: "All land of agricultural significance, or which can be used for agricultural production, comprises a unified state land fund, which is located in the management of the People's Commissariat of Agriculture and its local organs." *Agrarnaia politika sovetskoi vlasti*, 416.

133. It is not clear exactly *whom* Smirnov believed was pushing for private property in land. A year earlier the leaders of the Georgian Commissariat of Agriculture had drafted a proposal calling for the legalization of the purchase and sale of land, and this may have been one impetus for Smirnov's apprehension. See Carr, *Socialism in One Country*, vol. 1:287.

134. Quote by N. S. Izvekov, head of Narkomzem's Supreme Commission on Land Disputes, in "K desiatiletiiu Oktiabria. Zemel'nyi sud za desiat' let." *Sel'sko-khoziaistvennaia zhizn'*, 1927, no. 46:1–3.

135. See, for example, Carr, *Socialism in One Country*, vol. 1, 282–328.

CHAPTER 5

1. See, for example, George Yaney, *The Urge to Mobilize: Agrarian Reform in Russia, 1861–1930* (Urbana, 1982), 510–57; R. W. Davies, *The Socialist Offensive: the Collectivization of Soviet Agriculture, 1929–1930* (Cambridge, Mass., 1980); Naum Jasny, *Soviet Economists of the Twenties: Names to be Remembered* (Cambridge, Mass., 1972).

2. Iurii Poliakov, *Perekhod k NEPu*; Natalia Nosova, *Upravliat' ili komandovat'? Gosudarstvo i krest'ianstvo sovetskoi Rossii* (Moscow, 1993).

3. A conclusion of this chapter about the support of specialists for moderniztion proposals echoes David Shearer's argument that "Stalinist policies drew support across a wide spectrum of social and political groups: not just from the working class, but also and importantly, from within the middle-class professional strata of specialists, administrators, and planners in the state apparatus." Shearer, "The Language and Politics of Socialist Rationalization," in *Cahiers du monde russe et sovietique*, 32:4 (Oct.–Dec. 1991): 584.

4. See, for example, William G. Rosenberg and Lewis H. Siegelbaum, ed., *Social Dimensions of Soviet Industrialization* (Bloomington, 1993), especially the articles by R. W. Davies, "The Management of Soviet Industry, 1928–41" (105–23); David Shearer, "Factories within Factories: Changes in the Structures of Work and Management in Soviet Machine-Building Factories, 1926–34" (193–222); D. K. Rowney, "The Scope, Authority, and Personnel of the New Industrial Commissariats in Historical Context" (124–45); and Hiroaki Kuromiya, "The Commander and the Rank and File: Managing the Soviet Coal-Mining Industry, 1928–33" (146–65). Important work on the Soviet civil service has been done by Daniel Orlovsky, who has identified the "white-collar employees" *(sluzhashchie)* in the government apparatus as a serious subject for research. See, for example, his "Gimpelson and the Hegemony of the Working Class," *Slavic Review* 48:1 (Spring 1989): 104–6. See also his article, "State Building in the Civil War Era: The Role of the Lower Middle Strata," in Diane Koenker et al., eds., *Party, State, and Society in the Russian Civil War* (Bloomington: 1989), 180–209.

5. *Sel'sko-khoziaistvennaia zhizn'*, 1928, no. 11:15.

6. M. A. Shur, "Mestnyi agronom i VIKi," in *Sel'sko-khoziaistvennaia zhizn'*, 1926, no. 36:12.

7. Ibid.

8. On the low priority given to the rural health sector and the enormous disparity in health spending between rural and urban areas in the 1920s, see Christopher Davies, "Economic

Problems of the Soviet Health Service: 1917–1930," *Soviet Studies*, 35:3 (July 1983) 343–61.

9. See RGAE, f. 478, op. 1, d. 1139, l. 5–6 and d. 1801, ll. 27; also Stephen Sternheimer, "Administration" in Pintner and Rowney, eds., *Russian Officialdom*, 336.

10. RGAE, f. 478, op. 1, d. 961. For more on the penurious pay of local officials, see RGAE, f. 478, op. 1, d. 1139, l. 5–6 and d. 1801, ll. 27.

11. See Christine Ruane and Ben Eklof, "Cultural Pioneers and Professionals: The Teacher in Society," in Edith Clowes, Samuel Kassow, and James West, eds., *Between Tsar and People: Educated Society and the Quest for Public Identity in Late Imperial Russia* (Princeton, 1991), 199–211.

12. A. A. Alymov and S. Studenikin, "Rekonstruktsiia gosapparata," in E. Pashukanis, ed., *Piatnadtsat' let sovetskogo stroitel'stva* (Moscow, 1931), 253.

13. For an example of A. P. Smirnov bemoaning this phenomenon, see RGAE, f. 478, op. 15, d. 1, l. 12.

14. *Sel'sko-khoziaistvennaia zhizn'*, 1929, no. 28–29:15–16. Larry Holmes has noted similar turnover among teachers: "the flight of teachers from one school to another." *The Kremlin and the Schoolhouse: Reforming Education in Soviet Russia, 1917–1931* (Bloomington, 1991), 64. Daniel Peris has remarked on turnover among cadres of the League of the Militant Godless. *Storming the Heavens* (Ithaca, 1998).

15. *Sel'sko-khoziaistvennaia zhizn'*, 1927, no. 1:9.

16. Ibid., 1928, no. 26:5.

17. For more instances of turnover recorded in Rabkrin materials, see TsGA RSFSR, f. 406, op. 25, d. 362, l. 29.

18. *Sel'sko-khoziaistvennaia zhizn'*, 1927, no. 1:9.

19. Ibid., 1928, no. 17:3–4.

20. This instruction seems generally to have been ignored. A 1927 circular letter of the VTsIK Presidium (and a 1927 Sovnarkom instruction) to all provincial executive committees went unnoticed in many areas, according to a Narkomzem inspector.

21. *Sel'sko-khoziaistvennaia zhizn'*, 1927, no. 1: 8. In its report to the Congress of Soviets of the RSFSR in 1924, Narkomzem showed that, depending on the region, each of its agronomists was extraordinarily overburdened, being responsible for between 5,500 and 13,000 farms; the average was 8,000 to 9,000. *Otchet NKZ za 1923–24* (Moscow, 1925), 166. In 1927, there were only 18,500 agronomists in the entire USSR. In 1928, the USSR's thirty agricultural *vuzy* (higher educational institutions) and five agricultural departments in universities could satisfy only 28 percent of Narkomzem's demand for graduates. *K XVI S"ezdu VKP(b)* (Moscow, 1930), 130. See also *Sel'sko-khoziaistvennaia zhizn'*, 1927, no. 19:10.

22. *Sel'sko-khoziaistvennaia zhizn'*, 1927, no. 1:8.

23. Ibid., 1929, no. 28–29:16.

24. Terence Emmons's observation about the rural-urban divide in pre-revolutionary Russia provides us with a useful framework for conceptualizing these problems: "The zemstvo intelligentsia's persistent sense of isolation from the peasantry is a frequent refrain in these chapters, one which reminds us of the distance that, right up to the revolution, still separated the two cultures of Russia: the traditional culture of peasant Russia, and the European culture that emanated from its towns." Terence Emmons and Wayne S. Vacinich, eds., *The Zemstvo in Russia* (New York, 1982), 427.

25. See the VTSiK circular of July 23, 1925, on strengthening the agronomic *uchastok* as the fundamental base of agronomic measures, creating the material base and other conditions necessary for productively serving the peasantry. See also *Sel'sko-khoziaistvennaia zhizn'*, 1926, no. 36:12–13. In 1929, only 40 percent of aid stations had "tolerable" apartments.

26. Report of Bakhutov at Politburo session of September 1, 1925. A copy sent to deputy commissar of agriculture A. I. Sviderskii is located in RGAE, f. 478, op. 1, d. 1801, l. 55. Regarding graduates of the Timiriazev academy in 1924, Fomin reported to the VTsIK that students "graduate after a year and want to be scientific workers, but do not want to go to the village." *Biulleten' soveshchaniia krest'ian—chlenov VTsIK pri Narkomzeme RSFSR* (Moscow, 1924).

27. GARF, f. 374, op. 27, d. 702, l. 45. This phenomenon was also epidemic among teachers and doctors, and is very common among educated urban professionals in the developing world. See Samuel C. Ramer, "Feldshers and Rural Health Care," in Susan Gross Solomon and John F. Hutchinson, eds., *Health and Society in Revolutionary Russia* (Bloomington, 1990); Neil B. Weissman, "Origins of Soviet Health Administration," 113–14 in ibid.; and Mark Field, *Doctor and Patient in Soviet Russia* (Cambridge, Mass., 1957), 80. See also Larry Holmes, *The Kremlin and the Schoolhouse*, 64. The level of turnover is perhaps more striking with agronomists, who were trained, after all, to work with rural producers.

28. *Sel'sko-khoziaistvennaia zhizn'*, 1927, no. 46:26–27.

29. Ibid., 1929, no. 4:8–9. For an interesting perspective on this problem, see E. Ostrovskii, "Pereproizvodstvo agrospetsialistov ili neratsional'noe ikh ispol'zovanie," in *Sel'sko-khoziaistvennaia zhizn'*, 1927, no. 46:26–27. See also deputy commissar of agriculture Klimenko's statement at the Second All-Russian Agronomic Congress in early 1929 that "graduates of the *vuzy* as a rule do not want to go to the village." *Stenograficheskii otchet II-ogo vserossiskogo agronomicheskogo s"ezda* (Moscow, 1929), 48. Klimenko referred to them as "dilettantes."

30. *Sel'sko-khoziaistvennaia zhizn'*, 1926, no. 27:24–25.

31. RGASPI, f. 17, op. 85, d. 135, l. 85.

32. See the comments of Kharlamov, head of the Siberian *krai* land administration at the Fourth Congress of Land Workers. Russian SFSR, Narodnyi komissariat zemledeliia, *IV Soveshchane zemorganov RSFSR* (Moscow, 1929) 169.

33. *Sel'sko-khoziaistvennaia zhizn'*, 1926, no. 38:8.

34. Ibid., 1926, no. 36:12–13.

35. Report authored by Rabkrin and reported in *Sel'sko-khoziaistvennaia zhizn'*, 1928, no. 43:20–22.

36. On the campaign waged by Rabkrin for regularizing and reducing the "operational-statistical *otchetnost*" of land organs, see *Sel'sko-khoziaistvennaia zhizn'* 1926, no. 28: 14–17, and no. 42:6–7.

37. Some specialists blamed Narkomzem's constant requests for information, forwarding of myriad forms, and requests for monthly, quarterly, and annual reports. See comments of Glokhovskii of Tver province at the Second All-Russian Agronomic Congress. *Stenograficheskii otchet II-ogo vserossiskogo agronomicheskogo s"ezda*, 97. Tikhonov, an uezd agronomist from Tver, made the same argument (166).

38. For detailed reports on the train's tours, see *Otchet NKZ za 1924–5*, 205–7.

39. L. L. Slobodchikov, in *Sel'sko-khoziaistvennaia zhizn'*, 1927, no. 1:8.

40. *Sel'sko-khoziaistvennaia zhizn'*, 1928, no. 17:15.

41. Ibid., 1926, no. 36:12–13.

42. Ibid., 1929, no. 28–29:15.

43. For parallels, see Ramer, "Feldshers and Rural Health Care," 136; and on strained relations between physicians and local government in the late Imperial period, see Nancy Frieden, *Russian Physicians in an Era of Reform and Revolution, 1856–1905* (Princeton, 1981).

44. *Sel'sko-khoziaistvennaia zhizn'*, 1929, no. 38:18–19.

45. *Stenograficheskii otchet II-ogo vserossiskogo agronomicheskogo s"ezda*, 95. Viktorov, a

regional agronomist from the Urals, echoed this comment (99), as did others.

46. Matsuzato, "The Fate of Agronomists in Russia: Their Quantitative Dynamics from 1911 to 1916," *Russian Review* 55:2 (April 1996): 182.

47. The optimum version of the First Five Year Plan, adopted in April 1929 by the Sixteenth Party Conference, set a goal that 15.5 percent of gross production and up to 43 percent of extra-rural marketed grain from the harvests of 1932 and 1933 should come from collectives. It still assumed that at least 75 percent of peasants would remain outside the collectives. The point is not that collectivization brought increased modernity and efficiency, but rather that some specialists were prepared to believe this would result and hoped that increased modernity and efficiency would simultaneously improve greatly their working conditions and professional standing.

48. *Stenograficheskii otchet II-ogo vserossiskogo agronomicheskogo s"ezda*, 7.

49. See, for example, *Sel'sko-khoziaistvennaia zhizn'* 1928, no. 43:10.

50. The idea of state-directed economic transformation that would include the participation of specialists was also popular in the United States in the 1920s and 1930s. Thorsten Veblen proposed turning over power to "Soviets of Technicians" who would set up and administer a planned economy. For more details, see Bailes, *Technology and Society*, 95–140 and his "The Politics of Technology: Stalin and Technocratic Thinking among Soviet Engineers," *The American Historical Review* 79:2 (1974): 445–69. Indeed, engineers in many industrialized European countries also called for an important role in governance for their profession. See, for example, Edwin Layton, *The Revolt of the Engineers: Social Responsibility and the American Engineering Profession* (Cleveland, 1971), 6. As Lewin and Fitzpatrick have demonstrated, the economic debates of the 1920s helped to elevate the status of engineers, economists, and other experts, while cementing their position as authorities in the Soviet system. Moshe Lewin, *Political Undercurrents in Soviet Economic Debates* (Princeton, 1974), 73–96; Sheila Fitzpatrick, *Education and Social Mobility in the Soviet Union* (Cambridge, 1979).

51. *Stenograficheskii otchet II-ogo vserossiskogo agronomicheskogo s"ezda*, 327.

52. *Sel'sko-khoziaistvennaia zhizn'*, 1929, no. 40–41:3.

53. See, for example, *Sel'sko-khoziaistvennaia zhizn'*, 1928, no. 2:6. Experts declared that they preferred no longer to work as "agronomist-preachers," that is agitators, educators, or propagandists; they now desired to become "agronomist-organizers." *Stenograficheskii otchet II-ogo vserossiskogo agronomicheskogo s"ezda*, speech of Gosplan SSSR representative Wol'f, 31. See also speech of Klimenko, 36.

54. Kviring speaking at second agronomic congress. *Stenograficheskii otchet II-ogo vserossiskogo agronomicheskogo s"ezda*, 285. Antselovich's comment is on p. 18.

55. Present at this Congress were over a hundred delegates with careers in land work dating to before the revolution.

56. *Stenograficheskii otchet II-ogo vserossiskogo agronomicheskogo s"ezda*, 207.

57. David Shearer has discussed the appeal of modernization to engineers, in his *Industry, State, and Society*.

58. *IV Soveshchane zemorganov RSFSR*, 63-64, speech by Stepanov, Moscow province agronomist.

59. For example, *Stenograficheskii otchet II-ogo vserossiskogo agronomicheskogo s"ezda*, 90; *IV soveshchanie zemorganov RSFSR*, 57 (speech of Rodichev); 70 (speech of Filippov, agronomist from the Urals); 72-74, (speech of Nefidov, deputy chief of middle-Volga oblast' land administration).

60. For examples of suspicion about Narkomzem specialists, see TsGA RSFSR, f. 406, op.

25, d. 1165, ll. 118, "Letter to Informotdel zam RK VKP(b)" by Pal'gi, an agronomist, the secretary of the Narkomzem Party Cell and the head of the section of collective agriculture. Several speakers voiced their suspicions at the Second All-Russian Agronomic Congress in January–February 1929. See, for example, the speech of Lunacharsky on page 14.

61. A Rabkrin report (TsGA RSFSR, f. 406, op. 25, d. 1165, l. 172) finds individual cases of specialists' favoritism to kulaks, for example, though this phenomenon was particularly concentrated among *zemleustroiteli* (land reorganizers). In Nizhe-Volzhskii krai an agronomist Cherlaev was fired because a local Rabkrin investigator discovered that he had worked on the estate of Prince Golitsyn and that he was himself the son of a landowner and officer in the Tsarist army (l. 165).

62. *Stenograficheskii otchet II-ogo vserossiskogo agronomicheskogo s"ezda*, 15, speech of Lunacharsky.

63. Thirty-five percent were land reorganizers. RGAE, f. 478, op. 1, d. 2087, l. 20 ob.

64. TsGA RSFSR, f. 406, op. 25, d. 362, l. 22.

65. RGAE, f. 478, op. 1, d. 2087, l. 20 ob. The rest were removed for reasons of incompetence or as *byvshie liudi* (former people).

66. Speech of Kalinin. *IV Soveshchane zemorganov RSFSR* (Moscow, 1929), 8–12.

67. *Stenograficheskii otchet II-ogo vserossiskogo agronomicheskogo s"ezda*, 10, 188–9. At this point, Narkomzem's five-year plan called for only 10 percent of sown land to be inside collectives, either sovkhozy or kolkhozy.

68. *IV soveshchanie zemorganov RSFSR*, 12.

Chapter 6

1. The political developments of this period are discussed in Michal Reiman, *The Birth of Stalinism: The USSR on the Eve of the "Second Revolution"* (Bloomington, 1987); R. W. Davies, *The Socialist Offensive: The Collectivisation of Soviet Agriculture, 1929–1930* (Cambridge, Mass., 1980); E. H. Carr and R. W. Davies, *Foundations of a Planned Economy*, 2 vols. in 3 (New York, 1971).

2. See, for example, Smirnov's article in *Sel'sko-khoziaistvennaia zhizn'*, "Ocherednye zadachi razvitiia sel'skogo khoziaistva," 1927, no. 16:1; I. A. Teodorovich, "O planovoi rabote po sel'skomu i lesnomu khoziaistvu," in *Sel'sko-khoziaistvennaia zhizn'*, 1927, no. 28:7.

3. See, for example, "Vypiska informotdela OGPU iz doklada Samarskogo otdela OGPU o massovykh vystupleniiakh krest'ian ot 1 dekabria 1927 g." contained in *Sovetskaia derevnia glazami VChK-OGPU-NKVD*, tom 2 (Moscow, 2000), 618. See also idem 926.

4. Tables 6–9, in *Sovetskaia derevnia glazami VChK-OGPU-NKVD*, tom 2 (Moscow, 2000), 1032–36.

5. Jerry F. Karcz, ed., *The Economics of Communist Agriculture. Selected Papers* (Bloomington, 1979), 45, cited in Lewis Siegelbaum, *Soviet State and Society*, 190.

6. A. P. Smirnov, "Ocherdnye zadachi razvitiia sel'skogo khoziaistva," in *Sel'sko-khoziaistvennaia zhizn'*, 1927, no. 16:2.

7. A. P. Smirnov, "Vnimanie voprosam s.-kh. obrazovaniia i s.-kh. propagande," in *Sel'sko-khoziaistvennaia zhizn'*, 1927, no. 31:1 (emphasis in original).

8. He was referring to the Volga, the North Caucuses, and part of Siberia. RGAE, f. 478, op. 2, d. 371a, l. 1 ff.

9. See also Prof. N. I. Vavilov, "Puti povysheniia urozhainosti," in *Sel'sko-khoziaistvennaia zhizn'*, 1928, no. 31–32:6.

10. A. A. Manuilov, "Plan razvitiia promyshlennosti na 1926–27 god, s tochki zreniia interesov sel'skogo khoziaistva," in *Sel'sko-khoziaistvennaia zhizn'*, 1927, no. 5:1–3.

11. N. Rudin, "Eshche raz o formakh zemlepol'zovaniia," in *Sel'sko-khoziaistvennaia zhizn'*, 1927, no. 51:6–7.

12. A. A. Manuilov, "Plan razvitiia promyshlennosti na 1926–27 god, s tochki zreniia interesov sel'skogo khoziaistva," in *Sel'sko-khoziaistvennaia zhizn'*, 1927, no. 5:1–3.

13. See Rykov's speech at the 13th All-Russian Congress of Soviets in which he declared that prices for technical crops were too low. *Sel'sko-khoziaistvennaia zhizn'*, 1927, no. 19:3–5. Agricultural exports had stabilized at only about one third of the pre-war average by 1926–27. *Vneshniaia torgovlia SSSR za 1918–1940 gg. Statisticheskii obzor* (Moscow, 1960). On taxation, see f. 478, op. 1, d. 1428, ll. 1–5.

14. See I. F—N, "'My kruto vziali na povorote," in *Sel'sko-khoziaistvennaia zhizn'*, 1927, no. 6:22.

15. A. I. Sviderskii, "Na novykh putiakh," in *Sel'sko-khoziaistvennaia zhizn'*, 1927, no. 20:1–2.

16. He pointed out that progress was being made in terms of sown area under a multifield farming regime; the sorted seed fund was up to twenty million poods. The Soviet Union also had twenty-seven thousand tractors, 90 percent of which were in the hands of peasants.

17. "O planovoi rabote po sel'skomu i lesnomu khoziaistvu," in *Sel'sko-khoziaistvennaia zhizn'*, 1927, no. 28:5–7.

18. The details on shifting policies at the national level in 1927–29 can be found in several sources, most importantly Moshe Lewin, *Russian Peasants and Soviet Power* (New York, 1968); E. H. Carr and R. W. Davies, *Foundations of a Planned Economy*, vols. 1 and 2; R. W. Davies, *The Soviet Economy in Turmoil 1929–1930* (Houndmills, 1989), 95–153; James Hughes, *Stalin, Siberia, and the Crisis of the New Economic Policy* (Cambridge, Eng., 1991); and his *Stalinism in a Russian Province: A Study of Collectivization and Dekulakization in Siberia* (Houndmills, 1996).

19. N. S. Vlasov, "Organizatsionnye momenty voprosov truda i raspredeleniia v kokhozakh," in *Sel'sko-khoziaistvennaia zhizn'* 1927, no. 14:10–11.

20. See also M. Latsis, "Nashi zadachi v oblasti zemleustroistva v sviazi s resheniiami xv Parts,ezda," in *Sel'sko-khoziaistvennaia zhizn'*, 1927, no. 2:1–2.

21. A. P. Smirnov, "Novye zadachi kollektivizatsii derevni," in *Sel'sko-khoziaistvennaia zhizn'*, 1927, no. 50: 3–7.

22. M. Ustinov, "K voprosu of formakh zemlepol'zovaniia," in *Bol'shevik*, 1927, no. 19–20:143–49.

23. G. Zinov'ev, "Manifest kulatskoi partii," *Bol'shevik*, July 15, 1927, no. 13:33–47.

24. Robert V. Daniels, *The Conscience of the Revolution: Communist Opposition in Soviet Russia* (Cambridge, Mass., 1960), 352.

25. Speech of Molotov at the Fifteenth Party Congress, in *Sel'sko-khoziaistvennaia zhizn'*, 1928, no. 1:2.

26. See Lewin, *Russian Peasants and Soviet Power*. See also the documents on the procurement crisis collected in V. P. Danilov and Roberta Manning, eds., *Tragediia Sovetskoi derevni*, vol. 1, 1927–39 (Moscow, 1999). The documents in all volumes of this series are especially useful to historians. For a debate on levels of marketed produce between R. W. Davies and Jerry Karcz, see *Soviet Studies* 18 (1966–67): 399–434; *Soviet Studies* 21 (1969–70): 314–29; and *Soviet Studies* 22 (1970–71): 262–94.

27. Ironically, peasants reduced output or sold livestock to avoid being labeled as kulaks, and this was another factor that decreased grain production nationwide.

28. I. A. Teodorovich, "Osobennosti i nedochety khlebozagotovitel'noi kampanii," in *Sel'sko-khoziaistvennaia zhizn'*, 1928, no. 4:7–8. On the reversion to Civil War style requisitions

in 1928 and 1929, see Lewin, "Taking Grain," in *The Making of the Soviet System* (New York, 1985), 142–77.

29. See I. A. Teodorovich, "Osobennosti i nedochety khlebozagotovitel'noi kampanii," in *Sel'sko-khoziaistvennaia zhizn'*, 1928, no. 4:7–8.

30. Siegelbaum, *Soviet State and Society between Revolutions*, 192.

31. *Pravda* reported the end of Smirnov's five-year tenure on February 17, 1928. See also *Pravda*, March 2 and March 23, 1928. Sviderskii was appointed Commissar of Education.

32. TsGA RSFSR, f. 406, op. 75, d. 1165, l. 36.

33. In March 1928, Sovnarkom appointed him, together with Rabkrin's Ordzhonikidze, to be a plenipotentiary for the spring sowing campaign. *Ekonomicheskaia zhizn'*, June 24, 1928.

34. The professional revolutionary Klimenko was born in 1891 into "a peasant family" in Ukraine, though he left the village to study typography at the age of fourteen. Klimenko joined the Bolshevik Party in 1912 and was soon after arrested and exiled to Rostov-na-Donu. He was arrested again in the summer of 1913 and spent four months in prison, then was exiled to Poltava. During World War I, he hid in Siberia. Klimenko, a native Ukrainian, became People's Commissar of Agriculture for Ukraine in 1922. In 1925, he was selected a secretary of the Ukrainian Central Committee and became a candidate for membership in the All-Union Central Committee. Muralov, the second deputy commissar of agriculture, was an agricultural chemist by profession. He was born into the family of a small khutor farmer. He joined the party in 1905, and then enrolled in Moscow University. After spending time in jail, he became the zemstvo agronomist of Tula province in 1913–14 until the governor removed him as a "political undesirable." After the war, Muralov occupied various positions, including chair of the Nizhegorod provincial executive committee, until Sovnarkom appointed him to Narkomzem.

35. "Dostizheniia i nedochety v podgotovke vesennego seva," in *Sel'sko-khoziaistvennaia zhizn'*, 1928, no. 12:1.

36. Kulaks excluded from participating in the rural soviets were now forbidden to participate in the commune's village gathering, though they could remain members of the commune. "Obshchie nachala zemlepol'zovaniia i zemleustroistva," *Sobranie zakonov*, 1928, no. 69, art. 642.

37. "Posevnaia kampaniia i kollektivizatsiia zemledeliia (Rech' N. A. Kubiaka na zasedanii kollegii Narkomzema 23 fevralia 1928 g.)," in *Sel'sko-khoziaistvennaia zhizn'*, 1928, no. 9–10:2.

38. Mikhal Reiman, *Birth of Stalinism*, Appendix 6, 142–45, letter of Menzhinskii and Kubiak to Rykov.

39. Carr and Davies, *Foundations of a Planned Economy*, vol. 2:260.

40. See, for example, Klimenko's speech of March 15, 1928, in *Sel'sko-khoziaistvennaia zhizn'*, 1928, no. 13:12–13.

41. On March 23, 1928, the head of Rabkrin, Ordzhonikidze, wrote that many holdover "bourgeois specialists" were in fact "masked enemies" of Soviet power intent on reintroducing capitalism. Cited in Reiman, *Birth of Stalinism*, 150–51.

42. See Kendall Bailes, *Technology and Society under Lenin and Stalin* (Princeton, 1978), 81–87.

43. David Shearer has described purges in Vesenkha and the industrial trusts. *Industry, State, and Society in Stalin's Russia, 1926–34* (Ithaca, 1996), 189–90.

44. See the list "Spisok uvolennykh sotrudnikov NKZ b. dvorian i vykhodtsev iz dr. partii," TsGA RSFSR, f. 406, op. 25, d. 1165, ll. 39–40.

45. Chelintsev, "K voprosu o predmete, zadachakh, i metodakh organizatsii sel'skogo

khoziastva," in *Puti sel'skogo khoziastva*, 1928, no. 9:12–21; and his "K teorii organizatsii sel'skogo khoziastva massy krest'ianskikh khoziastva," in *Puti sel'skogo khoziastva*, 1928, no. 8:23–32; and A. V. Chaianov, "Ot klassovoi krest'ianskoi kooperatsii k sotsialisticheskoi rekonstruktsii sel'skogo khoziastva," in *Ekonomicheskaia zhizn'*, February 15, 1929:2–3. An article that appeared in 1935 captured the mood: "The Central Committee uncovered Right opportunistic practices in many agencies, in particular in Narkomzem and Zemplan, where the directors—A. P. Smirnov and I. A. Teodorovich—were a weapon in the counterrevolutionary *Kondrat'evshchina* [the scourge of Kondrat'ev]." N. Rubinshtein, in *Proletarskaia Revoliutsiia*, 1935, no. 6:94.

46. Two books that discuss Rabkrin's efforts to take over parts of economic planning in 1928–30 are David Shearer, *Industry, State, and Society*; and E. A. Rees, *State Control in Soviet Russia* (Houndmills, 1987).

47. Ia. A. Iakovlev, *Za kolkhozy*, 166–175; and E. A. Rees, *State Control in Soviet Russia*, 160. For a detailed discussion of clashes over plan figures in 1928, see Rees, 156–161. See also *Ekonomicheskaia zhizn'*, November 24, 1928.

48. Bukharin was expelled from the Politburo in November 1929; Rykov and Tomskii were removed in 1930. Kubiak was transferred out of Narkomzem RSFSR in December 1929.

49. A complete account of the purge process in the Commissariat of Agriculture must be based on archival materials produced by Rabkrin, the OGPU, and Narkomzem.

50. RGAE, f. 478, op. 1, d. 2087, l. 17 (Report of People's Commissar Kubiak). N. P. Nosova's assertion that "proletarian and peasant" promotees played an important role in the Commissariat is clearly an exaggeration, informed by official Soviet histories. Nosova, "Formirovanie," 8. See E. G. Gimpelson, *Rabochii klass v upravlenii Sovetskim gosudarstvom: noiabr' 1917–1920 gg.* (Moscow, 1982), for assertions similar to Nosova's. See also Orlovsky's comments in "Gimpelson and the Hegemony of the Working Class."

51. TsSU SSSR, *Gosudarstvennyi apparat SSSR*, 28. Within the entire Soviet state bureaucracy, only 9.4 percent of specialists at the okrug level were party members.

52. Bineman and Kheinman, *Kadry gosudarstennogo apparata*, 23, 26. The authors worried that the "mentalities" of two-thirds or even three-quarters of Narkomzem employees "were formed" before 1917. The age of state functionaries was indeed a common concern among inspectors who noted a troubling generation gap.

53. RGAE, f. 478, op. 1, d. 2087, l. 18. By leadership cadres, Kubiak meant the chiefs of the land reorganization, veterinary, and forest sections within land sections. In the same spirit, P. Lezhnev-Fin'kovskii, the head of Narkomzem's section for agronomic assistance, noted at a 1929 conference that many unsuitable people were still being sent to work in the land administration, including many who had been members of "other parties." His words were echoed by a comrade Tutskii. *Sel'sko-khoziaistvennaia zhizn'*, 1929, no. 38:18.

54. For the resolution launching the purge, see *KPSS v rezoliutsiiakh*, ii (1954), 594–97, 605–14. See also R. W. Davies, *Soviet Economy in Turmoil*, 61–62, 118–21.

55. The Plenum's resolution can be found in *KPSS v rezoliutsiiakh*, 4:143. The directive ordered the Inspectorate to begin this work parallel with the All-Union Rabkrin.

56. Letter of Il'in, "Moskovskoi RKI, Sev-Kavkazskoi RKI, Samarskoi RKI i Saratovskoi RKI," from December 31, 1928. TsGA RSFSR, f. 406, op. 25, d. 125, l. 3.

57. David Shearer makes this point in *Industry, State, and Society*, 196, as does Davies in *Soviet Economy in Turmoil*, 62, n. 21.

58. Rabkrin's conclusions as presented to Ordzhonikidze are found in "Rezul'taty chistki apparata v zemorganakh poslannykh t. Ordzhonikidze." Undated report, but probably March or early April 1929. No author, but probably written by the "Peters group." TsGA RSFSR, f.

406, op. 25, d. 362, ll. 18–29. Peters made it clear that he received his instructions from Ordzhonikidze.

59. This meant the Agriculture Administration, the Land Improvement and Reorganization Administration, and the Forest Administration.

60. GARF, f. 374 s.ch., op. 27s, d. 1382, l. 8.

61. For examples of offenses against the class line, see "Fakty iskazheniia klassovoi linii," author and date unknown, but most likely a product of Rabkrin in late 1928 or early 1929. TsGA RSFSR, f. 406, op. 25, d. 1165, l. 174.

62. Daniel Orlovsky argues that in light of the extreme social and occupational fragmentation after 1917, the state sought to cover up this messy reality by "developing the sociologically crude and reductive, but politically effective discourse of a class struggle among workers, peasants and the 'bourgeoisie.'" See Orlovsky, "The Hidden Class: White-Collar Workers in the Soviet 1920s," in Lewis Siegelbaum and Ronald G. Suny, eds., *Making Workers Soviet: Power, Class, and Identity* (Ithaca, 1994), 224.

63. "Analiz sostoianiia apparata NKZ RSFSR Proizvedennyi po 3-m upravleniiam (zemleustoristva i melioratsii, sel'skogo khoziaistva, upravleniia lesami)," no date, but data from January 1, 1929. GARF, f. 406, op. 25, d. 1165, l. 142–43 ob. "Materialy kharakterizuiushchie zasorennost' po upravleniiu sel'skogo khoziaistva," by Inspector of NK RKI SSSR, Vianes. GARF, f. 406, op. 25, d. 1165, ll. 138–41, 144. This total included the children of nobles, former landlords, and specialists who had lied about qualifications.

64. See Vianes's comments in "Protokol rasshirennogo zasedaniia biuro iacheiki VKP(b) s partorgami i adminstratorami ot 22 Fev. 1929." GARF, f. 406, op. 25, d. 1165, l. 156.

65. "Protokol zakrytogo zasedaniia biuro iach. VKP(b) NKZ RSFSR ot 10/I-29 goda." GARF, f. 406, op. 25, d. 1165, l. 115.

66. "V Prezidium TsKK VKP(b). Ob"iasnitel'naia zapiska k proektu predlozhenii, razrabotannomu Inspektsiey Sovetskogo stroitel'stva NK RKI RSFSR." No author and no date, but probably written inside Rabkrin in early 1929, no earlier than March.

67. Letter from Il'in of January 14, 1929, "O proverke raboty lichnogo sostava sovetskogo apparata vo vse kraevye, oblastnye i gub. RKI," GARF, f. 406, op. 25, d. 266, l. 1-10b.

68. Letter to TsKK-NK RKI SSSR, to tov. Peters, from the chair of the Oblast' Rabkrin, Studitov. GARF, f. 406, op. 25, d. 362, ll. 1–17.

69. See the anonymous letter to Peters denouncing the agronomist S. Chistiakov as alien, alcoholic, and engaged in speculation. GARF, f. 406, op. 25, d. 1165, l. 180. "Spravka dlia komissii po chistke apparata NKZema RSFSR," letter from P. Pleshkov, instructor at Timiriazev Agricultural Academy, of February 7, 1929. GARF, f. 406, op. 25, d. 1165, ll. 127–28.

70. Simonov and Figurovskaia, "Posleslovie," in *Osoboe mnenie*, 593, n. 75.

71. See, for example, "Spisok sotrudnikov upravleniia s/x, upr. zemlemeliozem i upravleniia lesami Narkomzema RSFSR na kotorykh imeetsia komprometiruiushchii material," by Markar'ian of OGPU. Information gathered between January 10 and February 1, 1929. GARF, f. 406, op. 25, d. 1165, ll. 107–8. See also the letter to Peters of September 4, 1929, from the economic administration of the OGPU, about the taking of bribes by S. Ia. Lapirov-Skoblo, the head of the collection section of the Forest Administration. TsGA, f. 406, op. 25 d. 1184, ll. 19–20.

72. "Spravka o polozhenii del v OZRa NKZ RSFSR," authored by Sheshnev of the sixth section of the EKU OGPU, December 4, 1928. RGAE, f. 478, op. 15, d. 38.

73. Kuromiya's discussion of the purges of 1928–29 is found in *Stalin's Industrial Revolution: Politics and Workers, 1928–1931* (Cambridge, 1988). M. David-Fox (*Revolution of the Mind*) and D. Shearer (*Industry, State, and Society in Stalin's Russia, 1926–1934*) use archival

materials to illustrate a degree of internal resistance to the purges.

74. "Spisok uvolennykh sotrudnikov iz NKZ v 1927 i 1928 gg., kak chuzhdykh i antisovetskikh elementov." This information was provided by Narkomzem's Uchraspred office. No date, but probably early 1929. GARF, f. 406, op. 25, d. 1165, ll. 36 ob.–38.

75. GARF, f. 406, op. 25, d. 1165, l. 162.

76. GARF, f. 406, op. 25, d. 362, l. 19.

77. GARF, f. 406, op. 25, d. 1165, l. 142.

78. GARF, f. 406, op. 25, d. 1165, l. 189 and ll. 142–43 ob.

79. Letter to Ordzhonikidze from Gerasimovich and Mironov, April 24, 1929, and May 3, 1929. GARF, f. 406, op. 25, d. 1184, l. 60.

80. GARF, f. 406, op. 25, d. 1165, ll. 142–43 ob.

81. Letter to Ordzhonikidze from Gerasimovich, May 3, 1929. GARF, f. 406, op. 25, d. 1184, l. 60.

82. Letter of Klimenko to Peters, undated but around March 1929. GARF, f. 406, op. 25, d. 1165, l. 158.

83. GARF, f. 406, op. 25, d. 1184, l. 60.

84. GARF, f. 406, op. 25, d. 1165, l. 143 ob.

85. *Shestnadtsataia konferentsiia VKP(b), Aprel' 1929g., Stenograficheskii otchet* (Moscow, 1962), 455.

86. Letter to Informotdel zam. RK VKP(b). "Kharakteristika ideologicheskogo sostoianiia spetsialistov Narkomzema RSFSR," by Pal'gi, responsible secretary of Narkomzem Party cell. GARF, f. 406, op. 25, d. 1165, ll. 116–18.

87. "Obshchie rezul'taty podgotovitel'nykh rabot po chistke zemel'nykh organov." No date, but probably produced in February or March 1929. GARF, f. 406, op. 25, d. 1165, l. 171.

88. *Shestnadtsataia konferentsiia VKP(b), Aprel' 1929g., Stenograficheskii otchet* (Moscow, 1962), 445.

89. GARF, f. 406, op. 25, d. 1165, l. 115.

90. "Vypiska iz protokola Zasedaniia Biuro Iacheiki VKP(b) Narkomzema s part. organami ot 7-ogo marta 1929," GARF, f. 406, op. 25, d. 1165, l. 159.

91. GARF, f. 406, op. 25, d. 363, l. 28.

92. Letter from People's Commissar of Ways of Communication Rudzutak to uezd branches, December 6, 1928, GARF, f. 406, op. 25, d. 363, l. 34.

93. RGAE, f. 478, op. 15, d. 38, ll. 24–25.

94. Shearer, *Industry, State, and Society in Stalin's Russia, 1926–34*, 189.

95. Unsigned report, "Vydvizhenchestvo," from 1929, located in GARF, f. 374, op. 28, d. 3061.

96. "O vydvizhencheskoi rabote v Narkomzeme," GARF, f. 406, op. 25, d. 1165, l. 194. In the Commissariat of Finance, a total of sixty-nine people from the working classes (peasants and workers) had been promoted into the Moscow offices between 1925 and 1928. None remained in 1929. There were 1,682 people in this organization in 1926, and 1,122 in 1929.

97. GARF, f. 406, op. 25, d. 1165, ll. 194–93.

98. GARF, f. 374, op. 28, d. 3061, l. 16.

99. *Ibid.*

100. In October 1928, the original peasant people's commissar, V. G. Iakovenko, wrote a despondent letter to Stalin detailing a visit to his home region of Kansk uezd, Eniseisk province. Iakovenko, who at that time worked in a typically marginal post for promotees—an assistant to Kalinin in charge of greeting peasant visitors and petitioners—described the horrible conditions prevailing in Kansk since the onset of grain confiscations in January 1928. See

Tragediia sovetskoe derevnia. Kollektivizatsiia i raskulachivanie: Dokumenty i materialy, 1927–1939. Tom 1, Mai 1927–Noiabr 1929 (Moscow, 1999), 398–401.

101. See, for example, RGASPI, f. 17, op. 74, d. 18, ll. 10–16. *Sel'sko-khoziaistvennaia zhizn'*, 1929, no. 38: 18.

102. *Pravda*, June 8, 1929.

103. *Izvestiia*, July 14, 1929.

104. On the Rabkrin investigations in industry of late 1929 and 1930 see Shearer, *Industry, State, and Society*; and Kuromiya, *Stalin's Industrial Revolution*.

105. Letter, "Predsedatel'iu tsentral'noi Komissii po chistke sov. apparata tov. Kokovikhinu." November 20, 1929, from assistant head of INFO OGPU, Zaporozhets. TsGA RSFSR, f. 406, op. 25, d. 125, l. 113.

106. At the November 1929 Central Committee Plenum, Molotov urged the creation of an all-union Narkomzem. The legislation creating Narkomzem SSSR is dated December 7, 1929. *KPSS v rezoliutsiiakh*, ii (1954), 653–56.

107. The Central Statistical Administration (TsSU) suffered a similar fate, as most of its functions were taken over by Gosplan's statistical economics sector. Rabkrin similarly reduced the Commissariat of Finance to an organization that collected revenues but had no say over budgets or expenditures. Kuromiya, *Stalin's Industrial Revolution*, 35.

108. *Shestnadtsataia konferentsiia VKP*, 445. The November 1929 Plenum of the Central Committee echoed this sentiment specifically with regard to agricultural workers. RGASPI, f. 17, op. 74, d. 18, l. 2.

109. Among the most important studies of the forced collectivization of agriculture are Lewin, *Russian Peasants and Soviet Power*; Sheila Fitzpatrick, *Stalin's Peasants: Resistance and Survival in the Russian Village after Collectivization* (New York, 1994); R. W. Davies, *The Socialist Offensive*; and Lynn Viola, *Peasant Rebels under Stalin: Collectivization and the Culture of Peasant Resistance* (New York, 1996).

110. *Kak lomali NEP: Stenogrammy Plenumov TsK VKP(b) 1928-1929 gg. v 5-ti tomakh*. Red. koll., V. P. Danilov, et al., eds. (Moscow, 2000).

111. RGASPI, f. 17, op. 2, d. 511, ll. 114–15. The incident probably occurred either at the very end of 1928 or in January or February 1929, since Bukharin, Rykov, and Tomskii presented their platform to the Politburo on February 9, 1929.

112. Rykov said this to the American journalist William Reswick, author of *I Dreamt Revolution*, 254.

113. Reiman, *Birth of Stalinism*, 100–101.

114. Several members of the joint 1933 Plenum mocked Smirnov for his illness. RGASPI, f. 17, op. 2, d. 511, l. 229.

115. *Osoboe mnenie*, 574, f. 2, citing FSB archives. The arrests were followed quickly by the publication of a number of books denouncing "bourgeois economists," "the ideologues of the kulaks," and, especially, "Kondrat'evshchina" (the scourge of Kondrat'ev) and its close relative "Chaianovshchina" (the scourge of Chaianov). See, for example, *Kondrat'evshchina, Chaianovshchina i Sukhanovshchina: Vreditel'stvo v sel'skom khoziastva* (Moscow, 1930); *Protiv Kondrat'evshchina. Klassovaia bor'ba v ekonomicheskoi teorii*. (Moscow, 1931); and *Kondrat'evshchina i bor'ba za kadry* (Moscow, 1931).

116. *Kondrat'evshchina*, 7.

117. *Pis'ma I. V. Stalina V. M. Molotovu, 1925–1936 gg. Sbornik dokumentov* (Moscow, 1995), 194, 211.

118. The trial's official stenographic report is contained in *Protsess Prompartii, 25 noiabria–7 dekabria 1930 g. Stenogramma sudebnogo protsessa i materialy priobshchennye k*

delu (Moscow, 1931). See also the wholly sympathetic (to the accusers): Andrew Rothstein, *Wreckers on Trial: A Record of the Trial of the Industrial Trial Held in Moscow, Nov.–Dec., 1930* (London, 1931).

119. *Protsess Prompartii*, 298–99.

120. *Osoboe mnenie*, kn. 2: 605–6. In August 1930, Chaianov signed a confession, obviously drawn up by the OGPU. Diane Koenker and Ronald D. Bachman, eds., *Revelations from the Russian* Archives (Washington, D.C., 1997), 241–42. In a series of unpublished letters to Khrushchev that were saved by family members, Makarov, who incredibly survived until 1980, explicitly renounced all statements he made at the trials. *Osoboe mnenie*, kn. 2, 601–4.

121. *Protsess kontr-revoliutsionnoi organizatsii Men'shevikov (1 mart–9 mart 1931 g.). Stenogramma sudebnogo protsessa, obvinitel'noe zakliuchenie i prigovor* (Moscow, 1931), 197. Kondrat'ev's testimony is on pages 194–210.

122. *Protsess*, 198. Stalin insisted that defendants testify that they desired foreign intervention. See Stalin's letter of October 1930 to OGPU's Menzhinskii. Koenker, ed. *Revelations*, 243. See also *Protsess Prompartii*, 11.

123. *Osobie mnenie*, kn. 2:608–9.

124. R. W. Davies's account of the causes and course of the famine is the most persuasive, balancing objective factors (weather and the poor harvest of 1931) with subjective ones (extremely ruthless collections and continuing export of scarce grain). R. W. Davies, *Crisis and Progress in the Soviet Economy, 1931–1933* (London, 1996); and R. W. Davies and Stephen Wheatcroft *The Years of Hunger: Soviet Agriculture, 1931–33* (Palgrave, 2003). See also the study by D'Ann R. Penner, "Stalin and the Ital'ianka of 1932–33 in the Don Region," *Cahiers du Monde Russe* 39:1–2 (January–June 1998), 27–68; N. A. Ivnitskii, ed., *Golod 1932–33 godov* (Moscow, 1995); V. V. Kondrashin, *Golod 1932–33 godov v derevne Povolzh'ia* (Kand. Ph.D. diss., Moscow, 1991).

125. See stenographic report of the January 1933 Plenum, RGASPI, f. 17, op. 2, d. 511, ll. 117–19. See also, for example, RGASPI, f. 17, op. 2, d. 511, ll. 103–11, 179, 227. Other pertinent materials on the "Antiparty group" can be found in RGASPI, f. 17, op. 2, d. 514, tom. ii; RGASPI, f. 589, op. 3, d. 9296, t. 1, ll. 358–61; and RGASPI, f. 589, op. 3, d. 9384, t. 1, l. 237–41.

126. *KPSS v rezoliutsiiakh*, iii (1954), 199.

127. Twenty years later, on July 17, 1958, A. P. Smirnov was posthumously rehabilitated into the ranks of the Communist Party.

Bibliography

BOOKS AND ARTICLES

Agronomicheskaia pomoshch' v Rossii. St. Petersburg, 1914.

Akademiia nauk SSSR. Institut Istorii. *Agrarnaia politika sovetskoi vlasti.* Moscow, 1954.

Alymov, A. A. and S. Studenikin. "Rekonstruktsiia gosapparata," in *Piatnadtsat' let sovetskogo stroitel'stva*, E. B. Pashukanis, ed. Moscow, 1931.

Anfimov, A. M. "On the History of the Russian Peasantry at the Beginning of the Twentieth Century." *Russian Review* 51:3 (July 1992): 396–407.

Antsiferov, Alexis et al. *Russian Agriculture during the War.* New Haven, 1930.

Argenbright, Robert. "Marking NEP's Slippery Path: The Krasnoshchekov Show Trial." *Russian Review* 61 (April 2002): 249–75.

Atkinson, Dorothy. *The End of the Russian Land Commune.* Stanford, 1983.

Avrich, Paul. *Kronstadt 1921.* Princeton, 1971.

Azrael, Jeremy. *Managerial Power and Soviet Politics.* Cambridge, Mass., 1966.

Bailes, Kendall. "The Politics of Technology: Stalin and Technocratic Thinking among Soviet Engineers." *American Historical Review* 79 (1974): 445–69.

———. *Technology and Society under Lenin and Stalin.* Princeton, 1978.

Ball, Alan. *Russia's Last Capitalists: The Nepmen, 1921–1929.* Berkeley, 1987.

———. "State Children: Soviet Russia's *Besprizornye* and the New Socialist Generation." *Russian Review* 52 April 1993): 228–47.

Barnett, Vincent. *Kondrat'ev and the Dynamics of Economic Development.* Houndmills, 1998.

Bechhofer, C. E. *Through Starving Russia.* Westport, 1977.

Beissinger, Mark. *Scientific Management, Socialist Discipline, and Soviet Power.* Cambridge, Mass., 1988.

Bineman Ia. M., and S. Kheinman. *Kadry gosudarstvennogo i kooperativnogo apparata SSSR.* Moscow, 1930.

Biulleten' soveshchaniia krest'ian-chlenov VTsIK pri Narkomzeme RSFSR, no. 3. Moscow, 1924.

Blum, Jerome. *The End of the Old Order in Rural Europe.* Princeton, 1978.

Bol'shakov, A. *Sovremennaia derevnia v tsifrakh.* Moscow, 1925.

Bonnell, Victoria E. *Iconography of Power: Soviet Political Posters under Lenin and Stalin.* Berkeley, 1997.

———. "The Representation of Women in Early Soviet Political Art," *Russian Review* 50:3 (1991): 277–87.

Carr, E. H. *The Bolshevik Revolution, 1917–1923.* 3 vols. New York, 1950–53.

———. *The Interregnum.* London, 1954.

———. *Socialism in One Country.* 3 vols. in 4. New York, 1958–64.

Carr, E. H., and R. W. Davies. *Foundations of a Planned Economy, 1926–1929.* 2 vols in 3. London, 1969–[78].

Chernov, V. M. *The Great Russian Revolution*. New Haven, 1936.
Chernyshev, I. *Sel'skoe khoziaistvo dovoennoi Rossii i SSSR*. Moscow, 1926.
Clowes, Edith W., Samuel D. Kassow, and James L. West. *Between Tsar and People. Educated Society and the Quest for Public Identities in Late Imperial Russia*. Princeton, 1991.
Cohen, Stephen F. *Bukharin and the Bolshevik Revolution: A Political Biography, 1888–1938*. Princeton, 1971.
———. "Bukharinism and Stalinism" and "Bukharin, NEP, and the Idea of an Alternative to Stalinism," in *Rethinking the Soviet Experience: Politics and History Since 1917* (New York, 1985).
Crozier, Michel. *The Bureacratic Phenonmenon*. Chicago, 1964.
Daniels, Robert V. *The Conscience of the Revolution: Communist Opposition in Soviet Russia*. Cambridge, Mass., 1960.
Danilov, V. P., ed., *Kooperativno-kolkhoznoe stroitel'stvo v SSSR, 1917–1922: Dokumenty i materialy*, vol. 1. Moscow, 1990.
———. "Pereraspredelenie Zemel'nogo fonda Rossii v rezul'tate velikoi oktiabraskoi revoliutsii," in I. I. Mints, ed., *Leninskii dekret o zemle*. Moscow, 1979.
———. *Sovetskaia dokolkhoznaia derevnia: Naselenie, zemlepol'zovanie, khoziaistvo*. Moscow, 1977.
Darnton, Robert. *Kiss of Larmourette: Reflections in Cultural History*. New York, 1990.
David-Fox, Michael. *Revolution of the Mind: Higher Learning among the Bolsheviks, 1918–1929*. Ithaca, 1997.
Davies, Christopher. "Economic Problems of the Soviet Health Service: 1917–1930." *Soviet Studies* 35:3 (1983): 343–61.
Davies, R. W. *Crisis and Progress in the Soviet Economy, 1931–1933*. London, 1996.
———. *The Development of the Soviet Budgetary System*. Cambridge, 1958.
———, ed. *From Tsarism to the New Economic Policy: Continuity and Change in the Economy of the USSR*. London, 1990.
———. *The Industrialisation of Soviet Russia*. Vol. 1. *The Socialist Offensive*. Cambridge, Mass., 1980.
———. *The Soviet Economy in Turmoil*. Houndmills, 1989.
Davies, R. W. and Stephen Wheatcroft. *The Years of Hunger: Soviet Agriculture 1931–33*. Palgrave, 2003.
Davies, R. W. et al., eds. *The Economic Transformation of the Soviet Union, 1913–1945*. Cambridge, Eng. 1993.
de Tocqueville, Alexis. *The Old Regime and the French Revolution*. Translated by Stuart Gilbert. New York, 1955.
Dekrety sovetskoi vlasti. Moscow, 1957.
Derevnia pri NEP'e: Kogo schitat' kulakom, kogo—truzhenikom. Chto ob etom govoriat krest'iane? Moscow, 1924.
Deutscher, Isaac. *The Prophet Unarmed: Trotsky, 1921–1929*. London, 1959.
Edmundson, Charles M. "The Politics of Hunger: The Soviet Response to the Famine of 1921." *Soviet Studies* 29: 4 (1977): 506–18.
———. "Soviet Famine Relief Measures, 1921–23." Ph.D. diss., Florida State University, 1970.
Efimkin, A. P. *Dvazhdy reabilitirovannye*. Moscow, 1991.
Emmons, Terence, and Wayne S. Vucinich, eds. *The Zemstvo in Russia*. New York, 1982.
Entsiklopediia mestnogo upravleniia i khoziaistrov. Moscow, 1927.

Erlich, Alexander. *The Soviet Industrialization Debate, 1924–1928.* Cambridge, 1960.
Eroshkin, N. P. *Istoriia gosudarstvennykh uchrezhdenii dorevoliutsionnoi Rossii.* Moscow, 1983.
Fainsod, Merle. *How Russia is Ruled.* Cambridge, 1953.
———. *Smolensk under Soviet Rule.* New York, 1963.
Felshtinskii, Iurii, comp. *Arkhiv Trotskogo: Kommunisticheskaia oppozitsiia v SSSR 1923–27.* Benson, 1988.
Field, Mark. *Doctor and Patient in Soviet Russia.* Cambridge, Mass., 1957.
Figes, Orlando. *Peasant Russia, Civil War: The Volga Countryside in Revolution (1917–1922).* New York, 1989.
———. *A People's Tragedy.* New York, 1996.
Fisher, H. H. *The Famine in Soviet Russia, 1919–1923: The Operations of the American Relief Administration.* New York, 1927.
Fitzpatrick, Sheila. "Ascribing Class: The Construction of Social Identity in Soviet Russia." *Journal of Modern History,* 65:4 (December 1993): 745–70.
———. *Education and Social Mobility in the Soviet Union.* Cambridge, 1979.
———. "Ordzhonikidzet's Takeover of Vesenkha: A Case Study in Soviet Bureaucratic Politics." *Soviet Studies* 37: 2 (April 1985): 153–72.
———. "The Problem of Class Identity in NEP Society," in Sheila Fitzpatrick, Alexander Rabinowitch, and Richard Stites, eds., *Russia in the Era of NEP: Explorations in Soviet Society and Culture.* Bloomington, 1991.
———. "Stalin and the Making of a New Elite, 1928–1939," in *The Cultural Front: Power and Culture in Revolutionary Russia.* Ithaca, 1992.
———. *Stalin's Peasants: Resistance and Survival in the Russian Village after Collectivization.* New York, 1994.
Frieden, Nancy. "The Politics of Zemstvo Medicine," in Terence Emmons, ed., *The Zemstvo in Russia: An Experiment in Local Self-Government.* Cambridge, 1982.
———. *Russian Physicians in an Era of Reform and Revolution, 1856–1905.* Princeton, 1981.
Frierson, Cathy. *Peasant Icons: Representations of Rural People in Late Nineteenth-Century Russia.* New York, 1993.
Gatrell, Peter. "The First World War and War Communism, 1914–1920," in *The Economic Transformation of the Soviet Union, 1913–1945.* Cambridge, 1994.
Genkina, E. B. *Lenin: Predsedatel' Sovnarkoma i STO.* Moscow, 1984.
Gershenkron, Alexander. *Economic Backwardness in Historical Perspective.* Cambridge, Mass., 1962.
Gimpelson, E. G. *Rabochii Klass vupravlenii Sovetskim gosudarstvem: noiabr' 1917–1920 gg.* Moscow, 1982.
Gladkov, I. A. *Sovetskoe Natodnoe Khoziaistvo (1921–1925).* Moscow, 1960.
Glavnyi politiko-prosvetitel'nyi komitet, *Chto govoriat tsifry o golode?* [N.p., n.d.].
Gorodetskii, E. N. *Rozhdenie sovetskogo gosudarstva.* Moscow, 1986.
Graziosi, Andrea. *The Great Soviet Peasant War: Bolsheviks and Peasants, 1917–1933.* Cambridge, Mass., 1996.
Hamm, Michael F. "The Breakdown of Urban Modernization: A Prelude to the Revolutions of 1917," in Michael F. Hamm, ed., *The City in Russian History.* Lexington, 1976.
Hardemann, Hilde. *Coming to Terms with the Soviet Regime: The Changing Signposts Movement among Russian Émigrés in the Early 1920s.* DeKalb, 1994.

Haslam, Jonathan. *The Vices of Integrity: E. H. Carr, 1892–1982*. London, 1999.
Heinzen, James W. "'Peasants from the Plow' to 'Professors from the Plow': The Cuture of the Soviet People's Commisariat of Agriculture, 1921–1929." *Journal of Peasant Studies* 25:2.
———. "Politics, Administration, and Specialization in the Russian People's Commissariat of Agriculture." Ph.D. diss., University of Pennsylvania, 1993.
Hoffman, David. *Peasant Metropolis: Social Identities in Moscow, 1929–1941*. Ithaca, 1994.
Holmes, Larry. *The Kremlin and the Schoolhouse: Reforming Education in Soviet Russia, 1917–1931*. Bloomington, 1991.
Holquist, Peter. "Information is the Alpha and the Omega of Our Work: Bolshevik Surveillance in Its Pan-European Perspective." *Journal of Modern History* 69:3 (1997): 415–50.
———. *Making War, Forging Revolution: Russia's Continuum of Crisis, 1914–1921*. Cambridge, Mass., 2002.
Huddleston, Sisley. *France*. New York, 1927.
Hughes, James. *Stalin, Siberia, and the Crisis of the New Economic Policy*. Cambridge, 1991.
———. *Stalinism in a Russian Province: A Study of Collectivization and Dekulakization in Siberia*. Houndmills, 1996.
Instruktsiia k sostavleniiu sel'sko-khoziaistvennykh kommun i dekret ob organizatsii i snabzhenii derevenskoi bednoty. Petrograd, 1918.
Ipatieff, V. N. *Life of a Chemist*. Stanford, 1946.
Iroshnikov, M. P. *Sozdanie sovetskogo tsentral'nogo gosudarstvennogo apparata. Sovet Narodnykh Komissarov i narodnye komissariaty (oktiahr' 1917g.–Ianvar' 1918)*. Moscow, 1966.
Itogi desiatiletiia sovetskoi vlasti v tsifrakh, 1917–1927. N.p. [1927].
Ivnitskii, N. A., ed. *Golod 1932–33 godov*. Moscow, 1995.
Jansen, Marc. *A Show Trial under Lenin: The Trial of the Socialist Revolutionaries, Moscow 1922*. The Hague, 1982.
Jasny, Naum. *Soviet Economists of the Twenties: Names to be Remembered*. Cambridge, Eng., 1972.
K soveshchaniiu gubernskikh zemelnykh upravlenii (tezisy dokladov upravlenii i khozorganov NKZ). Moscow, 1924.
Kabanov, V. V. *Krest'ianskoe khoziaistvo v usloviakh voennogo kommunizma*. Moscow, 1988.
Kak lomali NEP: stenogrammy plenumov TsK VKP(b) 1928–1929 gg. 5 vols. Edited by V. P. Danilov, et al. Moscow, 2000.
Kerans, David. *Mind and Labor on the Farm in Black-Earth Russia*. Budapest, 2001.
Khlevniuk, Oleg. *In Stalin's Shadow: The Career of 'Sergo' Ordzhonikidze*. Edited with an introduction by Donald Raleigh. Armonk, 1995.
Khriashcheva, A. I. *Gruppy i Klassy v krest'ianstve*, 2nd ed. Moscow, 1926.
Koenker, Diane, and Ronald D. Bachman, eds. *Revelations from the Russian Archives: Documents in English Translation*. Washington, D.C., 1997.
Kondrashin, V. U. *Golod 1932–33 godov v derevne Povolzh'ia*. Ph.D. dissertation, Moscow, 1991.
Kondrat'ev, N. D. *Osoboe mnenie*. Moscow, 1993.
———. *Rynok khlebov i ego regulirovanie vo vremia voiny i revoliutsii*. Moscow, 1922.

———. *The Works of Nikolai D. Kondrat'ev.* 4 vols. Translated by Stephen S. Wilson. Edited by Natalia Makasheva, et al. London, 1998.
Kondrat'ev, N. D., and D.I. Oparin. *Bol'shie tsikly kon'iunktury.* Moscow, 1928.
Kondrat'evshchina, Chaianovshchina i Sukhanovshchina: Vreditel'stvo v sel'skom khoziaistva. Moscow, 1930.
Kondrat'evshchina i bor'ba za kadry. Moscow, 1931.
Kotkin, Stephen. *Magnetic Mountain: Stalinism as a Civilization.* Berkeley, 1995.
———. "The State: Is It Us? Memoirs, Archives, and Kremlinologists." *Russian Review* 61:1 (January, 2002): 35–51.
Kotsonis, Yanni. *Making Peasants Backward: Agricultural Cooperatives and the Agarian Question in Russia, 1861–1914.* London, 1999.
Krupskaia, N. K. *Vospominaniia o Lenine.* Moscow, 1968.
Kuromiya, Hiroaki. "The Commander and the Rank and File: Managing the Soviet Coal-Mining Industry, 1928–33," in William G. Rosenberg and Lewis H. Sigelbaum, eds., *Social Dimensions of Soviet Industrialization.* Bloomington, 1993.
———. *Stalin's Industrial Revolution: Politics and Workers, 1928–1931.* Cambridge, 1988.
Kvashonkin, A. V. et al, eds. *Bol'shevistskoe rukovodstvo. Perepiska. 1912–1927.* Moscow, 1996.
Layton, Edwin. *The Revolt of the Engineers: Social Responsibility and the American Engineering Profession.* Cleveland, 1971.
Lenin, V. I. *Pol'noe sobranie sochinenii.* 5th ed. 55 vols. Moscow, 1958–65.
Lewin, Moshe. *The Making of the Soviet System.* New York, 1985.
———. *Political Undercurrents in Soviet Economic Debates.* Princeton, 1974.
———. *Russian Peasants and Soviet Power: A Study of Collectivization.* New York, 1968.
Lih, Lars. *Bread and Authority in Russia 1914–1921.* Berkeley, 1990.
———. *The Bolshevik Sowing Committees of 1920: Apotheosis of War Communism?* Pittsburgh, 1990.
Male, D. J. *Russian Peasant Organisation before Collectivisation: A Study of Commune and Gathering, 1925–1930.* Cambridge, Eng., 1971.
Matsuzato, Kimitako. "The Fate of Agronomists in Russia: Their Quantitative Dynamics from 1911 to 1916." *Russian Review* 55 (April, 1996): 172–200.
———. "Stolypinskaia reforma i rossiiskaia agrotekhnologicheskaia revoliutsiia." *Otechestvennaia istoriia* 6 (1992): 194–200.
McCannon, John. *Red Arctic: Polar Exploration and the Myth of the North in the Soviet Union, 1932–39.* Oxford, 1998.
Merl, Stefan. *Agrarmarkt und die neue okonomische Politik: die Anfange staatlicher Lenkung der Landwirtschaft in der Sowjetunion, 1925–1928.* Munich, 1981.
Merridale, Catherine. *Moscow and the Rise of Stalin: The Communist Party in the Capital, 1925–1932.* New York, 1990.
Meshcheriakov, V. *Organizatsiia Narkomzema.* Moscow, 1919.
———. *Zemel'naia politika kommunistov.* Petrograd, 1919.
Mikoian, A. I. *V nachale dverdtsatykh.* Moscow, 1975.
Mitrofanov, A. Kh. *Samodeiatel'nost krest'ianstva v velikuiu kampaniiu.* Moscow, 921.
Moon, David. *The Russian Peasantry, 1600–1930: The World the Peasants Made.* London: 1999.
Morgan, Gareth. *Images of Organization.* Beverly Hills, 1986.
Narodnyi komissariat zemledeliia. *IV Soveshchane zemorganov RSFSR.* Moscow, 1929.
———. *Materialy po perspektivnomu planu razvittia sel'skogo khoziastva RSFSR.* Mos-

cow, 1928.

———. *Osnovy perspektivnogo plana Razvitiia sel'skogo i lesnogo khoziaistva*. Mocsow, 1924.

———. *Sel'sko-khoziaistvennyi uchenyi komitet. Kratkii ocherk ego deiatel'nosti i zadach*. Moscow, 1919.

Nosova, Natalia P. "Formirovanie kadrov spetsialistov sel'skogo khoziaistva v sovetskoi dokolkhoznoi derevne (1917–29)," in R. P. Tolmacheva, ed., *Naselenie i trudovye resursy ural'skoi sovetskoi derevnia*. Sverdlovsk, 1987.

———. *Upravliat' ili komandovat'?: Gosudarstvo i krest'ianstvo sovetskoi Rossii, 1917–1929*. Moscow, 1993.

Orlovsky, Daniel T. "The Anti-Bureaucratic Campaigns of the 1920s," in Theodore Taranovski, ed., *Reform in Modern Russian History: Progress or Cycle?* New York, 1995.

———. "Gimpelson and the Hegemony of the Working Class," *Slavic Review* 48:1 (Spring 1989): 104–6.

———. "The Hidden Class: White-Collar Workers in the Soviet 1920s," in Lewis Siegelbaum and Ronald G. Suny, eds., *Making Workers Soviet: Power, Class, and Identity*. Ithaca, 1994.

———. *The Limits of Reform: The Ministry of Internal Affairs in Imperial Russia, 1802–1881*. Cambridge, Mass., 1981.

———. "Professionalism in the Ministerial Bureaucracy on the Eve of the February Revolution of 1917," in Harley Balzer, ed., *Russia's Middle Class: The Professionals in Russian History*. New York, 1996.

———. "State Building in the Civil War Era: The Role of the Lower Middle Strata," in Diane Koenker et al., eds., *Party, State and Society in the Russian Civil War*. Bloomington, 1989.

Osinskii, V. *Gousudarstvennoe regulirovanie krest'ianskogo khoziastva. Sbornik statei*. Moscow, 1920.

Osnovnye elementy sel'skokhoziaistvennogo proizvodstva SSSR 1916 i 1923–27 gg. Moscow, 1930.

O zemle: Sbornik statei o proshlom i budushchem zemel'no-khoziaistvennogo stroitel'stva. Vol. 1. Moscow, 1922.

Pallot, Judith. *Land Reform in Russia, 1906–1917*. Oxford, 1999.

Patenaude, Bertrand. *The Big Show in Bololand: The American Relief Expedition to Soviet Russia in the Famine of 1921*. Stanford, 2002.

———. "Bolshevism in Retreat: The Transition to the New Economic Policy, 1920–22." Ph.D. dissertation, Stanford University, 1987.

———. "Peasants into Russians: The Utopian Essence of War Communism." *Russian Review* 54:4 (October 1995): 552–70.

Penner, D'Ann R. "Stalin and the Ital'ianka of 1932–33 in the Don Region." *Cahiers du Monde Russe* 39:1–2 (Jan.–June 1998): 27–68.

Peris, Daniel. *Storming the Heavens: The Soviet League of the Militant Godless*. Ithaca, 1998.

Pershin, P. N. *Zemel'noe ustroistvo dorevoliutsionnoi derevnia*. Moscow, 1928.

Pethybridge, Roger. *One Step Backwards, Two Steps Forward*. Oxford, 1990.

———. *The Social Prelude to Stalinism*. New York, 1974.

Pintner, D. K., and Walter Rowney, eds. *Russian Officialdom: The Bureaucratization of Russian Society from the Seventeenth to Twentieth Century*. Chapel Hill, 1980.

Pipes, Richard. *The Russian Revolution*. Cambridge, 1990.

Pis'ma I. V. Stalina V. M. Molotovu, 1925–1936 gg. Sbornik dokumentov. Comp. by L. Koshelev et al. Moscow, 1995.
Poliakov, Iurii. 1921-i–Pobeda nad golodom. Moscow, 1975.
———. Perekhod k NEPu. Moscow, 1967.
Promyshlennost' SSSR: Statisticheskii sbornik. Moscow, 1964.
Protiv Kondrat'evshchina. Klassovaia bor'ba v ekonomicheskoi teorii. Moscow, 1931.
Protsess kontr-revoliutsionnoi organizatsii Men'shevikov (1 mart–9 mart 1931 g.). Stenogramma sudebnogo protsessa, obvinitel'noe zakliuchenie i prigovor. Moscow, 1931.
Protsess Prompartii, 25 noiabria–7 dekabria 1930 g. Stenogramma sudebnogo protsessa i materialy priobshchennye k delu. Moscow, 1931.
Radkey, Oliver. The Sickle under the Hammer. New York, 1963.
Raeff, Marc. "The Bureaucratic Phenomena of Imperial Russia, 1700–1905." American Historical Review 84, no. 2 (1979): 399–411.
Raleigh, Donald. Experiencing Russia's Civil War: Politics, Society, and Revolutionary Culture in Saratov, 1917–1922. Princeton, 2002.
———. Revolution on the Volga: 1917 in Saratov. Ithaca, 1986.
Ramer, Samuel C. "Feldshers and Rural Health Care," in Susan G. Solomon and John F. Hutchinson, eds., Health and Society in Revolutionary Russia. Bloomington, 1990.
Rasmussen, Wayne D., and Gladys L. Baker. The Department of Agriculture. New York: 1972.
Rees, E. A. State Control in Soviet Russia: The Rise and Fall of the Workers' and Peasants' Inspectorate, 1920–34. Houndmills, 1987.
Reiman, Michal. The Birth of Stalinism: The USSR on the Eve of the "Second Revolution." Bloomington, 1987.
Reswick, William. I Dreamt Revolution. Chicago, 1952.
Rieber, Alfred J. "The Reforming Tradition in Russian History," in Alfred J. Rieber and Alvin Z. Rubenstein, eds., Perestroika at the Crossroads. Armonk, 1991.
———. "The Sedimentary Society," in Edith W. Clowes, Samuel D. Kassow, and James L. West, eds., Between Tsar and People: Educated Society and the Quest for Public Identities in Late Imperial Russia. Princeton, 1991.
Rigby, T. H. Communist Party Membership in the USSR 1917–1967. Princeton, 1968.
———. Lenin's Government: Sovnarkom, 1917–1922. Cambridge, 1979.
———. "Staffing USSR Incorporated: The Origins of the Nomenklatura System." Soviet Studies 40:4 (1988): 523–37.
Robbins, Richard. Famine in Russia, 1891–92: The Imperial Government Responds to a Crisis. New York, 1975.
Rosenberg, William G., and Lewis H. Siegelbaum, eds. Social Dimensions of Soviet Industrialization. Bloomington, 1993.
Rosnitskii, N. Litso derevni. Moscow-Leningrad, 1926.
Rothstein, Andrew. Wreckers on Trial: A Record of the Trial of the Industrial Trial Held in Moscow, Nov.–Dec., 1930. London, 1931.
Rowney, D. K. "The Scope, Authority, and Personnel of the New Industrial Commissariats in Historical Context," in William G. Rosenberg and Lewis H. Siegelbaum, eds., Social Dimensions of Soviet Industrialization. Bloomington, 1993.
———. Transition to Technocracy: The Structural Origins of the Soviet Administrative State. Ithaca, 1989.
Ruane, Christine, and Ben Eklof. "Cultural Pioneers and Professionals: The Teacher in

Society," in Edith Clowes, Samuel Kassow, and James West, eds., *Between Tsar and People: Educated Society and the Quest for Public Identity in Late Imperial Russia*. Princeton, 1991.
Sbornik dekretov i postanovlenii po Narodnomu komissariatu zemledeliia, 1917–1920. Moscow, 1921.
Schapiro, Leonard. *The Communist Party of the Soviet Union*. New York, 1960.
Sel'sko-khoziaistvennoe vedomstvo za 75 let ego deiatel'nosti (1837–1912 gg.). Petrograd, 1914.
Shanin, Teodor. *The Awkward Class*. Oxford, 1972.
Shearer, David R. *Industry, State, and Society in Stalin's Russia, 1926–1934*. Ithaca, 1996.
———. "The Language and Politics of Socialist Rationalization: Productivity, Industrial Relations and the Social Origins of Stalinism at the End of NEP," *Cahiers du Monde Russe et Sovietique* 32: 4 (1991): 581–608.
Siegelbaum, Lewis. *Soviet State and Society between Revolutions, 1918–1929*. Cambridge, 1992.
Smirnov, A. P. *Na pomoshch' krest'ianskomu khoziaistvu*. Moscow, 1924.
———. *Nashi osnovnye zadachi po podniatiiu i organizatsii krest'ianskogo khoziastva*. Moscow, 1926.
———. *Zadachi nizovoi vlasti v oblasti sel'skogo khoziaistva*. Moscow, 1926.
Snabzhenie krestianskogo naseleniia sel'skokhoziaistvennymi mashinami i orudiiami. Moscow, 1925.
Solomon, Susan Gross. *The Soviet Agrarian Debate: A Controversy in Social Science, 1923–29*. Boulder, 1977.
Solomon, Susan Gross, and John F. Hutchinson, eds. *Health and Society in Revolutionary Russia*. Bloomington, 1990.
Sotsial'isticheskoe stroitel'stvo SSSR. Moscow, 1934.
Sovetskaia derevnia glazami VChK-OGPU-NKVD: Dokumenty i materialy. Tom 1. 1918–1922. Moscow, 1998; and *Tom 2. 1923–1929*. Moscow, 2000.
Spravochnik o spetsialistakh sel'skogo khoziastva SSSR. Moscow-Leningrad, 1924.
Stanziani, Alessandro. *L'economie en revolution: Les cas russe, 1870–1930*. Paris, 1998.
Starr, S. Frederick. *Decentralization and Self-Government in Russia, 1830–1870*. Princeton, 1972.
Stenograficheskii otchet II-ogo vserossiskogo agronomicheskogo s"ezda. Moscow, 1929.
Stenograficheskii otchet III-go vserossiiskogo soveshchaniia zemorganov 28 fevralia–7 marta 1926 g. Moscow, 1926.
Sternheimer, Stephen. "Administration for Development: The Emerging Bureaucratic Elite, 1920–1930," in D. K. Pintner and Walter Rowney, eds., *Russian Officialdom: the Bureaucratization of Russian Society From the Seventeenth to Twentieth Century*. Chapel Hill, 1980.
Stone, David. *Hammer and Rifle: The Militarization of the Soviet Union*. Lawrence, 2000.
Taranovsk, Theodore, ed. *Reform in Modern Russian History: Progress or Cycle?* New York, 1995.
Teodorovich, I. A. *K voprosu o sel'sko-khoziaistvennoi politike RSFSR*. [N.p.], 1923.
———. *O gosudarstvennoi regulirovanii krest'ianskogo khoziaistva*. Moscow, 1920.
Trotsky, Leon. *My Life*. New York, 1970.
The Trotsky Papers, 1917–1922, 2 vols. Edited and annotated by Jan M. Meijer. The Hague, 1964–1971.

Trudy Tsentral'nogo staticheskogo upravleniia, vol. 18. Moscow, 1925.
Tsentral'oe upravlenie zemledeliia i sovkhozov v svete Novoi Ekonomicheskoi Politiki. Moscow, 1921.
Tsentral'noe statisticheskoe upravlenie SSSR. *Gosudarstvennyi apparat SSSR, 1924–1928 gg*. Moscow, 1929.
Tsentral'noe statisticheskoe upravlenie SSSR. *Narodnoe khoziaistvo SSSR v 1961 godu. Statisticheskii ezhegodnik*. Moscow, 1962.
Tsentral'noe statisticheskoe upravlenie SSSR. *Sbornik statisticheskikh svedenii po Soiuzu SSSR, 1918–1923*. Moscow, 1924.
Tsentral'noe statisticheskoe upravlenie SSSR. *Trudy*. vol. 6, ch. 3, *Ekonomicheskoe rassloenie krest'ianstva v 1917 i 1919 g*. Moscow, 1922.
Tsk Pomgol, *Chto govoriat tsifry o golode?* n.p., n.d.
TsUNKhU Gosplana SSSR. *Zhivotnovodstvo SSSR za 1916–1938 gg., Statisticheskii Sbornik*. Moscow-Leningrad, 1940.
Valentinov, N. V. *Nasledniki Lenina*. Moscow, 1991.
———. *Novaia Ekonomicheskaia Politika i krizis partii posle Smerti Lenina*. Palo Alto, 1971.
Vasiaev, V. I. et al. *Dannye perepisi sluzhashchikh 1922 goda o sostave kadrov narkomatov RSFSR*. Moscow, 1972.
Viola, Lynn. *Peasant Rebels under Stalin: Collectiviation and the Culture of Peasant Resistance*. New York, 1996.
Vneshniaia torgovlia SSSR za 1918–1940 gg. Statisticheskii obzor. Moscow, 1960.
von Hagen, Mark. *Soldiers in the Proletarian Dictatorship: the Red Army and the Soviet State*. Ithaca, 1990.
von Laue, Theodore. *Sergei Witte and the Industrialization of Russia*. New York, 1969.
Wegren, Stephen K. *Agriculture and the State in Soviet and Post-Soviet Russia*. Pittsburgh, 1998.
Wehner, Markus. *Bauernpolitik im proletarischen Staat: die Bauernfrage als zentrales Problem der Sowjetischen Innenpolitik, 1921–1928*. Koeln, 1998.
———. "Golod 1921–22 v Samarskoi Gubernii i reaktsiia Sovetskogo praritel'stra." *Cahiers du Monde Russe* 38:1–2 (Janurary–June 1997): 223–242.
———. "Litsom k derevne: Sovetskaia vlast' i krest'ianskii ropros." *Otechestbennaia Istoriia* 5 (1993): 86–107.
Weissman, Benjamin M. *Herbert Hoover and Famine Relief to Soviet Russia, 1921–23*. Stanford, 1974.
Wheatcroft, Stephen. "Famine and Epidemic Crises in Russia, 1918–1922: The Case of Saratov." *Annales de Demographie Historique* (1983): 329–52.
Wheatcroft, Stephen et al. "Soviet Industrialization Reconsidered: Some Preliminary Conclusions about Soviet Economic Development between 1986 and 1941." *Economic History Review* 39:2 (1986): 264–94.
Williams, Christopher. "The 1921 Russian Famine: Centre and Periphery Responses." *Revolutionary Russia* 6:1 (December 1993): 277–314.
Wood, Elizabeth. *The Baba and the Comrade: Gender and Politics in Revolutionary Russia*. Bloomington, 1997.
Wortman, Richard. *The Development of a Russian Legal Consciousness*. Chicago, 1976.
Yaney, George. *The Urge to Mobilize: Agrarian Reform in Russia, 1861–1930*. Urbana, 1982.

Zaionchkovskii, P. A. *Pravitel'stvennyi apparat samoderzhavnoi Rossii v XIX v.* Moscow, 1978.
———. *Rossiiskoe samoderzhavie v kontse XIX stoletiia.* Moscow, 1970.
Zelenin, I. E. *Sovkhozy SSSR v gody dovoennykh piatiletok, 1928–1941.* Moscow, 1982.
———. *Sovkhozy v pervoe desiatiletie sovetskoi vlast', 1917–1927.* Moscow, 1972.
Zeml'no-planovaia komissiia. *Materialy po perspektivnomu planu razvitiia sel'skogo khoziaistva.* Moscow, 1928.

PERIODICALS, SERIES, AND NEWSPAPERS

XI Vserossiskii s"ezd sovetov RSFSR Stenograficheskii otchet. Moscow, 1924.
Bol'shevik, 1924–29.
Delo naroda, 1917–18.
Deviatyi s"ezd sovetov RSFSR, Stenograficheskii otchet. Moscow, 1922.
Dvenadtsatyi s"ezd rossiiskoi kommunisticheskoi partii (bol'shevikov): Stenograficheskii Otchet. Moscow, 1923.
Ekonomicheskii biulleten' koniunkturnogo instituta, 1927.
Ekonomicheskaia zhizn', 1920–28.
Izvestiia, 1918–29.
Kontrol'nye tsifry narodnogo khoziaistva SSSR na 1925–26 god. Moscow, 1925.
Kontrol'nye tsifry narodnogo khoziaistva SSSR na 1926–27 god. Moscow, 1926.
KPSS v rezoliutsiiakh, 1954.
League of Nations, Economic and Financial Section, *International Statistical Yearbook.* Geneva, 1926–29.
Na agrarnom fronte, 1925–30.
Narodnoe khoziaistvo SSSR, 1932–1958.
Odinadtsatyi s"ezd RKP (b), mart-aprel' 1922 goda. Stenograficheskii otchet. Moscow, 1961.
Otchet Narodnogo komissariata zemledeliia RSFSR (IX Vserossiiskomu s"ezdu sovetov) za 1921. Moscow, 1922.
Otchet Narodnogo komissariata zemledeliia za 1922 g. Moscow, 1923.
Otchet Narodnogo komissariata zemledeliia k XI s"ezdu sovetov za 1923 god. Moscow, 1924.
Otchet Narodnogo komissariata zemledeliia RSFSR XII-omu Vserossiiskomu s"ezdu sovetov za 1923–24 g. Moscow, 1925.
Otchet Narodnogo komissariata zemledeliia RSFSR za 1924–25 g. Moscow, 1926.
Piatnadtsatyi s"ezd VKP (b), dekabr' 1927 goda, stenograficheskii otchet. Moscow, 1961.
Pravda, 1918–29.
Proletarskaia Revoliutsiia, 1935.
Puti sel'skogo khoziaistva, 1925–29.
Sel'sko-khoziaistvennaia zhizn', 1922–29.
Shestnadtsataia konferentsiia VKP (b), aprel' 1929 goda: Stenograficheskii otchet, Moscow, 1962.
Sotsialisticheskoe khoziaistovo, 1925.
Statisticheskii spravochnik za 1927 g. Moscow, 1927.
Statistika zemlevladeniia 1905 g. St. Petersburg, 1907.
Vladimir Il'ich Lenin: Biograficheskaia khronika. Moscow, 1970–82.
Voennye arkhivy Rossii, vyp. 1, 1993.

ARCHIVES

Gosudarstvennyi Arkhiv Penzenskoi Oblasti (State Archive of Penza Oblast') [GAPO].
Gosudarstvennyi Arkhiv Rossiiskoi Federatsii (State Archive of the Russian Federation) [GARF].
Partiinyi arkhiv Penzenskoi Oblasti (Party Archive of Penza Oblast') [PAPO].
Rossiiskii Gosudartvennyi Arkhiv Ekonomiki (Russian State Archive of the Economy) [RGAE].
Rossiiskii Gosudarstvennyi Arkhiv Sotsial'noi i Politicheskoi Istorii (Russian State Archive of Social and Political History) [RGASPI].
Tsentral'ny Gosudarstvennyu Arkhiv Rossiiskoi Federatsii (TsGA RSFSR).

Index

Accounting, commercial, 81–82
Agrarian Marxists, 114, 116, 152, 154, 192, 262n59, 263n61
Agricultural Scholarly Committee, 42–43
Agriculture, 1, 4, 15, 163, 186; collective, 27–28, 38–39; communal, 10, 18, 44, 144, 165; development of, 12, 48, 50, 141, 152, 187, 190; expenditures on, 103–4; importance of, 13, 102, 106, 189; and industry, 197; recovery of, 56–57, 129–30, 140–41, 152, 186–88, 214, 222; and war, 3, 25, 47. *See also* Farming; Land tenure; Production, agricultural
Agriculture Administration, 112, 122, 129, 202
Agronomic aid, 17, 24–25, 44–46, 143–44, 151, 172, 222; network (uchastkovye punkty), 17, 137, 175, 249n152; and World War I, 19–20, 44
Alexander I, 22
Alien elements, 1, 133, 182, 197, 202–3, 206; personnel as, 10, 213; social, 119–21, 222
Allegiances, political, 85–86, 120
Antonov uprising, 76
Arrests, 85, 87, 94, 115, 186, 197; of specialists, 171, 216
Artel', 26, 164, 191
Attacks, 191–93, 214, 218–19; and legitimacy, 122; public, 217; on specialists, 115–19, 192. *See also* Purges
Austria-Hungary, 17
Autonomy, 66, 68, 92; of specialists, 89, 130, 263–64n73

Background: class, 85, 120–21; social, 123–24, 132, 198, 206–7, 213. See also Differentiation
Backwardness, 10, 12, 13–14, 48, 183, 222; agricultural, 60, 64–65, 136; economic, 45; peasant, 2, 58–60, 221
Belorussia, 163
Black Earth region, 13, 129
Black repartition, 24–25, 50, 147, 153
Bogdanov, Nikolai, 40
Bolsheviks, see Communist Party
Bourgeois specialists, 10, 28, 90–91, 116, 123, 134, 172, 182; prominence of, 68; protection of, 106; and purges, 205, 210; recruitment of, 66, 110; suspicions of, 2, 73, 87, 197. *See also* Specialists; Specialists, nonparty
Brest-Litovsk, Treaty of, 28
Briukhanov, N. P., 55
Brussilov, 117
Budgets, 38, 80–82, 102–4, 132, 143, 173. *See also* Resources
Budyennyi, S. M., 123
Bukharin, Nikolai, 6, 100, 156, 186, 194, 215–16
Bureaucracy, 7, 8, 30, 66, 126, 132, 205, 207, 223; and Bolshevik Party, 9, 45, 220; and continuities with the Old Regime, 29–32, 33, 43–45, 221–22; and interagency competition, 35–39, 45; local, 100, 172, 178; organization of, 21, 23, 27, 29, 42–43, 62, 93, 120; oversight of, 92, 108–14, 118–19, 133, 197–98, 200–1; and purges, 92, 172, 202; tsarist, 4–5, 13, 17, 22, 27–28. *See also* Personnel
Bureaucratism, 74, 108–9, 200–3, 213

Cadres, 2, 7, 31–32, 63, 80, 91, 104. *See also* Personnel
Categories, 154, 156, 201, 214, 223; class, 120–21, 132, 157, 185, 187, 206
Central Administration for Land Working (TsUZem), 47, 64, 67
Central Agricultural region, 84
Central Black Earth region, 15–16, 140, 144, 148
Central Committee, 35–36, 38, 95, 118, 139, 227; and peasant promotion, 76, 211; and personnel, 73, 88, 98–99, 111, 125–126, 195, 197; Plenum of, 68, 75, 105, 155, 200, 218–19; and policies, 106, 152, 189; and purges, 200, 205, 212; Secretariat of, 86, 111, 132, 191
Central Control Commission (TsKK), 108–9, 113, 116–19, 121, 218; and purges, 200, 212; and Rabkrin, 111, 120
Central Executive Committee (TsIK), 175; All-Russian, 24
Central Industrial Region, 15, 145–46
Central Producer region, 13, 49–50, 147
Central Statistical Administration, 139, 216, 278n107
Centralization, 62–63, 100, 120
Chaianov, A. V., 83, 171–72, 192, 198, 216–17,

291

220, 244–45n76, 278n115
Cheka, 28, 86. *See also* Main Political Administration
Chelintsev, A. N., 83, 115–17, 192, 198, 216
China, 186, 188
Civil War, 3, 11–12, 19, 27–28, 30, 32–34, 45–46, 53–54, 121, 132, 222
Class, 6, 7, 91, 105, 122, 138, 223; ascription of, 73, 121–23, 127, 246n95; and peasantry, 60–61; politics of, 2, 213. *See also* Categories
Class enemies, 36, 182, 211, 222
Class struggle, 39, 71–72, 152, 157, 192, 202, 225
Class warfare, 27–28, 181
Coercion, 12, 26, 39–41, 44, 48, 54–55, 88, 157
Collective farms (kolkhozy), 24, 39, 70–71, 84, 143, 149, 152, 160–61, 168, 172, 183; composition of, 196; establishment of, 3, 25–26, 41, 46, 51, 56, 163, 165–66, 169, 172, 189–91, 196, 224; as models, 151, 181, 191–92; resources of, 107, 150–52; and specialists, 183–84. *See also* Farming methods; Land tenure
Collectivization, 1, 9, 22, 134, 138, 165–66, 172, 196, 225; forced, 4, 6, 25–26, 39, 150–51, 191, 213, 216, 218, 223, 227; reactions to, 8, 179–84, 186, 219, 226, 271n47
Collegium, 28, 30, 52, 67–68, 75–76, 79, 136
Commissariats. *See* Peoples' Commissariats
Committee of Poor Peasants, 28, 39
Committee on Work in the Countryside, 152
Communes, 18, 56, 149, 196; and land policy, 23–24, 70, 166; preservation of, 143–44, 151, 160–62, 164–65, 167–69, 189, 224–25; repartitional, 15, 50, 163; separation from, 6, 70; and soviets, 158–59; traditional, 3, 39–40, 46
Communist Academy, 115
Communist Party, 3, 9, 11–12, 21, 72, 88, 91, 133, 215; anxiety within, 97, 199; and attitudes toward the countryside, 6, 48, 56, 63, 137, 160; and bureaucracy, 4, 8, 129–30; congresses of, 51, 53–54, 66, 102–3, 111, 190–92, 200–1, 208, 214; goals of, 182, 203, 213; and internal debates, 138–39; in localities, 159, 224, 98–99; membership, 4, 32–33, 63, 108–11, 199, 202; and NEP, 51, 118; and nonparty specialists, 50–51, 58–60, 89, 108–9, 112; opposition to, 27–28; and peasant promotion, 128–29
Communist Party, Right wing of, 6, 100–1, 103, 106, 115, 138–39, 149, 152, 156, 185–87, 190, 192, 198, 215–17, and commune, 164; and kulaks, 158
Communist Party cell, 110–11, 114, 117–18, 182; and purges, 204–5, 206–9
Communists. *See* Communist Party
Conflict, interagency, 20–21, 33–39, 44–45, 54–56, 118
Constituent Assembly, 20, 27–28, 83
Cooperatives, 40, 139, 150, 154, 161, 165
Council of Labor and Defense (STO), 69
Council of Ministers, 17, 19, 21
Council of Peoples' Commissars, see Sovnarkom
Countryside, 1, 3, 4, 13, 78, 183, 187; customs of, 160; development of, 11, 55, 138, 220; opinion in, 149; and urban relations, 73; vision of, 24,

135–37, 149. *See also* Peasantry; Village
Crop failure, 10, 81, 102, 129, 141; effects of, 55, 58, 85, 218; history of, 52–53, 64; and kulaks, 158; and requisitioning, 54. *See also* Famine
Crops, 15–16, 26, 40, 71, 139, 141, 189; industrial, 16, 50, 58, 145–47, 188, 190. *See also* Grain
Culture, 48, 57, 91, 95, 117, 177, 181, 183; bureaucratic, 4–5, 7, 31–32, 118, 134; institutional, 41, 65–66, 68, 89, 222, 224; peasant, 14, 171; political, 7, 9, 90, 138; of specialists, 182

Decentralization, 82, 87, 97
Decree on Land, 23–24
Denmark, 14, 188
Denunciations, 204. *See also* Purges
Department of Agriculture (Departament zemledeliia), 20, 31, 41
Development: agricultural, 141; economic, 138; rural, 6, 8, 168. *See also* Modernization; Transformation, rural
Differentiation: rural, 155, 168; social, 5, 71–72, 88, 149, 152–57, 181, 225–26. *See also* Class; Categories
Disease, 52, 55, 218. *See also* Famine
Drought, 129, 140. *See also* Famine
Dzerzhinskii, Feliks E., 100, 107, 115, 151, 156–57, 186, 251n12

Economy, 1, 3, 12–13, 34, 49, 196; and modernization, 11, 25; recovery of, 14, 51, 57, 101, 105, 173, 191, 222; rural, 4, 30, 44–45, 54, 59, 149, 161
Education, 18, 59, 71, 88, 137, 173, 243n43; and peasantry, 57–58, 60, 142–43; and specialists, 37–38, 136, 239n96
Eismont, N. B., 218–19
Emergency measures, 34, 194, 222
Enemies, 65, 89, 105, 112, 172; capitalist, 193; class, 122; internal, 186. *See also* Alien elements
England, 17
Enlightenment, 101, 169, 173. *See also* Education
Ethos, specialist, 99
Europe, 3–4, 13–16, 64–65
Expertise, 91, 134; importance of, 66, 132–33; institutionalization of, 48, 87, 89, 106, 110, 214, 223; politics of, 105–6, 193; subculture of, 41–43, 46. *See also* Specialists
Experts. *See* Bourgeois specialists; Specialists
Exploitation, 152–53, 156, 170, 181, 192

Face to the Countryside Campaign, 101–4
Famine (1891–92), 52, 81
Famine (1921–22), 1, 49, 52–53, 88, 129, 139, 141, 218; and farming methods, 16; and Narkomzem, 80–81; results of, 57–59, 73; threat of, 47, 54–55, 102
Famine (1932–33), 1, 218
Farming, 2, 139, 147, 188, 191, 224; livestock, 49, 144, 189; organization of, 151, 161, 163; practices of, 12, 15–16, 18; and quotas, 40–41; reorganization of, 137, 180; subsistence, 25, 50, 53, 65

Farming methods, 3, 148, 165–66; communal, 45, 88, 144, 152, 190–91, 221; and efforts to change, 57, 137, 141, 144–47, 154, 169, 171; European, 64–65; types of, 15–16, 24–25, 50, 57–58, 144–46, 160, 163, 177, 180, 189–90, 226, 234–35n16. *See also* Collective farms; Communes; Land tenure

First Five Year Plan, 181–82, 191, 215–16

Food supply, 35–36, 44, 61, 93, 95; brigades, 28, 33–37, 42–43, 54, 66, 96, 227; policy, 19–21, 34–35, 43, 49, 53. *See also* Peoples' Commissariat of Food Supply

Former people (byvshie liudi), 199, 201–3, 206

France, 11–12, 14, 17, 43–44

Georgia, 102

Germany, 14, 28, 188; as model, 63–64

Gosplan (State Planning Commission), 56, 67, 69, 80, 83, 187, 216

Gosudarstvennoe upravlenie zemleustroistva i zemledeliia (GUZiZ), 16

GPU. *See* Main Political Administration

Gradualism, 6, 10, 36, 48, 91, 149, 168, 186, 193, 227; attack on, 185; and collectivization, 7–8, 165, 181; and Lenin, 39, 139

Grain, 19, 54, 142, 185–86; exports of, 13, 54–55, 102, 140–41, 170, 218; monopoly, 20, 33–34; seizures of, 35, 218, 222; shortages of, 3, 10; yields, 13–14, 144, 188, 198, 225. *See also* Food supply; Requisitioning

Grain Procurement Crisis, 193–96, 198, 223

Great Britain, 14, 186

Groman, 217

Habsburg Empire, 14

Harvests, 13, 19, 52, 54, 140–41, 169, 190, 233n3. *See also* Crop Failure; Famine

Holdover specialists, 11–12, 41–42, 70, 133, 221–22; hostility toward, 44–45, 197, 201; influence of, 32–33, 68; in localities, 34, 85, 97–98, 199; replacement of, 74; unreliability of, 112. *See also* Bourgeois specialists; Specialists

Homesteads, 18, 70, 86, 165–67, 225, 266n115; and communes, 24–25, 50, 71, 162; and farming methods, 56, 88, 145, 160; popularity of, 163–64, 168

Households, 6, 14–15, 150, 159, 190–91; legal status of, 161–62, 166; resources of, 50, 148; splintering of, 145–46

Iakovenko, Vasilii Grigorevich, 77–79, 88, 90, 92–93, 95, 123–25, 131, 219, 247n115, 250n162, 277n100

Iakovlev, Ia. A., 198, 208–9, 213–14, 219

Identity, 74, 91, 121, 123–27, 131–32, 134, 149; bureaucratic, 7; professional, 172, 174, 182–83

Ideology, 7, 73, 88, 192–93

Ignorance, 65, 92, 116; Communist, 105–6, 226–27; peasant, 58, 60

Illiteracy, agronomic, 65, 177, 17

Incentives, 104–5, 153–54, 165, 225; market, 148; economic, 19, 40, 88, 147, 190, 195

Industrial Party Trial, 217

Industrialization, 4, 197, 201; of countryside, 180, 183; debates over, 138–39; pace of, 182, 186, 191, 193, 216

Industry, 4, 8, 49, 173, 186, 189–90; and prestige, 48, 174, 226

Intelligentsia, 7, 43, 47, 66, 74, 83–85, 173, 216

Intensification, agricultural, 144, 146–48, 154, 163, 171, 180, 188. *See also* Farming methods; Production, agricultural

Interests: bureaucratic, 4–5; institutional, 158, 167, 213, 224–25; of peasantry, 105

Intervention: foreign, 216–17; outside, 92, 99–100, 106, 113–14, 116–17, 126, 131, 133, 135, 149; state, 2, 21, 40–41, 58–59, 88, 221–22, 226

Investigations, 87, 96, 107–8, 185, 187, 198, 213, 223, 227; focus of, 208; methods of, 203–4; of personnel, 118–19, 200–3, 205–7; reactions to, 209–10, 212; resistance to, 209

Investment, 186–87, 226; capital, 146–48, 154; state, 180, 190

Italy, 14

Iurovskii, L. N., 216, 245n82

Kadets, 83, 85

Kaganovich, Lazar, 197, 111

Kalinin, Mikhail I., 56, 183

Kamenev, Lev, 187

Kazakhstan, 218

Khutor, 24, 50, 71, 143, 163–66, 196

Klimenko, Ivan Evdokimovich, 196, 207, 274n34

Knowledge, 88, 143; scientific, 105, 126, 131

Kolegaev, Lazar, 28, 237n60

Kommuna, 26, 164. *See also* Communes

Kondratíev, Nikolai D., 30, 68–70, 83, 100, 131, 136, 160–61, 219, 256n89; accusations against, 117, 192–93, 216–18, 278n115; arrest of, 86–87, 171–72; investigation of, 205; removal of, 195, 197

Krivoshein, A. V., 19

Kronstadt rebellion, 51, 76

Krzhizhanovskii, G., 56

Kuban, 130

Kubiak, Nikolai Afanasíevich, 196, 198–99, 219

Kuibyshev, 197

Kulak threat, 88, 139, 157–58, 168, 192

Kulaks, 60, 71–72, 152–58, 186–87, 211, 216, 225, 262n59; and agricultural policies, 10, 162, 169; and class struggle, 39, 181–82; conciliation of, 91, 105; definition of, 149–50, 153–55; and grain crisis, 194, 196, 198; liquidation of, 218, 221; numbers of, 25

Labor, 70–71, 145, 163; hiring of, 71, 86, 103, 115, 154, 170

Laboring Peasant Party (TKP), 216–17

Land, 5, 22, 166–67; lease of, 71, 86, 103, 115, 152; ownership of, 70; redistribution of, 16, 23–25, 50, 141, 146, 160–61, 163, 168, 225, 237n59; reorganization of, 17–18, 25, 38, 164, 180

Land Administration. *See* Peoples' Commissariat of Agriculture

Land Code of the RSFSR (1922), 70–73, 79, 160, 163–64, 189, 207, 268n132
Land committees, 20, 23–24, 27
Land reform, 12, 19–21, 28–30, 222
Land Reorganization and Improvement Administration, 41–42, 86, 189, 202, 205, 207
Land sections, local, 8, 22, 38, 62–63, 85, 87, 93, 100, 237n69; funding of, 81–82
Land tenure, 70–72, 115, 143, 160, 169; choice in, 3, 24, 51, 163–64, 168. *See also* Farming methods
Language, 78, 114, 130, 143, 164, 181, 193; bureaucratic, 31, 44; class, 119, 121; political, 224; and purges, 210; symbolic, 21–23
Larin, Iurii, 115–17
Latsis, M. I., 103, 164
Law on Socialization, 24, 30
Leadership, of Narkomzem, 10, 60, 67–68, 76–80, 84, 88, 90, 95, 107, 123, 182; attacks on, 185, 191; changes in, 193, 214; and loyalty, 92; and specialists, 106, 113, 205–9; strategy of, 105; vision of, 224
Left Opposition, 100–1, 106, 115, 138–39, 152, 155, 158, 185–87, 192–93
Legacies, 23, 30, 32, 44–46, 221
Legislation, 94, 115, 145, 150, 160–63, 169, 176; and land use, 23–24, 166
Lenin, V. I., 21, 35, 47, 53, 56, 85–86, 95; and building socialism, 51, 139; and bureaucracy, 31, 62, 87–88, 108, 114; and collective farms, 39, 40; and collectivization, 26, 70; and peasant promotion, 73, 75–78; and specialists, 61, 66–68, 74, 97, 120, 123, 247n115,121
Leveling, 25, 50, 153
Lezhava, 209–10
Lezhnev–Finíkovskii, P., 176, 208, 275n53
Literacy, 50, 58, 60–61
Living: conditions, 8, 36–38, 174–79, 226; standards, 89, 168–69, 190
Localism, 5
Localities, 5, 62–63, 96–97, 159; and personnel, 126, 133, 176
Loyalty, 92, 95, 202–4; of specialists, 33, 97, 112, 119–20, 182, 197; political, 7, 84, 133

Main Land Committee, 20, 30–31, 83
Main Political Administration (GPU/OGPU), 86, 101, 157–58, 186–87; and purges, 194, 200, 204–7, 212–13, 216, 218; and specialists, 115, 197–98
Makarov, N. P., 30, 83, 100, 104, 115–17, 136, 188, 192, 216–18, 255n85, 279n120
Manuilov, A. A., 188–90
Markets, 51, 55, 139–41, 145, 147, 163
Mechanization, agricultural, 88, 146–48, 172–73, 180, 183, 188, 190, 196, 199
Mensheviks, 83, 217
Mentalities, 1, 78, 97, 165
Menzhinskii, 196
Meshcheriakov, V. N., 29, 31, 35, 36, 237n68
Mesiatsev, Pavel, 70, 72
Middle peasants (serredniaki), 39, 154–56, 187, 192, 194, 211; and collective farms, 150, 196; conciliation with, 26, 51, 107; incentives for, 104, 153; numbers of, 25, 50
Miliutin, V. P., 216
Ministry of Agriculture, Imperial, 13, 17, 18, 20–21, 37; legacy of, 23, 30; and role in wartime, 19–20; and SRs, 27, 83
Modernization, 1, 12, 88, 138, 181, 213, 224, 226; approaches to 57, 60, 155, 168, 172, 179–80, 185, 221; and commune, 158, 160; and state, 2, 17. *See also* Transformation, rural
Molotov, Viacheslav, 99, 106, 111, 152, 159, 192–93, 217
Moral authority, 43, 56
Morosanov, A. N., 86
Myths, and peasant promotion, 76, 78

Na agronom fronte, 115–16, 256n89, 262n59
Narkomprod. *See* Peoples' Commissariat of Food Supply
Narkomzem. *See* Peoples' Commissariat of Agriculture RSFSR
Nationalization: of enterprises, 34; of land, 23–24, 225
Nepmen, 157, 186–87, 216
Netherlands, 14
New Economic Policy (NEP), 3, 7–8, 10, 12, 32, 41, 46, 47, 55, 66, 91–92, 106, 132, 137–39, 168, 185–86; Bolshevik attitude toward, 48, 61, 223; decline of, 170, 193, 220, 227; introduction of, 51, 54, 56, 67, 88; policies of, 6, 54, 63, 101, 156, 222–23; support for, 171–72
Nicholas II, 20
Nomenklatura, 109, 111, 129
North Caucuses, 45, 49, 52, 102, 146, 218
Northwest region, 15–16, 55, 145–46, 163–64

Oganovskii, Nikolai P., 72, 83, 85–86, 100, 198, 219, 256n89
OGPU. *See* Main Political Administration
Old Regime, 1, 21–22, 33, 44, 69, 79; bureaucracy of, 4–5, 11, 31, 221
Ordzhonikidze, G. K. "Sergo," 107, 200–2, 207
Orgburo, 85, 95, 111–12, 159, 193
Orgraspred, 112
Origins, 133, 202; social, 122, 127, 182, 198, 204, 208; concealment of, 120, 123, 205–6; peasant, 126, 257–58n111; of personnel, 2, 112–13. *See also* Background
Osinskii, V. V. (Valerian V. Obolenskii), 38–41, 63, 67–68, 72, 80–82, 86–87, 93, 95
Otrub, 24, 50, 71, 143, 163–64, 166
Output, agricultural, 13–14, 24–25, 149, 190; improvement of, 139–40, 144, 188, 220, 225

Party-state, 9–10, 12, 24, 32, 34, 75, 91–92, 99, 133, 138, 157
Patronage, 70, 73, 107, 110, 114–15, 118, 123, 134, 184, 195, 223; networks, 206–7
Peasant promotion, 2, 6–7, 74–80, 90, 123–30, 133–34, 210–12
Peasantry, 1, 9, 14–15, 18, 45–46, 72, 75, 124, 132–33, 138, 150–51, 159, 165, 172, 211; atti-

tudes toward, 60–61, 125, 128, 144, 211–12; backwardness of, 2, 58–60, 221; as capitalists, 9, 91, 223; and class, 73, 154–55; concessions to, 134, 158, 168, 195, 226; conciliation of, 6, 26, 185, 222; culture of, 57, 171, 183; and education, 60, 142–43; and grain crisis, 194–95; images of, 76–78, 90, 127; opinions of, 51, 102, 145, 149, 180, 219; and relationship with the state, 3–5, 51, 56–57, 61, 169, 186–87, 194, 225; and resistance, 169; and specialists, 176–77

Peoples' Commissariat of Agriculture RSFSR (Narkomzem), 2–7, 10, 44, 53, 59, 84, 86, 92–93, 102, 202, 222, 225–26; agenda of, 138, 213; congresses of, 164, 183, 176; decline of, 166–68, 194–95, 197, 213–14, 220, 227; organization of, 22–31, 42, 61–62, 87, 138, 193, 208, 221; mission of, 46, 58, 72, 79, 88, 96, 123, 129, 131, 137, 167, 189; and NEP, 55, 66, 139, 158, 214, 220; and peasantry, 56–57, 78, 105, 192; and politics, 49, 149, 169; reform of, 95–97, 132, 134–35; stature of, 12, 41, 44–46, 48, 54, 80, 82, 85, 89, 94–95, 102–3, 139, 161, 187, 193; and war, 34–36, 45–46

Peoples' Commissariat of Agriculture USSR, 22, 213

Peoples' Commissariat of Finance, 54–55, 80, 82–83, 103, 139, 189, 278n107

Peoples' Commissariat of Food Supply (Narkomprod), 28, 34–36, 39, 43, 45–46, 48, 54, 167–68; decline of, 55, 80, 89; and specialist personnel, 37–39; and war communism, 66

Peoples' Commissariat of Foreign Affairs, 32–33

Peoples' Commissariat of Internal Affairs, 32–33, 83

Peoples' Commissariat of Workers' and Peasants' Inspectorate (Rabkrin), 96, 108, 121–22, 132, 137, 162, 182, 197, 210; inspectors of, 118–20, 126; and peasant promotion, 123, 129, 211; and personnel reviews, 109, 111–15; and purges, 198, 200–201, 204–7, 209, 212–13

Peoples' Commissariats, 9, 33, 80, 93, 103, 109–10, 126

Personnel agencies, 123, 223

Personnel, bureaucratic, 1, 3, 8, 31–33, 55, 63, 91–95, 104, 106, 197–99, 213, 221–22, 236n43; background of, 2, 73–74, 122, 126, 199–200, 202, 246n96; and communist party membership, 97, 109–10; hiring of, 66, 68, 80, 85, 97–98, 113, 115–16, 119, 122, 132–34, 206; investigations of, 82, 107, 111–14, 182, 198, 200, 202; protection of, 7, 89, 92, 119–23, 135, 193, 223–24; and qualifications, 73, 129, 133, 206; shared beliefs of, 58, 60; suspicions of, 98, 214–15; turnover of, 20–21, 99, 104, 120–21, 174–75, 195–96, 205–6, 226

Peters, Iakov Khristorovich, 200–204, 207, 210

Petrograd, 20

Petty bourgeoisie, 5, 6, 165; peasantry as, 48, 220, 227

Planning, 62–63, 68–69, 198; and Perspective Plan, 155, 160, 163, 191; and State Regulation Plan, 39–41. *See also* Gosplan; Zemplan

Policy, 28–30, 53, 61, 83, 89, 92, 122, 148, 152, 169, 188, 194; agricultural, 48, 51, 56, 71, 84, 90, 100, 102, 132, 149, 165, 186–87, 226; and Narkomzem, 104–5, 117, 135, 138, 196, 225, 227; personnel, 99, 122; and specialists, 66, 68

Politburo, 35, 86, 103, 113, 139, 169, 193–94; and specialists, 98–99, 176

Politicization, 205, 207, 224

Poor peasants, 25, 71, 155–56, 162; and collective farms, 196; and cooperatives, 150; exploitation of, 152, 170, 181, 192; and kommuna, 26

Population, 4, 9, 49, 52, 188, 234n10; control over, 168; rural, 14–15, 19, 25, 50, 140, 146, 151, 153, 159

Pragmatism, 136, 141, 149, 224

Preobrazhenskii, Evgenii, 100, 106, 152, 186

Price policies, 19, 141, 148, 186, 189, 227; and purchase prices, 149, 169, 194–95, 225

Private property, 5, 6, 23, 162, 166–69, 225

Production, agricultural, 12, 49–50, 56, 138, 198, 213, 234n4; collectivization of, 39–40; forms of, 1, 6, 26–27, 57–58, 144, 148, 165, 188–89, 191; industrialization of, 180, 183; levels of, 3, 25, 43, 139–41, 190, 224; modernization of, 101, 158, 173, 186, 190; recovery of, 3, 18, 48, 97, 146–47, 188

Production, industrial, 49–50

Productivity, 4, 12, 15–16, 25, 35, 45, 191; agricultural, 13–14, 18–19, 224, 243n43; increases in, 18, 40, 168

Professors from the Plow, 131–32

Proletariat, 124, 226

Promotion, social, 7. *See also* Peasant Promotion

Propaganda, 76–77; agricultural, 142–43; and V. I. Lenin Agro-train, 178–79

Provisional Government, 11, 19–21, 28, 34, 69, 83, 221

Prussia, 17

Purges, 98–99, 133, 135, 172, 182, 185, 197, 200, 223; and Communist Party members, 108–10; excesses in, 203–4, 208–10; of nonparty specialists, 114, 198, 227; objectives of, 201–3; participation in, 212–13; of personnel, 119–21

Rabkrin. *See* Peoples' Commissariat of Workers' and Peasants' Inspectorate

Radek, Karl, 53, 218–19

Ramzin, Leonid, 217

Rationalization, 3, 47, 144–46, 148, 154, 160, 171, 180–81, 199

Rationing, 20, 37

Raw materials, 141, 186, 189, 223

Rebellions, 14, 51; peasant, 23, 27, 83, 101–3

Red Army, 102, 117, 214–15

Requisitioning, 20, 28, 34, 41, 63, 194–95, 218; wartime policies of, 25, 35, 51, 53–54, 56, 73, 168. *See also* Grain

Resources, 48, 59, 129, 150–51, 190, 194; allocation of, 17, 101–4, 107, 182; financial, 80–82; scarcity of, 12, 27, 36, 43, 45–46, 48, 57, 89, 173, 178, 191, 222–23, 226

Revolution, 11–12, 44; French, 22, 76, 221; and Left Opposition, 100–101; international, 49, 62, 92–93, 138; October, 2, 9, 25, 167

Rhetoric, 47, 56, 81, 96, 119, 153, 193, 248n128; class, 71, 157, 181, 201
Right deviation, 10, 91, 192–93, 197–98. *See also* Communist Party, Right wing of
Rudin, N. P., 70, 189, 207, 216
Rudzutak, R. E., 183, 209
Rybnikov, A. A., 86–87, 217
Rykov, Aleksei I., 98, 100, 102, 107, 114, 137, 156, 162, 166, 186–87, 190, 192, 194, 197, 215–16

Sabotage, 27–28, 33, 182, 196, 210, 216; political, 205, 207
Salaries, 37–38, 103–4, 174, 226, 251n10
Samara province, 188
Saratov province, 188
Savchenko, K. D., 126–27
Science, 3, 41, 43, 47, 55, 59, 66, 88–89, 137, 173, 222; agronomic, 142, 144; and collective farms, 181; and Germany, 64
Scissors crisis, 102, 190
Secret police, 82, 84, 201. *See also* Main Political Administration
Sel'sko-khoziaistvennaia zhizn', 85–86, 97, 102, 192
Senin, Vladimir I., 129–30
Serbia, 14
Sereda, A. P., 29, 46, 67
Shakhty Affair, 197, 205, 209
Shefler, M. E., 59–60, 63–64, 87
Shlikhter, A. G., 32
Shortages, 27, 41, 58, 140, 190, 194–95; equipment, 38, 147–49; food, 23, 49, 53–55; of specialists, 34, 36–37, 80, 82, 87, 104, 116, 123, 145, 173, 178, 227
Shvernik, Nikolai M., 112–14
Siberia, 130, 144
Skepticism, 61, 191; of peasantry, 78–79; of specialists, 68, 181–82
Sluzhashchie, 33, 73, 75, 127, 133, 206, 223
Smirnov, Alexander Petrovich, 90–96, 103, 131, 136, 138, 166, 168, 185–86, 190, 215–17, 219, 225; and agricultural policies, 102, 137, 167, 194, 219; and collective farms, 151–52, 191; criticism of, 118–19, 218–19; and communes, 160–62, 164–66, 169; and identity, 124–26, 128, 132–33; and kulaks, 152–57; leadership of, 105–6, 139; and Narkomzem reforms, 96–97, 134–35; and personnel, 99–101, 104, 109, 113–16, 120, 129–30, 223–24; and protection of specialists, 107–8, 110–11, 117, 123, 134, 206, 256n90; removal of, 195–98, 214, 227; and vision of countryside, 187, 193
Smolensk, 163
Smychka, 6, 46, 48, 56, 73, 75, 78, 194
Socialism, 1; building of, 12, 137–39, 186, 190; transformation to, 51, 169, 188, 224
Socialist Revolutionaries (SRs), 2, 84–85, 89, 122, 195, 199, 223; Left, 28–29; trial of, 83, 86
Socialization, 1, 158, 185, 224
Southeast region, 55, 84
Soviets: congresses of, 23, 28, 38, 80–81, 102, 192; local, 24, 62, 158–59, 162, 168, 171, 177–79, 224; opposition to, 192, 205, 207, 209

Sovnarkom (Council of Peoples' Commissars), 21–22, 27, 95, 138, 193, 198; and agricultural production, 25, 39; and bureaucracy, 62, 66; and food supply, 38; and legislation, 54, 161–62, 166; and Narkomzem, 30, 34–35, 37, 45, 69, 81, 132; organization of, 23; and personnel, 67, 73, 77; and specialists, 106, 175; and SRs, 28
Spain, 14
Specialist baiting, 106, 115–17, 179, 197, 202
Specialists, 3, 8, 10, 13, 38, 46, 80, 85, 97, 104, 132–33, 193, 214; arrests of, 86–88; attacks on, 98, 115–17, 187; and collective farms, 151, 183; and countryside, 4, 44–45, 48, 57, 194–95, 200; employment of, 37, 122, 137, 176; goals of, 42, 84, 173, 226; importance of, 42, 68, 130, 141–43, 208–9; influence of, 5, 223; and peasant promotion, 90, 130; professional interests of, 182; protection of, 106–7, 123, 135, 185, 192, 197; and role of, 18–20, 65, 181, 183, 222; and self-perception, 48, 134; tsarist, 12, 30, 32–33, 69, 221. *See also* Personnel; Specialists, local; Specialists, nonparty
Specialists, local 5, 7–8, 97–101, 176, 182, 199, 226; and local soviets, 177–79; and NEP, 171–72; status of, 173–75, 180–81, 183–84
Specialists, nonparty, 30, 41, 66, 70, 83, 92, 171–72, 179, 183, 213–14; and Communist Party, 9, 48, 58, 60, 68, 89, 109, 115–16, 220–22; hostility toward, 98–99, 106, 182; influence of, 61, 63, 101, 122, 199, 223; investigations of, 111–14; and patronage, 73, 96; and peasant promotion, 128–29, 210. *See also* Personnel
Specialization, 42, 79
Stalin, Josef, 86–88, 100–1, 110, 124, 132, 159, 161, 193, 201, 215–17, 227; victory of, 220; and grain crisis, 194; and industrialization, 188; and NEP, 195; and personnel, 197; and Rabkrin, 108
Starvation, 52, 55, 218
State, 12, 17, 43–44, 138, 213; administration of, 1, 4, 9, 66, 68, 74, 97; and countryside, 75, 199, 224; priorities of, 102, 173; regulation by, 39, 67; role of, 43, 48
State farms (sovkhozy), 23–27, 40, 84, 150–51, 166, 191. *See also* Collective Farms
Status, professional, 8, 180–81, 271n47
Stigmatization, 91, 154–55, 200; class, 123; institutionalization of, 214; social, 107
Stolypin reforms, 17–18, 24, 37, 143, 163–64
Strategy, 105, 137, 155, 193; Bolshevik, 42; and class, 123, 156; modernization, 158, 221; NEP as, 158; and protection of personnel, 106–7, 114–15, 119–22, 213, 223–24; resistance, 130
Sukhanov, N. N., 216–17, 267n122
Suspicion, 6, 89, 91, 157, 201; of nonparty specialists, 5, 33, 48–49, 132, 182, 207, 214
Sviderskii, A. I., 96, 103–4, 119, 121, 136, 152, 161–62, 190, 195–96, 219
Symbolism, 7, 75, 86–87; and peasant promotion, 78, 90

Taxation, 35, 54–55, 85, 101–2, 149, 154, 170, 186

Tax in kind, 51–52, 54–55, 89, 168
Technology, 13, 88, 154, 225; agricultural, 16, 57, 60, 147–48, 160, 191; and productivity, 12, 190, 222, 224
Teitel', A. V., 64, 67–68, 216
Teodorovich, Ivan A., 52, 68–69, 86–87, 96, 116, 136, 156, 191, 194, 219, 223, 244n76; attacks against, 110–11, 198, 217; as patron, 70, 76–78, 107, 215; removal of, 195–96, 207
Thirty Years War, 47, 64
Timiriazev Academy, 69, 176, 244–45n76
Tocqueville, Alexis de, 12, 22, 43–44, 46, 221
Tolmachev, V. N., 218
Tomskii, Mikhail, 100, 187, 215–16
Transformation, rural, 48, 60, 136, 138, 149, 173, 188; methods of, 55, 66, 137; obstacles to, 11, 171, 227; and specialists, 141–43, 179, 181, 183
Trials, 217; show, 197
Trotsky, Lev, 100–1, 105–6, 139, 152, 155, 186–87; campaign against, 111; supporters of, 107, 119, 192–93
Tsarist government, see Old Regime
Tsiurupa, A. D., 55, 87, 96
Tugan-Baranovskii, M. I., 69
Tukhachevsky, 117

Uchraspred, 111, 113, 118
Ukraine, 17, 52, 55, 102, 218
Underdevelopment, 58, 222; economic, 13–14; rural 6, 48, 60, 148
United States, 3–4, 13, 14, 17; and agronomic aid, 18; Department of Agriculture, 41–42
Uprisings. *See* Rebellions
Urals, 53, 163
Urals-Siberian method, 194

Vainshtein, A. L., 83, 85–86, 198
Valentinov, N. V., 84, 115, 156–57, 251n12
Vedomstvennosti, 5, 119, 133, 169, 193, 224
Verification Commission, 111–12, 114, 121–22

Verifications, 85, 108, 111–12, 119–20, 204. *See also* Purges
Vesenkha (Supreme Council of the National Economy), 32, 35, 54, 83, 187, 191, 203, 251n8
Village, 3, 14–15, 47, 83, 128, 138, 159–60; divisions within, 60–61, 88, 152–57, 226; policies toward, 26, 149, 196; vanguard, 18, 57, 72, 153, 155, 158, 225,
Violence, 36, 54, 194
Vitebsk, 163
Vol'skii, Nikolai Vladislavovich. *See* Valentinov, N. V.
Volga region, 13, 52–53, 55, 78, 84, 102, 129, 144, 148, 218
Voroshilov, K. Ye., 124

War Communism, 34, 55, 62, 194
War scare, 186
Wartime conditions, 25–26, 34–36, 44–45
Well-off peasants (zazhitochnye), 5, 72, 105, 107, 153–58, 187, 225–26; as models, 6; and specialists, 149, 178
Western region, 15–16, 145, 163–64
Western Siberia, 52, 78
White-Collar workers. *See* Sluzhashchie
Working class, 63, 74–75, 155
Working conditions, 8, 37–38, 104, 143, 171, 174–80, 183, 226, 271n47
World War I, 13– 15, 19, 21, 24, 37, 46, 57, 143; impact of, 3, 27, 53
Worldview, 4, 6, 9, 171, 224; of Bolsheviks, 63; of Narkomzem, 71, 96; of specialists, 89, 177

Yurovskii, L. N., 86–87

Zemplan (Land Planning Committee), 68–69, 86–87, 131, 164, 188, 216; and Land Code, 70, 73; specialists in, 83, 96, 112, 117, 149, 156, 223
Zemstvos, 13, 17, 18, 37, 160; and role in wartime, 19–20
Zinov'ev, G., 105, 187, 192